PROGRESS IN BEHAVIOR MODIFICATION

Volume 5

CONTRIBUTORS TO THIS VOLUME

Hal Arkowitz
Rex Forehand
Paul Karoly
S. H. Lovibond
N. McConaghy
Rosemery O. Nelson
Steven M. Ross
Dennis Upper

PROGRESS IN BEHAVIOR MODIFICATION

EDITED BY

Michel Hersen

Department of Psychiatry
Western Psychiatric Institute and Clinic
University of Pittsburgh School of Medicine
Pittsburgh, Pennsylvania

Richard M. Eisler

Department of Psychiatry and Human Behavior
University of Mississippi Medical Center
Jackson, Mississippi

Peter M. Miller

Weight Control Center
Hilton Head Hospital
Hilton Head Island, South Carolina

Volume 5

1977

ACADEMIC PRESS NEW YORK SAN FRANCISCO LONDON

A Subsidiary of Harcourt Brace Jovanovich, Publishers

ACADEMIC PRESS, INC.
111 Fifth Avenue, New York, New York 10003

United Kingdom Edition published by
ACADEMIC PRESS, INC. (LONDON) LTD.
24/28 Oval Road, London NW1

LIBRARY OF CONGRESS CATALOG CARD NUMBER: 74-5697

ISBN 0-12-535605-6

PRINTED IN THE UNITED STATES OF AMERICA

CONTENTS

Child Noncompliance to Parental Requests: Behavioral Analysis and Treatment
Rex Forehand

Behavioral Group Therapy: I. Emotional, Avoidance, and Social Skills Problems of Adults
Dennis Upper and Steven M. Ross

Behavioral Self-Management in Children: Concepts, Methods, Issues, and Directions
Paul Karoly

Assessment and Therapeutic Functions of Self-Monitoring
Rosemery O. Nelson

Behavioral Treatment in Homosexuality
N. McConaghy

LIST OF CONTRIBUTORS

Numbers in parentheses indicate the pages on which the authors' contributions begin.

HAL ARKOWITZ (1), Department of Psychology, University of Arizona, Tucson, Arizona

REX FOREHAND (111), Department of Psychology, University of Georgia, Athens, Georgia

PAUL KAROLY (197), Department of Psychology, University of Cincinnati, Cincinnati, Ohio

S. H. LOVIBOND (63), Department of Psychology, University of New South Wales, Sydney, Australia

N. McCONAGHY (309), School of Psychiatry, University of New South Wales, Sydney, Australia

ROSEMERY O. NELSON (263), Department of Psychology, University of North Carolina at Greensboro, Greensboro, North Carolina

STEVEN M. ROSS (149), Veterans Administration Hospital and University of Utah, Salt Lake City, Utah

DENNIS UPPER (149), Veterans Administration Hospital, Brockton, Massachusetts

PREFACE

Progress in Behavior Modification is a multidisciplinary serial publication encompassing the contributions of psychology, psychiatry, social work, speech therapy, education, and rehabilitation. In an era of intense specialization, it is designed to bring to the attention of all workers in behavior modification, in a yearly review format, the most timely issues and developments in the field. Inasmuch as several journals are presently devoted entirely to publishing articles on behavior modification, and in consideration of the fact that numerous other journals are now allowing an increased allotment of pages to articles dealing with behavioral techniques, even the most diligent reader will find it difficult to keep abreast of all new developments in the field. In light of the publication explosion in behavior modification, there is a real need for a review publication that undertakes to present yearly in-depth evaluations that include a scholarly examination of theoretical underpinnings, a careful survey of research findings, and a comparative analysis of existing techniques and methodologies. In this serial publication we propose to meet this need.

Theoretical discussion, research methodology, assessment techniques, treatment modalities, control of psychophysiological processes, and ethical issues in behavioral control will be considered. Discussions will center on a wide spectrum of child and adult disorders. The range of topics will include, but will not be limited to, studies of fear behavior, measurement and modification of addictive behaviors, modification of classroom behaviors, remedial methods for the retarded and physically handicapped, descriptions of animal analogs, the effects of social influences on behavior, the use of drugs in behavioral approaches, and the contribution of behavior therapy to the treatment of physical illness.

Progress in Behavior Modification will present a diversity of views within the field. We will, on occasion, solicit discussions from theoreticians, researchers, or practitioners not directly associated with behavior modification. Cross-fertilization of ideas, *when maintained at the empirical level,* can be most rewarding and often leads to refinements in theory, research, and practice. In short, we propose not only to review critically developments in behavior modification at a particular point in time, but also to identify new directions and point toward future trends at all levels of inquiry.

Michel Hersen
Richard M. Eisler
Peter M. Miller

CONTENTS OF PREVIOUS VOLUMES

PROGRESS IN BEHAVIOR MODIFICATION

Volume 5

MEASUREMENT AND MODIFICATION OF MINIMAL DATING BEHAVIOR

HAL ARKOWITZ
Department of Psychology
University of Arizona
Tucson, Arizona

I. INTRODUCTION

In recent years, there has been a growth of interest in the application of behavior modification to interpersonal problems. Behavioral researchers and practitioners have moved away from a focus on relatively isolated analog problems, such as small animal and insect phobias, and have begun to address themselves to more clinically relevant problems that are also more firmly embedded in an interpersonal context. This trend may be clearly seen in the recent advances of behavioral treatment approaches to subassertiveness (e.g., Hersen, Eisler, & Miller, 1973; McFall, 1976); child and family interaction problems (Patterson, Reid, Jones, & Conger, 1975; Reisinger, Ora, & Frangia, 1976); marital problems (Weiss, Hops, & Patterson, 1973); sexual dysfunction (Masters & Johnson, 1970); and depression (Lewinsohn, 1975). One area of social functioning that has recently received much attention is that of minimal dating. This chapter will review the research on the assessment and treatment of problems relating to minimal dating and offer some suggestions for future research and practice in this area.

The constructs of social competence and social skill have played important roles in many formulations of psychopathology. Zigler and Phillips (1960) found systematic relationships between measures of social effectiveness and particular groups of symptoms. Argyle (1969) has documented the lack of social competence in most major categories of neurosis and psychosis. Argyle, Trower, and Bryant (1974b) assessed the social competence of applicants for treatment at a mental hospital using behavioral and peer-rating measures. The authors concluded that 28% of their sample could be considered socially inadequate. In addition, factor analytic studies of the Fear Survey Schedule have typically found an interpersonal anxiety factor accounting for a large percentage of the variance in the responses of both outpatients and inpatients (e.g., Landy & Gaupp, 1971).

The more specific problems of minimal dating, lack of social skill, and negative self-evaluations are significant problems for a large percentage of our population. In our culture, adolescence is often a period fraught with anxiety, particularly with respect to feelings about the opposite sex. In addition, due to such life changes as divorce or death of a spouse, many formerly married men and women are faced with the search for a new partner and for an extended social environment. For many people, marriage has served to insulate them from having to deal directly with heterosexual relationships involving attraction. With the loss of their spouse, many individuals are subsequently faced with problems in relating to the opposite sex (Johnson, 1976).

Minimal dating is a major problem for many college students and other young adults. The nature and extent of these problems have been well-documented in a number of recent survey studies. Borkovec, Stone, O'Brien, and Kaloupek (1974) surveyed undergraduates in introductory psychology courses at the University of Iowa. They found that 15.5% of the men and 11.5% of the women reported some degree of fear of being with a member of the opposite sex. In addition, 32% of the men and 38.5% of the women reported some degree of fear of meeting someone for the first time. Klaus, Hersen, and Bellack (in press) found that their sample of undergraduates rated the item "finding possible dates" as one of the most difficult. Shmurak (1973; also cited in Glass, Gottman, & Shmurak, 1976) conducted a survey of undergraduates at the University of Indiana. For men, Shmurak found that of the social situations with which they had difficulty, 54% concerned dating; the corresponding figure for females was 42%. In England, Bryant and Trower (1974) conducted a survey at the University of Oxford. Their survey involved 30 specific social situations ranging from casual interactions to more intimate ones. Their subjects were asked to rate the difficulty of each situation. Bryant and Trower found that 75% of their sample rated six or more of the situations as at least "moderate" in difficulty, and ratings of great difficulty were made by 40% of the sample for an average of between two and three of the situations. A factor analysis further revealed that over 25% of the variance concerned items that reflected actively seeking contact with strangers, particularly of the opposite sex. Finally, Zimbardo, Pilkonis, and Norwood (1975) developed a shyness survey and administered it to over 800 undergraduates and high school students. The construct of shyness was broadly defined and included assertiveness, initiation of contacts with members of the same and opposite sex, group situations, and public speaking situations. The findings indicated that over half of the subjects indicated that they felt they could use therapeutic help for their perceived problem with shyness.

The results of these survey studies document the degree to which social anxieties and inhibitions are significant life problems for high school and college students. These results also bear on the issue of the "analog status" of problems relating to minimal dating. Most of the studies which have been conducted in the area of minimal dating have employed college students as subjects. In many areas of research, college students have been used as an analog population to approximate some other clinical population of interest. In this sense, research on minimal dating college students may serve as an analog to generate tentative conclusions that might apply to other populations with this problem (e.g., adult outpatients). However, in addition to the potential value of studying minimal dating college students as a possible analog to clinical populations, the study is clinically meaningful in itself. The survey results discussed above demonstrate that minimal dating and social anxiety often constitute significant and central life problems for many college students, apart from the merits of the analog. Thus, studies concerned with the measurement and modification of minimal dating in college students have direct and immediate implications for clinical work with distressed minimal dating college students. The merits of studying minimal dating in college students as an analog to similar problems in other populations is a far more complex question. The validity of any generalization from a college population to an adult inpatient or outpatient population obviously depends on how accurately the analog population approximates relevant parameters in the clinical population. In this regard, many factors become important in assessing the adequacy of the analog, such as the severity of the problem of minimal dating, the presence of other life problems, and questions relating to motivation (e.g., whether the target individuals volunteered for an experiment for remuneration or whether they sought out treatment for their problem). Obviously, the greater the difference between the analog population and the clinical population on these and other relevant variables, the less adequate the analog.

II. MODELS OF MINIMAL DATING

Recently, there have been several models proposed to account for the etiology and maintenance of problems relating to minimal dating. The different models were originally presented as unidimensional explanations of the etiology and maintenance of minimal dating. Each model emphasizes a particular factor as primary, and views other aspects of the problem as secondary derivatives of the primary factor. The main models that have been proposed are discussed below.

A. Social Skill Deficit

In this model, the minimal dater is assumed to lack specific social skills which are thought to be required for successful heterosexual interactions and dating (e.g., MacDonald, Lindquist, Kramer, McGrath, & Rhyne, 1975; Twentyman & McFall, 1975). The anxiety and avoidance of the minimal dater is seen as reactive in that the attempts of the minimal dater at heterosexual approach are typically met by failure and rejection. Thus, in this model, the focus is on the inadequate social behaviors of the minimal daters which in turn lead to anxiety and avoidance. Rather than being "irrational," the anxiety experienced by the minimal daters is seen as a natural response to the negative interpersonal consequences of their social behavior. MacDonald *et al.* (1975) have further stated that the negative self-evaluations of anxious minimal daters constitute *appropriate* appraisals of their inadequate social performance. This conceptualization leads naturally to treatment strategies based on social skills training rather than anxiety reduction or modification of cognitions.

B. Conditioned Anxiety

In this view, the anxiety and avoidance of the minimal dater are seen as the result of direct or vicarious classic conditioning experiences. Cues relating to heterosexual interaction become elicitors of anxiety due to their past association with such aversive experiences as rejection and failure. In this model, the individual's social skill is seen as adequate, but through past experience, heterosexual approach behaviors have acquired conditioned anxiety properties in much the same way as a phobia might be established through classic conditioning. The anxiety leads to avoidance, and avoidance is reinforced through the reduction of anxiety, thus maintaining the pattern of minimal dating and heterosexual avoidance. The main distinction between the social skills deficit model and the conditioned anxiety model is that the former assumes that the social skills of the minimal dater are inadequate and the latter assumes that the social skills of the minimal dater are adequate. The conditioned anxiety model has grown out of the findings of several treatment studies for minimal dating which demonstrate the effectiveness of systematic desensitization for this problem (e.g., Curran, 1975; Curran & Gilbert, 1975; Hokanson, 1971).

C. Cognitive Models

There are several different cognitively oriented models of social anxiety and minimal dating. These models emphasize different aspects of cognition and information processing to account for the anxiety and avoidance of the minimal dater. In these views, as in the conditioned anxiety view, the social skills of the minimal dater are considered to be adequate. The anxiety and avoidance of the minimal dater are viewed as the result of faulty cognitive appraisals and information processing relating to heterosexual social interaction. Different investigators have discussed different cognitive processes which might be involved. These have included: overly negative self-evaluations of social performance (Clark & Arkowitz, 1975; Glasgow & Arkowitz, 1975); negative covert self-statements (Glass *et al.*, 1976; Meichenbaum & Turk, 1976); excessively high standards for performance (Bandura, 1969); selective attention and memory for negative versus positive information about oneself and one's social performance (O'Banion & Arkowitz, in press); and pathological patterns of attribution for social success and social failure (Miller & Arkowitz, in press). The faulty information processing leads to a negative appraisal of one's performance or of the outcome of the interaction which in turn is hypothesized to mediate the anxiety and avoidance of the minimal dater.

D. Physical Attractiveness

Berscheid and Walster (1973) reviewed the extensive literature on physical attractiveness and have concluded that one's physical attractiveness is a very powerful determinant of interpersonal attraction. It appears that physical attractiveness strongly influences the degree to which others will perceive an individual as a desirable dating partner, particularly on first impressions. More positive characteristics are attributed to more physically attractive individuals, and this in turn influences the way others respond to the individual (Berscheid & Walster, 1973). Further, the responses of others will exert considerable impact on our own behavior and feelings about ourselves. In this formulation, the major difficulty of minimal daters consists of their relatively low physical atrractiveness. Because of this, their heterosexual advances are not likely to be met by success, and they are less likely to be sought out by others for dates. Thus, in this view, the low physical atrractiveness of minimal daters is primary, and any anxiety, social skill deficiency, or negative appraisals are secondary results of their low physical attractiveness.

E. Comments on Models of Minimal Dating

Each of the views discussed above emphasizes one aspect or response system as primary, and sees the other problems found in minimal daters as secondary. However, real-life situations are rarely as simple or unidimensional as these models. In a discussion of the first three models presented above, Curran (1977) has correctly pointed out that it is unlikely that these models are mutually exclusive explanations of minimal dating. I agree fully with this point and with the further point that it is likely that there are considerable individual differences among those who manifest a problem in minimal dating. The four models presented above point to relevant possible determinants of minimal dating problems in any particular individual. However, it is likely that some individuals are characterized by problems that can accurately be described by one or more of these component processes. The determinants of the problem for any individual may well involve a complex interaction among some or all of the processes. It appears most likely that minimal dating is indeed a complex problem which can come about and be maintained by a variety of factors. Further, while there may be considerable individual differences *within* any particular population, there may also be differences that apply across different populations. For example, the major determinants of minimal dating for men may be different than those for women, or may involve a different weighting of the factors already mentioned. Physical attractiveness may be a more important determinant of dating for women than for men. College students may show a different pattern or emphasis on the component processes than might a population of adult outpatients or inpatients. Thus, individual difference variables are important to examine both within and across populations to determine those factors most heavily influencing the minimal dating problem. However, for the clinician faced with a patient whose problem is minimal dating, this discussion would suggest that each of the relevant components be assessed. The more accurately we can assess the particular determinants of the individual client's problems, the better we can design individually tailored treatment programs to fit the individual's needs. This is particularly important in view of the fact that there are treatment procedures available that primarily address each of the problem areas discussed. In the next section, we will critically review the major methods and measures used in assessing for minimal dating.

III. ASSESSMENT FOR MINIMAL DATING

Most of the measures for minimal dating have been developed in the context of treatment outcome studies. Measures are often selected or devised based on their apparent validity, with little or no attempt to provide adequate reliability or validity data or to refine the measure psychometrically. The emphasis on treatment studies in this area has been at the expense of careful development of appropriate measures for assessment. In addition, investigators typically select from the few established measures in the area and develop or adapt other measures for the purposes of their study. This has led to considerable variation in assessment procedures across studies, making comparisons among studies difficult. In many instances, pretreatment to posttreatment changes on the measure are taken as indirect evidence for the validity of the measure. Hersen and Bellack (1977) have provided an excellent review of the assessment of social skill and point out that significant pretreatment to posttreatment changes on a particular measure are, at best, only a weak index of its validity. If such changes are found, they would be consistent with the notion that the instrument is valid, although this would not be a direct demonstration of its validity. However, as Hersen and Bellack point out, if such changes are not found, this may mean *either* that the instrument is not a valid measure *or* that the treatment was ineffective in changing what the instrument was intending to measure.

The weaknesses in the area of assessment of minimal dating may be a temporary reflection of the recency of research in this area, where investigators have not had the benefits of other research on which to build their assessment procedures and measures. In fact, the majority of studies on the assessment and treatment of minimal dating did not appear until 1975. Nonetheless, there are a number of sound instruments available for assessment in minimal dating, and a number of promising directions emerging. The main instruments of measurement which have been employed in this area are self-report, behavioral, self-monitoring, and peer-rating measures.

A. Self-Report Measures

A detailed outline of the major self-report measures which have been used in the assessment of minimal dating is presented in Table I. This table lists each measure, the studies in which it was employed, the population in the study, information regarding reliability and validity of each scale, and brief comments, and serves as a summary and guide for this section of the chapter.

Self-report measures have exclusively emphasized the assessment of social anxiety. The Social Avoidance and Distress Scale (SAD), developed by Watson and Friend (1969), is one of the most carefully constructed and well-validated self-report measures. It is a 28-item true–false scale tapping social anxiety and avoidance in same and opposite sex interactions, group and public speaking situations, and interactions with "authority figures." It was standardized on a population of undergraduate men and women. The items are general (e.g., "I tend to withdraw from people") and do not provide diagnostic information about specific situational areas of distress and avoidance that would be useful in planning treatment. However, as a broad measure of social anxiety and avoidance, it seems quite useful both as a screening instrument for studies on social anxiety and as an outcome measure in treatment studies. The scale was carefully constructed, with attention to developing appropriate psychometric properties. In addition, scores on the SAD have been shown to adequately discriminate between high- and low-frequency daters (Arkowitz, Lichtenstein, McGovern, & Hines, 1975; Glasgow & Arkowitz, 1975) and to correlate in the expected direction with behavioral and peer-rating measures of social skill and anxiety (Arkowitz *et al.*, 1975). The correlations in this latter study were generally high. In addition, Royce and Arkowitz (1976) found that SAD scores correlated significantly with self-monitoring measures of frequency ($r = -.46$) and range ($r = -.44$) of heterosexual interactions during a 7-day assessment period. The SAD has also been shown to be sensitive to changes due to treatment, as shown in a number of studies with college students (see Table I). However, in one study involving an adult outpatient population (Marzillier, Lambert, & Kellett, 1976), no significant treatment changes were obtained on the SAD. It should be noted that other measures in this study also showed either small or nonsignificant changes with treatment. Finally, as Table I indicates, the SAD has been used to make theoretical predictions in a number of experiments relating to social anxiety. The fact that most of these predictions have been confirmed may be taken as support for the predictive validity of the SAD. While the SAD appears to be a very good self-report measure of social anxiety for a college population, normative and validational data on other populations, particularly clinical populations, are notably lacking.

The Fear of Negative Evaluation Scale (FNE) was developed by Watson and Friend (1969) at the same time as the SAD. The FNE is a 30-item true–false scale intended to measure the degree to which one is fearful about receiving negative evaluations from others. The scale was developed and standardized on a population of undergraduate men and women. While the scale has several desirable

TABLE I

Self-Report Measures for the Assessment of Minimal Dating

Measure	Experiment	Population	Reliability data	Validity data	Comments
Social Avoidance & Distress Scale (SAD) (Watson & Friend, 1969)	Watson & Friend (1969)	Undergraduate men and women	Yes—adequate	Yes—confirmed behavioral predictions using SAD; correlations with related scales	A 28-item true–false scale appropriate for both men and women
	Arkowitz, Lichtenstein, McGovern, & Hines (1975)	Undergraduate men	No	Yes—differences between high- and low-frequency daters on the SAD and correlations with behavioral and rating measures	
	Glasgow & Arkowitz (1975)	Undergraduate men and women	No	Yes—differences between high- and low-frequency daters on the SAD	
	Bander, Steinke, Allen, & Mosher (1975); Christensen & Arkowitz (1974); Christensen, Arkowitz, & Anderson (1975); Curran, Gilbert, & Little (1976a), Kramer (1975); McGovern, Arkowitz, & Gilmore (1975)	Undergraduate men and women	No	Yes—significant changes with treatment	Bander, Steinker, Allen, & Mosher (1975) used modified form of SAD
	Marzillier, Lambert, & Kellett (1976)	Adult outpatients—men and women	No	Yes—but insignificant changes with treatment	
	Clark & Arkowitz (1975); O'Banion & Arkowitz (1975); Smith (1972)	Undergraduate men and women	No	Yes—various predictions concerning social anxiety confirmed using the SAD	

	Royce & Arkowitz (1976)	Undergraduate men and women	No	Yes—significant changes with treatment and correlations self-monitoring measures	
Fear of Negative Evaluation Scale (FNE) (Watson & Friend, 1969)	Watson & Friend (1969)	Undergraduate men and women	Yes—adequate	Yes—confirmed behavioral predictions relating to fear of negative evaluation using FNE	A 30-item true–false scale appropriate for use with both men and women
	Arkowitz, Lichtenstein, McGovern, & Hines (1975)	Undergraduate men	No	Yes—differences between high- and low-frequency daters	
	Curran, Gilbert, & Little (1976a)	Undergraduate men and women	No	Yes—but no significant changes with treatment	
	Kramer (1975); McGovern Arkowitz, & Gilmore (1975)	Undergraduate men	No	Yes—significant changes with treatment	
	Marzillier, Lambert, & Kellett (1976)	Adult outpatients—men and women	No	Yes—insignificant changes with treatment	
	Smith & Campbell (1973); Smith & Jeffery (1970); Smith & Sarason (1975)	Undergraduate men and women	No	Yes—various predictions concerning fear of negative evaluation confirmed using FNE	
Situation Questionnaire (SQ) (Rehm & Marston, 1968)	Rehm & Marston (1968)	Undergraduate men	No	Yes—differences between volunteers for social anxiety treatment with nonvolunteers; changes with treatment	A 30-item scale with 7-point ratings of discomfort for each item; for men only
	Curran (1975); Curran & Gilbert (1975); Curran, Gilbert, & Little (1976a)	Undergraduate men and women	No	Yes—pre- to posttreatment changes	
	Borkovec, Stone, O'Brien, & Kaloupek (1974)	Undergraduate men	No	Yes—correlations with other self-report measures and with ratings of behavioral effectiveness from a laboratory interaction	

(*continued*)

TABLE I (*contd.*)

Measure	Experiment	Population	Reliability data	Validity data	Comments
	Curran, Gilbert, & Little, (1976a); Curran, Wallander, & Fishetti (1976b)		No	Yes—various predictions relating to social anxiety confirmed using the SQ	
Survey of Heterosexual Interactions (SHI) (Twentyman & McFall, 1975)	Twentyman & McFall (1975)	Undergraduate men	No	Yes—differences between extreme scoring subjects on the SHI on behavioral, rating, and physiological measures, and measures of social activity; changes with treatment	A 20-item scale, each rated on a 1–7 scale (1: unable to respond; 7: able to carry out interaction); for men only
	McGovern, Arkowitz, & Gilmore (1975)	Undergraduate men	No	Yes—significant changes with treatment	
Fear Survey Schedule (FSS) (Wolpe & Lang, 1964) Items relating only to dating or interpersonal anxiety	Curran (1975); Curran & Gilbert (1975); Curran, Gilbert, & Little (1976a); Rehm & Marston (1968)	Undergraduate men and women	No	Yes—Curran & Gilbert (1975) and Rehm & Marston (1968) found significant changes with treatment; however, no such changes were obtained by Curran, Gilbert, & Little (1976a)	Reliability and validity data on entire FSS available elsewhere, but not on specific items used in these studies

	Borkovec, Stone, O'Brien, & Kaloupek (1974)	Undergraduate men	No	Yes—differences between high and low anxious subjects on other self-report measures, physiological arousal, and ratings of effectiveness derived from a laboratory interaction	
Modified S-R Inventory of Anxiousness (adapted from Endler, Hunt, Rosenstein, 1962)	Arkowitz, Lichtenstein McGovern, & Hines (1975)	Undergraduate men	No	Yes—differences between high- and low-frequency daters	Describes 5 hetero-sexual situations and requires 14 different ratings per situation; for men only
	Christensen & Arkowitz (1974); Christensen, Arkowitz, & Anderson (1975); Kramer (1975); McGovern, Arkowitz, & Gilmore (1975)	Undergraduate men and women	No	Yes—changes with treatment	
	MacDonald, Lindquist, Kramer, McGrath, & Rhyne (1975)	Undergraduate men	No	Yes—insignificant changes with treatment	Used a different modification of the Inventory than did above studies

features from a psychometric point of view, specific validational data are still relatively sparse, as can be seen from an examination of Table I. Arkowitz *et al.* (1975) demonstrated that high- and low-frequency daters differed on the FNE, and several additional studies have provided evidence consistent with the predictive validity of the FNE (Smith & Campbell, 1973; Smith & Jeffery, 1970; Smith & Sarason, 1975; Watson & Friend, 1969). Two studies have found significant changes on the FNE with treatment (Kramer, 1975; McGovern, Arkowitz, & Gilmore, 1975) and two others failed to find any treatment effects (Curran, Gilbert, & Little, 1976a; Marzillier *et al.*, 1976). As with the SAD, normative and validational data are lacking for populations other than college students. The correlation between the FNE and the SAD is moderately high ($r = .51$), as demonstrated by Watson and Friend (1969). This suggests considerable overlap between the two scales. The FNE appears to be useful in instances where treatment or predictions are specifically aimed at this construct. However, the constructs of social anxiety and avoidance as measured by the SAD seem more directly relevant to the problem of minimal dating.

The Situation Questionnaire (SQ), developed by Rehm and Marston (1968), consists of 30 items relating specifically to heterosexual interactions. The content of the scale makes it appropriate for males only. Subjects are asked to rate on a 7-point scale the amount of discomfort they would feel in each situation described on the questionnaire. There has been no evaluation of the reliability of the SQ. Apart from studies showing that scores on the SQ are sensitive to changes with treatment (Curran, 1975; Curran & Gilbert, 1975; Curran *et al.*, 1976a), there have been several studies supporting the validity of the scale. Borkovec *et al.* (1974) found that scores on the SQ correlated significantly and in the expected direction with other self-report measures of general and social anxiety. In addition, SQ scores also correlated negatively with confederates' ratings of the "effectiveness" of the subjects' conversational skills based on a laboratory interaction with a female confederate. Curran *et al.* (1976a) and Curran, Wallander, and Fishetti (1976b) have confirmed various predictions relating to social anxiety using the SQ as a selection instrument. Thus, these studies provide some support for the concurrent and predictive validity of the SQ.

Twentyman and McFall (1975) have developed the Survey of Heterosexual Interactions (SHI). This scale consists of 20 specific heterosexual situations which are described on the questionnaire. Subjects rate each item on a 1 to 7 scale, with a score of 1 indicating "unable to respond" and a score of 7 indicating "able to carry out interaction." The scale is appropriate for men only and was developed for an undergraduate population. The SHI was designed to assess subjects' ability to initiate and carry out interactions with women in specific social situations. The authors also present normative data for the SHI. In addition, they conducted a well-designed study comparing high and low scorers on the SHI with other self-report, self-monitoring, behavioral, and physiological measures relating to social anxiety and social skill. Scores on the SHI were good predictors of these other behaviors. In addition, scores on the SHI have shown significant changes with treatment in two studies (McGovern *et al.,* 1975; Twentyman & McFall, 1975). Although this is a new and relatively unresearched scale, it appears highly promising on several dimensions. Apart from its apparent validity, the scale is highly specific to heterosexual interactions. In this respect, it is similar to the SQ and unlike the SAD. A major advantage of the SHI as well as the SQ is that subjects' responses to specific situations can potentially be used to plan treatment in specific areas and situations in which the subjects are deficient. In addition, the specificity of the situations in both the SHI and the SQ can have a direct link to treatment in a related manner. The specific problem situations for any individual can be used as the basis for hierarchies for anxiety reduction or as the basis for behavior rehearsal and social skill training situations. While both the SHI and the SQ have this desirable specificity, the SHI appears to have been more carefully developed than the SQ, although the SQ has more validity research associated with it so far. Unfortunately, no corresponding situation-specific questionnaires have as yet been developed for women.

There have been several other measures which have been used in various treatment studies. The heterosexual anxiety items from the Fear Survey Schedule (Wolpe & Lang, 1964) have been employed by Curran (1975), Curran and Gilbert (1975), Curran *et al.* (1976a), and Rehm and Marston (1968). In addition, Borkovec *et al.* (1974) have shown that subjects differing on heterosexual anxiety (as measured by the Fear Survey items) also differed on other self-report measures, as well as physiological arousal and behavioral ratings of effectiveness derived from a laboratory heterosexual interaction. Finally, several investigators have employed a modified form of Endler, Hunt, and Rosenstein's S-R Inventory of Anxiousness (SRIA). The situations in the original inventory were modified to make them appropriate to heterosexual anxiety. Arkowitz *et al.* (1975) demonstrated that high- and low-frequency daters differ on the SRIA. In addition, this measure has been used in a number of treatment outcome studies indicated in Table I.

In summary, the SAD appears to be a promising and reasonably well-researched general measure of social anxiety that is useful as a screening instrument for studies on social anxiety as well as a treatment outcome measure. It is also one of the few available measures that can be used for both men and women. The FNE appears to overlap with the SAD, but might be useful for more basic studies specifically concerned with the construct of fear of negative evaluation. The SHI and SQ are less well-researched than the other two instruments and are for men only. However, the SHI and the SQ have an important advantage in the situation-specific quality of the items for specific diagnosis and for treatment planning. The SAD and FNE both have more general items that would not be as useful for these purposes. The FSS items and the modified SRIA have much less research associated with them. However, the FSS items might serve well as a screening instrument for subject selection. It has the advantage of being extremely brief. There is a clear need for more situation-specific questionnaires appropriate for women. One major limitation that applies to all the self-report instruments reviewed is that they were developed using undergraduate populations. The appropriateness of these measures and corresponding norms for other populations such as adult outpatients and inpatients remain to be determined.

B. Behavioral Methods and Measures

Most of the studies involving assessment of minimal dating have utilized some form of simulated laboratory heterosexual interactions. These methods have taken the form of either discrete situation tests or extended interaction tests. In discrete situation tests, subjects are presented with a series of specific simulated heterosexual situations utilizing trained confederates in either live or taped presentations. In extended interaction tests, the subject is typically asked to interact with a live opposite-sex partner (who may be either a confederate or another subject). The context of the situation is general and involves 5 or 10 minutes of conversational interaction. In these extended situation tests, the focus is on the extended flow of behavior during the course of the conversation rather than on specific segments of heterosexual interaction.

1. DISCRETE SITUATION TESTS

The majority of the discrete situation tests have involved audiotaped presentations of the situations. Rehm and Marston (1968) were the first to use this format for minimal dating. Their situation test involved 10 social situations presented and enacted on audiotape and was for males only. A male voice initially described the background of a situation (e.g., "As you are leaving a cafeteria, a girl taps you on the back and says. . . ."). Following this, a female voice came on the tape with a line of dialogue (e.g., "I think you left this book"), to which subjects were asked to respond aloud. Subjects' responses were recorded on a second tape recorder. Various rating and behavioral measures are typically derived from the subjects' responses. These have included latency of response, number of words per response, and ratings of anxiety, skill, effectiveness, and likability. Melnick (1973) used videotaped presentations of the situations, and Twentyman and McFall (1975) and MacDonald *et al.* (1975) used live interactions with confederates for presentations.

Rehm and Marston (1968) found significant differences between a group of volunteers for treatment and a "normal" population on the following measures derived from their taped situation test: self-ratings of anxiety, raters' anxiety ratings, latency of response, and anxiety signs. Number of words per response did not discriminate between the two groups. Arkowitz *et al.* (1975) used a different taped situation test and found significant differences between high- and low-frequency daters on both latency and number of words. In addition, one or both of these measures (i.e., latency and number of words) correlated significantly with self-report, behavioral, and peer-rating measures of social skill and social anxiety. Twentyman and McFall (1975) found significant differences between shy and confident subjects (as determined by the SHI) on length of response, pulse rates, and ratings of anxiety and skill derived from their discrete situation test. In addition, a number of studies have shown some changes with treatment on measures derived from discrete situation tests (Christensen, Arkowitz, & Anderson, 1975; Gambrill, 1975; Glass *et al.*, 1976; MacDonald *et al.*, 1975; Melnick, 1973; Twentyman & McFall, 1975).

Rhyne, MacDonald, McGrath, Lindquist, and Kramer (1974) have developed a situation test that involves three discrete 4-minute live interactions with trained confederates. The test is appropriate for men only and has the advantage of sampling more of the flow of interaction and reciprocity in heterosexual interaction than do discrete situation tests involving only situation and response. The confederate's behaviors are clearly specified to insure relatively standardized confederate behaviors in the interaction. Criteria for scoring are based on specific behaviors designated as appropriate by the experimenters, and on observable anxiety signs derived from a modified form of the Timed Behavioral Checklist (Paul, 1966). Reliability of the measures in the Rhyne *et al.* study was quite high. In addition, Rhyne *et al.* (1974) demonstrated that high- and low-frequency daters differed significantly on the measures of social skill but did not differ on the observable anxiety signs. Further, the measures of social skill on this test have been demonstrated to be sensitive to treatment change (MacDonald *et al.*, 1975) while the results for the anxiety measures were less clear.

With only two exceptions, the discrete situation tests are appropriate for male undergraduate populations only. Gambrill (1975) developed a test for women and Goldsmith and McFall (1975) developed one appropriate for psychiatric inpatients. However, apart from results showing changes with treatment, no further validity data are available for either of these tests.

The situation tests discussed thus far have been guided by the experimenter's judgments in determining item content and response scoring methods. There are two situation tests that are noteworthy exceptions. The tests developed by Glass *et al.* (1976) and Goldsmith and McFall (1975) both employed a "behavioral-analytic" test construction strategy, as outlined by Goldfried and D'Zurrilla (1969). This construction involves situational analysis, response enumeration, and response evaluation. Each step is guided by data derived from the criterion population. Thus, in these tests, the item pool, the response alternatives, and criteria for response evaluation were derived from information from the criterion populations rather than from the experimenter's judgment. The behavioral-analytic strategy insures that the situations and scoring criteria are appropriate for the populations of interest. While no validational data are available for either of these situation tests other than changes with treatment, they warrant further attention because of the strong test construction strategy employed.

One potential liability of all these discrete situation tests is that they take the subject's behavior out of context and deal only with specific situation–response episodes, rather than with the flow of reciprocal interaction that takes place in naturalistic situations. This may limit the generality and validity of behavior samples derived from such tests. A study by Martin (1971) on parent–child interaction raises some potential problems with discrete situation tests and the degree to which they may be an adequate sample of how subjects respond in more naturalistic situations. Martin studied the responses of parents to a "programmed child" presented in various situations. He coded the parents' behavioral responses to the situation test with an identical coding system he employed to code the parents' actual behaviors with their own children in similar situations at home. He found little or no relationship between parental response to the situation test and their response to similar behaviors emitted by their own children in the home situation. This suggests that data from discrete situation tests should not be accepted on face validity alone. Independent demonstrations of the validity of these situation tests are needed.

1. EXTENDED INTERACTION TESTS

Extended interaction tests are designed to approximate a naturalistic "boy-meets-girl" situation in the laboratory. Various rating and specific behavioral measures are coded from the subject's performance during a 5- to 10-minute laboratory interaction. In one of the first systematic studies of an extended interaction test, Borkovec *et al.* (1974) compared the performance of high and low socially anxious men during an interaction with a female confederate. The high-anxious men showed significantly greater heart rate and were rated as significantly less "effective" in their performance than were low anxious men. However, no significant differences were found on behavioral measures of observable anxiety signs. The Borkovec *et al.* study is also the only one that has evaluated the effects of task demands during an extended interaction test. Borkovec and co-workers found that subjects' performance during extended interaction was not influenced by a demand manipulation, which had previously been shown to exert significant influence on the assessment of snake-fear behavior (Borkovec, 1973). These findings suggest that the demand effects which have plagued other areas of anxiety assessment (cf. Bernstein, 1973) may not be present in the assessment of social anxiety in extended interaction tests.

Arkowitz *et al.* (1975) compared the performance of high- and low-frequency dating men during an extended interaction test with a female confederate. This exploratory study was to try to empirically determine those behaviors that discriminated between high- and low-frequency daters during the extended interaction test. Subjects' performance was evaluated on a large number of behavioral and rating measures gleaned from the literature on social skill and social anxiety. These included a number of specific nonverbal behaviors such as eye contact, head nods, and smiles, as well as numerous verbal behaviors based on an elaborate system for coding the content and flow of conversation. In addition, subjects' performances were rated on social skill by trained observers. While the reliability of most measures was reasonably high, the only behavioral measure to discriminate between the groups was the frequency of "awkard" silences, that is, silences of 10 or more seconds. Nonetheless, high-frequency daters were rated as significantly more socially skilled than low-frequency daters by the trained observers. In a subsequent study, Glasgow and Arkowitz (1975) suggested that measures of simple output may not discriminate between the groups, and focused instead on measures based on reciprocity. They compared high- and low-frequency dating men *and* women on reciprocal measures (e.g., eye contact given partner talk) derived from an extended interaction test. None of the measures significantly differentiated between high- and low-frequency daters. This was true for both men and women. However, the high-frequency dating women were rated as significantly more socially skilled than the low-frequency dating women, while no such differences were obtained for the two groups of men. Twentyman and McFall (1975) also used an extended interaction test and compared the performance of shy and confident men (as measured by the SHI) on behavioral, physiological, and rating measures. Shy men showed more observable anxiety signs, and were rated as significantly more anxious and less skilled than confident men. Pulse rate measures on this task did not discriminate between the groups.

The studies reviewed are the only ones which have employed contrasted groups on the extended interaction test. There have been numerous other studies which have used such tests for the assessment of treatment outcome, with mixed but generally positive results (Bander, Steinke, Allen, & Mosher, 1975; Christensen & Arkowitz, 1974; Christensen *et al.*, 1975; Curran, 1975; Curran & Gilbert, 1975; Curran *et al.*, 1976a; Kramer, 1975; Marzillier *et al.*, 1976; Melnick, 1973; Twentyman & McFall, 1975). The findings of the studies employing contrasted groups generally indicate that anxiety measures (observable anxiety signs, ratings of anxiety, physiological measures) do discriminate among the groups, but behavioral measures thought to reflect social skill do not. The lack of behavioral differences on social skill measures is surprising in view of the relatively consistent finding that raters do discriminate between the groups on general ratings of social skill. Obviously, the observers are responding differentially to some behavioral factor, which is reflected in their social skill ratings. However, the nature of what they are responding to is unclear. It may be that social skill differences are present, but the behavioral measures selected have not been the appropriate ones. Or, it may be that the groups do not differ in social skill in this task and that the observers' ratings are reflecting another dimension, such as physical attractiveness.

Clarification of whether or not the subjects are in fact deficient in social skills is an important question with implications for treatment. This issue will be considered more fully in Section VI. For the more practical purposes of assessment, however, specific behavioral indices of social skill have not proved useful in extended interaction tests, while measures of anxiety and general ratings of social skill do appear valid.

Observer ratings of social anxiety and social skill have been used in most of the assessment and treatment studies in this area. There are several problems with this method of determining these ratings. First, as mentioned, the ratings are derived from live observations of the subjects and may be influenced by the subject's physical attractiveness. The findings that minimal daters are less physically attractive than more frequent daters (Glasgow & Arkowitz, 1975) and that positive socially desirable characteristics are attributed to physically attractive individuals (Dion, Berscheid, & Walster, 1972) suggest that this may indeed be the case. Any biasing effects due to physical attractiveness could be handled through the use of audiotapes of conversations for generating the social skill ratings. However, this would result in loss of nonverbal behaviors for coding. A second problem with the way in which rating measures have been used relates to the use of the same raters of both social anxiety and social skill. It seems likely that a rater's first rating may artifactually influence his subsequent ratings. Thus, a subject first rated as high on social skill may be likely to receive a low social anxiety rating, apart from any signs of anxiety the subject might show. Some data from a study by Rotter and Wickens (1948) are relevant to this point. They found that when a subject's role-played responses to two different situations were rated by the same raters, the average correlation of the ratings across situations was .78. However, when two different sets of raters were used for two situations, the average correlation dropped to .55. This suggests that there may well be a halo effect determined by the first rating, and this poses a serious problem for ratings of extended interaction tests. This problem may be handled through counterbalancing the order of ratings. The use of different sets of raters for each different rating would be even more desirable. This discussion also raises some interesting theoretical questions as to whether social skill and social anxiety are two discriminably different constructs. Most definitions of social skill imply low anxiety. This latter problem cannot adequately be dealt with until we have a clear and empirically generated definition of social skill. Since most of the treatment procedures in the area are based on a social skills training paradigm, the need for such a definition is clear. One promising direction in this regard is a coding system developed by Argyle, Bryant, and Trower (1974a) for interactional behavior. This system consists of 17 5-point rating scales representing elements of social skill previously described and studied by Argyle (1969). The rating scale includes voice quality (e.g., tone and clarity), verbal signals (e.g., content, interest in self, and emotional content), and non-verbal signals (e.g., facial expression, posture, and appearance). While the scale was generated from past research on social skill, no validational data for this scale have as yet been presented. Further, because of possible halo effects discussed earlier, separate raters would be needed for each dimension. While this would be a time-consuming undertaking, this scale appears to be the most promising one available.

The extended interaction tests which have been employed have several other limitations. First, they have almost exclusively involved subjects' behavior once the subject is placed in an interaction with an opposite-sexed partner, and have focused only on this initial conversation. However, there are many other aspects of social skill this situation does not tap. These include such skills as discovering ways that maximize the likelihood of meeting people, making the first overture to a conversation, asking for a date, dealing with real or perceived rejection, and more complex issues relating to longer term and more intimate relationships. While these aspects are often the focus of social skills training programs, they have not typically been assessed in any of these studies. Naturalistic assessment of some of these might better be accomplished through such procedures as a dance or social gathering given by the experimenters during which subjects' behaviors are unobtrusively coded (cf. Berscheid, Dion, Walster, & Walster, 1971). A second limitation of the usual extended interaction test relates to the situational lack of consequences. Such consequences, however, are present in more naturalistic situations. For example, a male minimal dater might perform differently in a laboratory interaction with a confederate where there are no consequences involving acceptance or rejection which might influence subsequent contact with the female. However, if the assessment situation did have such consequences, the behaviors of subjects might more closely approximate their behavior in the naturalistic situation. Thus, if the situation was structured in such a way that the impression that the subject made on his partner would have consequences in terms of further dating contact with her, it would more closely approximate the consequences present in naturalistic heterosexual interactions. A procedure developed by Glass *et al.* (1976) approximated more naturalistic consequences. In this study, female undergraduates were recruited who volunteered for a study of "telephone conversations." They did not know that the male subjects who were to telephone them were volunteers for a treatment program for minimal dating. The male subject was given the names of two women and asked to telephone the woman during the week in order to practice becoming acquainted with a woman. Measures derived from this task were based on a questionnaire sent to the women to find out which of the subjects had in fact telephoned. In addition, the questionnaire asked for ratings by the woman of the skillfulness of each man she had spoken to and an indication of which man she would most like to meet. This assessment task appears to be very promising since it involves naturalistic interaction and can be structured so that the consequences (relating to further contact) are similar to those present in the naturalistic situation. Twentyman and McFall (1975) have used a related telephone assessment task that also holds promise.

C. Self-Monitoring Measures

Self-monitoring measures have been used in the assessment of a variety of target behaviors, including smoking (McFall, 1970), food intake (Bellack, Rozensky, & Schwartz, 1974), study activities (Johnson & White, 1971), and time spent outside by agoraphobics (Emmelkamp, 1974). This method has been used in minimal dating by asking subjects to record their dates and casual heterosexual interactions in a diary for some specified assessment period, usually from 7 to 10 days. Considerable care is required to define clearly for the subjects those interactions that qualify for inclusion or exclusion.

Typically, fairly detailed instructions and examples are given, as in the diary employed by Christensen *et al.* (1975). In most cases, the derived measures from such self-monitoring involve frequency of heterosexual contacts as well as the range or number of different people with whom the subject interacted.

Twentyman and McFall (1975) compared shy and confident subjects (as determined from the SHI) on various measures derived from their social activity diary. They found that confident subjects had significantly higher frequency and range scores, and spent more total time interacting with women in more situations than did shy subjects.

Self-monitoring measures are open to criticism based on their accuracy (e.g., Nelson, 1977) since typically no objective external check on the accuracy of these scores is available. However, there are some data which bear on this issue for minimal dating. In the Twentyman and McFall (1975) study, male subjects were given the opportunity to telephone and have a "coke date" with female volunteers. The authors noted that those subjects who actually made the telephone call (as verified by the female volunteers) also recorded these contacts in their diary; those who did not telephone did not record any such contact. In addition, diary scores also correlated significantly with measures from other modalities including scores on the SHI, observer ratings of anxiety during an extended interaction test, and other self-report measures. Royce and Arkowitz (1976) found that diary scores correlated significantly with scores on the SAD ($r = -.46$, $p < .01$) and with peer-ratings of the subjects' social activity ($r = .65$, $p < .01$). This latter correlation is particularly interesting since the peers have the opportunity to observe the subjects' social activities in the natural environment and may be considered to be external accuracy checks. Measures derived from social activity diaries also have been shown to be sensitive to changes with treatment (e.g., Christensen & Arkowitz, 1974; Christensen *et al.*, 1975; Hokanson, 1971; Kramer, 1975; Twentyman & McFall, 1975).

Thus, self-monitoring measures are to be recommended in assessment and treatment studies for minimal dating. The frequency and range of the subjects' heterosexual interactions certainly are relevant to the assessment of minimal dating, perhaps even more so than laboratory derived measures of anxiety and skill. However, self-monitoring measures are also highly reactive. Nelson (1977) has provided an excellent discussion of the accuracy and reactivity of self-monitoring measures. The reader is referred to this contribution for ways in which self-monitoring measures might be improved.

D. Peer-Rating Measures

One useful but infrequently used method of assessment consists of ratings of the subject by their friends and acquaintances. In some respects, these ratings can be considered as a form of direct observation in the natural environment, using as coders individuals who are naturally a part of the subject's social environment. However, these ratings are limited by the fact that the peers observe only a small and limited portion of the subject's social behavior, and are open to the possibility of bias in trying to present the subject in a "good light." Nonetheless, their naturalistic base still makes them valid assessment instruments.

Arkowitz *et al.* (1975) found significant differences between high- and low-frequency dating men on peer-rating measures of social skill, social anxiety, and social activity. In addition, significant correlations in the expected direction were obtained between peer ratings of social skill, and self-report measures of social anxiety and behavioral measures derived from a discrete situation test. The peer rating measures did not show any significant correlation with measures derived from an extended interaction test. Royce and Arkowitz (1976) also found that peer-rating measures correlated significantly with SAD scores and self-monitoring measures of frequency of social activity. In addition, peer-rating measures have been used in several treatment outcome studies and have been sensitive to treatment effects (Christensen & Arkowitz, 1974; Christensen *et al.*, 1975; Royce & Arkowitz, 1976).

While use of peer-ratings is still in a preliminary stage, these ratings have one characteristic that recommends further work on these measures. Apart from the "correctness" of the peers' evaluations, it is likely that these evaluations will influence the way in which they respond to the subject. If they see the subject as shy and inhibited, this evaluation decreases the likelihood that the subject will be included in social activities with the peers; the reverse would be true for subjects whom the peers consider confident and socially skilled. Thus, the peers are likely to treat the subject in ways consistent with their evaluation of the subject, further perpetuating subjects' behaviors consistent with that evaluation.

E. Dating Frequency Measures

The target of minimal dating leads directly to a consideration of using the subjects' own retrospective estimates of their dating frequency as a measure in minimal dating studies. Clearly, if an accurate estimate of the subject's past dating frequency were available, it would constitute a relevant dependent variable for treatment studies and may also serve as one selection criterion for both assessment and treatment studies in the area. Such retrospective estimates have been employed in several studies and usually involve asking the subject to estimate their frequency of dating in the past 3–6 months. Curran and Gilbert (1975) have discussed the use of dating frequency as a measure in treatment outcome studies and have criticized its use on several grounds. These included possible inaccuracy in recall, the possibility of temporal fluctuations in dating frequency (e.g., due to weather and time of school year), and difficulties in defining a date. They point out that inaccuracies in recall should be randomly distributed across groups. In using pretreatment to posttreatment changes in dating frequency in treatment outcome studies, temporal variations should be relatively constant across groups. However, the possibility of such variations suggests that such pre- and posttreatment estimates should occur at equivalent periods in the school year and season. The difficulty in defining a date may be a more serious problem. If different individuals have different conceptions of what is meant by "date," then considerable inaccuracy will be introduced into any measures of this kind. Usually, investigators provide subjects with some general definition of a date. For example, Curran and Gilbert (1975) defined a date as "an arranged interaction that may lead to romantic involvement" (p. 519). However, findings that subjects differing in their retrospective estimates of dating frequency also differed on self-report, behavioral, and rating measures (Arkowitz *et al.*, 1975) suggest that such retrospective estimates may have some validity.

Curran and Gilbert (1975) make one point concerning dating frequency that is quite important and which has been virtually neglected. They point out that parametric statistics are inappropriate for the analysis of dating frequency scores, since extreme scores of a few subjects may unduly influence the mean. For example, a subject who has completed a treatment program may still be deficient in social skills, but may have fortuitously found a steady dating partner. The observed increase in dating frequency of this subject would bias the mean for their group. Further, such a subject's dating frequency may decrease drastically if that relationship is terminated. For these reasons, Curran and Gilbert recommend nonparametric analyses of dating frequency data. This recommendation is one that should be followed by researchers in this area.

While there are several problems with retrospective estimates of dating frequency, it would seem important to try to address these problems as well as we can, and include this measure in studies of minimal dating, since it is certainly an index which is important to the subjects, perhaps even more so than laboratory-based measures of social skill and social anxiety. Dating frequency is clearly a meaningful criterion and can serve as a measure of generalization of treatment effects. The inclusion of such measures for minimal dating is to be highly recommended. It would also seem worthwhile to develop measures of "quality" or satisfaction in addition to "quantity" or simple frequency. Subjects may date frequently with different partners, but may still be unable to form satisfying relationships with any of them, and such a phenomenon suggests that measures of quality are worth pursuing.

F. Conclusions

Despite the recency of assessment and treatment research in minimal dating, there are a number of sound instruments and methods available in this area. Most studies have taken a multimethod assessment approach and used some or all of self-report, self-monitoring, peer-rating, behavioral, and dating frequency measures. This multimethod approach is appropriate in light of the complexity of the determinants of minimal dating. However, more research directed specifically at assessment is needed, not just in the context of treatment studies, but to specifically evaluate different methods and instruments that can be used in this area.

While there are many good procedures available to assess treatment outcome, specific methods for behavioral diagnosis are still lacking. Such methods would serve to pinpoint the specific areas of difficulty for the particular individual and to aid in the planning of treatment. The best measures are self-report, self-monitoring, and peer-rating measures. In addition, general ratings derived from live interaction tests have also proved useful. However, specific and valid behavioral measures of social skill are not yet available. Further theoretical and empirical work on the construct of social skill is necessary before such measures can be developed. While live extended interaction tests seem an appropriate context in which to measure social skill, most that have been employed thus far relate to only a restricted situation involving "boy-meets-girl." Assessment situations tapping other skills and including the potential for naturalistic consequences are needed. Further, the weakness of specific behavioral measures from live interaction tests should serve as a caution to clinicians who plan their treatment based on assessment of the patient's social skill from such tasks. Until we know what behaviors we should observe that relate to social skill, we should be cautious in accepting specific behavioral observations of subjects' task performances as the basis for assessment and treatment planning.

IV. THE TREATMENT OF MINIMAL DATING

Treatment research in the area of minimal dating has paralleled the work on subassertiveness (e.g., McFall, 1976) in that it emphasizes a social skills-deficit model. Consistent with this model, most research has been aimed at the evaluation of social skills training programs for minimal daters. These programs have typically involved some or all of the following elements: behavior rehearsal, feedback, modeling, coaching, and homework assignments. A second set of studies has emphasized an anxiety model of minimal dating and has emphasized anxiety reduction procedures such as systematic desensitization or variations of *in vivo* desensitization. Finally, several recent treatment studies have been explicitly derived from a cognitive model of minimal dating and have emphasized cognitive modification procedures derived from the work of Meichenbaum (1973). These studies will be reviewed under each of these categories. The majority of studies have employed college student volunteers as the target population. The relatively few studies which have been done with patients will be reviewed separately.

A. Social Skill Training

Twentyman and McFall (1975) compared a social skills training program with a waiting-list control group for male minimal daters. Subject selection criteria consisted of a dating frequency of not more than one date per month and a score on the Survey of

Heterosexual Interactions no higher than one standard deviation above the mean score of the normative population. This study is noteworthy in its use of physiological measures and the careful assessment of the validity of each of the dependent measures employed through the use of comparisons with a contrasted group of subjects who scored high on the Survey of Heterosexual Interactions. Pre- and posttreatment assessment consisted of the Survey of Heterosexual Interactions, self-monitoring measures over a 7-day period, and measures derived from several discrete and extended interaction tests. These measures included observer ratings of anxiety and skill, ratings of overt anxiety signs, pulse rate, avoidance behavior (number of situations to which the subject did not respond), and time spent in each situation.

Treatment consisted of three individual sessions. The social skills training subjects were presented with problematic situations described by the therapist. Subjects were asked to covertly rehearse their response. After this, subjects received coaching, modeling via the presentation of the responses of two competent models, and overt behavioral rehearsal. This sequence was repeated several times for each of the situations. In addition, subjects were given homework assignments involving telephone conversations with female confederates. While pretreatment scores for the two groups were equivalent, the findings indicated that treated subjects did better than controls at posttest on observer ratings of skill and anxiety, ratings of overt anxiety signs, physiological responsivity, avoidance behaviors, and scores on the Survey of Heterosexual Interactions. While the findings were not significant for all the specific measures in each category, most of the measures showed this pattern. On the self-monitoring measures, treated subjects spent significantly more time with significantly more women in significantly more situations, and also tended to interact with a greater number of different women than did the control group. A 6-month follow-up was included in the design. However, only 50% of the subjects could be located or responded to the follow-up, making any interpretation of follow-up differences tenuous.

These results are impressive, particularly in view of the relatively brief duration of treatment. Although this study lacks an attention placebo group, several subsequent studies, which we shall review, have not found any significant changes with attention placebo manipulations. The clear demonstration that the subjects in this study were indeed more anxious, less skilled, and less socially active than a group of confident subjects on the dependent measures makes the results of this study even more impressive. Such a comparison provides validity data for the measures and also demonstrates that the subjects were deficient in the areas to which treatment was addressed. Only one of the remaining studies which we will review (Rehm & Marston, 1968) included such a comparison with a contrasted group. Since selection criteria vary considerably across studies, this leaves open the possibility of whether the subjects in the other studies were in fact more anxious, less skilled, and less socially active than their peers. The unfortunate attrition in the follow-up of the Twentyman and McFall (1975) study limits any conclusion about maintenance and generalization (in terms of long-term changes in dating frequency) of the treatment effects.

MacDonald *et al.* (1975) have also evaluated a social skill training program for men. A major strength of this study consists of the stringent selection criteria employed. Subjects were accepted into the study only if they reported having less than four dates in the past year and having a desire to change. Social skill training consisted of six 2-hour group sessions. Treatment included hierarchically arranged behavior rehearsal, group discussion, coaching, and feedback. In addition, one of the two social skill training groups also received intersession homework assignments coordinated with the content of each session. The two social skill training groups were compared to an attention placebo and a waiting-list control group. Therapists were two women, each of whom served as therapist for one group in each treatment condition. Assessment consisted of self-report measures of social anxiety as well as observer ratings of anxiety signs and a social skill score based on the discrete situation test developed by Rhyne *et al.* (1974). Finally, estimates of dating frequency were obtained during a 1-week period before and after treatment.

The strongest results were for the social skill scores from the situation test. Both social skill training groups showed significant improvements on this measure while neither of the control groups showed any such changes. However, the strength of these results is attenuated somewhat by therapist differences in which one of the therapists' social skill training groups did not show significant change on this measure. No clear differences between treatment and control groups emerged on the anxiety measure from the interaction test. There were no differential treatment effects for two of the self-report anxiety measures employed. On a third self-report measure, the social skill training groups improved more than the controls. Finally, there were no significant effects for the dating frequency measure. In general, both social skills groups did equally well, suggesting that homework assignments did not enhance treatment effectiveness.

The most interesting finding was the result that social skill training led to increased social skill scores on the interaction test. However, the improvement on this measure of social skill was not matched by any corresponding increase in dating frequency, suggesting that the changes that did occur may not have generalized beyond the laboratory. The lack of any follow-up further leaves open any question about the maintenance of obtained changes.

Melnick (1973) conducted one of the few studies which evaluated the incremental effects of various components of social skill training programs. The design consisted of six groups which were combined into adjoining pairs for data analysis due to lack of clear differences among these pairs. The first two were control groups, consisting of a waiting-list control group and a group that received the same equivalent therapy time as the treatment groups, but which received insight and reflective techniques without any specific behavioral intervention. The second two were "intermediate" therapy groups. Both received modeling in which they were exposed to video tapes of college students in progressively more intimate interactions with women. In addition, one of these groups also received behavior rehearsal and feedback after the modeling, using live interactions with female confederates. The remaining two groups were "self-observation" groups. Subjects in these two groups also received modeling, behavior rehearsal, and feedback. In addition, both had the opportunity to observe their performance through the use of videotape feedback. One of these groups also received intermittent reinforcement contingent on appropriate behaviors displayed on the videotape playback. Treatment consisted of four 40-minute sessions of individual therapy with a female therapist.

Assessment included behavioral and rating measures derived from a discrete and an extended interaction test. The discrete interaction test was a videotaped version of Rehm and Marston's situation test. The extended interaction consisted of a conversation with a female confederate. Behavioral measures consisted of latency of response and speech dysfluencies derived from the discrete situation test. In addition, observers rated the subjects' performances on both situation tests on dimensions of appropriateness, masculine assertiveness, anxiety, and overall pleasantness. Finally, the Gough Adjective Checklist was used as a measure of self-concept.

The subjects were male volunteers for a dating study. While these subjects differed significantly in their retrospective estimates of dating frequency compared to a normal control group, by no means could they be considered minimal daters. Subjects were accepted if they reported a dating frequency of no more than two dates a week. The actual frequencies of the various groups were not given. This excessively liberal selection criterion limits any generalization of the results to populations of what most would consider to be minimal daters.

The results generally favored the self-observation groups. Subjects in these groups performed better than the control groups on all four rating measures from the extended interaction test and better than the intermediate treatment groups on two of these measures. There were no significant differences on any of these four measures between the intermediate and control groups. On the discrete situation test, the self-observation groups did better than the intermediate groups on two of the rating measures. However, on these measures, neither the self-observation nor intermediate treatment groups were significantly different from the controls. Finally, there were no significant effects on the two behavioral measures (latency and speech dysfluencies) and the self-concept measure.

There are numerous problems with the interpretation of the results of this study. The major one involves the overly liberal selection criterion. In addition, the lack of any follow-up and the fact that the only significant changes were in rating rather than overt behavioral measures limit the interpretation of results.

Curran and his associates have conducted a series of studies evaluating social skill training procedures. In the first study, Curran (1975) compared social skill training, imaginal desensitization, attention placebo, and a waiting-list control group. Subjects were undergraduate male and female volunteers who responded to a newspaper advertisement. No objective screening criteria were employed for subject selection. The dating frequency characteristics of the sample were not fully described. Curran reported that 50% of the subjects reported 20 or fewer dates in their lives. However, the recent dating frequency status and the dating frequency of the remaining 50% of the subjects were not given. The social skill training procedure consisted of providing subjects with instructional material, videotape modeling, behavior rehearsal, group and videotape feedback, and homework assignments. The skills in which the subjects were trained included: giving and receiving of compliments, listening skills, feeling talk, assertion, nonverbal methods of communicating, training in planning dates, and methods of enhancing physical attractiveness. The social skill training, desensitization, and attention placebo groups received six 75-minute sessions in a group setting. Assessment consisted of several self-report questionnaires (including the Situation Questionnaire and Fear Survey Schedule) and a live extended interaction test with an opposite-sexed confederate. Observers of the videotapes of the live interaction test rated subjects on social anxiety and social skill. The results showed that all four groups showed significant improvement on all measures. However, the social skill training and desensitization groups showed significantly greater improvement on observer ratings of anxiety and skill than did either of the two control groups.

This initial study had several methodological problems which weakened the acceptance of the results. These included the relatively small number of subjects (between 6 and 9 per condition), subject attrition of greater than 20% which occurred differentially across groups, and the lack of clear selection criteria, follow-up, and assessment of changes in dating frequency.

Despite the problems with the Curran (1975) study, the results were sufficiently encouraging to warrant a second improved study subsequently conducted by Curran and Gilbert (1975). The overall design of this study and the assessment procedures were basically similar to the previous one with several important exceptions. The overall number of subjects was increased, clearer and more objective screening criteria were employed, the number of treatment sessions was increased, dating frequency was included in the assessment, and a follow-up was included. Subjects were included only if they fell within the upper third of the distribution of scores on the Fear Survey heterosexual items and the Situation Questionnaire from a larger sample of 854 persons. The study compared social skills training, desensitization, and a waiting-list control group, omitting the attention placebo control group used in the first study. The results of this study demonstrated that the skills training and desensitization groups showed significantly greater improvements than the control group on all of the self-report measures of anxiety. These differences persisted at a 6-month follow-up. On the behavioral ratings derived from the live extended interaction test, the results were more mixed. At posttreatment assessment, there was only one significant between-groups difference. The social skill training group was rated as significantly more skilled than the control group. At follow-up, the social skills group was rated as significantly more skilled than both the desensitization and control groups. Regarding the anxiety ratings from the extended interaction test, there were no significant between-groups differences at posttest. However, at follow-up, both the skill training and desensitization group were rated as significantly less anxious than the control group.

The findings that both groups improved on anxiety, but only the social skills training group improved on the skill ratings are interesting and suggest that the social skill program was specific in its effects. While this might be true, there was no demonstration that the subjects were initially deficient in social skills. Curran and Gilbert seem to acknowledge this point and indicate that while many subjects did seem deficient in social skills, others seemed adequate in their skills and were characterized instead by excessive anxiety or overly negative self-evaluations. While social skill training may lead to increased social skill, it would appear important to demonstrate that subjects were indeed lacking in social skill through a comparison of pretreatment levels of social skill with a normal control group. Otherwise, it is possible that social skill training may be increasing the social skills of already skilled individuals who might better benefit from some alternative treatment. This interpretive problem is not unique to the Curran and Gilbert study, but is present in most of the studies on social skill training.

Curran and Gilbert also assessed dating frequency. Regarding this measure, as with the anxiety reduction measures, the results pointed to the effectiveness of both the social skill training and desensitization procedures. Both groups showed significant increases in dating frequency compared to the control group, and these differences were maintained at follow-up. However, the subjects could not be characterized as minimal daters. Pretreatment dating frequencies of the subjects averaged about one date per month. Nonetheless, the Curran and Gilbert study was well-designed, showed clear and significant changes on both laboratory measures and dating frequency, and documented positive effects over a 6-month follow-up period.

In the third study in this series, Curran *et al.* (1976a) compared their social skill training procedure with a sensitivity training program developed by Berzon, Reisal, and Davis (1969). Their results indicated that while both treatment groups improved significantly on self-report measures of social anxiety, only the social skill training group showed significant improvements on ratings of skill and anxiety derived from the extended interaction test.

Bander *et al.* (1975) have also evaluated social skill training procedures for minimal dating men. They report that their subjects were screened for self-reports of anxiety and low dating frequency, but they do not give either the screening criteria or the mean pretreatment levels of either anxiety or dating frequency. However, they report that their subjects differed significantly from a randomly selected comparison group regarding social anxiety and dating frequency. One group of subjects received eight weekly sessions of social skill training, which involved behavior rehearsal with female assistants who provided feedback and information about dating behaviors and norms. Homework assignments were also given paralleling the rehearsed situations. The situations were dealt with hierarchically, starting with the least difficult ones. A second group received a combination of the social skill training procedure described above with imaginal desensitization. Treatment for this group also consisted of eight sessions, necessitating use of an abbreviated form of the social skills training program. These two behavioral procedures were compared to a microlab procedure that emphasized sharing, clarifying, and expressing of feelings relating to members of the opposite sex. The groups also included women who were not aware that the men were subjects in a dating treatment study. The microlab procedure was conducted during one 4-hour session. The three treatment groups were compared to placebo and waiting-list control groups. Assessment consisted of pre- and posttreatment self-report measures of social anxiety, and a posttreatment administration of an extended live interaction. Three behavioral measures (smiles, eye contact, and 10-second silences) and two rating measures (anxiety and adequacy) were coded from this interaction. No significant differences among groups were found on any of the rating or behavioral measures derived from the live interaction. On self-report measures derived from a modified version of the Social Avoidance and Distress Scale, the three main treatment groups (social skill training, social skill training + desensitization, and microlab) showed significantly greater improvement than did either of the two control groups. However, no differences among groups were obtained on the Situation Questionnaires. The follow-up was only of three weeks duration and consisted of a newly developed self-report questionnaire which supported the pattern of results at posttest. Thus, the only significant changes in this study occurred on the self-report measures. The authors concluded that desensitization was superfluous to treatment effectiveness, since the addition of desensitization to social skills training did not lead to significantly greater improvements. They point out that both behavioral treatments involved hierarchically based behavior rehearsal, and that desensitization may be redundant when other hierarchically structured behavioral techniques are employed. However, the combination group received only abbreviated forms of both desensitization and social skill training in order to equate treatment time with the social skill training group. The use of systematic desensitization during relatively small portions of eight sessions does not appear to be an adequate test of the effectiveness of desensitization. In addition, these results differed from those of Curran (1975) and Curran and Gilbert (1975), who obtained clear-cut improvements with desensitization. Overall, the outcome of this study was weak, with the only changes occurring on self-report measures, many of which were of undetermined validity. In addition, the authors served as therapists, introducing possible bias into the results. Thus, given the weaknesses of the study and the weak changes obtained, this study does not provide clear support for the social skill training program employed.

McGovern *et al.* (1975) conducted an evaluation of social skill training for men. In this study, there were three treatment groups, each of which received two common treatment components. The first component was a dating manual developed by McGovern (1972) over the course of discussions with groups of high dating frequency women. The manual focused on specific situations, behaviors, and consequences in heterosexual interactions. The second element was contact with female trainers. The women were present at each of the group meetings and served to facilitate discussion and provide information and corrective feedback. In addition, they served as confederates for the two groups who received behavior rehearsal. These two behavior rehearsal groups were identical except for the physical setting of the behavior rehearsal scenes. For one group, the scenes were rehearsed in the office setting while for the second group these scenes were rehearsed in naturalistic settings (e.g., the student union) with one other subject and a female trainer present. A third group received no specific behavior rehearsal or social skill training other than the manual and discussion of material in the manual. Thus, while the content of what each of the groups dealt with was similar, the mode of treatment differed across these three groups. The three treatment conditions received six meetings of 1 hour and 45 minutes each in a group context. These three treatment groups were compared to a waiting-list control group.

Assessment consisted of self-report questionnaires (Social Avoidance and Distress Scale, Fear of Negative Evaluation Scale, Survey of Heterosexual Interactions, modified S-R Inventory of Anxiousness) as well as retrospective estimates of dating frequency.

Subjects were male volunteers for a dating treatment program who were selected on the basis of dating frequency and dissatisfaction with dating behaviors. However, the dating frequency criterion was excessively liberal and required that subjects dated no more than three times in the past month and seven times in the past six months. While none of the changes on the self-report questionnaires was significant for the waiting-list control group, 11 of the 18 comparisons for the three treatment groups showed significant pre- to post-treatment changes. No clear differences emerged among the three treatment groups, suggesting that the common elements of the manual and contact with female trainers may have accounted for improvements rather than the social skill training emphasizing behavior rehearsal. The three treatment groups all showed trends toward increased dating frequency compared with the control group.

There were several problems with this study. These include the almost exclusive reliance on self-report measures, the author serving as therapist for all groups, the absence of an attention placebo control group, the overly liberal selection criteria, and the lack of any follow-up. Within the context of these limitations, the results do not point to the superiority of behavior rehearsal over simple discussion, exposure to a dating manual, and to female trainers. Further evaluation of the dating manual appears warranted since it could potentially provide an economical adjunct to ongoing treatment programs.

Two studies have been conducted which have evaluated some form of "self-reinforcement" therapy in the context of social skills training. The first, conducted by Rehm and Marston (1968), was one of the earliest studies on minimal dating. While no screening criteria were used for subject selection, the subjects were compared to a normal group on the measures employed. These consisted primarily of self-report questionnaires (Situation Questionnaire, Fear Survey Schedule, Taylor Manifest Anxiety Scale, and Gough Adjective Checklist) as well as self-rating, observer rating, and behavioral measures derived from subjects' responses to a discrete taped situation test. The two groups differed significantly on all but two measures—number of words and adequacy ratings derived from the taped situation test. Subjects were randomly assigned to one of three groups. The first was a group receiving training in self-reinforcement as well as graded homework assignments based on a hierarchy of anxiety-arousing heterosexual situations. Subjects assigned themselves points based on the adequacy of their performance during the extrasession homework assignments. Individual meetings with a therapist focused on evaluation of the subjects' behaviors in the homework assignments, along with discussions between the therapist and subject to determine appropriate numbers of points when a discrepancy existed between the subject and the experimenter's evaluations. This self-reinforcement group was compared to a non-specific therapy group that received treatment based on clarification and reflection. Finally, a minimal treatment control group was included. This group met with a therapist individually for the same number of sessions as did subjects in the other groups and received encouragement for self-help, but did not receive any active therapy treatment. The findings indicated that the self-reinforcement group showed significantly greater improvement than the control groups on most self-rating and self-report measures. However, with only one exception, there were no significant group differences on any of the measures derived from the discrete situation test (rated anxiety, rated adequacy, rated likability, anxiety signs, and latency). The only significant group difference on the behavioral measures was on number of words per response—a measure on which treatment and normal control subjects did not initially differ significantly. Post-therapy reports of dating frequency from the subjects suggested that the self-reinforcement group was dating more frequently than either of the control groups. However, no pretreatment assessment was done on this measure and absolute rates of dating frequency were not given. A follow-up was conducted between 7 and 9 months after treatment. Follow-up measures generally favored the self-reinforcement groups except for the measure of estimated dating frequency. Although there was a trend for the self-reinforcement group to be dating more often than the follow-up control subjects (two dates a month vs. one date a month), this did not reach statistical significance. The treatment changes obtained in this study were largely restricted to self-report measures, and the absolute amounts of change were generally small. The lack of clear selection criteria and the lack of specification of subjects' dating frequency status further clouded the interpretation of the study's results.

Gambrill (1975) has conducted one of the few studies directed specifically to women. Subjects were female volunteers from the community at large, only a small percentage of whom were college students. The age range of the women was from 19 to 34. The treatment was not aimed specifically at dating, but more generally at increasing initiations and contacts with members of both sexes. Subjects were selected on the basis of their desire to change and their low rate of initiating contacts. They ranged from 0 to 4 on frequency of initiating social contacts during a 1-week self-monitoring assessment period.

In this study, three treatment groups were compared to a waiting-list control group. In the "manual" group, subjects were given a training manual which included information about behavior change, ways to initiate conversations, and information about choosing places to go to meet people. This group was also given homework assignments directed toward increasing social activities, and were instructed to self-monitor during the course of treatment. The manual + self-reinforcement group received all of the elements of the first group, with the addition of instructions to covertly compliment and award themselves points for behaviors which pleased them. A self-help group was also included. This group discussed the same topics as the two other treatment groups but did not receive either the manual or instructions for self-reinforcement. However, they were instructed to self-monitor their social behaviors during treatment and received encouragement to carry out homework assignments.

Assessment consisted of self-monitoring measures and behavioral and rating measures derived from a discrete situation test. The results demonstrated that the manual group was significantly more successful in increasing the frequency and range of their social contacts over the course of the treatment program. The changes on these measures for the remaining three groups were not significant. Subjects in the self-reinforcement group initiated a higher proportion of social contacts than did subjects in either the self-help or waiting-list control groups. The self-reinforcement group did not differ significantly from the manual group on this measure. At the 3-month follow-up, both the manual and self-reinforcement groups showed significant increases on the proportion of social contacts initiated over their baseline level. However, no significant follow-up effects are reported for measures of frequency and range of social contacts. In addition, self-reinforcement subjects showed significant improvements on observer ratings of social skill while no significant changes occurred on this measure for any of the three remaining groups. No significant effects were found for either latency or number of words per response on the discrete situation test. Thus, while there are different findings for different measures, the results point to the efficacy of both the manual and self-reinforcement condition, with the social skill rating and follow-up measures favoring the self-reinforcement group. Overall, however, the changes were relatively small, and several of the measures did not show any significant changes.

In addition to the studies reviewed above, there are two other studies with minimal dating college students which have reported significant changes with social skill training (Glass *et al.*, 1976; Kramer, 1975). Since both of these studies also involved comparisons with other procedures, they will be reviewed separately in Section IV,C.

COMMENTS ON SOCIAL SKILL TRAINING

While there is evidence supporting the effectiveness of social skill training procedures, the evidence is considerably weakened by several considerations. First, and most important, is the issue of subject selection. The majority of studies have used either unspecified or excessively liberal subject selection criteria. These range from the very stringent criterion of no more than four dates in the past year (MacDonald *et al.*, 1975) to the very liberal criterion of no more than two dates in the past week (Melnick, 1973). In fact, the majority of studies deal with "not so minimal" daters, with a few noteworthy exceptions. Clearly, more stringent screening criteria are needed, including dating frequency as well as some objective and validated screening measure such as the Survey of Heterosexual Interactions.

A second consideration is the fact that most studies have obtained changes on laboratory measures but far fewer studies have either employed generalization measures (e.g., self-monitoring, dating frequency, peer-ratings, measures derived from extrasession behaviors). Those that have employed generalization measures (usually dating frequency) have only obtained significant changes in a few studies. While self-report and behavioral measures from laboratory tasks do have some validity, it is still not clear to what extent the treatment procedures effect changes in aspects of the subjects' behavior or social activity outside the laboratory setting.

A related consideration is that while many studies report statistical significance, these changes are often of very small absolute magnitude (e.g., a 1-point change on a 7-point scale of social skill or social anxiety). Studies in this area should be read more carefully with regard to the absolute amounts of changes effected by the treatment intervention. Statistical significance is too often equated with clinical significance. Clearly, statistical significance is necessary. But such changes may only demonstrate some amount of change in the person's life, and not anything approximating a desirable adjustment.

Another issue is that relating to the goal of "social skill training." This term implies that subjects are deficient in social skills and that this deficiency is primary. However, no study has yet adequately demonstrated that subjects are deficient in social skills. The subjects are often quite socially anxious and avoidant, but the only direct evidence for social skills deficits comes from observer ratings of social skill, which are prone to halo effects based on physical attractiveness. While procedures labeled as social skill training do appear to have some effect, this is not necessarily due to the acquisition of new and more effective social skills in deficient subjects. Most social skill training programs incorporate a hierarchy of situations and live behavior rehearsal with females. This hierarchically arranged real-life exposure may serve to reduce anxiety in socially skilled subjects rather than to explicitly train them in new social skills (cf. Marks, 1975). This observation brings us back to a point raised in Section III,F. We do not as yet have adequate behavioral assessment techniques for the measurement of social skill, and until we do, we will be unable to specifically diagnose a subject's particular deficit. As discussed earlier, the deficit may well be different for different subjects, ranging from excessive anxiety to social skill deficits to negative cognitive appraisals. Such individual differences have not yet been addressed.

It is more than likely that at least some subjects will be characterized by a deficit in social skills. Yet an examination of the content of social skill training programs needs to be made. Twentyman and McFall (1975) have made the excellent point that the skills in which subjects are trained are typically generated from the life experience and common sense of the experimenter. Clearly, a more systematic analysis of what are effective social skills is needed to help structure the content of social skill training programs more meaningfully.

B. Anxiety Reduction Procedures

There have been only a few studies dealing directly with imaginal desensitization. The two studies by Curran and his associates (Curran, 1975; Curran & Gilbert, 1975) reviewed earlier showed positive support for the effectiveness of desensitization for minimal daters. In addition, a study by Mitchell and Orr (1974) showed significant changes for two groups receiving brief courses of desensitization compared to relaxation-only and waiting-list control groups. However, this latter study employed only self-report anxiety measures.

Most of the work in this area has involved a procedure based on "real-life practice" which can be viewed as a form of *in vivo* desensitization. Martinson and Zerface (1970) reported the first study of this kind. Subjects were male volunteers who were selected on the basis of self-reports of heterosexual anxiety and no dating during the past month. Subjects were assigned to either an arranged interaction, individual counseling, or waiting-list control group. In the arranged interaction group, each male subject was matched randomly each week for 5 weeks, with a different female drawn from a population of volunteers interested in improving their conversational skills. The subjects were instructed to arrange a meeting with one another, and to discuss problems and personal concerns with their partners. This condition might also be viewed as a form of peer counseling. The individual counseling group received "eclectic" nonbehavioral individual treatment from an experienced counselor. Subjects in this condition were scheduled for five sessions of treatment but due to early terminations these subjects averaged only slightly over three sessions. Assessment consisted of a self-rating of heterosexual anxiety, the Willoughby Personality Schedule, and reports by the subjects of whether they had a date during an 8-week period after the end of treatment. The results showed no significant differences among groups on the Willoughby Schedule. In addition, subjects in the arranged interaction condition reported significant decreases in social anxiety compared to the remaining two groups. More subjects in the arranged interaction group reported that they were dating after treatment than subjects in either of the two remaining groups. While this study lacked any behavioral measurement and had liberal selection criteria, the results were promising.

Christensen and Arkowitz (1974) independently developed a related procedure which they called "practice dating" based on real-life exposure to dating situations. The first study was a pilot investigation involving a single group assessed before and after treatment. The practice dating procedure differs in several respects from the one used by Martinson and Zerface. First, the interactions are clearly structured as practice dates and do not involve any interactions to discuss personal concerns. Second, both the men and women in the study are volunteers for a program to increase dating comfort, effectiveness, and frequency, and know that their partners are also volunteers. While the practice dating procedure has been varied somewhat across different studies, the basic procedure involves a series of weekly practice dates, each with a different partner who is also a volunteer for the program. Apart from an initial orientation meeting and assessment, the procedure takes place entirely in naturalistic settings outside the laboratory with no professional personnel present. Each week, subjects are sent the name and telephone number of their partner for that week. Their only instruction is that a meeting should occur before the end of that week. All details of the date—including where to go, how long the date should be, what to talk about, and so on, are left entirely to the subjects. Even the decision as to who makes the call to arrange the date is left entirely to them. Unlike computer dating services, the subjects are told that the goal of the program is to provide them with "dating practice" rather than helping them find some ideal mate. Consistent with this view, there is no attempt to match subjects on any ideal characteristics, and the partners are randomly selected with a few rare exceptions not involving personality characteristics. After each date, subjects are instructed to fill out a form which inquires about various details of the date and calls for ratings of themselves and their partners on social anxiety and social skill. Other than the initial orientation meeting and assessment, there is no contact between the subject and any experimental personnel or therapist.

Christensen and Arkowitz (1974) used the basic practice dating procedure described above with the addition of partner-generated feedback. For the feedback manipulation, each partner filled out a form that called for positive and negative aspects of their partners' behavior during the date. These forms were sent to their partners a few days after the date. Subjects were male and female undergraduate volunteers for the program and were selected from a larger pool or volunteers, based primarily on their relatively lower dating frequency. Nonetheless, the initial dating frequency of the subjects was quite high (over one date per week). Results were analyzed separately for a subgroup of lower frequency daters (who averaged 1.5 dates per month). Pre- and posttreatment assessment consisted of three self-report questionnaires (the Social Avoidance and Distress Scale, Fear of Negative Evaluation Scale, and modified S-R Inventory of Anxiousness) and self-monitoring of date and casual heterosexual interactions over a 12-day assessment period. Significant pre- to posttreatment changes were obtained on the Social Avoidance and Distress Scale and the modified S-R Inventory of Anxiousness. Subjects showed significant changes in the frequency and range of dates and a trend toward increased frequency of casual heterosexual interactions. Christensen and Arkowitz also evaluated whether this increase in dating reflected dates with partners met through the program or contacts with new partners. They found that 65% of the posttreatment dates and 88.9% of the posttreatment casual interactions were with new partners. This demonstrated that the program did more than merely provide the subjects with dating partners, and pointed to involvement of some active behavior change mechanism.

No clear conclusions could be drawn from this pilot study due to the lack of any control groups, the lack of any behavioral measures other than self-monitoring, and the relatively high dating frequency status of the subjects. Nonetheless, the results were sufficiently encouraging to warrant a controlled evaluation of the practice dating procedure, which was conducted by Christensen *et al.* (1975). In this study the practice dating and feedback procedure was compared to a practice dating without feedback condition and a waiting-list control group. Once again, volunteers were chosen with the lowest dating frequency. However, these subjects still had a fairly high dating frequency, and averaged one date per month prior to treatment. Subjects were 30 men and 30 women who were divided as homogeneously as possible, with respect to age, self-reported dating frequency, and reported heterosexual anxiety, into blocks of three same-sexed members. Each member of a block was randomly assigned to one of the three groups. This randomized blocking of pretreatment scores allowed for a posttest only design. However, two self-report questionnaires (Social Avoidance and Distress Scale and modified S-R Inventory of Anxiousness) were given before and after treatment. Assessment consisted of these self-report questionnaires, self-monitoring measures taken during a 2-week period, partner and observer ratings of social skill and social anxiety derived from an extended interaction test, and behavioral measures of pulse rate, awkward conversational silences, and latency of response derived from discrete and extended interaction tests.

The results of this study provided clear support for the superiority of the practice dating groups over the control group. The practice dating groups were superior to the control group on the self-report measures, behavioral measures from the discrete and extended interaction test, and self-monitoring measures of frequency and range of casual and date interactions. Only the observer and partner ratings of anxiety derived from the live extended interaction test did not show significant differences among groups. In addition, the absolute amounts of change in dating frequency were considerable. On measures of posttreatment dating frequency, the control subjects were averaging 1.2 dates per month and the combined practice dating groups were averaging 4 dates per month. Once again, the overwhelming majority of the posttreatment dates and casual interactions were with new partners (78% of the dates and 96% of the casual interactions), with the percentages closely paralleling those found in the first experiment. Thus, while the program failed as a computer dating service, it did seem to provide subjects with changes that allowed them to find new dating partners for themselves. This study also includes the longest follow-up of any study of minimal dating. Follow-up information was collected 15 months after the termination of treatment. Follow-up consisted of the Social Avoidance and Distress Scale and retrospective estimates of dating frequency. The follow-up indicated that changes in social anxiety and dating frequency were maintained.

The two practice dating groups did equally well with a few exceptions. On the behavioral measures (latency of response, pulse rate, and awkward conversational silences), the practice dating only group did better than the practice dating with feedback group. In addition, the practice dating programs worked equally well for male and female subjects.

Process data were available through the self-ratings and partner ratings of social skill and social anxiety collected from the participants after each date. Significant decreases in self- and partner ratings of anxiety occurred from the first three to the last three practice dates, while no changes occurred in the self- or partner ratings of social skill. These data suggest that the practice dating procedure may work primarily through anxiety reduction rather than through any acquisition of new social skills. However, these data can only be taken as suggestive, and the mechanisms involved in the practice dating procedure remain to be elucidated. Descriptively, the mechanism seems best to fit a form of *in vivo* desensitization involving the repetition of a moderately anxiety-arousing situation. Performance anxiety on the practice dates is likely reduced due to the knowledge that the partner is also a volunteer for the program and that asking for a date will not be met by rejection. The main limitations of the studies on practice dating presented thus far are the overly liberal subject selection criteria in terms of dating frequency and the lack of an attention placebo control group. It may be that mildly distressed subjects can benefit from this procedure for anxiety reduction, but that more distressed and less frequent daters may also require social skill training.

Kramer (1975) has conducted a well-designed study comparing practice dating with other behaviorally oriented treatment procedures for male and female minimal daters. In this study, the practice dating group received five weekly practice dates, similar in form to the procedure described above, but with one exception involving the fact that the practice dating subjects also had three 1-hour group meetings to deal with administrative procedures and to discuss their experiences on the practice dates. A second treatment group received an identical series of practice dates, but was also given five weekly group meetings aimed primarily at cognitive restructuring based on the work of Ellis (1962) and Meichenbaum (1973). The group meetings focused on changing self-verbalizations, cognitions, and irrational beliefs which would interfere with effective dating behaviors. Subjects were given homework assignments to note their self-verbalizations during practice dates. These formed the basis of discussion for the cognitive restructuring condition. The two practice dating groups were compared to a social skill training group. This group received five 2-hour weekly group meetings with a therapist emphasizing behavior rehearsal, feedback, coaching, and encouragement to try out the new behaviors discussed during the week. These three treatment groups were compared to a waiting-list control group.

Assessment consisted of pre- and posttreatment administration of several self-report questionnaires, including the Social Avoidance and Distress Scale, and self-monitoring measures of frequency and range of heterosexual contacts over a 10-day assessment period. In addition, a posttest extended interaction test was conducted. Behavioral measures of anxiety signs and approach behavior were coded.

Unfortunately, as in the other practice dating studies, the volunteers were fairly high in initial dating frequency, averaging slightly less than one date a week.

While there were different results for different measures, the overall pattern of results showed that the three treatment groups all improved significantly or did better than the waiting-list control group, with few significant differences among the three treatment groups. Thus, it appears that the addition of cognitive restructuring to the practice dating procedure did not enhance treatment effectiveness. In addition, practice dating and social skill training were equally effective. This latter finding is particularly interesting in view of the fact that social skill training required 10 hours of therapist time while practice dating required no contact with a therapist. While a 6-week follow-up was included in the original design, the return rate for follow-up was only approximately 50%, precluding any interpretation of these results. Even though Kramer's study suffers from an overly liberal selection criterion and a lack of an attention placebo control group, the overall design was strong.

Royce and Arkowitz (1976) employed the paradigm of practice interactions and applied it to a closely related problem—social isolation with respect to same-sex friendship interactions. Subjects for this study were selected on the basis of self-reports of anxiety, dissatisfaction, and a desire to change. In addition, those subjects were selected who only fell into the lowest 15% of the 1,000 undergraduates surveyed for frequency of social activity with friends. There were four main groups in the study. The first group received practice interactions only. This procedure closely paralleled the practice dating procedure with the exception that the interactions were between same-sex pairs. Each week, the subject and partner met for two practice interactions, for a total of 12 interactions with six different partners. A second group received the same practice interaction procedure with the addition of six weekly 1-hour group meetings. These meetings were conducted by a therapist and emphasized feedback from group members with whom the subject had practice interactions as well as social skill training. Social skill training consisted of readings from a social interaction manual, behavior rehearsal, modeling, and feedback. A minimal treatment group was included to control for expectancy and placebo effects. This group also received six $1\frac{1}{2}$-hour group meetings with a therapist and the same social interaction training manual. However, treatment for this group focused on discussion and verbal counseling, with no specific social skill training procedures employed. Finally, the design included a waiting-list control group.

Assessment was conducted before and after treatment and included the Social Avoidance and Distress Scale, self-monitoring measures, behavioral and rating measures derived from an extended interaction test, and peer-ratings. The peer-rating form was sent to peers of the subjects and called for ratings of anxiety, skill, and activity in same-sex social interactions. Because it seemed likely that there would be a substantial lag between changes in the subjects' behavior and their peers' perceptions of these changes, the peer ratings were taken at pretreatment and again at the 8-week follow-up. The peer-rating form also asked for ratings of social skill, anxiety, and activity in opposite-sex social situations. Self-monitoring measures also included frequency and range of opposite-sex interactions.

Since there were no significant differences between the group receiving practice interactions only and practice interactions + social skills training on any of the measures of improvement, these two groups were combined for purposes of further data analysis. Subjects in the two practice interaction groups showed significantly greater improvements than any of the other groups on the Social Avoidance and Distress Scale and self-monitoring measures. Less than 2% of the posttreatment interactions of the practice groups were with partners whom they had met through the program. On peer ratings, the practice interaction groups improved significantly more than an untreated control group, but the comparison of practice interaction groups with the minimal treatment group only approached an acceptable level of significance. On the behavioral and rating measures derived from the extended interaction test, the practice interaction groups did not show any greater improvements than did either of the control groups. Self-monitoring and peer-rating measures relating to opposite-sex interactions did not yield any significant treatment effects. Treatment gains, as measured by the Social Avoidance and Distress Scale and peer ratings, were maintained at 8-week follow-up. A 15-month follow-up, using the SAD and retrospective estimates of frequency and range of social interactions, yielded mixed results. The long-term follow-up for the SAD was significant. In addition, subjects also reported having significantly more friends at follow-up compared to baseline. While the treated groups did show an increase in their frequency of interactions at this follow-up, this difference did not reach significance.

The results of this well-designed study provide further support for the effectiveness of real-life practice in the treatment of social inhibitions. The precise mechanism by which the real-life practice procedure works still remains to be clarified. Process and outcome data point more clearly to anxiety reduction rather than to social skill acquisition. Since there has not yet been any clear demonstration that minimal dating college students are indeed deficient in specific social skills, real-life practice may serve to reduce anxiety which subsequently leads to increased frequency of social interaction. Glasgow and Arkowitz (1975) have demonstrated that male minimal daters perform as well as high-frequency daters in an extended interaction test. They suggest that the main differences between these groups may be due to anxiety and avoidance rather than social skill deficiencies. For those minimal daters for whom this is the case, an anxiety-reduction procedure such as practice dating would be the treatment of choice. However, it is important to keep in mind that most of the practice dating studies have not employed subjects who are extreme minimal daters. It may well be that more infrequent daters will manifest a social skill deficit that would require explicit social skill training. In such cases, practice dating procedures might serve as useful adjuncts to treatment. In addition to the apparent efficacy of the practice dating procedure, no therapist time is required and the procedure can be administered on a large scale by someone with only clerical skills. The practice dating treatment program also takes place in naturalistic situations within the subject's environment so that concerns about generalization from the laboratory to these natural situations are minimized. However, further evaluation of practice dating procedures is warranted with subjects who are truly minimal daters. Such studies are presently being conducted by the author.

C. Cognitive Modification Procedures

The use of cognitive modification procedures is consistent with a cognitive model of minimal dating in which negative self-appraisals and negative "self-talk" are seen as mediating the anxiety and avoidance of the minimal dater. The work of Meichenbaum (1973) has provided a solid base for the development and application of cognitive modification techniques to the problem of minimal dating. While Kramer (1975) used cognitive modification procedures in conjunction with practice dating, there has been only one study which specifically has evaluated a cognitive modification procedure for minimal dating. This was a well-designed study by Glass *et al.* (1976). Subjects for this study were undergraduate and graduate men who volunteered for a treatment program. Unfortunately, no selection criteria were employed. The study compared a cognitive modification program, a social skill training program, and a combined group receiving both cognitive modification and social skill training. The design included a waiting-list control group. In addition, there were two other groups that controlled for the longer training time the combined group received. Social skill training consisted of a semi-automated procedure. Situations were presented on audiotape, followed by behavioral rehearsal, modeling, feedback, and coaching. The cognitive modification group was presented with the same situations. The focus of this procedure was to train subjects to verbalize their negative self-talk and to learn to change from this to more positive self-talk. After each situation, a model of effective self-statement responses was presented and subjects were reinforced for making positive self-statements themselves. Treatment took place in the context of individual meetings with a therapist.

A noteworthy aspect of this study was the use of an empirical method for generating the training situations, the socially skilled responses, and the positive self-statements. These were all determined through the behavioral-analytic method of Goldfried and D'Zurilla

(1969), based on information collected from undergraduate populations. This method insured that the content of the training situations and the responses in which subjects were trained were relevant to the criterion population.

Assessment consisted of a discrete taped situation test (described earlier) which was also developed according to the behavioral-analytic model. The total situation test consisted of 24 situations. Eleven of these were also used in the training phase, so that the remaining 13 situations served as a test of generalization of treatment effects. The situation was given at pretest, posttest, and again at 6-month follow-up. Responses were scored on the adequacy of the response derived from empirically generated scoring criteria. In addition, a telephone task was included which involved asking the subject to call female volunteers. The females provided information regarding which of the subjects actually called, and rated the subjects' conversational skills on several dimensions, including the impression the subject made on the female. The assessment task was administered at the posttest and 6-month follow-up. Finally, retrospective estimates of dating frequency were taken at the 6-month follow-up. There were no significant differences among any of the groups at pretest assessment. Posttest analyses of the discrete situation test revealed that all treatment groups were superior to the waiting-list control group in regard to adequacy ratings on the trained situations. However, only the cognitive modification group showed significant improvement regarding the untrained situations. This suggests that cognitive modification procedures enhance generalization to new situations. At follow-up, the cognitive modification group and combined groups were superior to the waiting-list control regarding the untrained situations, but these differences were not significant. At posttest, the cognitive modification group made significantly more calls and made a significantly better impression on the women than all other goups. While the cognitive modification group also made a significantly better impression at follow-up, the number of telephone calls they made was not significantly different from the other groups. Finally, there were no significant differences among groups regarding dating frequency at follow-up.

Although the social skill training group showed significant improvements in trained situations, the findings clearly supported the cognitive modification procedure in effecting generalization to untrained situations. In addition, the cognitive modification subjects were more likely to make telephone calls to females and made a more favorable impression. An important implication of these findings is that cognitive modification procedures seem to enhance generalization, which is reasonable, since such procedures train subjects in skills they can utilize in new situations. The results for social skill training were more limited to the specific trained situations, and this group showed little generalization on any of the measures. However, the fact that no selection criteria were used for subjects limits an otherwise well-designed study. In addition, the lack of any significant changes on the dating frequency measure suggests that changes did not generalize to behaviors and situations in subjects' lives. Consistent with the multidimensional view of minimal dating discussed earlier, this result may be caused by the fact that some subjects are characterized primarily by cognitive deficits and they would therefore be ideal candidates for the cognitive modification procedure. These individuals already possess adequate levels of social skill. However, even for subjects who are socially unskilled, the addition of cognitive modification procedures to a social skill training program may well enhance generalization of treatment effects.

V. SOCIAL SKILL TRAINING IN CLINICAL POPULATIONS

While the focus of this chapter is on minimal dating in college students, a consideration of the treatment research in this area inevitably leads to questions concerning the extent to which the positive treatment effects with college students might also occur using similar treatment procedures with clinical populations. Most of the work with patient populations has emphasized social skill training procedures. A comprehensive review of research in this area is beyond the scope of this chapter. Several excellent reviews are available in papers by Hersen and Bellack (1976), Hersen and Eisler (1976), and Marzillier (1976). In this section, we will make a few brief comments about treatment research with clinical populations and review one study which comes closest to extending the work done with minimal daters to a clinical population.

While there have been numerous controlled studies using clinical populations, the majority have been directed at effecting specific changes in a limited class of problem behaviors by using short-term behavioral treatments. Most provide important starting points for demonstrating that social skill training can lead to specific behavioral changes in patient populations. However, these studies fall short of demonstrating that the treatment procedures lead to significant changes in patients' overall social adjustment. The social skill treatment procedures have typically involved modeling, behavior rehearsal, coaching, and feedback. The dependent variables utilized in most of these studies have involved specific responses to discrete or extended situation tests in the laboratory (e.g., Eisler, Hersen, & Miller, 1973; Goldsmith & McFall, 1975; Goldstein, Martens, Hubben, vanBelle, Schaff, Wiersma, & Goedhart, 1973; Gutride, Goldstein, & Hunter, 1973; Hersen, Eisler, & Miller, 1974). While most of these studies show significant changes in behavioral and rating measures derived from the situation tests and have provided valuable information about the efficacy of various components of social skill programs, the dependent variables have largely been restricted to laboratory assessment procedures. As a result, we do not have information concerning the extent to which these treatment programs have led to statistically and clinically significant changes in patients' behavior outside the laboratory. Typically, there are no measures of generalization of change outside the laboratory, and no follow-up.

While several reports evaluating social skill training with patients have been reported by Argyle and his associates (Argyle *et al.*, 1974a, 1974b), the obtained changes have usually been small and generalization of changes has not been assessed. Marzillier *et al.* (1976) have conducted a well-controlled outcome study of social skill training and desensitization using an outpatient population. This study was noteworthy in its comprehensive assessment, which included methods derived from self-report, laboratory, interview, and self-monitoring domains. In addition, the treatment closely approximated that employed in behavioral clinical practice: the therapist was highly experienced, the treatment was tailored to the needs of each patient, and a sufficient number of sessions (15) was employed in order to provide an adequate test of the clinical effectiveness of the different treatment procedures.

Marzillier *et al.* (1976) compared social skill training with systematic desensitization and a waiting-list control group. The subjects were outpatient referrals whose major problems consisted of social or interpersonal difficulties. Patients whose social difficulties were secondary to some other disorder were not included in the sample. The patients ranged from 17 to 43 years of age. Treatment consisted of 15 weekly individual sessions with an experienced clinical psychologist. Social skill training consisted of behavior rehearsal, modeling, feedback, and encouragement to try out new behaviors between sessions. The situational targets of treatment differed for each patient depending on their areas of social difficulty, but the treatment procedures always included the elements mentioned above. The desensitization group received the same number of sessions involving imaginal desensitization and occasional instances of *in vivo* desensitization. Subjects were randomly assigned to one of these two treatment groups or a waiting-list control group. From the initial sample of patients, seven dropped out of treatment. This left eight patients in the social skill training group, six in the desensitization group, and seven in the control group. Unfortunately, most of the attrition occurred in the desensitization group.

Assessment was comprehensive and included self-report measures (including the Social Avoidance and Distress Scale and the Fear of Negative Evaluation Scale), observer ratings of social skill and social anxiety from an extended interaction test, self-monitoring measures of social activities and contacts, and ratings of social adjustment made by a psychiatrist who was unaware of the subject's treatment condition. These ratings included evaluations of the patient's adjustment in such areas as sexual functioning, family, social and work adjustment, and anxiety and depression evaluated with the Social Adjustment Rating Scales developed by Gelder and Marks (1966). In addition, retrospective reports of social activities and social contacts were taken. Assessment was conducted before and after treatment. A follow-up was also included using the self-monitoring and self-rating measures.

On most measures, neither treatment led to significantly greater improvement compared to the waiting-list control group. All patients, including those in the waiting-list control group, showed some improvement from pre- to posttest. However, on most measures, there were not significant differences in the amount of improvement shown by the treated groups compared to the control group. The only significant difference among groups was that both treatment groups showed a significant increase in their range of social activities, with the social skill group also showing a significant increase in their range of social contacts. Frequency measures did not yield any significant effects. The measure of range of social activities also showed significant maintenance at follow-up.

As Marzillier *et al.* (1976) acknowledge, their study was weakened by several methodological problems. The major one involved the first author serving as therapist for all patients. However, the therapist's stated expectation was that both treatment conditions would be equally effective, and that they would be more effective than the control. The other problems related to the relatively small number of subjects and the considerable and differential attrition rates. Clearly, we need more studies evaluating behavioral treatment procedures with clinical populations. This study was discussed in detail because it came closest to approximating clinical treatment procedures that might be used in actual practice, and because the assessment was broad and comprehensive. Although we have reviewed positive findings with social skill training and desensitization for college student volunteers, these changes have often been of small magnitude. Consistent changes have not occurred across all studies, and measures of generalization often have not been significant. These considerations, taken in conjunction with the Marzillier *et al.* study, suggest that we by no means have any clearly effective behavioral treatment for social difficulties in clinical populations. However, the research does suggest that we have made a promising start in that direction.

VI. CONCLUDING COMMENTS

Despite the relative recency of behavioral research on the measurement and modification of minimal dating, considerable advances have occurred. Even though this review has been generally critical in tone, the contributions of the research on both assessment and treatment have been considerable. Yet, due to the preliminary state of research in these areas, there remain a number of problems and future directions for further research and practice.

One of the major issues relates to differential diagnosis and treatment. It appears most likely that minimal dating is not a unidimensional problem. Some individuals may be characterized by social skill deficits, some by unrealistic anxiety, and some by overly negative cognitive appraisals. While there appear to be effective treatment procedures that fit each of these areas of difficulty, we do not as yet have adequate methods for assessment and diagnosis to evaluate individual differences. Virtually all the treatment studies have randomly assigned subjects to groups, and have not attended to these individual differences. It is striking, therefore, that treatment studies have found such clear treatment effects. As we develop a methodology to measure these areas of individual differences, it is likely that our treatment effects will be considerably stronger, since individuals will be assigned to those forms of treatment best designed for their particular problem.

Physical attractiveness is also an area that warrants further attention in view of the differences in physical attractiveness between high- and low-frequency daters (Glasgow & Arkowitz, 1975). In this study, high- and low-frequency daters were compared on a number of behavioral and rating measures derived from an extended interaction with an opposite-sexed subject. A stepwise multiple regression equation was formed using the seven behavioral and rating measures to predict partners' ratings of their attraction to the subject. Even the best linear combination of these measures turned out to be a relatively poor predictor of attraction. By contrast, the single measure of partners' ratings of subjects' physical attractiveness did as well or better in predicting attraction than this linear combination. This finding held true for both male and female subjects. This study, as well as the studies reviewed by Berscheid and Walster (1973), point to the powerful effects of physical attractiveness in determining how others respond to us, particularly in first impressions. In fact, one writer was so impressed with the power of physical attractiveness that he seriously suggested plastic surgery as an adjunct or alternative to psychotherapy for some patients (Cavior, 1970, cited in Berscheid & Walster, 1973). While I would not go so far as to advocate plastic surgery, I would like to suggest that physical attractiveness may be modified by other, less drastic means. A person's appearance, in terms of dress, grooming, hairstyle, and so on, may in fact modify his or her physical attractiveness (cf. Liza Doolittle in *My Fair Lady*). My guess would be that a person's rated physical attractiveness is not a fixed aspect of his or her physical characteristics, but may well be modifiable through training to improve one's appearance. This idea can easily be tested. We can pay more attention to "appearance training" in our treatment programs for minimal daters and the use of professional consultants or even "attractive" peers for this purpose might be a useful addition to our programs. Curran and Gilbert (1975) have been the only ones who have explicitly mentioned that appearance training was a part of their treatment program. Research evaluating the effects of such appearance training would be useful.

Another area in which we need further theoretical and empirical advances relates to the construct of social skill. Thus far, the research has not yet pointed to any specific behavioral components of social skill. Most attempts at the measurement of social skill have emphasized either global ratings or the frequency of verbal and nonverbal behaviors. Simple frequency counts of behaviors probably do not adequately reflect the subtleties relating to timing and reciprocity of interactional behavior. There is a considerable need to develop measures of social skill which take into account these more subtle aspects of interpersonal behaviors. In addition, most research and theoretical definitions of social skill have emphasized the content of the responses, and have not adequately included response consequences. By contrast, Lewinsohn (1975) has defined socially skilled behavior entirely in terms of the consequences of the behavior. Lewinsohn's approach suggests that we at least ought to include an evaluation of the response consequences of interpersonal behavior as part of our definition of socially skilled behavior, rather than emphasizing the content of the behaviors only. We need coding systems for interpersonal behaviors in heterosexual interactions. These would include the timing, reciprocity, and consequences of behaviors and would resemble the coding system developed by Lewinsohn and his associates (Lewinsohn, Alper, Johansson, Libet, Rosenberry, Shaffer, Sterin, Stewart, & Weinstein, 1968) for depression. In addition, our definition and measurement of social skill needs to go beyond the "boy-meets-girl" interaction to include such factors as ways to meet people, formation of a peer group environment that would facilitate meeting members of the opposite sex, and ways of dealing with rejection and the more complex aspects of a longer term intimate relationship. Considerable empirical and theoretical work is needed in the area of social skill before we have an adequate definition and methodology for measurement which can usefully guide assessment and treatment.

Another area where further research is needed is on models of minimal dating and on factors relating to the etiology and maintenance of dating problems. Most of the models of minimal dating have been derived from treatment outcome studies. For example, the finding that social skill training programs are effective has led investigators to propose that social skill deficiencies must therefore be the cause of subjects' minimal dating. Davison (1968) has elegantly discussed the circularity of inferring etiology from treatment effectiveness. With regard to minimal dating, it may be that social skill training programs are effective because they remediate a social skill deficit. However, social skill programs are often hierarchically organized, and behavior rehearsal can also be viewed as a form of *in vivo* desensitization. Thus, it is just as likely that social skill training programs may work primarily through anxiety reduction rather than through social skill acquisition. Similarly, the findings that anxiety reduction and cognitive procedures are effective are not clear evidence for each of these respective models of minimal dating. Basic research on factors relating to the etiology and maintenance of minimal dating is needed, other than speculations derived from treatment studies.

Finally, we should consider the extent to which minimal dating problems may be part of a broader network of interpersonal problems. There are two areas in particular that seem closely related to minimal dating–depression and subassertiveness. Lewinsohn (1975) has demonstrated that low rates of social activity are characteristic of depressed patients and has developed a theory based on the lack of response-contingent positive reinforcement as a cause of depression. Since dating is one important area of social activity, this theory suggests that at least some minimal daters may also be depressed. Further, there is considerable overlap between the problems of assertiveness and minimal dating. In fact, a study by Orenstein, Orenstein, and Carr (1975) demonstrated strong negative correlations between scores on an assertion inventory and scores on Fear Survey items relating to social fears. These findings suggest that minimal dating may well be part of a broader network of interpersonal problems that should be assessed. If such is the case, treatment of minimal dating might constitute one treatment component that would be a part of a broader multidimensional treatment approach.

The area of minimal dating is rich and exciting. However, with the likely proliferation of research in this area, it is likely that our review of the data on dating will soon be outdated. That speaks well for the advances that have been and will be made regarding minimal dating.

REFERENCES

Argyle, M. *Social interaction.* Chicago: Aldine, 1969.

Argyle, M., Bryant, B., & Trower, P. Social skills training and psychotherapy. *Psychological Medicine,* 1974, **4**, 435–443. (a)

Argyle, M., Trower, P., & Bryant, B. Explorations in the treatment of personality disorders and neuroses by social skills training. *British Journal of Medical Psychology,* 1974, **47**, 63–72. (b)

Arkowitz, H., Lichtenstein, E., McGovern, K., & Hines, P. The behavioral assessment of social competence in males. *Behavior Therapy,* 1975, **6**, 3–13.

Bander, K. W., Steinke, G. V., Allen, G. J., & Mosher, D. L. Evaluation of three dating specific treatment approaches for heterosexual dating anxiety. *Journal of Consulting and Clinical Psychology,* 1975, **43**, 259–265.

Bandura, A. *Principles of behavior modification.* New York: Holt, 1969.

Bellack, A. S., Rozensky, R., & Schwartz, J. A. Comparison of two forms of self-monitoring in a behavioral weight reduction program. *Behavior Therapy,* 1974, **5**, 523–530.

Bernstein, D. Behavioral fear assessment: Anxiety or artifact? In H. Adams & P. Unikel (Eds.), *Issues and trends in behavior therapy.* Springfield, Ill.: Thomas, 1973. Pp. 225–267.

Berscheid, E., Dion, K., Walster, E., & Walster, G. W. Physical attractiveness and dating choice: A test of the matching hypothesis. *Journal of Experimental Social Psychology,* 1971, **7**, 173–189.

Berscheid, E., & Walster, E. Physical attractiveness. In L. Berkowitz (Ed.), *Advances in experimental social psychology* (Vol. 7). New York: Academic Press, 1973. Pp. 158–215.

Berzon, B., Reisal, J., & Davis, D. P. PEER: An audiotape program for self-directed small groups. *Journal of Humanistic Psychology,* 1969, **9**, 71–86.

Borkovec, T. D. The effects of instructional suggestion and physiological cues on analogue fear. *Behavior Therapy,* 1973, **4**, 185–192.

Borkovec, T. D., Stone, N. M., O'Brien, G. T., & Kaloupek, D. G. Evaluation of a clinically relevant target behavior for analogue outcome research. *Behavior Therapy,* 1974, **5**, 503–511.

Bryant, B. M., & Trower, P. E. Social difficulty in a student sample. *British Journal of Educational Psychology,* 1974, **44**, 13–21.

Christensen, A., & Arkowitz, H. Preliminary report on practice dating and feedback as treatment for college dating problems. *Journal of Counseling Psychology,* 1974, **21**, 92–95.

Christensen, A., Arkowitz, H., & Anderson, J. Practice dating as treatment for college dating inhibitions. *Behaviour Research and Therapy,* 1975, **13**, 321–331.

Clark, J., & Arkowitz, H. Social anxiety and self-evaluation of interpersonal performance. *Psychological Reports,* 1975, **36**, 211–221.

Curran, J. P. Social skills training and systematic desensitization in reducing dating anxiety. *Behaviour Research and Therapy,* 1975, **13**, 65–68.

Curran, J. P. Skills training as an approach to the treatment of heterosexual-social anxiety. *Psychological Bulletin,* 1977, **84**, 140–157.

Curran, J. P., & Gilbert, F. S. A test of the relative effectiveness of a systematic desensitization program and an interpersonal skills training program with date anxious subjects. *Behavior Therapy,* 1975, **6**, 510–521.

Curran, J. P., Gilbert, F. S., & Little, L. M. A comparison between behavioral training and sensitivity training approaches to heterosexual dating anxiety. *Journal of Counseling Psychology,* 1976, **23**, 190–196. (a)

Curran, J. P., Wallander, J. L., & Fishetti, M. *The importance of behavioral and cognitive factors in heterosexual-social anxiety.* Unpublished manuscript, Purdue University, 1976. (b)

Davison, G. C. Systematic desensitization as a counterconditioning process. *Journal of Abnormal Psychology,* 1968, **73**, 91–99.

Dion, K., Berscheid, E., & Walster, E. What is beautiful is good. *Journal of Personality and Social Psychology,* 1972, **24**, 285–290.

Eisler, R. M., Hersen, M., & Miller, P. M. Effects of modeling on components of social skill training. *Journal of Behavior Therapy and Experimental Psychiatry,* 1973, **4**, 1–6.

Ellis, A. *Reason and emotion in psychotherapy.* New York: Lyle Stuart, 1962.

Emmelkamp, P. M. G. Self-observation versus flooding in the treatment of agoraphobia. *Behaviour Research and Therapy,* 1974, **5**, 606–613.

Endler, W. S., Hunt, J. McV., & Rosenstein, A. J. An S-R Inventory of Anxiousness. *Psychological Monographs,* 1962, **76**(17, Whole No. 536).

Gambrill, E. A. *A behavioral program for increasing social interaction.* Unpublished manuscript, University of California, Berkeley, 1975.

Gelder, M. G., & Marks, I. M. Severe agoraphobia: A controlled prospective trial of behavior therapy. *British Journal of Psychiatry,* 1966, **112,** 309–319.

Glasgow, R., & Arkowitz, H. The behavioral assessment of male and female social competence in dyadic heterosexual interactions. *Behavior Therapy,* 1975, **6,** 488–498.

Glass, C. R., Gottman, J. M., & Shmurak, S. H. Response acquisition and cognitive self-statement modification approaches to dating skills training. *Journal of Counseling Psychology,* 1976, **23,** 520–526.

Goldfried, M. R., & D'Zurilla, T. J. A behavior-analytic model for assessing competence. In C. D. Spielberger (Ed.), *Current topics in clinical and community psychology* (Vol. 1). New York: Academic Press, 1969.

Goldsmith, J. B., & McFall, R. M. Development and evaluation of an interpersonal skill-training program for psychiatric inpatients. *Journal of Abnormal Psychology,* 1975, **84,** 51–58.

Goldstein, A. P., Martens, J., Hubben, J., vanBelle, H. A., Schaff, W., Wiersma, H., & Goedhart, A. The use of modeling to increase independent behavior. *Behaviour Research and Therapy,* 1973, **11,** 31–42.

Gutride, M. E., Goldstein, A. P., & Hunter, G. F. The use of modeling and roleplaying to increase social interaction among asocial psychiatric patients. *Journal of Consulting and Clinical Psychology,* 1973, **40,** 408–415.

Hersen, M., & Bellack, A. S. Social skills training for chronic psychiatric patients: Rationale, research findings, and future directions. *Comprehensive Psychiatry,* 1976, **17,** 559–580.

Hersen, M., & Bellack, A. S. Assessment of social skills. In A. R. Ciminero, K. S. Calhoun, & H. E. Adams (Eds.), *Handbook for behavioral assessment.* New York: Wiley, 1977. Pp. 509–554.

Hersen, M., & Eisler, R. M. Social skills training. In W. E. Craighead, A. E. Kazdin, & M. J. Mahoney (Eds.), *Behavior modification: Principles, issues, and extensions.* Boston: Houghton, 1976. Pp. 361–375.

Hersen, M., Eisler, R. M., & Miller, P. M. Development of assertive responses: Clinical, measurement, and research considerations. *Behaviour Research and Therapy,* 1973, **11,** 505–521.

Hersen, M., Eisler, R. M., & Miller, P. M. An experimental analysis of generalization in assertive training. *Behaviour Research and Therapy,* 1974, **12,** 295–310.

Hokanson, D. T. *Systematic desensitization and positive cognitive rehearsal treatment of social anxiety.* Unpublished doctoral dissertation, University of Texas at Austin, 1971.

Johnson, S. M. *First person singular.* Unpublished manuscript, University of Oregon, 1976.

Johnson, S. M., & White, G. Self-observation as an agent of behavior change. *Behavior Therapy,* 1971, **2,** 488–497.

Klaus, D., Hersen, M., & Bellack, A. S. Survey of dating habits of male and female college students: A necessary precursor to measurement and modification. *Journal of Clinical Psychology,* in press.

Kramer, S. R. *Effectiveness of behavior rehearsal and practice dating to increase heterosexual social interaction.* Unpublished doctoral dissertation, University of Texas, 1975.

Landy, F. J., & Gaupp, L. A. A factor analysis of the Fear Survey Schedule—III. *Behaviour Research and Therapy,* 1971, **9,** 89–94.

Lewinsohn, P. M. The behavioral study and treatment of depression. In M. Hersen, R. M. Eisler, & P. M. Miller (Eds.), *Progress in behavior modification* (Vol. 1). New York: Academic Press, 1975. Pp. 19–64.

Lewinsohn, P. M., Alper, T., Johansson, S., Libet, J., Rosenberry, C., Shaffer, M., Sterin, C., Stewart, R., & Weinstein, M. *Manual of instructions for the behavior rating used for the observation of interpersonal behavior.* Unpublished manuscript, University of Oregon, 1968.

MacDonald, M. L., Lindquist, C. U., Kramer, J. A., McGrath, R. A., & Rhyne, L. L. Social skills training: Behavior rehearsal in groups and dating skills. *Journal of Counseling Psychology,* 1975, **22,** 224–231.

Marks, I. M. Behavioral treatments of phobic and obsessive–compulsive disorders: A critical appraisal. In M. Hersen, R. M. Eisler, & P. M. Miller (Eds.), *Progress in behavior modification* (Vol. 1). New York: Academic Press, 1975. Pp. 65–158.

Martin, S. *The comparability of behavioral data in the laboratory and natural settings.* Unpublished doctoral dissertation, University of Oregon, 1971.

Martinson, W., & Zerface, J. Comparison of individual counseling and a social program with non-daters. *Journal of Counseling Psychology,* 1970, **17,** 36–40.

Marzillier, J. S. *Social skills and assertive training: A critical review of outcome research.* Unpublished manuscript, University of Birmingham, 1976.

Marzillier, J. S., Lambert, C., & Kellett, J. A controlled evaluation of systematic desensitization and social skills training for socially inadequate psychiatric patients. *Behaviour Research and Therapy,* 1976, **14,** 225–238.

Masters, W. H., & Johnson, V. E. *Human sexual inadequacy.* Boston: Little, Brown, 1970.

McFall, R. M. Effects of self-monitoring on normal smoking behavior. *Journal of Consulting and Clinical Psychology,* 1970, **35,** 135–142.

McFall, R. M. Behavioral training: A skill-acquisition approach to clinical problems. In J. T. Spence, R. C. Carson, & J. W. Thibaut (Eds.), *Behavioral approaches to therapy.* Morristown, N.J.: General Learning Press, 1976. Pp. 227–259.

McGovern, K. B. Development and evaluation of a social skills training program for undergraduate male nondaters. Unpublished doctoral dissertation, University of Oregon, 1972.

McGovern, K. B. Arkowitz, H., & Gilmore, S. K. Evaluation of social skill training programs for college dating inhibitions. *Journal of Counseling Psychology,* 1975, **22,** 505–512.

Meichenbaum, D. Cognitive factors in behavior modification: Modifying what clients say to themselves. In C. M. Franks & G. T. Wilson (Eds.), *Annual review of behavior therapy: Theory and practice* (Vol. 1). New York: Brunner/Mazel, 1973. Pp. 416–431.

Meichenbaum, D., & Turk, D. The cognitive-behavioral management of anxiety, anger, and pain. In P. O. Davidson (Ed.), *The behavioral management of anxiety, depression, and pain.* New York: Brunner/Mazel, 1976. Pp. 1–34.

Melnick, J. A comparison of replication techniques in the modification of minimal dating behavior. *Journal of Abnormal Psychology,* 1973, **81,** 51–59.

Miller, W. R., & Arkowitz, H. Anxiety and perceived causation in social success and failure experiences: Disconfirmation of an attribution hypothesis in two experiments. *Journal of Abnormal Psychology,* in press.

Mitchell, K. R., & Orr, F. E. Note on treatment of heterosexual anxiety using short-term massed desensitization. *Psychological Reports,* 1974, **35,** 1093–1094.

Nelson, R. O. Methodological issues in assessment via self-monitoring. In J. D. Cone & R. P. Hawkins (Eds.), *Behavioral assessment: New directions in clinical psychology.* New York: Brunner/Mazel, 1977.

O'Banion, K., & Arkowitz, H. Social anxiety and selective memory for affective information about the self. *Social Behavior and Personality,* in press.

Orenstein, H., Orenstein, E., & Carr, J. E. Assertiveness and anxiety: A correlational study. *Journal of Behavior Therapy and Experimental Psychiatry,* 1975, **6,** 203–207.

Patterson, G. R., Reid, J. B., Jones, R. R., & Conger, R. E. *A social learning approach to family intervention* (Vol. 1), *Families with aggressive children.* Eugene, Ore.: Castalia Publishing, 1975.

Paul, G. L. *Insight versus desensitization in psychotherapy.* Stanford: Stanford University Press, 1966.

Rehm, L. P., & Marston, A. R. Reduction of social anxiety through modification of self-reinforcement: An instigation therapy technique. *Journal of Consulting and Clinical Psychology,* 1968, **32,** 565–574.

Reisinger, J. J., Ora, J. P., & Frangia, G. W. Parents as change agents for their children: A review. *Journal of Community Psychology,* 1976, **4,** 103–123.

Rhyne, L. D., MacDonald, M. L., McGrath, R. A., Lindquist, C. U., & Kramer, J. A. The roleplayed dating interactions (RPDI): An instrument for the measurement of male social dating skills. JSAS *Catalog of Selected Documents in Psychology,* 1974, **4,** 42.

Rotter, J. B., & Wickens, D. D. The consistency and generality of ratings of "social aggressiveness" made from observations of role playing situations. *Journal of Consulting Psychology,* 1948, **12,** 234–239.

Royce, W. S., & Arkowitz, H. *Multi-modal evaluation of* in vivo *practice as treatment for social isolation.* Unpublished manuscript, University of Arizona, 1976.

Shmurak, S. H. *A comparison of types of problems encountered by college students and psychiatric inpatients in social situations.* Unpublished manuscript, Indiana University, 1973.

Smith, R. E. Social anxiety as a moderator variable in the attitude-similarity-attraction relationship. *Journal of Experimental Research in Personality,* 1972, **6,** 22–28.

Smith, R. E., & Campbell, A. W. Social anxiety and strain toward symmetry in dyadic attraction. *Journal of Personality and Social Psychology,* 1973, **28,** 101–107.

Smith, R. E., & Jeffrey, R. W. Social-evaluative anxiety and the reinforcement properties of agreeing and disagreeing attitude statements. *Journal of Experimental Research in Personality,* 1970, **4,** 276–280.

Smith, R. E., & Sarason, I. G. Social anxiety and the evaluation of negative interpersonal feedback. *Journal of Consulting and Clinical Psychology,* 1975, **43,** 429.

Twentyman, C. T., & McFall, R. M. Behavioral training of social skills in shy males. *Journal of Consulting and Clinical Psychology,* 1975, **43,** 384–395.

Watson, D., & Friend, R. Measurement of social-evaluative anxiety. *Journal of Consulting and Clinical Psychology,* 1969, **33,** 448–457.

Weiss, R. L., Hops, H., and Patterson, G. R. A framework for conceptualizing marital conflict, a technology for altering it, some data for evaluating it. In L. A. Hammerlynck, L. C. Handy, & E. J. Mash (Eds.), *Behavior change: Methodology, concepts, and practice.* Champaign, Ill.: Research Press, 1973. Pp. 309–342.

Wolpe, J., & Lang, P. J. A fear survey schedule for use in behavior therapy. *Behaviour Research and Therapy,* 1964, **2,** 27–30.

Zigler, E., & Phillips, L. Social effectiveness and symptomatic behaviors. *Journal of Abnormal and Social Psychology,* 1960, **61,** 231–238.

Zimbardo, P., Pilkonis, P., & Norwood, R. The silent prison of shyness. *Psychology Today,* 1975, **8,** 69–72.

BEHAVIORAL CONTROL OF EXCESSIVE DRINKING

S. H. LOVIBOND
Department of Psychology
University of New South Wales
Sydney, Australia

I. INTRODUCTION

Several excellent reviews of recent work on the behavioral control of excessive drinking are available (Briddell & Nathan, 1976; Lloyd & Salzberg, 1975; Nathan & Briddell, 1976). Rather than duplicate this work, the present chapter will attempt an evaluation of current methods of behavioral control in light of developments in a number of fields of experimental psychology. Despite the relative success of behavioral procedures in modifying some addictive behaviors, our knowledge of the conditions and mechanisms of addictive behavior and its control is still limited. Since it would seem beyond dispute that a better understanding of addiction and the mode of operation of behavioral control procedures would open the way for the development of more effective control measures, particular emphasis will be placed on behavioral theories of addictions in general and excessive drinking in particular.

If it is accepted that behavior modification, or behavior therapy, represents the application of the methods and findings of experimental psychology as a whole to clinical problems, it behooves the behavior modifier to study developments in the basic discipline, particularly in areas that impinge most directly on the field of applied interest. The implications of recent work in two areas of animal behavior, animal models of excessive drinking, and taste aversion, will be discussed.

Since attempts to understand and to modify other behavioral excesses would likely provide valuable leads for those working in the field of alcohol abuse, some pertinent studies in the control of obesity and opiate addiction will be examined.

Finally, some current multifaceted behavioral programs for the management of alcohol abuse will be evaluated, and, in light of earlier discussions, an attempt will be made to delineate the courses that might be pursued with the greatest gain in the further development of modification strategies.

II. BEHAVIORAL DEFINITION OF RESPONSIBLE AND EXCESSIVE DRINKING

The central assumptions of what has become the traditional, nonbehavioral approach to the problems associated with excessive use of alcohol are: (a) that alcohol abuse is a symptom of a disease called alcoholism, and (b) that persons suffering from the disease alcoholism (alcoholics) have an abnormal reaction to alcohol such that once they begin to drink alcohol, they are unable to refrain from further drinking (Alcoholics Anonymous, 1953; Jellinek, 1960; Keller & Efron, 1955; Williams, 1959). Widespread acceptance of the traditional view of alcohol abuse has had the following effects:

1. Excessive use of alcohol has come to be regarded as essentially a problem for the medical practitioner and the spiritual counselor.

2. The alcohol abuser has been seen as clearly differentiated from the "normal" or social drinker.

3. The public identification of abnormal drinking with derelicts or chronic inebriates has not been corrected.

4. Because of the public stereotype of the alcoholic and the difficulty of establishing irrefutable signs of the disease state alcoholism, there has been a reluctance to diagnose the disorder and prescribe treatment.

5. In the absence of criteria of excessive drinking short of chronic alcoholism, levels of alcohol consumption which clearly place the individual's health, safety, and social relationships at risk have been accepted as normal.

6. It has been generally accepted that the only conceivable goal of treatment for excessive drinking is total abstinence.

7. Many grossly excessive drinkers have been prevented from seeking help to modify their drinking patterns because of a reluctance to associate themselves with the common stereotype of the alcoholic, and to accept the treatment goal of total abstinence.

8. Persons with grave drinking problems have been encouraged to believe that they have an inherent defect, and consequently have no hope of controlling their drinking behavior.

9. Because it is believed to be impossible to differentiate between "normal social drinkers" and "early alcoholics," social, and particularly governmental agencies have been reluctant to foster the development of behavior modification programs that could be offered in lieu of statutory penalties to persons whose excessive drinking brings them into conflict with the law.

An alternative, and potentially more fruitful approach to the problem of alcohol abuse can be derived from the principles of behavior modification. The central assumption of a behavioral approach is that although excessive consumption of alcohol eventually produces medical symptoms, in essence it is a social/behavioral problem. Further, excessive drinking, as any other behavior, can be modified. (If excessive drinking has been continued to the point where definite medical pathology is present, the resources required for change may, of course, make a program of behavior modification impracticable.)

As in the case of any other behavior, criteria of acceptable and unacceptable drinking behavior may be defined in terms of frequency and/or intensity. Although for many problem behaviors any frequency or intensity above zero may be unacceptable to the individual, to society, or to both, in the case of alcohol intake, acceptable criteria for frequency and intensity may well be above zero. If it is assumed that levels of alcohol consumption which involve very low risks to health, work efficiency, and capacity for responsible social behavior are acceptable, levels of reasonable or responsible drinking behavior can be defined in terms of peak blood alcohol concentration (BACs) and absolute quantities of alcohol consumed per unit time.

A. Responsible Drinking

The suggested criterion of acceptable or responsible drinking is that use of alcohol which rarely results in BACs greater than .07–.08% (70–80 mg/100 ml). Usually not more than six drinks will be consumed on a single occasion, and not more than eight drinks per day (1 drink = 10 oz. beer, 4 oz. table wine, 2 oz. fortified wine, 1 oz. spirits). Blood alcohol concentrations of .07–.08% produce a measurable effect on driving performance, but even when reached daily over long periods, are not usually associated with impairment of social relations, work efficiency, or health. The drinking behavior of the responsible drinker remains fully under his control (i.e., the individual can cease drinking for prolonged periods without undue effort).

B. Excessive Drinking

Two levels of excessive drinking may be distinguished:

Level I. Level I excessive drinking behavior may be defined as drinking which consistently results in BACs approaching or exceeding .15% (150 mg/100 ml). Often more than 10 drinks will be consumed on a single occasion, and daily intake is likely to average 10 drinks or more. Drinking at such levels is unlikely to result in physical dependency but is associated with a high risk of accident to self or others. In the long term this level is associated with a high risk of impairment of family and other social relations and decreased work performance. Moreover, deterioration of health due to tissue damage is virtually certain.

Level II. Level II excessive drinking behavior may be defined as drinking which consistently results in BACs of .20–.30% (200–300 mg/100 ml) or higher. Drinking may occupy most waking hours such that a BAC of zero is seldom attained, or periods of abstinence may alternate with periods of binge-type drinking. Tolerance may have been developed to the point where a BAC of .15% (150 mg/100 ml) results in no obvious signs of drunkenness. Physical dependence is likely to be present to some degree. Continued over a sufficient period, Level II excessive drinking inevitably results in personality disintegration, destruction of family and other social relations, and marked deterioration of work performance and health.

It should be noted that the above definitions dispense with the terms alcoholic, prealcoholic, problem drinker, social drinker, and the like, and are quite independent of normative data. Custom is, of course, likely to insure the continued currency of the term alcoholic, and it offers a convenient way of referring to the Level II excessive drinker, providing the behavioral criteria are kept in mind.

III. THE GOALS OF A MODIFICATION PROGRAM

From the viewpoint of conventional, nonbehavioral theories of alcohol abuse, the only conceivable goal of any intervention program is total abstinence. In the first place, the alcohol abuser is suffering from a disease and, although the disease is incurable, its course can be arrested by total abstinence. Second, the alcohol abuser is irresistibly compelled to continue drinking once he begins. Hence drinking in moderation must remain an unattainable goal for such a person.

The conventional view has been challenged by workers other than behaviorally oriented psychologists. In the 1960s, following an early report by Davies (1962), Pattison (1966, 1967) reviewed evidence that a proportion of alcoholics who had undergone abstinence-oriented programs, or no therapy at all, returned voluntarily to moderate levels of drinking, and made a satisfactory life adjustment.

From the behavioral point of view, excessive consumption of alcohol is a learned pattern of behavior that has been acquired and is maintained in accordance with the same principles that govern other behaviors. Consequently, if certain levels of alcohol intake are defined as acceptable, it becomes a reasonable goal to train excessive drinkers to moderate or control their drinking behavior and maintain chosen levels of consumption. It was with such considerations in mind that Lovibond and Caddy (1970) undertook a behavioral program designed to train alcohol abusers to moderate their drinking.

The specific target set for the subjects was that of keeping their BACs below the designated level of 65 mg/100 ml.

More recently, an increasing number of investigators have made controlled drinking the goal of behavior modification programs using a variety of techniques (e.g., Cohen, Liebson, Faillace, & Allan, 1971; Mills, Sobell, & Schaeffer, 1971; Pickens, Bigelow, & Griffiths, 1973; Silverstein, Nathan, & Taylor, 1974; Sobell & Sobell, 1973b). Lloyd and Salzberg (1975) have reviewed the evidence relating to the controlled drinking versus abstinence issue, and have concluded that:

> There seems to be no clear-cut experimental evidence to support the belief that loss of control and a heavy drinking bout are inevitable consequences of an alcohol abuser's consumption of an initial drink. On the contrary, the literature has shown that alcohol abusers can learn to exercise considerable control over their drinking behavior, and that treatment programs can be oriented toward establishing and maintaining controlled drinking. [pp. 834–835]

Lloyd and Salzberg (1975) go on to observe that:

> Some evidence does exist to suggest that alcohol abusers are more likely to succeed at establishing controlled drinking than at establishing strict abstinence. [p. 835]

Nathan and Briddell (1976) have discussed the considerations that might lead to a decision to adopt controlled or moderate drinking as the goal of a behavior modification program. Advocating the development of predictors of response to treatments with abstinence or controlled drinking goals, Nathan and Briddell suggest that attention should be paid to the following: (a) evaluation of the functional relationship between excessive drinking and choice of treatment goal; (b) assessment of pretreatment consumptive behavior as a predictor of treatment response; (c) assessment of the patient's social support systems as an adjunct to posttreatment planning; (d) evaluation of prior treatment experiences; (e) assessment of the patient's expectations about changes required for successful treatment as a predictor of treatment choice.

It is difficult to quarrel with the view that attention should be given to the above issues and that a thorough behavioral assessment should be conducted for each individual patient. On the other hand, there are good grounds for taking issue with Nathan and Briddell when they assert that controlled drinking should not be chosen as a treatment goal for a patient unless that patient has previously tried and failed in abstinence-oriented programs.

Our own experience with both controlled and abstinence-oriented training programs has led us to believe that controlled drinking should be the goal of choice unless it is contraindicated by any of the following considerations:

1. The person is currently able to remain abstinent.
2. The person's state of health is such that it would be medically unwise for him or her to consume more alcohol.
3. The person chooses abstinence as a program goal after a thorough examination of the issues in light of a behavioral assessment of his or her problem.

In our view, the above rules may be applied across the whole spectrum of alcohol abuse. In the case of Level I excessive drinkers, however, there are strong pragmatic reasons for emphasizing controlled drinking. There can be few young persons in this category who would voluntarily enter programs designed to turn them into total abstainers for the rest of their lives, and it would be ludicrous to deny them access to controlled drinking training unless they had already failed abstinence-oriented programs.

As Lloyd and Salzberg (1975) have pointed out, however, a controlled drinking goal has many potential advantages for other excessive drinkers:

1. For the majority of alcohol abusers, abstinence is an undesirable goal that has proved unattainable.
2. In most developed countries the controlled consumption of alcohol is normal behavior and gains more social reinforcement than abstaining behavior.
3. In controlled drinking programs, the alcohol abuser is treated as a person with a particular behavior problem which, with help, he can learn to control. The excessive drinker is thus offered the opportunity to develop responsible control over his own behavior and to be accepted as normal.

We believe, however, that any alcohol abuser who has been able to achieve abstinence should be assisted to remain abstinent, and that any excessive drinker who is able to accept the Alcoholics Anonymous (AA) philosophy and treatment goals should be encouraged to enter AA programs.

In the absence of systematic prediction-oriented research, it is possible to offer only clinical impressions of the significance of the sorts of background factors listed by Nathan and Briddell. Our own experience suggests that the most important predictor of success in *any* program is the degree to which the person concerned can be helped to achieve satisfying work and interpersonal relations when his drinking is no longer a problem. All too often the individual's ability to attain these objectives is limited by lack of intellectual and job skills, by social and cultural barriers, and by the lack of significant others to provide social support.

IV. THE TARGET GROUP

One of the fundamental problems in the behavioral control of alcohol abuse is the reluctance of excessive drinkers to accept the need for modification of their drinking behavior. Thus, treatment resources typically are brought to bear at a time when excessive consumption of alcohol has been maintained to the point where the destruction of health, job performance, and social relationships are serious problems. Usually the period of excessive drinking has extended over 20 years or more, and the problems of change are so great that the individual concerned is likely to be recycled through a number of treatment agencies. Almost always, behavior modification is well down on the list of treatment priorities, and by the time patients find their way into behavioral programs they are likely to have failed in previous intervention programs.

It would seem that one of the few potential mechanisms for getting young excessive drinkers into modification programs is the legislation that exists in most communities against the operation of a motor vehicle with a BAC above a prescribed limit.

There is no evidence that the usual court-imposed penalties of fines, license suspensions, and, in extreme cases, jail sentences result in any significant modification of the drinking behavior of the persons involved. Nevertheless, breath and blood analysis legislation have permitted a more adequate definition of the problem of excessive drinking. As an example, in the State of New South Wales, Australia, approximately 15,000 drivers are prosecuted annually for driving with more than the prescribed limit of alcohol in the blood (80 mg/100 ml). The average BAC of the convicted drivers, almost all of whom are male, is 160 mg/100 ml, and the variation from year to year is extraordinarily small. Approximately 50% of prosecuted drivers are below 25 years of age and, from samples already studied, it can be estimated that at least half of the younger drivers are Level I excessive drinkers.

The University of New South Wales currently has a behavior

modification program designed to train volunteer drinking drivers from this group to moderate their drinking behavior (Lovibond, 1975). Initially, referral was via the offender's legal counsel, but recently the courts have instituted a procedure whereby convicted persons are given the option of joining prior to sentencing one of several available programs.

There seems little doubt that, as a target for modification programs, young Level I excessive drinkers offer a greater potential return in relation to cost than any other group.

V. BEHAVIORAL THEORIES OF THE ETIOLOGY OF EXCESSIVE DRINKING

Although behavioral theories of the etiology of alcohol abuse have not been well articulated, there are some differences in emphasis which are associated with different treatment orientations.

A. Extrinsic Control

The essential feature of most behavioral theories is that they view excessive consumption of alcohol as an instrumental act (i.e., behavior which is maintained chiefly by reinforcement other than that provided by the intrinsically rewarding effects of the drug itself). As Nathan and Briddell (1976) have noted, most current theories are variations on the theme that drinking is a learned means of reducing anxiety. The chief difference between such a view and that of the traditional psychodynamicist lies in the presumed origins of the anxiety. For the behaviorist, the anxiety is conditioned, whereas for the psychodynamicist, the anxiety arises from inner conflicts.

A variant of extrinsic control theory emphasizes the role of positively reinforcing events in the external world rather than negatively reinforcing events within the subject. Thus, the excessive consumption of alcohol is said to be maintained by such social reinforcers as peer acceptance and approval.

Miller and Eisler (1976) have recently outlined a "social learning theory" of the etiology of alcoholism which may be regarded as an all-inclusive view of alcohol abuse as instrumental behavior.

> Within a social-learning framework, alcohol and drug abuse are viewed as socially acquired, learned behavior patterns, maintained by numerous antecedent cues and consequent rein-

forcers that may be of a psychological, sociological or physiological nature. Such factors as reduction in anxiety, increased social recognition and peer approval, enhanced ability to exhibit more varied spontaneous social behavior, or the avoidance of physiological withdrawal symptoms, may maintain substance abuse. . . . [p. 380]

Such statements are, of course, theoretical orientations rather than theories, but they nevertheless guide the practice of behavior modification in some particular directions rather than others. Thus, emphasis on the anxiety-reducing role of alcohol is likely to lead the behavior modifier to eschew aversion therapy on the grounds that it may simply exacerbate the subject's anxiety, and to direct attention toward the anxiety rather than the drinking behavior.

A belief that excessive drinking is maintained principally by interpersonal reinforcement suggests that attention should be directed to environmental changes which will eliminate identifiable cue stimuli and reinforcers for excessive drinking and which will encourage new socially reinforced behaviors incompatible with drinking.

The foregoing strategies, individually or severally, may make a contribution to an integrated therapeutic program designed to control excessive drinking, but there is some doubt whether they can carry a significant part of the therapeutic burden.

The view that excessive consumption of alcohol may be a learned means of reducing anxiety has immediate intuitive appeal. The idea loses its plausibility, however, when it is recognized that the major anxiety-reducing function of alcohol is probably achieved at BACs around 100 mg/100 ml or lower. The typical chronic alcoholic habitually achieves BACs two to three times higher than this value.

In a behavioral study conducted by Nathan and O'Brien (1971), it was found that the anxiety levels of alcoholics increased following an initial 12- –24-hour period of drinking, although levels of anxiety decreased modestly while the alcoholics were actually drinking.

In a review of relevant studies carried out with both animal and human subjects, Cappell (1974) concluded that the tension reduction model of alcohol consumption has been unable to account for the drinking patterns of alcoholics. This is not to assert, of course, that levels of alcohol consumption are not increased by anxiety. Indeed, it has been demonstrated that under some circumstances of increased tension the alcohol intake of some subjects, both animal and human, increases. However, the instrumental tension reduction model cannot fully account for the alcohol consumption of excessive drinkers.

There is no direct evidence concerning the validity of the social reinforcement model of alcohol abuse, but the model has led to some interesting laboratory studies of the extent to which the drinking behavior of chronic alcoholics can be brought under the control of various reinforcement contingencies (Bigelow, Liebson, & Griffiths, 1974; Cohen *et al.*, 1971; Mello & Mendelson, 1965, 1970; Nathan, Titler, Lowenstein, Solomon, & Rossi, 1970). It was shown that in-patient alcoholics who were exposed to freely available alcohol do not exhibit loss of control after their first drink. Although the alcoholic when he was drinking felt that alcohol was profoundly reinforcing to him, his drinking behavior could be brought under the efficient control of reinforcers such as money and access to an enriched environment. In some cases drinking was controlled by the opportunity for social contact, but some alcoholics preferred to drink in social isolation.

It is, of course, one thing to show that the drinking behavior of alcoholics in a controlled environment, removed from the usual context of drug abuse, can be brought under the control of social reinforcers. It is quite another thing to demonstrate that the consumption of alcohol by Level I excessive drinkers is normally controlled by such contingencies, and it is something else again to show that the grossly excessive alcohol intake of Level II alcohol abusers in their usual drinking environment is so controlled. Nevertheless, the studies in question are highly significant inasmuch as they have made it clear that the drinking of chronic alcoholics is not uncontrollable once it has begun.

B. Intrinsic Control

A striking feature of most behavioral theories of the etiology of excessive drinking is the virtual absence of any mention of the positive reinforcing properties of alcohol per se. Subjective descriptions of the positive effects of alcohol include feelings of warmth, relaxation, social ease, and general euphoria. There can be little doubt that most responsible drinkers drink in order to enjoy the positive behavioral changes alcohol produces. It is at least arguable that most excessive (but not physically dependent) drinkers initiate drinking for precisely the same reasons, and the real problem is that of understanding why responsible drinkers stop drinking at moderate blood alcohol concentrations and excessive drinkers do not. One possibility is that the responsible drinker is more sensitive to the aversive effects of large doses of alcohol, and that his drinking comes under the control of such aversive effects relatively early. In the case of the excessive drinker, however, drinking may remain under the control of the initiating events for much longer periods, and often may be brought to an end by environmental changes (liquor supplies running out, bars closing, drinking companions leaving). In the case of the physically dependent alcoholic, the aversive effect of not continuing to drink when high BACs are reached enters as an additional control over drinking. Emphasis on the role of alcohol as a powerful pharmacological reinforcer is likely to lead the behavior modifier to the view that, in the control of excessive drinking, the highly reinforcing effects of alcohol should be modified directly; for example, by aversive procedures.

C. Stimulus Control of Excessive Drinking

With some exceptions (notably Wikler, 1971a, 1971b), behavioral psychologists and psychiatrists have not emphasized the role of drinking-associated stimulus patterns in the control of drinking. If the consumption of alcohol is an instrumental act, the stimuli consistently associated with drinking may simply become discriminative stimuli (i.e., stimuli that signify extrinsic reinforcements are forthcoming if the instrumental act of drinking is performed).

If, however, drinking is intrinsically reinforcing or self-reinforcing, stimulus sequences consistently culminating in drinking may take on positive incentive properties. In other words, the stimuli in question subjectively may come to elicit the desire to drink, and behaviorally may elicit alcohol-seeking activity.

There is little direct evidence concerning the stimulus control of alcohol consumption, but the experience of users of the more addictive drug heroin is instructive. O'Brien, Raynes, and Patch (1972) have described the treatment of two heroin addicts by behavioral procedures, including aversion therapy. Because the subjects reported that stimuli associated with drug use triggered a desire for heroin, O'Brien and his co-workers devised a scale to measure therapeutic changes in "craving cued by drug-associated stimuli." The five points on the scale were defined as follows: (a) evoking a strong and uncontrollable desire to heroin use; (b) evoking a strong and controllable desire to heroin use; (c) evoking an easily changed desire to take heroin; (d) evoking no desire to use heroin; and (e) evoking an aversion to the use of heroin.

Stories which contained the stimuli associated with acquisition and use of heroin were presented to the patients in their own jargon.

This pattern of CS's was considered the complex behavioral chain of drug use. . . . The presentation of the CS's was reinforced (paired with the shock UCS) initially after presentation of the complex behavioral chain. . . . Progressively smaller segments of the behavioral chain were reinforced until individual events and items were used. [O'Brien *et al.*, 1972, p. 58]

Patient 1, after her 21st treatment session, returned to her drug usage environment while on a pass and experienced confusion, loneliness, and physiological cravings. After the 27th session, Patient 1 had no desire to use heroin and was discharged. Reports obtained from the patient and her employer 14 months later, which were substantiated by the absence of track marks, indicated that the patient had remained free of heroin use. The second patient was reported to have developed an aversion to heroin after following the same procedures.

The article by O'Brien and his co-workers is of particular interest because it presents clear evidence of the positive incentive value (or craving eliciting characteristics) of the stimuli associated with drug use. The contribution also provides clear evidence of the role of aversive stimulation in reducing the reinforcing value of such stimuli. The authors, however, described their motivational change procedure as extinction of the response of heroin use.

Experimental investigations with rats of the role of stimuli paired with administration of opiates have been carried out by Wikler and his associates. In one experiment (Wikler, Pescor, Miller, & Norrell, 1971), a pharmacologically inactive chemical, anise flavor, was paired with the suppression of morphine abstinence phenomena in rats, which was achieved by their drinking etonitazene solution. In subsequent tests on 17 occasions at variable intervals through the 137th day after the cessation of morphine injections, experimental animals drank significantly more anise-flavored water than controls. The difference was no longer significant after the 137th day. The authors interpreted their findings as indicating "that repeated suppression of morphine abstinence phenomena with a constantly associated sensory stimulus can endow the latter with secondary–appetitively reinforcing properties that persist long after drug withdrawal" (p. 115).

In an earlier experiment, Wikler and Pescor (1967) observed a persistent tendency for rats, previously made dependent on morphine (but no longer physically dependent), to relapse into further morphine ingestion when placed in an environment consistently associated with drug intake. It should be noted that there is as yet no experimental demonstration of the development of positive incentive properties in stimuli paired with drug dosages that produce purely appetitive reinforcing effects and no signs of physical dependence.

A further line of evidence strongly suggesting the importance of stimulus controls in addictive behavior comes from sensory deprivation experiments. In early experiments outlined by Vernon (1963), addicted smokers undergoing sensory deprivation reported an absence of any desire to smoke while in the experimental chamber and for some time afterwards. In an experiment conducted by Suedfeld and Ikard (1974) to examine the effects of persuasive communications under conditions of sensory deprivation, similar effects were observed. Five addicted smokers, who normally smoked 35–50 cigarettes per day, underwent 24 hours of sensory deprivation with periods of taped messages designed to change attitudes toward smoking. All five subjects reported that their cravings for cigarettes disappeared during, and for some time after, treatment.

In a further study using a similar procedure, subjects were randomly assigned to one of four conditions: sensory deprivation with messages (24 hours of sensory deprivation plus messages every 1½ hours), sensory deprivation with no messages, messages with no sensory deprivation, and no sensory deprivation with no messages. The subjects were 35 addicted smokers (persons who experienced a craving for cigarettes whenever not in the act of smoking) and 42 preaddictive smokers (symptoms less severe, but "close to addiction").

It was emphasized to the subjects that the sensory deprivation experience would be relaxing and not unpleasant. Subjects were required to lie on a hospital bed wearing night attire (but without cuffs, earphones, or goggles) in a completely dark, sound-reducing chamber. Instructions to the subjects emphasized the need to remain fairly still and quiet except when using the chemical toilet provided. Subjects were told that they could leave by walking out, but would not be permitted to return. No subject reported distress in the debriefing. Smoking behavior showed almost 100% abstention by all subjects for a week after the treatment procedure. During the second week posttreatment, however, the proportion of totally abstinent subjects was close to 100% in the sensory deprivation groups and close to zero in the no sensory deprivation groups. Twelve months after the treatment session, the reduction in smoking rates from pretreatment baseline was virtually identical for the two no sensory deprivation groups (15% and 17%) and quite similar for the two sensory deprivation groups (45% and 52%).

A study of the effects of sensory deprivation on excessive drinking is clearly needed. The technique may provide a baseline against which the effects of incentive stimuli can be assessed, and it may prove to be a useful adjunct to behavioral programs in the control of alcohol abuse.

VI. ANIMAL MODELS OF ALCOHOL ADDICTION

Many investigators working over a long period have attempted to devise ways of inducing high levels of voluntary ethanol intake in animals. The essential purpose of this work has been to develop an animal analog, or model, of alcoholism in man in the hope that such a model might permit a detailed experimental analysis of the conditions and mechanisms of addiction. From the point of view of the behavior modifier, the possibility of investigating behavioral control procedures in the laboratory is particularly appealing.

The previously discussed influences that have been postulated as operating to initiate and maintain drug seeking and drug using behavior are summarized in Table I. It would appear that all of the influences listed, other than Social Reinforcement, are, in principle at least, open to meaningful study in the animal laboratory. For example, the objective signs of intoxication in animals include ataxia and drowsiness. Withdrawal signs include tremor, lowered startle threshold, extreme irritability, hyperactivity, tail arching, spasticity, rigidity, and convulsions when handled. Current work suggests that a differentiation can be made in terms of BACs over time between levels of ethanol intake that result in gross intoxication only, and levels that result in gross intoxication plus "physical dependence," or abstinence phenomena when the drug is withdrawn. Interestingly enough, the BAC levels are close to those that have been suggested as differentiating Level I and Level II excessive drinkers. Thus, BACs of about 150 mg/100 ml achieved in the rat for a short period (e.g., an hour) daily result in gross intoxication, but not abstinence phenomena, even when maintained for many months. However, BACs of around 250 mg/100 ml, if sustained throughout the 24 hours for only 2–3 days, result in withdrawal signs following cessation of drug intake.

Recent reviews of the literature by Mello (1972) and Myers and

TABLE I
Influences Initiating and Maintaining Drug-Seeking and Drug-Using Behavior

1. Pharmacological reinforcement
   Increased probability of occurrence (and recurrence) of drug-seeking and drug-using behavior consequent upon certain effects of the drug on the organism
   A. Intrinsic effects
      Intoxication (warmth and relaxation, social ease, euphoria)
   B. Extrinsic instrumental effects
      (i) Pharmacological suppression of drug-induced aversive states (abstinence phenomena)
      (ii) Pharmacological suppression of nondrug-induced aversive states (anxiety, depression, boredom)
2. Incentive stimulus control
   Increased probability of occurrence (and recurrence) of drug-seeking and drug-using behavior consequent upon presentation of stimuli consistently associated with drug-seeking and drug-using behavior
3. Social reinforcement
   Increased probability of occurrence (and recurrence) of drug-seeking and drug-using behavior consequent upon social approval of drug use

Veale (1972) make it clear that the chief problem in the development of adequate animal models of addiction has been the natural aversion most animals appear to have for the taste of ethanol.

A. Methods Used to Establish Addiction in Animals

Among the procedures used by different investigators to overcome the taste aversion problem are the following: (a) induction of ethanol polydipsia by appropriate arrangement of the feeding schedule with ethanol solutions available instead of water; (b) restriction of diet to liquid containing ethanol; (c) provision of ethanol during stimulation of the lateral hypothalamus; (d) injection of ethanol into the stomach by various intubation procedures; (e) intravenous ethanol infusion; and (f) injection of minute quantities of ethanol directly into brain structures.

Most of the methods listed have induced ethanol tolerance and abstinence phenomena in the animal subjects, and many have produced an increase in alcohol preference (or a decrease in aversion for alcohol), but none has resulted in sustained voluntary intake of ethanol at levels that might reasonably be regarded as addictive.

One of the most promising techniques is that developed by Deutsch and Koopmans (1973) in which the animal is permitted to drink palatable sweet water while injecting itself intragastrically with ethanol. The level of fluid in the animal's drinking tube is monitored, and when it is lowered by drinking, the intragastric pump is turned on. Initially the animal may be given large periodic doses of ethanol intragastrically to induce rapid physical dependence on the drug. The method requires care because even preferred substances have been shown to have readily conditionable aversive effects when injected directly into the animal's stomach. An advantage of the method is that it retains the natural drinking behavior, but bypasses the gustatory–olfactory system that is sensitive to ethanol.

Predictably, work in the field of animal models of alcoholism has placed a great deal of emphasis on the development of physical dependence with its consequent behavioral signs of withdrawal. There is good reason to believe that the emphasis on physical dependence has been misplaced. Mello (1972), in discussing the "ambiguous relationship" between physical dependence and subsequent self-administration of drugs in both animals and men, makes the following observation:

> Human alcoholics, given an opportunity to work for alcohol at a simple operant task, frequently alternate drinking episodes of 3–6 days with relatively abstinent work periods of 2–3 days. These abstinent periods are usually associated with partial withdrawal signs and symptoms. Intravenous alcohol self-administration in monkeys is also punctuated by periods of spontaneous abstinence which are associated with withdrawal signs. [p. 97]

Other evidence quoted by Mello (1972) underscores the role of the intrinsic reinforcing effects of drugs in maintaining self-administration:

> (1) Monkeys will self-administer intravenous doses of opiates at levels below those required to produce physical dependence; (2) Responding for intravenous alcohol (by monkeys) under conditions in which physical dependence cannot be produced (i.e., a 3-hr access paradigm) is more consistent than in the 24-hr access paradigm that produces physical dependence. [p. 98]

In contrast to ethanol-addicted monkeys, however, monkeys physically dependent on narcotics do appear to maintain responding in order to avoid withdrawal symptoms. In general, animal studies have confirmed clinical impressions that ethanol is a less addictive drug than narcotics.

B. General Requirements for an Animal Model of Excessive Drinking

From the point of view of the behavior modifier, an animal model of the excessive drinker who does not exhibit abstinence phenomena is required. We have seen that the contribution of "physical dependence" to the reinforcing properties of alcohol (as distinct from the opiates) is by no means clear-cut for either animals or humans. As Mello (1972) has stated: "Existing data do not support the notion that the presence or absence of physical dependence influences the rate of response for drug (ethanol) in the same way that presence or absence of food deprivation affects the rate of response for food" (p. 98).

In any case, most excessive users of the drug ethanol (Level I excessive drinkers) do not develop classic physical dependence, and these people offer by far the best prospects for effective behavioral intervention. The criteria suggested by Lester and Freed (1973) for an adequate animal model of alcoholism offer a convenient starting point for a discussion of an animal model of excessive drinking. The criteria are as follows:

1. Oral ingestion of alcohol without food deprivation.
2. Substantial ingestion of alcohol with competing fluids available.
3. Ingestion directed to the central intoxicating character of alcohol substantiated by determination of circulating blood alcohol levels.
4. Work performed, even in the face of aversive consequences, to obtain alcohol.
5. Intoxication sustained over a long period.
6. Production of withdrawal syndrome and physical dependence.
7. After abstinence, reacquisition of drinking to intoxication, and reproducibility of the alcoholic process.

There can be no quarrel with Criterion 1, provided "self-administration" is substituted for "oral ingestion" of alcohol. It seems reasonable to regard oral ingestion as essentially a convenient way for the alcoholic to get ethanol into his blood stream, and hence into his brain. Since animals' aversion for the taste of alcohol is stronger than man's, and indeed is a constant problem in establishing animal models of alcoholism, it seems reasonable to bypass the animal's gustatory system. The major self-administration methods then become intragastric and intravenous dosing procedures initiated either by the drinking of nonaversive fluids, or by lever press or the like. The advantage of using consumption of a palatable fluid as the initiator of self-administration is that Criterion 2 of Lester and Freed can stand.

Criteria 3 and 4 are crucial, and while Criterion 3 has been met in numerous studies, Criterion 4 appears not to have been fully achieved in any investigation to date. Provided Criterion 5 is read to mean frequent intoxication sustained over a long period, it too is crucial although difficult to achieve. For the present purpose, Criterion 6 must be deleted as physical dependence and withdrawal are to be avoided, and reference to the alcoholic process must be deleted from Criterion 7.

If further work substantiates the importance of the role of drug-associated stimuli, it will be possible to add a further criterion (i.e., performance of work to obtain alcohol facilitated by presence of salient stimuli consistently associated with drug use).

What conditions might be necessary to facilitate the development of an animal model of excessive drinking that meets the foregoing criteria? We have already discussed the crucial bypassing of the gustatory system. The next critical condition would seem to be the circumstances of drug use. The human excessive drinker (as distinct from the physically dependent chronic alcoholic who may prefer to drink alone) typically drinks repeatedly in a drinking environment which itself carries the reinforcements of relaxation and companionship. (What is being suggested here is that, rather than drinking being triggered by a need for relaxation, relaxation triggers drinking in the population with which we are concerned.) It would be difficult to establish a rat analog of companionship and social acceptance, but an environment offering relative security, comfort, and satisfaction of bodily needs would not be difficult to devise. Thus, drinking might be confined to a distinctive environment into which the animal escapes from mild stress, has its needs for food and sex satisfied, and in which it spends only a limited period of the day. Whether or not such an environment would be more or less conducive to excessive drinking is a matter that may be decided empirically.

Given the establishment of a satisfactory animal model of excessive drinking, many questions of interest to the behavior modifier immediately arise. For example: What classes of stimuli most readily control drinking? Under what conditions is such control most likely to develop? What are the most effective procedures for reducing stimulus control?

VII. TASTE AVERSION LEARNING IN ANIMALS

The recent work on taste aversion learning in animals is of particular relevance to the problem of modifying excessive drinking by aversive behavioral procedures. The essential finding of the classic experiment conducted by Garcia and Koelling (1966) was that pairing of perceptible cues with effective reinforcers is not a sufficient condition for efficient associative learning. Rather, efficient learning will occur only if the cue is appropriate for, or relevant to, the consequences that follow. Two specific cues, auditory–visual and gustatory–olfactory, were paired with two aversive consequences, pain produced by electric shock, and illness or malaise produced by ionizing radiation. Learning occurred readily when the auditory–visual stimulus was linked with pain, and when the gustatory–olfactory stimulus was paired with illness or malaise. By contrast, learning when auditory–visual cues were paired with illness, and gustatory–olfactory cues were paired with pain was extremely slow. Further work has made it clear that it is the gustatory rather than the olfactory stimulus that is most readily linked with illness or malaise.

Garcia and his associates have emphasized, however, that gustatory-illness learning is not simply an association. Thus, if the gustatory stimulus paired with illness is a sweet flavor, after conditioning the sweet flavor does not signal illness, but *becomes distasteful even in situations remote from that in which illness occurred.* By contrast, true associative learning occurs when an auditory stimulus is paired with pain; that is, the auditory stimulus now signals the onset of shock and elicits many of the components of the response to shock. Furthermore, the learned association is limited in its generalization to situations closely resembling the original learning situation.

Taste Aversion Conditioning and the Effects of Aversion Therapy

There are some interesting parallels between the development of conditioned aversions in animals and the effects produced by aversion therapy in human subjects. The most frequently observed response in animals following illness conditioning associated with food is a disgust reaction. In other words, the substance paired with illness is no longer food. The substance has an unpleasant taste for the animal, and the taste aversion may become linked with associated olfactory and visual stimuli. As noted by several authors (Hallam & Rachman, 1972; Lovibond, 1970, 1976; Rachman & Teasdale, 1969), the most common report of patients following aversion therapy is that the deviant stimulus or addictive drug loses its attraction for them. In most cases there is reduced interest or indifference rather than aversion, although conditioned nausea reactions have been obtained. Interestingly enough, during interviews, some of the patients of Hallam and Rachman (1972) "spontaneously reported that the smell and taste of alcohol had become 'flat,' 'repulsive,' or 'bitter.' "

Typically, most of the effects observed in animals following pairing of illness with food intake are stronger than those resulting from aversion therapy. The differences may well reflect the greater susceptibility of animals to conditioned taste aversions. However, most of the animal studies have averted the subjects to novel flavors, and novelty has been shown to be a variable favoring the development of taste aversions (Kalat & Rosin, 1973; Revusky & Bedarf, 1967). The alcoholic undergoing aversion therapy is, of course, thoroughly habituated to the flavor of alcoholic beverages. A point of some interest is that, whereas animals show little evidence of conditioned taste aversion or "stimulus devaluation" when electric shock is the aversive stimulus, some effects of this nature can be observed in most human alcoholics following electric shock aversion therapy.

VIII. AVERSIVE METHODS IN THE CONTROL OF EXCESSIVE DRINKING

A. The Choice of the Aversive Event

The taste aversion experiments suggest rather strongly that, in attempts to develop aversive control of excessive drinking, it may be more appropriate to use illness and malaise as the aversive event rather than electrical stimulation.

The aversive procedures found to be most effective in taste aversion conditioning with animals, exposure to ionizing radiation and ingestion of lithium chloride, are ruled out for clinical work because of their hazardous nature. Two other agents are currently available, emetic drugs and sickness-inducing motion. Emetic drugs, such as apomorphine, are not without risk of accidental death, and they have the disadvantage of acting as central nervous system depressants, a characteristic that is likely to impede learning. A more acceptable procedure clinically is to induce a degree of motion sickness in the patient by subjecting him to appropriate vestibular stimulation. For example, rotation in a special chair at 25–50 r.p.m. for 2–15 minutes has been found to produce long-lasting nausea without vomiting in almost all subjects (Lovibond, 1976).

Garcia, Hankins, and Coil (1976) have suggested that the ideal agent for the conditioning of aversive illness effects may be one that produces a rapid illness and a slow recovery. The authors suggest that because gustatory-visceral conditioning is relatively insensitive to delays of up to an hour between food intake and illness, and a flavor given prior to a brief intense illness may still be present during recuperation, the flavor thus may be conditioned to a positive "medicinal" effect. (Positive taste conditioning has been demonstrated when the ingestion of substances that correct dietary deficiency malaise has been associated with a distinct flavor.)

Presumably the possibility of positive conditioning to the flavor of alcohol when recovering from illness during aversive conditioning could be obviated by having the subject rinse his mouth at the height of the malaise and then drink a substitute drink, such as orange juice, when there are signs that the recuperative process is under way.

B. Method of Presentation of the Aversive Event

There has been a good deal of discussion of the appropriate mode of presentation of the aversive event in the aversive control of undesired appetitive behaviors (see esp. Hallam & Rachman, 1972; Rachman & Teasdale, 1969). The clinical use of aversive procedures has rested on three classes of assumption: (a) those concerning the nature of the learning to be sought, (b) those concerning the learning model to be employed (usually classical conditioning, active avoidance or punishment), (c) those concerning the applicability of empirical generalizations (e.g., relating to optimal stimulus relations) derived from laboratory studies of learning.

1. WHAT IS TO BE LEARNED?

Most workers who have used aversive procedures to control unwanted appetitive behaviors have sought to develop conditioned aversions to the drug or stimulus in question. In other cases, however, the aim has been to condition a response of avoidance of the stimuli concerned, whether or not any form of aversion is developed as a further consequence of the procedures used. It is argued, however, that the essential aim of aversive procedures should be to produce a motivational shift (i.e., a loss of interest in the performance of the undesired behavior).

2. WHICH LEARNING MODEL?

If the learning required is essentially motivational change, so-called avoidance procedures become irrelevant, and the distinction between classical conditioning and punishment procedures becomes irrelevant. Punishment, or the presentation of an aversive event in close proximity to the consummatory behavior (eating, alcohol consuming, etc.) becomes a procedure for reducing the appetitive value of stimuli closely associated with the consummatory act, rather than a method of suppressing a response.

There are clinical as well as theoretical reasons for making motivational shift the aim of programs using aversive stimuli. From the clinical viewpoint it is clearly preferable for a patient to lose interest in the performance of the deviant or excessive behavior rather than to remain strongly motivated while inhibited from performing by conditioned fear or a conditioned retching response. If, of course, the change in motivation is dramatic enough to produce a disgust reaction and consequent avoidance, there should be no particular problem, but such an outcome is likely to be seen rather seldom.

3. WHAT ARE THE STIMULUS TIME RELATION RULES?

In seeking to apply a classical conditioning model to the problem of aversive control of appetitively motivated behavior, most workers (see Rachman & Teasdale, 1969) have made the conventional assumptions that: (a) efficient classical conditioning can be obtained only when the aversive event follows the conditioned stimulus by a very short interval (less than one second), and (b) any conditioned stimulus–unconditioned stimulus combination is as likely to enter into association as any other. The studies of learned taste aversions in animals suggest that the conventional assumptions should be called into question. Insofar as learned taste aversions can be regarded as examples of conditioned motivational change rather than associative learning, however, the conventional assumptions simply may not be relevant.

From the standpoint of clinical practice in reducing appetitive motivation by aversive procedures, the conventional rules for efficient classic conditioning do not seem to apply. For more specific guidance, the practitioner must await the outcome of research directed to the problem of the optimum conditions for changing appetitive motivation by aversive means.

IX. IMPLICATIONS OF THE BEHAVIORAL CONTROL OF OVEREATING

Work in the field of overeating would seem to be pertinent to problems in the control of excessive drinking if, as suggested by Hebb (1949), there is an addictive component in eating behavior.

Some findings of a group of workers at the University of Arizona are of particular interest. The conclusions members of the group have derived from recent studies may be summarized as follows:

1. The eating patterns of normal, overweight, and obese persons do not differ significantly (Schisslak & Blake, 1976). The hypothesis under investigation was that, by comparison with persons of normal weight, obese persons take fewer and larger bites of their food, chew their food less, and eat more rapidly. Dependent measures, which included total number of bites, chews per bite, and total time spent chewing, did not differentiate between normal, overweight, and obese subjects (N = 96) whose eating behavior was observed in a natural setting.

A further study by Luera and Albright (1976) produced essentially similar results.

2. High levels of anxiety do not facilitate eating in the obese (Reznik & Dannenfelser, 1976). A comparison of the amount of eating engaged in by normal weight and obese subjects (N = 64), under conditions of high and low experimentally induced anxiety, demonstrated a nonsignificant tendency for high levels of anxiety to inhibit eating in the obese. There was no suggestion of such an effect in normals.

3. The eating behavior of obese persons shows significantly greater external stimulus control than the eating behavior of normal subjects (Bustamante & Mossay, 1976). Schachter (1971) has pro-

posed that the eating behavior of the obese is controlled chiefly by external stimuli, whereas the eating behavior of normal weight persons is controlled chiefly by internal physiological stimuli.

In order to test Schachter's hypothesis, Bustamante and Mossay (1976) developed a scale to measure external stimulus control of eating. Twenty items were found to discriminate between the obese and the nonobese. The discriminating items concerned temporal factors associated with eating, the triggering of eating by the sight, aroma, and taste of food, the amount of food available, and social and emotional factors controlling eating.

Obese subjects indicated that they tended to eat more if they were upset, depressed, or nervous, although, as has been stated, Reznick and Dannenfelser (1976) were unable to demonstrate such influences experimentally.

Perhaps the most striking finding was the willingness of obese subjects to endorse items demonstrating the capacity of external stimuli to control their eating even when they were "full" or had just eaten (e.g., "Watching someone else eat makes me hungry even if I've just had a meal"; "When I smell something good cooking, I feel compelled to eat even when I'm already full").

The secondary reinforcing or positive incentive value of external stimuli is clearly demonstrated here. Also of interest is the inability of the obese to stop eating even when reasonable bodily needs have been met (e.g., "I have a tendency to eat everything on my plate regardless of the amount of food that is served"; "I tend to eat leftovers before leaving the dinner table"; "The more food is available, the more I eat").

It is interesting to note that even in nonobese subjects, a high degree of stimulus control of eating was demonstrated. Nevertheless, the externality of control of eating in the obese was significantly greater. What emerges is a picture of the obese as persons whose eating behavior is triggered by a wide range of stimulus conditions associated with eating. Furthermore, once eating begins, it continues to be controlled by the same stimulus conditions in addition, presumably, to feedback stimuli from the performance of the consummatory act itself. Rather than eating being brought to an end by an internal mechanism of satiety, it is brought to an end by changes in the external environment, e.g., all available food consumed, eating companions finished and ready to go, social pressure from others present (e.g., "The presence of other people influences the amount of food I eat").

The picture of the obese person that emerges is strikingly reminiscent of the one drawn earlier of the excessive drinker. In both cases there is susceptibility to external stimulus control and the tendency for the consummatory behavior to continue once it has begun. In neither case, however, is there a consumption impulse immune to situational influence. The obese person's eating behavior is inhibited by immediate social influences, as is the drinking behavior of the excessive drinker. In both cases, however, the control is temporary and disappears as soon as the influences are withdrawn.

The results of the studies of obesity under consideration have a number of implications for the treatment of overeating.

1. There is little to be gained by attempting to train the obese to adopt the eating style of the nonobese (take smaller bites, chew more, etc.).

2. There is unlikely to be much return from therapeutic strategies which focus on the reduction of negative affects in the patient. Negative affect controls eating, but only to a minor degree. Thus, modification of negative affect is likely to be of minimal therapeutic significance.

3. By far, the greatest impact is likely to be made by directing attention to the stimulus control of eating. The basic strategies are two in number: (a) the use of aversive procedures to reduce the positive reinforcing value of both incentive stimuli and stimuli associated with the act of consuming high calorie foods; and (b) the reduction of external stimulus control by avoidance of triggering stimuli, restriction of eating to certain situations and certain times, increasing awareness of and control by internal stimuli, and training in self-management procedures to insure continued control over controlling stimuli.

X. OBJECTIVE ASSESSMENT OF OUTCOME

To date most assessments of treatment outcome have relied on some form of self-report from the subject (Bowman, Stein, & Newton, 1975; Emric, 1974). In order to overcome the problem of possible unreliability of self-report data, some workers have sought corroborative evidence from significant others, or have used elaborate procedures which permit cross-checking, but require frequent follow-up interviews. The problem of the reactivity of measures soon becomes acute, however, when the latter strategy is adopted.

Attempts to develop more objective methods of assessing drinking behavior have proceeded along several different lines. Some workers have measured drinking behavior under controlled conditions; others have obtained breath samples for BAC analysis, and still others have sought physiological evidence of drinking behavior.

A. Behavioral Assessment of Drinking under Controlled Conditions

Several investigators have studied the drinking of alcoholics under laboratory or controlled hospital ward conditions, for example, by monitoring free drinking behavior over periods of some weeks, and by recording the rates of operant responses emitted to earn alcohol (Mello & Mendelson, 1965, 1970; Miller, Hersen, Eisler, & Elkin, 1974; Nathan & O'Brien, 1971). Another behavioral assessment procedure has been developed by Marlatt and his co-workers (Higgins & Marlatt, 1973; Marlatt, Demming, & Reid, 1973). Subjects are required to "taste" a number of alcoholic and nonalcoholic beverages, and to rate the beverages on a number of dimensions. The interest of the experimenter centers on how much of the beverages the subject consumes in the course of making the test ratings. The taste test procedure has been used to study some of the environmental conditions controlling drinking in alcoholics, and to evaluate response to treatment.

Although the behavioral assessments conducted in laboratories and other controlled environments have produced valuable data on drinking behavior, they suffer from the very considerable disadvantage that the usual triggering or incentive stimuli for excessive drinking are absent. After the initial drying out phase, alcoholics who are treated on an in-patient basis frequently appear to be relatively untroubled by a period of enforced sobriety in an environment usually associated with an absence of drinking. Quite often, prior to discharge, a patient will declare his intention of remaining abstinent, only to resume his habitual pattern of alcohol consumption on returning to his usual environment. Not infrequently such "relapses" are interpreted as evidence of insincerity on the part of the patient. It seems reasonable to hypothesize, however, that aspects of the habitual heavy drinking environment (e.g., previously frequented bars, taverns or clubs, and the presence of drinking companions of long standing) provide powerful incentive stimuli which substantially increase the probability of drinking behavior, whatever the patient's intentions. For this reason, assessments of pre- and posttreatment drinking behavior in the natural environment are likely to remain of critical importance.

B. Measurement of BACs

A potentially useful procedure involves periodic breath testing of subjects. The subject's consent is obtained prior to the commencement of treatment when it is explained that objective evidence of drinking behavior during and subsequent to treatment is essential to therapeutic planning. The investigator makes periodic unannounced visits to the subject's home to obtain a breath sample for test. Visits are not strictly random, but are based on a knowledge of the subject's drinking habits, and are designed to maximize the chances of obtaining a high BAC reading. Such a procedure is currently in use on a small scale at the University of New South Wales. While the method is labor intensive, it is probable that repeated brief visits for the purposes of breath analysis will yield greater returns than repeated interviews.

A study conducted by Harris, Walter, and Keding (1976) has produced some preliminary evidence on the relationship between measured BAC and self-report of drinking on the day of testing. In a follow-up of alcoholic clients, self-reports of the quantity of alcohol consumed during the day of the interview were obtained without any mention of BAC measurement. The estimates of intake were converted to expected BACs at the time of interview. Finally, expected BACs were correlated with actual BACs measured late in the interview. The obtained correlation of +.63 is probably higher than most workers in the field of alcoholism would have expected.

C. Serum Liver-Enzyme Levels

It is well established that prolonged excessive consumption of alcohol is associated with liver damage (e.g., Goldberg & Watts, 1965; Rollason, Pincherle, & Robinson, 1972; Rosalki & Rau, 1972). Laboratory evidence of such damage is usually derived from assays of a number of enzymes, including aspartate aminotransferase (AST), alanine aminotransferase (AIT), ornithine carbamoyltransferase

(OCT), isocitrate dehydrogenase (ICD), and alkaline phosphatase (ALP).

AIT and OCT appear to be the most specific indicators of liver damage, but neither is particularly sensitive (Goldberg & Watts, 1965; Patel & O'Gorman, 1975). Recent work has suggested that another enzyme, gamma glutamyl transpeptidase (GGTP), is a highly sensitive indicator of liver cell dysfunction (Patel & O'Gorman, 1975; Zein & Discombe, 1970). According to Zein and Discombe (1970), GGTP is principally an indicator of reversible liver cell dysfunction following exposure to a noxious agent, whereas the transaminases are indicators of an acute lesion, or necrosis of the liver.

Patel and O'Gorman found raised levels of GGTP in 48% of 67 chronic alcoholics who had been admitted to an alcoholism clinic during or immediately after a heavy bout of drinking. Zein and Discombe (1970) observed abnormally high levels of GGTP in all 14 of their sample of alcoholics who had continued to drink regularly. Normal levels of GGTP were found in 5 alcoholics who had been abstinent for a month or more. The authors noted that 80 gm of alcohol, consumed during a 5-hour drinking session, resulted in a marked elevation of GGTP levels. Within 18 hours there was a 40% increase to well above normal limits.

The evidence thus suggests that, in the absence of liver or kidney diseases known to be associated with increased production of GGTP, abnormally high levels of GGTP may be taken as evidence of recent heavy consumption of alcohol.

The work of Hennessy (1976) provides further evidence of the potential value of GGTP as an objective indicator of recent excessive alcohol consumption. The levels of three liver enzymes, GGTP, ALP, and AST, were determined in 96 males convicted of driving a motor vehicle with BACs of .15% or higher. The examinations were made prior to sentencing after an initial court hearing. With very few exceptions the subjects were free of any signs of cirrhosis or other tissue damage usually associated with chronic alcoholism.

Abnormal levels of GGTP were found in 55% of the subjects. Abnormal levels of the other enzymes were observed in significantly fewer cases (AST, 34%; ALP, 14%).

While the evidence presently available must be regarded as only suggestive, there would seem to be grounds for believing that GGTP assays are capable of providing objective supportive evidence of recent heavy drinking behavior. Such assays are likely to prove particularly useful in work with Level 1 excessive drinkers, as earlier defined. A comparative follow-up study of GGTP determinations, repeated BAC measurements, self-reports, and corroborated self-reports, would be most instructive.

XI. MULTIFACETED CONTROL-ORIENTED PROGRAMS

A. The Patton Research Program

In a series of papers, Sobell and Sobell (1973a, 1973b, 1976) have reported the rationale, design, treatment, procedures, and first- and second-year outcome results of the "first large-scale clinical research investigation in the United States to explore the use of controlled drinking as a treatment objective" (Sobell & Sobell, 1976). The behavioral treatment program, which was carried out at Patton State Hospital, San Bernardino, California, represents a refinement of procedures employed by Mills and his co-workers (1971).

The basic assumptions of the investigatiors were: (a) heavy, abusive drinking of alcoholic beverages can be considered a discriminated operant behavior, that is, behavior occurring in particular settings and acquired and maintained as a result of its consequences; (b) that controlled drinking represents a feasible treatment goal for some alcohol abusers; and (c) that experimental treatment procedures should be tailored whenever possible to each individual's learning history.

The treatment goals were to suppress inappropriate, abusive drinking, to train each subject to identify crucial stimulus variables (stressors) that in the past had been associated with the decision to drink, and to teach effective and socially appropriate behaviors that could be used as alternative responses to the stressful situations. One of the alternative responses was drinking in a controlled manner.

Seventy male *gamma* (Jellinek, 1960) alcoholics, who were inpatients at Patton State Hospital, volunteered to serve as subjects in the experimental program. Subjects were assigned by staff decision to one of two treatment goal conditions: nondrinking (abstinence), N=40; or controlled drinking, N=30. Volunteers who were able to identify with Alcoholics Anonymous, who preferred the goal of abstinence, and who were judged to have insufficient social support to maintain controlled drinking, were allocated to the abstinence group. Those who did not find the AA philosophy appealing and requested controlled drinking, and/or had attempted controlled drinking in the past, were allocated to the controlled drinking group if it was considered they had sufficient support in their environment to make controlled drinking a feasible objective.

Subjects in each of the two treatment groups were then allocated at random to experimental or control groups to give four experimental conditions: (1) Controlled Drinker Experimental (CD-E), N=20; (2) Controlled Drinker Control (CD-C), N=20; (3) Nondrinker Experimental (ND-E), N=15; and (4) Nondrinker Control (ND-C), N=15. Subjects in the two experimental groups received 17 behavioral treatment sessions, and control group subjects received conventional hospital treatment (AA groups, chemotherapy, physiotherapy, and industrial therapy). The behavioral treatment program took the following form: *Sessions 1 and 2* (Video Recording). Pairs of subjects drank to the point of intoxication by consuming up to 16 oz. of liquor, and, while in an intoxicated state, took part in discussions with staff members concerning the origins of their drinking problems, their behavior while drunk, and their expectations and apprehensions concerning treatment. Video recordings of the sessions were made. *Session 3* (Treatment Planning). During the third session, the treatment program was explained in detail, and controlled drinking subjects were trained to identify and recognize the separate components of mixed drinks. *Sessions 4 and 5* (Videotape Replaying). In the fourth and fifth sessions, subjects viewed video recordings of their own behavior while intoxicated in Session 1. The purpose of the video replays was to confront the subjects with the inappropriateness of their behavior while intoxicated, in the hope of increasing motivation for behavioral change. *Session 6* (Failure Experience). Immediately prior to Session 6, subjects were asked to complete a series of tasks that were impossible to complete, thus guaranteeing an experience of failure. In the treatment session that followed, attention was directed toward the subjects' maladaptive responses to the experimentally induced failure stress, and to real-life stress. The assumption made here was that maladaptive responses to stress were likely to be an integral part of the subjects' pattern of alcohol abuse. *Sessions 7–16* (Behavioral Training). During the 10 treatment sessions, the Nondrinker Experimental subjects underwent electric shock aversive training via an avoidance paradigm. The subject received a 1-second shock delivered on a variable ratio schedule to the fingers for ordering any type of drink, and received continuous shock from the time of touching the drinking glass until the time of releasing it.

The shock avoidance contingencies that were operative in the case of the CD-E subjects were explained to each subject. Subjects were permitted to engage in controlled drinking with impunity (ordering and sipping mixed drinks to a limit of 3 drinks, and ordering nonalcoholic drinks thereafter). The subject was shocked for inappropriate drinking behavior (ordering, sipping, or gulping straight drinks, gulping mixed drinks, and drinking beyond 3 drinks).

In the section of the training program directed toward the development of alternative, socially acceptable coping responses to situations associated with drinking, modeling and role-playing techniques were employed. All experimental subjects underwent training of this type.

Session 17 (Summary: Videotape Contrast). During the final session, in which no alcoholic drinks were available, patients viewed excerpts from the video recordings of their intoxicated behavior in Sessions 1 and 2. By way of contrast, they then viewed recordings of their own sober behavior in Session 16. Following a general discussion of their treatment progress, subjects were given a card containing lists of "Do's" and "Don'ts" dealing with responses to the setting events associated with excessive drinking. After completion of the program, the subject was discharged from hospital, usually within 2 weeks.

In summary, the four components of the behavioral program were: (a) aversive shock conditioning; (b) training in the identification of crucial stimulus variables (stressors) that in the past had been associated with drinking; (c) training in socially acceptable alternative behaviors to heavy drinking; (d) feedback of intoxicated behaviors to demonstrate inappropriate behaviors and to motivate change.

Follow-up data obtained after 6, 12, 18, and 24 months are available. Immense effort was expended to secure adequate follow-up data, both in terms of numbers of subjects evaluated and the amount and validity of data obtained from each subject. Contact was made with the subject and with each of three collateral sources at least every 3–4 weeks. The data obtained related to drinking disposition (abstinent, controlled drinking, drunk, incarcerated), general adjustment, vocational and occupational status, use of outpatient therapeutic supports, marital status, and physical health.

Data were obtained from 67 of the original 70 subjects at the 2-year follow-up. Daily drinking dispositions of abstinent and controlled drinking were combined to operationally define days "functioning well." Days "not functioning well" were defined as the sum of drunk days and days incarcerated in a hospital or a jail as a result of drinking. Applying these measures to the second year follow-up data, it was found that the CD-E subjects functioned well on a significantly greater number of days than the CD-C subjects (CE-E, N=20, mean = 85.17% of all days; CD-C, N=19, mean = 42.27% of all days; $p < .001$). The difference between ND-E and ND-C subjects was not significant (ND-E, N=14, mean = 64.15% of all days; ND-C, N=14, mean = 43.23% of all days). Approximately 11 to 13 of the 20 CD-E subjects controlled their drinking nearly all the time. By comparison, only one of the CD-C subjects did so. Typically, controlled drinking days represented consumption of 2 to 4 oz. of 86-proof liquor.

Detailed drinking profiles indicated that subjects who successfully engaged in controlled drinking typically drank in a controlled manner in a social context or in their own homes. Lapses tended to occur when the subject drank alone or away from home. Measures other than drinking behavior indicated that the experimental subjects, particularly the CD-E subjects, adjusted better socially and vocationally.

Several authors (e.g., Lloyd & Salzberg, 1975; Nathan & Briddell, 1976), while praising the quality of the Patton research, have offered a number of methodological criticisms.

1. Treatment factors were confounded. Certainly it is impossible to draw any conclusions about the relative contributions of the four treatment components mentioned earlier, but this is properly a further research step.
2. Because of the nonrandom allocation of subjects to controlled drinking versus abstinence training, no valid comparisons between the two procedures can be made. It is obviously the case that practical considerations prevented the possibility of a strictly valid comparison between the two experimental groups, but this was a secondary consideration. The experiment was concerned primarily with the effectiveness of behavioral procedures designed to train subjects in controlled drinking.

Of more moment are the criticisms that apply to the controlled drinking (experimental and control) comparisons.

1. The experimental subjects received more hours of treatment and more attention than the controls, thus giving rise to the possibility of attention placebo effects. While there were undoubtedly differences in treatment time between the experimental and control groups, the possibility that this difference played any important part in the outcome would seem to be extremely remote.

2. The lengthy, intensive follow-up, involving almost weekly contact between a single worker and the subjects may have influenced the outcome. Many of the subjects viewed the follow-up as aftercare, and the attention subjects received for controlled drinking and nondrinking could have distorted the data as reflections of the inpatient treatment.

There is an important point here, as it is well established that many patients attribute considerable significance to continued contacts with follow-up interviewers in their efforts to maintain controlled drinking or abstinence. As very extensive follow-up contact is not practical in the normal clinical service situation, the contribution such contact makes to the long-term outcome of training programs should be explored by research.

3. Follow-up data were generated from self-reports of drinking behavior which are susceptible to experimenter bias and subject unreliability. Two points can be made here. In the first place, the investigators went to considerable pains to obtain collateral information, and obtained data which permitted cross-checking. Second, it is highly probable that the unreliability of *corroborated* self-reports has been exaggerated. Research on the problems of follow-up is currently being conducted (Harris *et al.*, 1976; Sobell & Sobell, 1975), and the results should assist future workers to forestall criticism of the crucial follow-up phase of their work.

4. All follow-up data were collected by a single person who was one of the principal investigators, thus introducing the possibility that experimenter bias and demand characteristics influenced the results. In response to this criticism, the researchers have reported plans for a blind follow-up by two independent teams of investigators.

5. The CD-C subjects received inconsistent treatment by being sent to AA meetings after being selected for a goal of controlled drinking, and, in general, the control subjects may have received less than comparable treatment.

It must be agreed that there is a certain inconsistency in setting a goal of controlled drinking for some subjects and then placing them in treatment programs run by workers violently opposed to the whole concept of controlled drinking. Since it is the efficacy of specific behavioral procedures designed to train subjects in controlled drinking that is under investigation, the most appropriate control group is one which receives nonspecific supportive counseling, preferably from persons who believe (a) that controlled drinking is a reasonable goal, and (b) that subjects can be assisted to attain such a goal by appropriate counseling.

Despite some justifiable criticisms, we can agree with Lloyd and Salzberg (1975) that the Patton research "demonstrated very convincingly that controlled drinking could be learned, practiced, and maintained by many persons formerly abusing alcohol" (p. 828). Interestingly enough, the controlled drinking results were very similar to those obtained by Lovibond and Caddy (1970), using rather different procedures. We cannot agree, however, that the Patton study demonstrated that an avoidance-conditioning paradigm (whereby an appropriate alternative response may occur in place of the punished response) was effective in changing drinking behavior (Lloyd & Salzberg, 1975). As Lloyd and Salzberg themselves point out, the four treatment effects and the aftercare effects were confounded in the design.

It would seem appropriate at this point to comment on the overall Patton research strategy in light of the conclusions reached in the earlier sections of this contribution.

1. It is clear that the research was conducted within a theoretical framework which placed a good deal of emphasis on the extrinsic reinforcement produced by the consumption of alcohol. Thus, in training the subject to discriminate stimuli that previously elicited excessive drinking, and in training alternative responses to such stimuli, the emphasis was on stress conditions.

As indicated earlier, there is reason to believe that the delineation of positive incentive stimuli, followed by an attempt to devalue the incentive stimuli, is likely to be a more fruitful strategy.

2. The use of finger shock, in an attempt to shape either controlled drinking or abstinence via an avoidance paradigm, indicates an emphasis on the *response* of drinking which, it has been argued earlier, is misplaced.

3. In the absence of an experimental analysis of the program to delineate the effective components, it can only be a matter of judgment whether the remaining procedures made any worthwhile contribution. The present judgment is that the time spent on feedback of intoxicated behavior, failure experience and the like, would almost certainly have been better spent on alternative procedures (see later for specific suggestions). On balance, then, it is suggested that, despite the favorable results achieved by the Patton group, we are now in a position to formulate more powerful behavioral programs to control excessive drinking.

B. The University of New South Wales Program

The program developed at the Behavior Modification Center, University of New South Wales, was designed primarily to train alcohol abusers to become controlled or responsible drinkers. If, however, the subject chooses abstinence as the training goal, the program can be suitably modified.

From the first contact with the patient, the disease or illness concept of alcoholism is implicitly rejected. The term alcoholism is never used, and in discussions with the patient the problem is referred to as excessive drinking. The subject is at all times treated as an essentially normal person who has a particular behavioral problem to overcome. Thus, the responsibility of the subject as an active participant in the program of behavioral change is emphasized at all times. He is told that, although the procedures to be used at the Center can assist his efforts at self-control, and that he will receive assistance from significant others, he will be taught techniques that he must use himself, and ultimately the responsibility for maintaining a pattern of responsible drinking will be his. The relationship with the subject is a training relationship in which the subject is helped to learn new skills. He is told the precise nature of the training procedures to be used, the precise goals of training, and the results achieved with the program to date.

The subject is encouraged to recognize that, when he first comes to the Center, he is unable to make decisions about his alcohol intake. The essential goal of training is to bring his drinking back under his control so that he is free to make decisions about it. For the time being, it has been agreed that the goal is to become a moderate or responsible drinker, but later the subject will be able to choose abstention if he so desires.

The program, as originally devised, includes a number of separable components:

1. *BAC Discrimination Training.* The subject initially is trained to discriminate his own BAC within the range from 0 to .08% (80 mg/100 ml) by periodically feeding back breathalyzer readings to the subject while he consumes alcohol over a 2-hour session.

2. *Discriminated Aversive Conditioning.* Following BAC discrimination training, aversive shock is made contingent upon further drinking when the BAC has reached a designated level (usually .05–.06%). As long as the BAC remains below the chosen level, the subject is permitted to drink without aversive consequences. High

shock levels have been used, with electrodes attached to the cheek and neck.

3. *Training in Self-Regulation.* Heavy emphasis is placed on self-regulation of behavior as an essential component of the program. Not only is the subject encouraged to assume responsibility for his own drinking behavior, but he is taught specific techniques aimed at developing self-control.

4. *Education Relating to Alcohol.* The subject is given detailed information about alcohol and its effects on behavior and health. He is taught the relationship between intake of various alcoholic beverages and BAC, and the essentials of responsible and excessive drinking.

5. *Incidental Counseling and Relaxation Training.* As part of the interaction that develops with the subject during the course of the training program, supportive counseling in relation to particular personal problems is offered. When indicated by the patient's general state of tension, relaxation training may be given.

Usually the program involves 8 to 10 weekly sessions, each of 2 to $2\frac{1}{2}$ hours duration. Most of the training is given individually, but some components lend themselves to group training.

The first investigation of the outcome of the program was carried out with 31 subjects who had, on the average, a 10-year history of alcohol abuse and many periods of hospitalization. All but 30 of 31 experimental subjects completed the full program. Eight of 13 control subjects given noncontingent shock dropped out. At the conclusion of treatment and at follow-up 16–60 weeks later, 21 of the 28 experimental subjects were maintaining a pattern of controlled drinking and exceeding the designated BAC limit only occasionally. By contrast, the control group subjects showed a sharp initial drop in alcohol consumption which was not maintained. By the end of the third week, the alcohol intake of the control subjects was significantly higher than that of the experimental subjects.

In addition to changes in drinking behavior, most experimental subjects showed a marked improvement in health and general adjustment.

Although the initial aim was to develop a discriminated conditioned aversion (i.e., to make drinking aversive if, but only if, the designated BAC had been exceeded), most subjects simply reported a loss of desire to drink beyond 3–4 drinks. Only about 20% of the subjects developed any semblance of a conditioned aversion, and no conditioned aversion was at all marked. In brief, the experiment demonstrated that significant numbers of alcohol abusers, who have been diagnosed as chronic alcoholics, are able to maintain controlled drinking patterns when they have undergone a behavioral training program designed to assist them to become responsible drinkers.

Criticisms of the study have centered mainly on the reliance on self-report for outcome data. The reports were corroborated in almost all cases by a family member and otherwise by another collateral source, whose cooperation had been sought from the start, and who had attended the initial treatment sessions. Whenever feasible, follow-up interviews were conducted with the collateral source present. As suggested earlier, it is quite likely that *some* reports obtained in this manner will be optimistic, but, given the necessary experience, skill, and dedication on the part of the interviewers, the chances that the data will be seriously vitiated are remote.

Nevertheless, it will obviously be a worthwhile enterprise to develop the most efficient means of obtaining BACs from subjects to put the issue of posttreatment drinking behavior beyond doubt.

A further criticism has concerned the validity of the initial BAC discrimination learning. Lloyd and Salzberg (1975) have stated: "There was no control to test the validity of the internally cued discrimination learning in the first phase. The subjects might have done as well merely counting the number of drinks consumed, bringing into question the validity of the outcome measures, which were, in part, merely a verbal report of subjective measures of BAC" (p. 823).

There are several misconceptions here. First, the subject initially consumes ethanol in fruit juice and is unaware of the quantity consumed. The purpose here is to direct attention to internal cues. Later, when the subject changes to consuming his normal alcoholic beverage, he is *encouraged* to relate his BAC, estimated and actual, to the number of drinks he has consumed; that is, the subject is trained to use all cues to estimate his BAC in the interests of controlling his alcohol intake. Discriminated aversive training is, of course, related to the subject's *actual* BAC.

Finally, outcome data were not in any way dependent on the subject's BAC estimates. The primary data presented were weekly alcohol intake means expressed in ounces of pure alcohol. A supplementary data figure showed the estimated mean number of times subjects' BACs exceeded .07% before, during, and after treatment, the estimates being derived from the intake data.

1. DRINKING DRIVER TRAINING

Although the controlled drinking program achieved encouraging results with Level II excessive drinkers, it was clear that the program was particularly suitable for use with young Level I excessive drinkers. Accordingly, the program was offered to persons convicted of driving a motor vehicle with a BAC of 150 mg/100 ml or higher, who were found usually to attain BACs in this region on drinking days. In most cases the referral was made by the subject's legal counsel after an adjournment of the case. (For an interim report, see Lovibond, 1975.)

In an initial study, 43 drinking drivers participated in a program essentially the same as that described by Lovibond and Caddy (1970). By comparison with the total population of drinking drivers convicted in New South Wales over a period 1968–1974, the sample was closely matched in terms of age range, BAC on arrest, and occupation (there was a high proportion of unskilled and semiskilled workers). The frequency of prior convictions, however, was much higher in the sample than the population (81% cf. 25%). Approximately 20% of the cases were rejected on the grounds of lack of (a) ability to speak English, (b) adequate social supports (family or relatives), or (c) motivation to undertake training.

Training was conducted by two graduate research assistants who had prior experience in the training of Level II excessive drinkers by similar methods. Follow-up was conducted by two graduate assistants who were unaware of the variables under investigation. Particular emphasis was placed on the need (a) to obtain detailed information concerning the drinking pattern to permit cross-checking for consistency, and (b) to conduct the follow-up interviews with family members or other collateral sources actually present.

Comparable data were obtained from 16 control subjects matched with the first 16 experimental subjects on the criteria of age, marital status, occupation, BAC at time of arrest, number of prior convictions, and approximate date of arrest. The control subjects had been dealt with by the courts in the usual manner (fines and/or license suspension) but had received no other treatment.

In the case of the control subjects, information concerning drinking patterns prior to the court appearance was obtained in a single interview conducted at the time of the follow-up of the experimental subjects.

At follow-up, after 12 months, 66% of the experimental subjects were maintaining controlled drinking (i.e., their intake of alcohol was within the limits of responsible drinking previously defined). Older subjects (33–66 years) tended to do less well than young subjects (18–32 years), but not significantly so. By contrast, very few members of the control group had modified their drinking behavior in any way following their arrest and court appearance.

Although our sample was selected on the basis of criteria of relevance to the legal counsels, it is unlikely that it differed in any critical way from the total population of convicted drinking drivers. Our sample had a much higher frequency of prior convictions, but, as the detection rate for drinking drivers is very low, it is likely that our drivers were simply those whom the luck of the draw had not favored. However, they could have been better motivated to change than their fellows who had fewer prior convictions. Certainly, the possibility of a long license suspension (which is highly aversive to the group in question) increases markedly as the number of prior convictions increases.

Despite these uncertainties, it seems reasonable to conclude that the drinking behavior of a substantial proportion of drinking drivers can be moderated by a suitable behavioral program. In the interest of widening the possible application of the program, every effort has been made to develop the nonaversive procedures to the point where they alone form an effective treatment package.

2. DEVELOPMENTS IN THE PROGRAM

Further work, as yet unpublished, has sought to determine the contributions made to the effectiveness of the total package by the components of self-regulation and discriminated electric shock aversive conditioning. In brief, it has been found that both aversive conditioning and self-regulation training contribute significantly to the efficacy of the program when the subjects are Level II excessive drinkers. When the subjects are Level I excessive drinkers, however, electric shock aversive conditioning does not appear to add significantly to the effects of the remainder of the treatment package.

It should be pointed out, however, that recent changes in the program require further experimental analyses of the contributions of the various components. In that part of the program which seeks to reduce the probability of excessive drinking by the use of aversive procedures, there has been a shift of emphasis from direct response suppression by response-contingent aversive stimulation to reduction of incentive motivation. In other words, the main focus of attention has shifted from the response itself (i.e., the act of drinking) to the controlling stimuli.

In current work, exclusive reliance on electrical stimuli as the aversive agent has given way to emphasis on rotating the subject in a special chair in order to induce sickness or malaise. The details of the procedure, which is being developed with Dr. J. C. Clarke, have been described elsewhere (Lovibond, 1976). As a consequence of our general clinical experience, as well as the results of direct experimental investigation, an even greater emphasis has come to be placed on self-regulation. Self-regulation entails not only development of self-management skills based on learning principles, but important cognitive components as well. Thus we have found that, for many alcohol abusers who have earned the label alcoholic, with the implication of inherent defect and helplessness, it is profoundly gratifying to be treated as ordinary human beings, and to find that they *can* exert control over their own drinking behavior.

When aversive procedures are used in the modified program, one of the explicit aims is to produce conditioned motivational change by pairing of stimulus conditions of heavy drinking with aversive events. The stimulus conditions can be divided into several classes:

(a) Stimuli directly associated with the act of consuming alcoholic beverages. In probable order of importance the stimuli include: the taste, aroma, and other properties of alcohol while it is taken into the mouth and swallowed; the internal stimuli associated with rising BACs; and the sight and aroma of alcohol prior to consumption.

(b) Stimuli associated with the drinking environment. This class of stimuli includes particular physical and social environments, for example, public bars and club rooms, drinking companions and their social responses, particular foods, and smoking, or in the home, a particular room, an easy chair, the television, and smoking.

(c) Temporal and imaginal stimuli; for example, stimuli associated with the approach of lunch time and the time of leaving work, memories of the companionship of past drinking occasions, thoughts of the rewarding effects of alcohol consumption, images of frothing tankards, or the bouquet of wine.

All of the above classes of stimuli are likely to become linked in behavioral chains, that is, sequences of events in which external stimuli and imaginal processes interact with and reinforce successive components of alcohol-seeking and consuming behavior. An early task is the delineation of the behavioral chains in each individual case.

In practice, reduction of the stimulus control of drinking by aversive means may be achieved by associating the stimuli with aversive events either *in vivo,* or in the imagination. While it would appear that, in principle, training *in vivo* is superior, the pairing of evoked images with aversive events seems to have been successful in controlling a variety of behaviors (Rachman & Teasdale, 1969). The advantage of the use of imaginal processes, of course, is the range of stimulus situations that becomes accessible. Further, the imaginal events can be formed into chains that closely mirror the stimulus-behavior-image sequences that occur in actual situations. Finally, instructions to form images can be given in response to an accompanying narrative, as in the procedure used by O'Brien *et al.* (1972).

Such a procedure is obviously convenient for dealing with the behavioral chains that lead to the drinking situation. Concerning the drinking environment itself, the question of whether or not a simulated bar offers advantages over an imaginal reproduction of the particular bars frequented by the subject is a matter that must be decided by experiment.

Certainly the stimuli directly associated with the consumption of alcohol should be presented *in vivo,* and the detailed procedure must depend on whether controlled drinking or abstinence is the ultimate goal. If controlled drinking is sought, the aversive training can be combined with BAC discrimination training, using the biofeedback procedures developed by Lovibond and Caddy (1970). The purpose of BAC discrimination training is to sensitize the individual to the internal and external cues of the BAC as the basis for a decision to stop or drastically slow down drinking. The purpose of the aversive procedures is to provide an automatic mechanism to reinforce or assist the decision to stop drinking when the BAC limit has been reached. As part of the procedure, the subject can be taught the essentials of responsible social drinking, including ordering mixed drinks, sipping, and spacing drinks.

a. Rules for the Use of Aversive Procedures. Until further research evidence is obtained, it is suggested that, in the control of excessive drinking by aversive procedures, the following rules should be applied.

1. Illness produced by motion (e.g., rotational) and/or by chemical means should be the aversive event of choice, with electrical stimulation a possible supplementary procedure.

2. Drinking should occur before malaise induction and should occur again during the phase of acute malaise.

3. The subject's mouth should be rinsed before the acute period of malaise passes, and orange juice or other nonalcoholic drinks should be given judiciously when recovery is well under way.

4. Narrative-supplemented imaginal construction of the chains of events immediately preceding heavy drinking on an habitual basis should systematically be associated with malaise in the manner of O'Brien *et al.* (1972). For this purpose, malaise should be established first, and then reinforced by suggestions of sickness as the narrative proceeds.

5. If reduction in incentive to drink beyond a chosen BAC (say 50 mg/100 ml) is sought, then after BAC discrimination training drinking can be allowed to occur with impunity as long as the BAC remains below the chosen value. Aversive procedures can then be instituted when the BAC rises above the designated value.

6. Treatment sessions should not be programmed more often than once per day, and preferably should occur less frequently.

7. The number of treatment sessions should be determined on the basis of each individual's response.

8. In the conditioning of motivational change, it may be an advantage to begin by serving the alcoholic beverage at room temperature when it is to be associated with malaise, and then to "fade" to normal chilled temperature as learning proceeds.

9. If practical, some trials should be given in the habitual drinking situation, for example, by first inducing malaise and then, after taking the subject into his favorite drinking place, requiring him to sip a drink and leave a few minutes later.

If aversive procedures are not to be used, stimulus control of drinking must be reduced as far as practicable by avoidance of the critical stimulus conditions. In the case of public drinking, what may be required is a change in drinking companions and in places of drinking. Such changes not only permit avoidance of incentive stimuli for heavy drinking, but insure the development of new incentive stimuli for reduced or controlled drinking. Such a tactic is desirable even when aversive procedures are used, but in the case of subjects from lower socioeconomic groups, the required changes may be difficult to achieve in practice.

In the case of drinking in the home, it may be necessary to limit the amount of liquor in the house, and to drink in another room or in a different chair without television and without smoking, at least until the new pattern of reduced drinking is thoroughly established. It may then become possible to incorporate some of the old stimuli into the new pattern associated with controlled drinking, without untoward consequences. Obviously, however, great care is called for here.

b. Other Components. The emphasis on self-regulation has already been discussed and no further comment is called for, as no new developments have occurred. Although experimental evidence is lacking, it is our firm impression that education concerning alcohol is an important component in self-regulation. Certainly, excessive drinkers typically know very little about the drug they consume, and indeed resist the very idea that alcohol is a drug. Many subjects, however, later evaluate the educational component of the program as an important positive influence.

We continue to seek the aid of the spouse or other family member as a cotherapist who reinforces the subject's new pattern of controlled drinking. In many cases, however, we have achieved little beyond nonspecific support from the spouse.

Some incidental counseling is an inevitable component of an intensive individually based program, as is occasional help with a specific problem, such as anxiety or depression. We believe that in the majority of cases, however, anxiety and depression are likely to be consequences rather than causes of excessive drinking, and nothing is calculated to improve the general well-being of subjects more than bringing their drinking under their own control.

In a similar vein, we believe the critical "alternative behavior to cues preceding drinking" which alcohol abusers need to be taught is reduced drinking. Inasmuch as alcohol abusers may previously have occupied most of their time with heavy drinking, however, they may need help to acquire new behaviors.

REFERENCES

Alcoholics Anonymous. *12 steps and 12 traditions.* New York: Harper, 1953.

Bigelow, G., Liebson, I., & Griffiths, R. Alcoholic drinking: Suppression by a brief time-out procedure. *Behaviour Research and Therapy,* 1974, **12,** 107–115.

Bowman, R. S., Stein, L. I., & Newton, J. R. Measurement and interpretation of drinking behavior. *Journal of Studies on Alcohol,* 1975, **36,** 1154–1172.

Briddell, D. W., & Nathan, P. E. Behavior assessment and modification with alcoholics: Current status and future trends. In M. Hersen, R. M. Eisler, & P. M. Miller (Eds.), *Progress in behavior modification* (Vol. 2). New York: Academic Press, 1976. Pp. 1–51.

Bustamante, A., & Mossay, P. *Development of a scale measuring externally controlled eating behavior.* Paper read at the Western Psychological Association, Los Angeles, April 1976.

Cappell, H. An evaluation of tension models of alcohol consumption. In Y. Israel *et al.* (Eds.), *Research advances in alcohol and drug problems.* New York: Wiley, 1975. Pp. 177–209.

Cohen, M., Liebson, I. A., Faillace, L. A., & Allen, R. P. Moderate drinking by chronic alcoholics. *Journal of Nervous and Mental Disease,* 1971, **153,** 434–444.

Davies, D. L. Normal drinking in recovered alcohol addicts. *Quarterly Journal of Studies on Alcohol,* 1962, **23,** 94–104.

Deutsch, J. A., & Koopmans, H. S. Preference enhancement for alcohol by passive exposure. *Science,* 1973, *179,* 1242–1243.

Emrick, C. D. A review of psychologically oriented treatment of alcoholism. *Quarterly Journal of Studies on Alcohol,* 1974, **35,** 523–549.

Garcia, J., Hankins, W. G., & Coil, J. D. Koalas, men and other conditioned gastronomes. In N. S. Milgram, L. Krames, & T. Allowan (Eds.), *Food aversion learning,* New York: Plenum, 1976.

Garcia, J., & Koelling, R. A. Relation of cue to consequence in avoidance learning. *Psychonomic Science,* 1966, 4(3), 123–124.

Goldberg, D. M., & Watts, C. Serum enzyme changes as evidence of liver reaction to oral alcohol. *Gastroenterology,* 1965, **49,** 256–261.

Hallam, R., & Rachman, S. Theoretical problems of aversion therapy. *Behaviour Research and Therapy,* 1972, **10,** 341–353.

Harris, R. N., Jr., Walter, J., & Keding, A. *Alcoholism follow-up as a clinical procedure: How much is enough?* Paper read at the Western Psychological Association, Los Angeles, April 1976.

Hebb, D. O. *The organization of behavior.* New York: Wiley, 1949.

Hennessy, W. B. *Serum liver-enzyme estimations in drinking drivers.* Paper read at a Research Seminar, St. Vincent's Hospital, Sydney, October 1976.

Higgins, R. L., & Marlatt, G. A. The effects of anxiety arousal upon the consumption of alcohol by alcoholics and social drinkers. *Journal of Consulting and Clinical Psychology,* 1973, **41,** 426–433.

Jellinek, E. M. *The disease concept of alcoholism.* New Haven: College and University Press, 1960.

Kalat, J., & Rosin, P. "Learned safety" as a mechanism in long delay taste-aversion learning in rats. *Journal of Comparative and Physiological Psychology,* 1973, **83,** 198–207.

Keller, M., & Efron, V. The prevalence of alcoholism. *Quarterly Journal of Studies on Alcohol,* 1955, **16,** 619–644.

Lester, D., & Freed, E. X. Criteria for an animal model of alcoholism. *Pharmacology, Biochemistry, and Behavior,* 1973, **1,** 103–107.

Lloyd, R. W., & Salzberg, H. C. Controlled social drinking: An alternative to abstinence as a treatment goal for some alcohol abusers. *Psychological Bulletin,* 1975, **82,** 815–842.

Lovibond, S. H. Aversive control of behavior. *Behavior Therapy,* 1970, **1,** 80–91.

Lovibond, S. H. Use of behavior modification in the reduction of alcohol-related road accidents. In E. Thomson (Ed.), *Applications of behavior modification.* New York: Academic Press, 1975. Pp. 399–406.

Lovibond, S. H. Aversive control of addictive behaviour. *Australian Psychologist,* 1976, **2,** 25–41.

Lovibond, S. H., & Caddy, G. Discriminated aversive control in the modification of alcoholics' drinking behavior. *Behavior Therapy,* 1970, **1,** 437–444.

Luera, L., & Albright, D. *The effects of ethnicity on eating styles of obese and non-obese subjects.* Paper read at the Western Psychological Association, Los Angeles, April 1976.

Marlatt, G. A., Demming, B., & Reid, J. B. Loss of control drinking in alcoholics: An experimental analogue. *Journal of Abnormal Psychology,* 1973, **81,** 233–241.

Mello, N. K. Behavioral studies of alcoholism. In B. Kissin & H. Begleiter (Eds.), *The biology of alcoholism* (Vol. 2). New York: Plenum, 1972. Pp. 219–291.

Mello, N. K., & Mendelson, J. H. Operant analysis of drinking patterns of chronic alcoholics. *Nature (London),* 1965, **206,** 43–46.

Mello, N. K., & Mendelson, J. H. Experimentally induced intoxication in alcoholics: A comparison between programmed and spontaneous drinking. *Journal of Pharmacology and Experimental Therapeutics,* 1970, **173,** 101–116.

Miller, P. M., & Eisler, R. M. Alcohol and drug abuse. In W. E. Craighead, A. E. Kazdin, & M. J. Mahoney (Eds.), *Behavior modification: Principles, issues, and applications.* Boston: Houghton, 1976. Pp. 376–393.

Miller, P. M., Hersen, M., Eisler, R. M., & Elkin, T. E. A retrospective analysis of alcohol consumption on laboratory tasks as related to therapeutic outcome. *Behaviour Research and Therapy,* 1974, **12,** 73–76.

Mills, K. C., Sobell, M. B., & Schaeffer, H. H. Training social drinking as an alternative to abstinence for alcoholics. *Behavior Therapy,* 1971, **2,** 18–27.

Myers, R. D., & Veale, W. L. The determinants of alcohol preference in animals. In B. Kissin & H. Beglieter, (Eds.), *The biology of alcoholism* (Vol. 2). New York: Plenum, 1972. Pp. 131–168.

Nathan, P. E., & Briddell, D. W. Behavioral assessment and treatment of alcoholism. In B. Kissin & H. Beglieter (Eds.), *The biology of alcoholism* (Vol. 5). New York: Plenum, 1976. Pp. 301–349.

Nathan, P. E., & O'Brien, J. S. An experimental analysis of the behavior of alcoholics and non-alcoholics during prolonged experimental drinking: A necessary precursor of behavior therapy? *Behavior Therapy,* 1971, **2,** 455–476.

O'Brien, J. S., Raynes, A. E., & Patch, V. D. Treatment of heroin addiction with aversion therapy, relaxation training and systematic desensitization. *Behaviour Research and Therapy,* 1972, **10,** 77–80.

Nathan, P. E., Titler, N. A., Lowenstein, L. M., Solomon, P., & Rossi, A. M. Behavioral analysis of chronic alcoholism. *Archives of General Psychiatry,* 1970, **22,** 419–430.

Patel, S., & O'Gorman, P. Serum enzyme levels in alcoholism and drug dependency. *Journal of Clinical Pathology,* 1975, **28,** 414–417.

Pattison, E. M. A critique of alcoholism treatment concepts with special reference to abstinence. *Quarterly Journal of Studies on Alcohol,* 1966, **27,** 49–71.

Pattison, E. M. Abstinence criteria in alcoholism treatment. *Addictions,* 1967, **14,** 1–19.

Pickens, R., Bigelow, G., & Griffiths, R. An experimental approach to treating chronic alcoholism. A case study and one-year follow-up. *Behaviour Research and Therapy,* 1973, **11,** 321–325.

Rachman, S., & Teasdale, J. *Aversion therapy and behaviour disorders.* London: Routledge & Kegan Paul, 1969.

Revusky, S. H., & Bedarf, E. W. Association of illness with prior ingestion of novel foods. *Science,* 1967, **155**, 219–220.

Reznick, H., & Dannenfelser, S. *The effects of anxiety level and response cost on the eating behavior of normal and obese subjects.* Paper read at the Western Psychological Association, Los Angeles, April 1976.

Rollason, J. G., Pincherle, G., & Robinson, D. Serum gamma- glutamyl transpeptidase in relation to alcohol consumption. *Clinical Chimica Acta,* 1972, **39**, 75–80.

Rosalki, S. B., & Rau, D. Serum gamma-glutamyl transpeptidase activity in alcoholism. *Clinical Chimica Acta,* 1972, **39**, 41–47.

Schachter, S. *Emotion, obesity, and crime.* New York: Academic Press, 1971.

Schaeffer, H. H., Sobell, M. B., & Mills, K. C. Baseline drinking behaviors in alcoholics and social drinkers. *Behaviour Research and Therapy,* 1971, **9**, 23–27.

Schisslak, C., & Blake, S. *Naturalistic observations of eating patterns in humans: Relationships between obesity and eating styles.* Paper read at the Western Psychological Association, Los Angeles, April 1976.

Silverstein, S. J., Nathan, P. E., & Taylor, H. A. Blood alcohol estimation and controlled drinking by chronic alcoholics. *Behavior Therapy,* 1974, **5**, 1–15.

Sobell, L. C., & Sobell, M. B.. *Training responsible drinking with state hospitalized alcoholics.* Paper read at the American Psychological Association, Chicago, September 1975.

Sobell, M. B., & Sobell, L. C. Alcoholics treated by individualized behavior therapy: One year treatment outcome. *Behaviour Research and Therapy,* 1973, **11**, 599–618. (a)

Sobell, M. B., & Sobell, L. C. Individualized behavior therapy for alcoholics. *Behavior Therapy,* 1973, **4**, 49–72. (b)

Sobell, M. B., & Sobell, L. C. Second year treatment outcome of alcoholics treated by individualized behavior therapy: Results. *Behaviour Research and Therapy,* 1976, **14**, 195–215.

Suedfeld, P., & Ikard, F. F. Use of sensory deprivation in facilitating the reduction of cigarette smoking. *Journal of Consulting and Clinical Psychology,* 1974, **42**, 888–895.

Vernon, J. A. *Inside the black room.* New York: Potter, 1963.

Wikler, A. Present status of the concept of drug dependence. *Psychological Medicine,* 1971, **1**, 377–380. (a)

Wikler, A. Some implications of conditioning theory for problems of alcohol abuse. *Behavioral Science,* 1971, **16**, 92–97. (b)

Wikler, A., & Pescor, F. T. Classical conditioning of a morphine-abstinence phenomenon, reinforcement of opioid-drinking behavior and "relapse" in morphine-addicted rats. *Psychopharmacologia,* 1967, **10**, 255–284.

Wikler, A., Pescor, F. T., Miller, D., & Norrell, H. Persistent potency of a secondary (conditioned) reinforcer following withdrawal of morphine from physically dependent rats. *Psychopharmacologia,* 1971, **20**, 103–117.

Williams, R. J. Biochemical individuality and cellular nutrition: Prime factors in alcoholism. *Quarterly Journal of Studies on Alcohol,* 1959, **20**, 452–463.

Zein, M., & Discombe, G., Serum gamma-glutamyl transpeptidase as a diagnostic aid. *Lancet,* 1970, **II**, 748–750.

CHILD NONCOMPLIANCE TO PARENTAL REQUESTS: BEHAVIORAL ANALYSIS AND TREATMENT

REX FOREHAND
Department of Psychology
University of Georgia
Athens, Georgia

I. INTRODUCTION

"Johnny will not obey me!" "Susie never comes to dinner when I call her!" "Billy refuses to make up his bed!" "Cindy will not do anything I tell her to do!" These parental statements are familiar to professionals who engage in parent counseling and training since parents frequently complain that their children fail to comply with requests.

An examination of the literature suggests that noncompliance is a pervasive childhood behavior problem. For example, in extensive naturalistic observations in the homes of 33 nonclinic "normal" children, Johnson, Wahl, Martin, and Johansson (1973) found that among 13 "deviant" child behaviors, noncompliance was the most frequent response and occurred among more children than any other deviant behavior. Among children referred to clinics for treatment of behavior problems, noncompliance is also a frequent presenting complaint of parents. Patterson and Reid (1973) reported that all 11 of the parents they trained at the Oregon Research Institute, Eugene, selected noncompliance as one of the target behaviors to be modified. In a more recent statement from the Oregon Research Institute, Taplin and Reid (1975) indicated that noncompliance was the most frequently designated child problem, as 24 of 25 parents who referred their children for treatment reported difficulties with this behavior. Christophersen, Barnard, Ford, and Wolf (1976) similarly reported noncompliance to be a major problem of children they treated. Working with mothers of retarded children, Tavormina, Henggeler, and Gayton (1976) found that noncompliance was perceived by these parents as the most significant behavior problem they experienced with their children. Consistent with these data, Johansson (1971) noted that noncompliance typically has been identified as a primary characteristic of several classifications of child psychopathology. In addition, Landauer, Carlsmith, and Lepper (1970) and Rudestam, Fisher, and Fiester (1974) indicate that children are less compliant to commands from their own parents than from strangers.

The frequency with which child noncompliance is perceived and experienced by parents as a problem indicates the need to develop, implement, and assess treatment procedures for this specific problem. While three reviews (Berkowitz & Graziano, 1972; Johnson & Katz, 1973; O'Dell, 1974) provide evidence that training parents as behavior therapists for their own children is an effective and efficient treatment approach for modifying child behavior problems, many investigators (e.g., Patterson, 1974) have not examined individual child behavior problems, but rather total deviant child behavior. Although deceleration of total deviant behavior is the goal of most behavior therapists who train parents, combining various child behaviors into a total deviant behavior category produces data interpretation and treatment evaluation problems. For example, a substantial decrease in a low-rate, highly noxious behavior resulting from treatment may be masked by the failure of a higher rate, less noxious behavior to change with treatment implementation (Weinrott, 1975). Also, particular treatment approaches or training models may be differentially effective with different deviant child behaviors—a fact that would be obscured by combining various child behavior categories into a total deviant behavior score.

As noncompliance has been identified as a primary behavior problem of children, this chapter will focus on the behavioral analysis and treatment of this one problem. Included in the chapter will be a review of (a) various definitions of noncompliance which investigators have employed, (b) hypotheses concerning the development of noncompliance, (c) normative data, (d) analog studies examining the effects of various variables on noncompliance, (e) treatment outcome studies with noncompliant clinic-referred children, and (f) ethical issues involved in the treatment of noncompliance. The focus of the chapter will be on the treatment of preadolescent children, as some data (e.g., Patterson, 1976; Tavormina *et al.*, 1976) suggest that noncompliance to parental commands diminishes with age. However, it should be noted that when noncompliance to parental commands exists in the adolescent years, behavioral treatment approaches often have been less than successful (e.g., Weathers & Liberman, 1975).

II. DEFINITIONS

A number of investigators have examined noncompliant behavior of children but, perhaps unfortunately, they have employed various definitions of compliance and noncompliance. In order to interpret the data presented in later sections, it is important to sample the definitions that have been used and to attempt to reach some conclusions about their similarities and differences.

Patterson, Ray, Shaw, and Cobb (1969) recorded compliance when "a person does what is asked of him" and noncompliance when "a person does not do what is requested of him" (pp. 8, 10). Johnson (1975) used a similar definition but incorporated a time criterion: Compliance to a command was coded in the 10-second time block in which the command occurred or in the immediately following 10-second time block. If compliance did not occur in that time period, noncompliance was coded. Bernal, Kreutzer, North, and Pelc (1973) allowed the child 30 seconds to comply to a command.

Each of the above definitions appears to require child compliance to a parental command to be completed before compliance is scored. In contrast, the definition for compliance used by this writer and his colleagues (e.g., Forehand, Gardner, & Roberts, 1976a; Forehand & King, 1977; Forehand, Peed, & Roberts, 1975b) involves only initiation of compliance. For example, Forehand *et al.* (1975b) defined compliance as the presence of an observable cue reflecting initiation of compliance within 5 seconds of the termination of the parental command. Noncompliance was the absence of such a cue.

Wahler, House, and Stambaugh (1976) scored both initiation and maintenance of compliance using an interval scoring system. After a parental command was presented, the child's behavior was scored as compliant (termed "cooperative" by Wahler *et al.*) or noncompliant (termed "oppositional") for each 10-second interval until the command was completed or a new command was issued. In order for compliance to be scored in the first 10-second interval following the command, the child must have complied with the command during that interval. Subsequent 10-second intervals were scored if the command specified an act of indefinite length (e.g., "Clean up your room"). Compliance was scored in each of these intervals in which there was an instance of compliance; otherwise, noncompliance was scored. Although Wahler and his colleagues have not analyzed their data in such a manner to allow a comparison of initiated versus maintained compliance, Forehand and Scarboro (1975) have demonstrated that the data generated in this type of coding system are amenable to such an analysis.

Terdal, Jackson, and Garner (1976) developed a scoring system which also allows a comparison of initiated versus maintained compliance to parental commands. They termed their two categories immediate and long-term efficiency. The former was defined as the proportion of commands followed by compliance within the 15-second interval immediately following parental issuance of a command, whereas the latter was defined as the number of 15-second intervals in which compliance to a command was maintained.

A survey of studies to be reviewed in the following sections of this chapter suggests that most investigators have used one of three definitions for scoring compliance: (a) completion of compliance within a predetermined time period, usually 20–30 seconds; (b) initiation of compliance within a predetermined time interval, usually 5 seconds; or (c) initiation and maintenance of compliance that is scored in consecutive 10-second time blocks. In each study, noncompliance was the failure of compliance to occur during the specified time period. Intuitively, it would seem logical that different criteria for compliance (or noncompliance) would lead to different results; however, such a hypothesis has yet to be examined.

Noncompliance represents a unique form of deviant child behavior in that the antecedent variable is constant; that is, noncompliance or compliance is preceded by a parental command. Since the command is an integral part of the compliant/noncompliant response, it is important to review briefly the types of command definitions that have been used by various investigators. Some researchers (e.g.,

Wahler, 1969a, 1969b) have simply defined parental commands as instructions or requests directed at the child. Other investigators have further specified the definition. For example, Forehand, King, Peed, and Yoder (1975a) defined a command as an order, demand, direction, or suggestion requiring motor response.

Several investigators have delineated different types of commands. Forehand *et al.* (1975b) differentiated commands into those to which a motoric response is appropriate and feasible (alpha commands) and those to which there is no opportunity for compliance as the command is too vague, interrupted by parental verbiage, or is complied to by the parent (beta commands). Wahler *et al.* (1976) scored aversive and nonaversive commands. The two types of commands differed in that the former was judged to be aversive because of the quality of voice in which it was delivered, its content, and/or the assertive behavior of the speaker. Patterson *et al.* (1969) coded four types: (a) command (a direct, reasonable, and clearly stated request or command is made); (b) command negative (commands in which someone is told to stop doing something); (c) aversive command (commands which explicitly threaten aversive consequences if compliance is not forthcoming); and (d) command prime (commands for which compliance or noncompliance cannot be readily assessed). Bernal *et al.* (1973) also delineated four types of commands: (a) original command (a direct, reasonable request to do or stop doing something); (b) negative command (an original command given in a threatening, humiliating, angry, or nagging fashion); (c) repetitions (an original or negative command is repeated); and (d) delayed command (a command that doesn't require compliance or initiation of compliance immediately). Although Patterson *et al.* (1969) and Wahler *et al.* (1976) have delineated potentially important dimensions of commands, they have not reported the differential effects of the various types of commands on compliance. The types of commands differentiated by Forehand *et al.* (1975b) and Bernal *et al.* (1973) have been examined and will be discussed in later sections.

III. HYPOTHESES CONCERNING THE DEVELOPMENT OF NONCOMPLIANCE

Few investigators have presented hypotheses concerning the development of compliance and noncompliance. Holmes (1969) has proposed that young children are helpless and dependent on their parents. In order to cope with their helplessness, children incorporate the parent into their childlike world and view the parent as omnipotent. Subsequently, they "identify" with the parent and "introject" the demands of the parent, thus making them their own. By this process, obedience to parental demands is hypothesized to occur. While such an account of how compliance develops is intellectually stimulating, it is quite safe from disproof and rejection; in fact, it is untestable.

On a more behavioral level, Milgram (1974) has proposed that rewards for compliance and punishment for noncompliance are significant factors in the development of compliance. Along this line, Patterson (1976) has presented the coercion hypothesis to account for the development of deviant child behavior, including noncompliance. Patterson proposes an S-R-C (aversive stimulus–child response–removal of aversive stimulus) paradigm which, for noncompliance, can be conceptualized as parent command–child noncompliance plus other possible deviant child behaviors (e.g., negativism, yelling, crying)–removal of parent command.[1] Most researchers (e.g., Wahl, Johnson, Johansson, & Martin, 1974) have assumed that certain types of parental commands are aversive to children. The child can terminate a parental command by compliance; however, coercive behaviors such as noncompliance and negativism may also terminate the aversive parental command. Over a period of time, the deviant child learns to repeat or escalate the intensity of his or her coercive behaviors (e.g., whining and crying) in order to terminate parental commands. The parent, in turn, may either withdraw the command (i.e., fail to punitively respond to noncompliance and other coercive behaviors), thus negatively reinforcing the noncompliance and other behaviors, or respond with coercive behaviors (e.g., yelling) of his or her own. If the latter occurs, the child may respond by complying, thus reinforcing the parental coercive behavior, or by intensifying his or her own coercive behaviors. Consequently, as a function of such experiences, parent–child interactions that are initiated by a parent command eventually are characterized by high-rate coercive *parent and child* behaviors, including noncompliance. As is evident, negative reinforcement (i.e., the removal of an aversive stimulus) plays a critical role in increments in the rate and intensity of coercive

[1] The following application of Patterson's coercion hypothesis to noncompliance is based on the present writer's interpretation of the hypothesis. Consequently, any faulty reasoning detected in the account is his burden to bear.

behaviors in such a system. Patterson (1976) has suggested that both the prevention and treatment of such interactions require parents to *consistently* punish coercive behaviors and to be more contingent in their use of social reinforcers.

IV. NORMATIVE DATA

Many investigators now believe there is a need for the establishment of normative data regarding child deviant behavior. Such data allow therapists to determine if a child actually is deviant and/or if, after treatment, his or her level of deviance is within "normal limits." Some investigators (e.g., Eyberg & Johnson, 1974; Patterson, 1976) recently have reported using normative data for such purposes.

Johansson (1971) has conducted an extensive investigation involving 33 families in which there was a child between the ages of 4 and 6 having no history of treatment for behavior problems. Each family was observed five times in the home for 45 minutes on each occasion. The results indicated that the children complied (as defined by Johnson, 1975) to 74% of their parents' commands, with little variance associated with which parent gave the command (75% compliance to father and 72% compliance to mother). Furthermore, compliance did not vary significantly with the age or sex of the child. Whether the command was presented positively ("Pick up the blocks") or negatively ("Stop hitting your brother") also did not affect the percentage of compliance. Both parents responded significantly more positively and significantly less negatively to the children's compliance than to their noncompliance. There was also a consistent positive relationship between parental reinforcement rate for compliance and the percentage of compliance received by the parent, but this relationship was significant only for fathers. Finally, a significant positive relationship was found between other deviant child behaviors (e.g., destructive behavior, crying, tantrum) and noncompliance to paternal commands. Although the relationship between other deviant child behavior and noncompliance to maternal commands did not reach significance, the trend was in the same direction as for fathers.

Simmons and Schoggen (1963) quantified data collected from 12 to 14 hours of observer-recorded transcripts for each of 11 parents and children observed in their homes. These investigators found that the children failed to comply to 20% of the commands issued by mothers and 18% of the commands issued by fathers. Compliance to only one type of parental command was examined: an authoritarian command in which the parent handled a conflict situation with the child by making no attempt to justify, quality, or explain his or her demand. Although fathers encountered conflict situations with their children significantly less often than mothers, they used authoritarian commands a significantly greater percentage of the time to handle conflicts.

The Johansson (1971) and Simmons and Schoggen (1963) investigations represent two of the few studies in which fathers were included. In both studies, child compliance did not differ significantly between commands issued by mothers and fathers. Nevertheless, Johansson found that the relationship between parental reinforcement and child compliance differed for mothers and fathers, whereas Simmons and Schoggen found that paternal and maternal use of authoritarian commands differed. These findings suggest the importance of including fathers when data on child compliance are being collected.

Forehand *et al.* (1976a) conducted a laboratory investigation in which 32 middle-class mothers issued a standard set of commands to their 3- to 6-year-old children. The results indicated that the children complied with 51% of the maternal commands. However, the children did not have an opportunity to comply with 35% of the maternal commands as the mothers verbally interrupted the 5-second interval following their command, thus preventing the child from having sufficient time to comply. The interruption was most often in the form of a repetition of the command. When maternally interrupted commands were removed from the calculation of compliance, the percentage of compliance was 89%. Maternal consequences were also examined: mothers ignored (failed to respond to) child compliance 27% of the time and attended positively to compliance 30% of the time. Child noncompliance was followed by a repetition of the command 60% of the time and never received positive attention. These data should be viewed only as pilot results since naturalistic observations of parent–child interactions, such as those obtained by Johansson (1971), are needed.

A number of studies have compared the compliance of nonclinic (presumably normal) children to that of children referred to a clinic for treatment of behavior problems. These studies have typically been conducted for one or more of the following three reasons: (a) to demonstrate that the clinic children and their parents differ prior to treatment from the normal population; (b) to provide data indicating that the clinic children and their parents are within normal limits after treatment; and/or (c) to demonstrate that a particular coding system is sensitive to differences in behavior problem and normal children.

Patterson (1976) reported that 27 behavior problem children, ages 5 to 15, referred for treatment were more noncompliant in the home, as determined by 6 to 10 observations by independent observers, than a nonproblem sample of 27 children. The problem sample was termed "aggressive" but, as mentioned earlier, a primary presenting problem of most of Patterson's clients was noncompliance.

Forehand *et al.* (1975a) compared 20 mothers and their 4- to 6-year-old children (referred to a clinic for treatment of noncompliance) with 20 mothers and their nonclinic children. Both the clinic and nonclinic groups were differentiated into middle and lower socioeconomic status groups. One observation of each parent–child interaction was conducted in a laboratory setting and indicated that the clinic–nonclinic factor, but not socioeconomic status, was a significant variable in determining the parent–child interaction. In a situation in which the mothers were instructed to structure the child's activities (command situation), nonclinic children complied to significantly more of their mother's commands than did clinic children (means of 62% vs. 42% compliance). In a free play situation, mothers of the clinic-referred children issued significantly more commands and criticisms than mothers of nonclinic children. Examining data they collected in both laboratory and home settings, Lobitz and Johnson (1977) have reported similar differences in parents of clinic and nonclinic children.

Delfini, Bernal, and Rosen (1976) compared 21 5- to 7-year-old children referred by their parents for noncompliance and disruptive behavior in the home to 21 normal children. Four observations were conducted for each child in the home with all family members present. The normal group was more compliant to parental (mother plus father) commands than was the clinic-referred group (means of 80% vs. 69% compliance). In examining parental commands, the investigators found that parents of the clinic-referred children gave more total commands than parents of nonclinic children. Further analysis of parental commanding revealed that parents of the clinic children emitted more negative commands (e.g., commands presented in a threatening, angry, humiliating, and nagging manner) than parents of nonclinic children. These results would suggest that not only the number, as reported by Forehand *et al.* (1975a) and Lobitz and Johnson (1977), but also the type of parental command is important in differentiating parents of clinic-referred and nonclinic children.

Two studies have provided data comparing the compliance of nonclinic children to that of children referred to clinics for reasons other than noncompliance. Doleys, Cartelli, and Doster (1976) found that a group of children labeled as learning disabled complied significantly less than a nonclinic normal group (means of 31% vs. 69%) but equivalent to a noncompliant clinic group (means of 31% vs. 32%).

Terdal *et al.* (1976) compared 40 normal children and 42 developmentally delayed children in a laboratory setting. In order to assess changes over chronological age, both groups were subdivided. The normals were divided into three chronological age (CA) groups: 2- to 4-year-olds; 4- to 6-year-olds; and 6- to 8-year-olds. The developmentally delayed (retarded) children were divided into three groups such that their mental age (MA) approximated the CA of the three normal groups. The mean compliance to commands was 41% for the low MA retarded group, 76% for the middle MA retarded group, and 68% for the high MA retarded group. For the normals, the compliance means were 65%, 69%, and 77% for the low, middle, and high CA groups. The low MA retarded group differed significantly from the low CA group and from the middle and high MA retarded groups. The significant change in the compliance percentage over MA levels for the developmentally delayed group corresponds with the data collected by Tavormina *et al.* (1976) on problems presented by parents of retarded children: compliance is less of a problem with older than younger retarded children. The Terdal *et al.* data for normals indicate a similar trend for nonretarded children.

The findings of Terdal *et al.* suggest that if one wishes to establish norms for compliance, an examination of age, as well as other subject characteristics, may be important. Simmons and Schoggen (1963) also found a positive relationship between age and compliance. Patterson (1976) reported that noncompliance of children appeared to decrease by age five. He hypothesized that the decrement in noncompliance did not occur until age five because parents tolerated the behavior and failed to punish its occurrence until that age. As mentioned earlier, Johansson (1971) did not find that compliance to parental commands varied with the age of the child. Relative to other studies (e.g., Terdal *et al.*, 1976), Johansson used a more restricted age range (4–6 years), thus perhaps accounting for her finding.

Data also suggest that compliance at certain ages can serve as a predictor of compliance at later ages. Based on parental interviews and parent-completed questionnaires, Kagan and Moss (1962) examined, among other child behaviors, changes in child obedience to parent and teacher requests and rules over the first 14 years of life. Measures used to assess changes included ratings of narrative reports obtained from home and school visits and interviews with the child, parent, and teacher. Obedience in the first 3 years of life was significantly and positively correlated with obedience during the 3–6 age range, but not during the 6–10 or 10–14 age ranges. Compliance during the 3–6 age range correlated significantly with compliance during both the 6–10 and 10–14 age ranges, whereas obedience during the 6–10 ages was correlated significantly with obedience during the 10–14 age period. The Kagan and Moss findings would suggest that noncompliance during the 3–6 age range can serve as an indicator for compliance problems during later years of childhood. While important, these data do not provide the extent of change in compliance that may occur across ages, but rather only the relationship between compliance rates at different age levels.

The effects of sex and socioeconomic status on children's compliance to parental commands also have been examined. The Johansson (1971) study, cited earlier, suggested that sex may not be an important variable in determining compliance. Neither the sex of the parent nor of the child affected the child's compliance rate. Simmons and Schoggen (1963) also found that sex of the parent did not affect child compliance, whereas Landauer *et al.* (1970) found that compliance did not vary significantly with sex of the child. The failure to find boys to be more noncompliant than girls is surprising as investigators typically have reported that most clinic-referred noncompliant children are males (e.g., Forehand & King, 1974, 1977). Nevertheless, based on available data, sex does not appear significant when establishing child compliance norms.

Another subject characteristic that may affect child compliance and should be taken into account when compliance norms are considered is socioeconomic status of the family. Conflicting results have been reported. Johansson (1971) failed to find a significant relationship between father's occupational level and child compliance but did find a significant negative correlation between family income level and compliance. As mentioned previously, Forehand *et al.* (1975a) reported social class did not affect the compliance rate of either clinic-referred or nonclinic children. In contrast, Zegiob and Forehand (1977) found that lower-class children complied significantly more than middle-class children to maternal commands. Interestingly, lower-class parents issued significantly more direct commands (e.g., "Pick up the toys") whereas middle-class parents issued significantly more suggestions or indirect commands (e.g., "Would you pick up the toys now?"), suggesting that compliance differences that may exist between children from different socioeconomic classes may, at least partially, be a function of the type of parental command.

Data regarding compliance norms lead to several conclusions. First, compliance to parental commands for nonclinic normal samples ranges from approximately 60% to 80%. Considering the range of experimental settings and compliance definitions employed, the agreement across studies is respectable and provides some estimates for compliance norms. Second, children for whom noncompliance is one reason for referral to a clinic differ in their percentage of compliance to parental commands from children not referred to a clinic for treatment. Third, both number and type of parental commands appear to differentiate parents of nonclinic children and parents of noncompliant clinic-referred children. Fourth, some clinic populations whose primary presenting problem is one other than noncompliance (i.e., retardation and learning disabled) also differ from nonclinic normal samples in terms of compliance to parental commands. Fifth, data are available to indicate that age and socioeconomic status exert significant effects on child compliance, whereas neither sex of child nor parent have been demonstrated to significantly affect child compliance to parental commands.

V. ANALOG STUDIES

A number of studies have been conducted with nonclinic children in laboratory settings in order to specify treatment variables that are effective in modifying noncompliance. The selection of nonclinic children appears to be a function of the desire for experimental control and experimenter convenience. Extraneous variables that may systematically or unsystematically affect child compliance in the home are controlled as the analog studies are typically conducted in the laboratory setting. Furthermore, the experimenter can withdraw, as well as introduce, treatment conditions (e.g., ABAB designs), can examine the effectiveness of novel treatment procedures, and does not have to concern him- or herself with generalization of treatment effects to the home. Also, subjects are more easily recruited and can be paid for their participation, thus relieving the researcher of further obligation.

The primary question that arises in examining the analog studies is whether the findings generalize to noncompliant clinic-referred children. For example, if 2-minute and 5-minute time-outs are equally effective in reducing noncompliance of nonclinic children in a laboratory setting, does this indicate that the shorter time-out is sufficient to use with noncompliant clinic-referred children in the home? This question as yet is unanswered; however, at least two arguments can be advanced to suggest that the answer may be less than critical. First, the position can be taken that the results of analog studies are important regardless of whether or not generalization of conclusions to clinic-referred populations is possible, as we need to begin to focus our attention on procedures that can be used by parents in the general population; that is, the procedures, which are shown to be effective in analog studies, may be viewed as good child-rearing techniques which should be used by all parents. Risley, Clark, and Cataldo (1976) recently advocated this position as they pointed out the need to develop, package, and disseminate child-rearing advice for normal families. Such an approach would fit well into what Rosen (1976) has labeled nonprescription behavior therapy: self-help programs that can be self-administered. The recent growth and popularity of such therapy for weight reduction, toilet training, and sexual dysfunction suggests that analog work with nonclinic children may lead to the packaging of good nonprescription behavioral child-rearing techniques.

Second, although differences in nonclinic and clinic-referred child samples exist in terms of compliance to parental commands, there is overlap in their percentage of compliance (Delfini *et al.*, 1976). This suggests that nonclinic and clinic noncompliant samples represent different points on the same continuum; consequently, procedures effective with one sample also may be effective with the other.

Most analog studies have examined the effects of various parental consequences on child compliance and noncompliance. However, in at least three studies the effects of parental antecedent events have been investigated. Forehand and Scarboro (1975) requested mothers to issue 12 standard commands to their children in a laboratory setting. A comparison of compliance to the first six versus the second six commands indicated significantly less compliance to the latter commands. Further analysis of the first and second six commands revealed that the difference in compliance occurred only during the first 30 seconds (three 10-second intervals) following parental issuance of a command. During 15 subsequent 10-second intervals following each command, there were no differences in compliance to the first and second six commands. Number of commands appear to affect compliance initiation only.

Other studies suggest that number of commands is not related to compliance. Johnson and Lobitz (1974) instructed parents to make their child look "bad" on three days during an observation period and "good" on three other days. Results indicated a significant increase in parental commands on "bad" days but not a corresponding significant increase in noncompliance. In an investigation of observer effects in parent–child interactions, Zegiob and Forehand (1977) also failed to find a decrease in compliance when commands increased. Using a laboratory setting, mothers were observed under informed and uninformed conditions. Relative to the uninformed condition, maternal commands increased significantly during the informed condition but child compliance did not vary significantly across the two conditions.

The inconsistent findings may be explained, at least in part, by the fact that parent behaviors other than commands did not vary across the first and second six commands in the Forehand and Scarboro (1975) study. In contrast, in both the Johnson and Lobitz (1974) and Zegiob and Forehand (1977) investigations, other parent behaviors (e.g., playing interactively in the Zegiob and Forehand study) also varied across experimental conditions, possibly masking an effect of increased commands.

The primary emphasis in analog studies of child compliance has been on parental consequences to child compliance and noncompliance. All of these studies have been conducted in laboratory settings, used a bug-in-the-ear to cue the mother as to how to respond to the child, and used 3- to 6-year-old children. In one study (Toepfer, Reuter, & Maurer, 1972), the effects of contingent maternal reinforcement on child compliance were examined. Two types of reinforcement for compliance were manipulated simultaneously across phases: maternal proximity (within one arm's length) to the child and maternal verbal reinforcement (statements of praise or correctness). Child noncompliance resulted in the mother increasing her distance from the child and withdrawing her attention. Analysis of the data revealed significant increases in maternal proximity and verbal reinforcement during three reinforcement conditions relative to each of two baseline conditions. A session-by-session analysis of compliance indicated that this child's behavior increased significantly above baseline during one of the eight reinforcement sessions, leading the authors to conclude that maternal reinforcement affects child compliance. However, the results at best provide only minimum support for such a conclusion, as only one of eight treatment sessions differed from baseline.

Although the Tropfer *et al.* data are not compelling in terms of the effects of maternal social reinforcement on child compliance, results are available in a laboratory setting to indicate that maternal social reinforcement exerts a significant effect on child behavior other than compliance (Bernhardt & Forehand, 1975). Furthermore, in other settings, such as preschools, teacher attention has been shown to significantly affect child compliance (Goetz, Holmberg, & LeBlanc, 1975).

A series of studies has been conducted by this writer and his colleagues examining the effects of time-out (a period of time in which one or more reinforcers are removed) on child noncompliance to maternal commands. The studies were undertaken after a review of the literature indicated that most investigators utilizing time-out have not employed adequate experimental methodology (Forehand & MacDonough, 1975) and that most parameters of time-out (e.g., location of time-out, contingent vs. noncontingent release from time-out, presence vs. absence of a verbalized reason for the time-out prior to its onset) have not been examined (MacDonough & Forehand, 1973).

Scarboro and Forehand (1975) compared a within-room and an out-of-room time-out procedure. After a baseline, mothers assigned to the within-room procedure were instructed to issue a warning ("If you do not ____, I am not going to play with you for awhile") if the child did not initiate compliance within 5 seconds after a maternal command. If the child did not initiate compliance within 5 seconds after the warning, the mother moved away from the child and withdrew all her attention from him or her for 2 minutes plus a 5-second quiet contingency prior to returning her attention. The procedure for the out-of-room time-out was similar except for the warning ("If you do not ____, I am going to take the toys and leave the room") and the actual time-out administration in which the mother took the toys and left the room for 2 minutes plus a 5-second quiet contingency. During training, mothers in both groups were cued by way of a bug-in-the-ear as to when and how to issue commands and warnings and to implement time-out. Relative to a control group in which the mothers issued the same commands but did not use time-out, both time-out procedures significantly increased compliance to maternal commands. The two procedures did not differentially affect compliance; however, the within-room procedure required significantly more administrations of time-out than the out-of-room procedure, suggesting that the latter is more efficient than the former. Finally, in a posttraining period, without cueing from the experimenter regarding when to issue warnings or implement time-out, the mothers in both time-out groups maintained child compliance at the levels previously achieved during training. The accuracy (i.e., consistency) with which the mothers used time-out following noncompliance during this phase was not examined.

A more recent study (Gardner, Forehand, & Roberts, 1976), using a methodology similar to Scarboro and Forehand (1975), examined the consistency with which mothers used time-out in a posttraining period. Although during the posttraining phase child compliance was maintained at the level achieved during training, mothers used time-out for only 50% of their children's noncompliance. These results suggest that brief training (30 minutes) in time-out is not sufficient to enable parents to consistently use time-out for noncompliance. Nevertheless, at least in a laboratory setting, the consistent use of time-out is not necessary to maintain a previously established high percentage of compliance to maternal commands.

Gardner *et al.* also examined the addition of a verbalized reason ("You did not do what I said, so I am going to take all the toys and not play with you") to time-out in facilitating or inhibiting the effectiveness of time-out in suppressing noncompliance to maternal commands. A comparison of groups receiving time-out only, a verbalized reason followed by time-out, and time-out followed by a verbalized reason failed to reveal any significant differences. However, all three were associated with less noncompliance than a control group for which time-out was not implemented.

Although a verbalized reason does not alter the effectiveness of time-out, studies by Hobbs and Forehand indicate that duration and type of release are important parameters of time-out. In one study (Hobbs, Forehand, & Murray, 1977), children were assigned to either a control group or one of three experimental groups: 10 seconds, 1 minute, or 4 minutes of time-out (standing in a corner) for each noncompliance to a maternal command. Relative to a control group, all three time-out durations were effective in suppressing noncompliance; however, the 4-minute time-out duration was more effective in decelerating noncompliance than the 10-second or 1-minute groups. Furthermore, during a subsequent recovery (return to baseline) period, the noncompliance of the subjects in the 4-minute group remained at a significantly lower level than that of the other two time-out groups.

In a second study, Hobbs and Forehand (1975) found that contingent release from time-out is important when modifying noncompliance. A comparison of contingent release (15 seconds of quiet were required prior to the mother reentering the room in an out-of-room time-out procedure) and noncontingent release (subjects were yoked to those in the contingent release group in terms of length of time-out) groups suggested that less disruption occurred during time-out and less noncompliance to maternal commands occurred outside of time-out for the former than for the latter group.

In contrast to the above studies in which various parameters of time-out were manipulated, Nay (1975) manipulated the method of conveying instructions to mothers implementing time-out for child noncompliance. Four instructional techniques were compared: (a) written presentation, (b) lecture presentation, (c) videotaped modeling presentation, and (d) modeling plus role-playing. All approaches were equally effective as determined by a questionnaire assessment of knowledge of time-out; however, assessment of the parent's ability to correctly apply time-out to audiotaped presented situations that simulated the home environment showed modeling plus role-playing to be superior to either written presentation or lectures, but not to modeling alone. Unfortunately, the assessments used in this study did not provide an actual *in vivo* measure of the parent's ability to use time-out with her child.

Although time-out is an effective procedure for modifying child noncompliance (e.g., Scarboro & Forehand, 1975), recent investigations have examined other techniques that may also be used by parents. In the first of two experiments, Forehand, Roberts, Doleys, Hobbs, and Resick (1976b) examined the effects of negative attention and repeated commands on child noncompliance to parental commands. Negative attention consisted of a verbal reprimand ("You did not do what I said right away; I do not like it when you disobey me") followed by a brief period (1 minute) in which the mother glared intently at the child. The rationale for examining negative attention was that the procedure eliminated the need for a special time-out area and the difficulty in placing and maintaining a child in the area. Repeated commands involved the mother twice reissuing each command to which the child did not comply originally. The rationale for examining this procedure was that informal observations of parent–child interactions suggested that parents frequently repeat commands in an attempt to obtain child compliance, but the effectiveness of the technique is unknown. Parent–child pairs were assigned to one of the following four groups: (a) negative attention, (b) repeated commands, (c) negative attention plus repeated commands, and (d) control (neither negative attention nor repeated commands). Following baseline, the appropriate treatment was implemented for each mother–child pair in each group. The results indicated that the contingent use of negative attention decreased noncompliance of the child, whereas the simple repetition of a command did not serve as an aversive stimulus to decrease noncompliance to subsequent commands.

In the second experiment of the study, negative attention was compared to isolation (out-of-room time-out as defined by Scarboro and Forehand, 1975, and reported above), ignoring (in-room time-out as defined by Scarboro and Forehand), and a combination condition in which isolation, ignoring, and negative attention were used alternately with each mother–child pair in this experimental group. Seven mother–child pairs were assigned to each group, and, as in earlier studies, the mothers issued a series of standard commands to their children. Following three baseline sessions, the respective treatment for each experimental group was implemented for three sessions for child noncompliance. Subsequently, a recovery condition (return to baseline) was implemented for four sessions. Results indicated that each of the four treatment procedures significantly reduced noncompliance from baseline levels; however, negative attention was associated with a lower level of noncompliance than ignoring during recovery, whereas the combination condition was the only procedure that maintained noncompliance at the treatment level during recovery. These findings indicate that negative attention may be a feasible disciplinary procedure for child noncompliance. The effectiveness of the combination condition suggests that it is not necessary to consistently use one type of discipline to suppress noncompliance. Neither the effects of negative attention nor a combination of disciplinary procedures have been examined with parents and their noncompliant children outside a laboratory setting.

In summary, the results from analog studies provide support for the hypothesis that time-out is an effective procedure for child noncompliance to parental commands. Furthermore, data support the use of certain parameters or types of time-out, such as contingent release from time-out and time-out durations above 1 minute. In addition, isolation of the child may not be necessary, since simply ignoring the child is effective, at least in an analog setting. One other aversive consequent procedure, negative attention, also is effective in suppressing noncompliance. The data examining the effectiveness of parental social reinforcement with child compliance are less compelling than the data supporting the effectiveness of time-out. Finally, consistent data demonstrating a negative relationship between number of commands and child compliance have not been reported.

VI. OUTCOME STUDIES

A number of studies have been conducted to examine the effects of behavioral treatment on children labeled as noncompliant by their parents. In the majority of these studies, both positive reinforcement for compliance and time-out for noncompliance were used. For review purposes, investigations have been grouped into the following categories: (a) studies in which treatment of noncompliance was undertaken in a clinic (laboratory) setting and outcome measures were restricted to the clinic setting; (b) studies in which treatment was undertaken in a clinic setting but outcome measures were collected in the home; and (c) studies in which intervention was conducted in the home and outcome measures were recorded in the home. The relative merits of studies in these three categories are debatable; however, the contribution of those studies in which outcome measures are recorded only in the clinic is questionable, especially as Forehand, Wells, and Sturgis (1977) have demonstrated that compliance in a clinic setting is not an effective predictor of compliance in the home. Treatment in the clinic is advantageous over treatment in the home in terms of efficiency; however, effectiveness of treatment is probably the more critical factor at this time.

A. Clinic Treatment and Clinic Outcome Measures

In one of the earliest studies, Wahler, Winkel, Peterson, and Morrison (1965, Case 3) taught a mother in a laboratory setting to ignore noncompliance and reinforce compliance with a smile and praise. This procedure failed to produce a substantial and stable increase in compliance; consequently, a five-minute isolation was imposed for noncompliance while compliance continued to be reinforced. A marked increase in the child's compliance occurred. Subsequent conditions of reinforcement for noncompliance and then reinforcement for compliance were associated with decreases in compliance, whereas a final condition of reinforcement for compliance and isolation for noncompliance again increased the target behavior. Green, Budd, Johnson, Lang, Pinkston, and Rudd (1976, Study 2) reported a similar finding in that ignoring noncompliant behavior was ineffective whereas a time-out condition did reduce such behavior. It should be noted that both of these studies contradict the conclusion reached in the preceding section that ignoring is effective in reducing noncompliance.

Whereas the studies by Wahler *et al.* (1965) and Green *et al.* (1976, Study 2) involved the manipulation of consequences for compliance and noncompliance, several studies have dealt with both parental antecedents and consequences to compliance and noncompliance. Budd, Baer, and Green (1974) examined the effects of decelerating each of the following maternal behaviors: (a) repetition of instructions, (b) instructions contingent on inappropriate child behavior, (c) physical intervention which preempted the child's opportunity to comply, and (d) physical and verbal prompts. The first two procedures had little effect on the child's correct response to the mother's instructions, whereas the third procedure accelerated correct responding to instructions and the fourth procedure maintained the increased percentage of compliance. Subsequently, a 3-minute time-out was instituted for noncompliance. This procedure increased correct responding to parent instructions to almost 100%. These results suggest that simply allowing a child sufficient time to comply can increase compliance rate; however, the use of a parent consequence, such as time-out, for noncompliance is most effective. In another study examining the effects of parent's antecedents and consequences to compliance, Mash and Terdal (1973) reported an increase in child compliance after five groups of 8–10 parents were trained to reduce the number of commands they issued and to increase their positive social reinforcement for child compliance.

Hanf (1972) has devised a systematic parent training program incorporating, among other things, a reduction in parental commands and an increase in parental social reinforcement for compliance. The treatment program consists of two phases. During the reinforcement phase of treatment (Phase I) the parent is taught to be a more effective reinforcing agent by increasing the frequency and range of his or her social rewards and by reducing verbal behavior, such as commands and criticisms, which is associated with deviant child behavior (Johnson & Lobitz, 1974). First, the parent is taught to attend to the child's behavior. Moreover, he or she is taught to reduce the number of commands, questions, and criticisms directed to the child. Subsequently, the parent is taught how to use rewards contingent on compliance and other appropriate child behavior. Throughout Phase I, the use of contingent attention to increase child compliance and other behaviors that the parent considers desirable is emphasized. The parent is required to develop programs for use outside the clinic to increase several child behaviors using the laboratory-acquired reinforcement skills.

The second phase of the treatment program (Phase II) consists of training the parent to use a time-out procedure to decrease noncompliant behavior exhibited by the child. The parent is trained to give direct, concise commands and to allow the child sufficient time to comply. If compliance is initiated within 5 seconds of the command, the parent is taught to reward the child. If compliance is not initiated, the parent is trained to use a time-out procedure consisting of a warning, placing the child in time-out in a corner if he or she does not comply to the warning, and using two quick spanks to punish the child for leaving the chair. The child is required to remain in the chair for approximately 2 minutes. Subsequently, he or she is returned to the uncompleted task and the initial command is repeated. Compliance is followed by contingent attention from the parent. The parent also develops a list of nonclinic situations in which child noncompliance occurs. He or she is instructed how to use the time-out technique in each setting to reduce the noncompliant child behavior.

Reinforcement and time-out skills in the Hanf program are taught to parents by way of didactic instruction, modeling, and role-playing. In addition, the parent practices the skills in a laboratory setting with his or her child and receives prompting and feedback from a therapist by way of a bug-in-the-ear.

Using the program, Hanf and Kling (1973) have altered the interactions between 40 pairs of mothers and their severely physically handicapped, noncompliant children. A comparison of baseline to treatment data indicated that mothers significantly increased their use of verbal rewards and decreased their use of commands and questions. In addition, there was a significant increase in child compliance. All gains were maintained at a 3-month follow-up. Similar success was reported by Forehand and King (1974) in the treatment of eight noncompliant preschool children and by Forehand, Cheney, and Yoder (1974) in the treatment of a noncompliant deaf child and his mother.

Forehand and King (1977) subsequently used the program developed by Hanf in the treatment of 11 physically normal, preschool children and their mothers. Parent attitude measures as well as observational data on the mother–child interaction in the clinic were obtained prior to and after treatment. Results indicated that after treatment the mothers used significantly more rewards and fewer commands and questions than prior to treatment. In addition, the children complied significantly more after treatment. Attitude changes also occurred from pre- to posttreatment as mothers perceived their children as better adjusted after treatment. Both the behavior and attitudinal gains were maintained at a 3-month follow-up. Relative to a nonclinic normal sample, the treated children were less compliant prior to treatment and more compliant after treatment. Furthermore, prior to treatment, parents of the treated children perceived their children as less well adjusted than parents of the nonclinic children. However, following treatment, the two groups of parents did not differ significantly in their perception of their children. These studies suggest the feasibility of this particular parent training program for the modification of child noncompliance. Data presented in the following section indicate that the results produced in the clinic setting generalize to the home.

Three studies have been reported in which different strategies to modify noncompliance were compared. Green *et al.* (1976) reported three single subject studies in which a different training procedure was used in each to modify noncompliance. An examination of each study revealed that each of the training procedures (written and verbal instructions, instructions plus cueing, and modeling) was successful in teaching parents to use reinforcement and time-out techniques to modify child noncompliance. However, in terms of professional intervention time, the authors recommended the written and verbal instructions training procedure as the most efficient.

In two additional studies, two training procedures to modify noncompliance were compared. In contrast to the previous investigations reviewed in this section, both of these studies taught child management skills to groups of parents rather than to individual parents. Glogower and Sloop (1976) compared a group of four mothers (who read a book on social learning principles, received instructions on how to modify specific target behaviors, and received lectures on behavior management principles) to a second group of four mothers who received the first and second components, but not the lectures, of the first group's treatment. All mothers were parents of behavior problem children. The results indicated that from pre- to posttreatment laboratory observations, children in the first group increased in percentage of compliance to maternal commands whereas children in the second group decreased in percentage of compliance. Only mothers in the first group increased their use of praise for compliance from pre- to posttreatment. As a result of the small sample size and the authors' failure to subject their data to statistical analysis, these results can only be viewed as suggestive.

Tavormina (1975) compared the effectiveness of behavioral counseling groups and reflexive counseling groups in modifying, among other behaviors, child and maternal compliance. The former groups were taught how to apply principles of operant conditioning for problems presented by their children, whereas the latter groups received training in Ginott's (1959) principles of reflecting feelings, setting appropriate limits, and providing appropriate alternate activities. Comparing pre- to posttreatment mother–child interactions, Tavormina found that the behavioral groups increased in number of compliances relative to the reflexive group. It should be noted that Tavormina scored and analyzed together both child compliance to maternal commands and maternal compliance to child commands, thus making it impossible to examine child compliance alone.

The studies reviewed in this section indicate that when both treatment and outcome measures of treatment effectiveness are conducted in a clinic setting, child compliance to maternal commands can be increased. In all the studies reviewed, more than one treatment procedure (usually positive reinforcement for compliance and time-out for noncompliance) was used. In some studies, only parental consequences were manipulated, whereas in others both parent antecedents and consequences were altered.

B. Clinic Treatment and Home Outcome Measures

Although studies in the preceding section provide evidence that child compliance can be modified in a laboratory setting, the failure to assess whether concomitant changes occurred in the home makes an evaluation of their effectiveness difficult. The studies reviewed in this section used a clinic setting to effect change but assessed changes in compliance in the home.

Using the program developed by Hanf (described in the preceding section), Peed, Roberts, and Forehand (1977) compared six mother–child pairs placed on a waiting list (control group) to six treated mother–child pairs. Five 40-minute pretreatment, five 40-minute posttreatment home observations, and three 20-minute pre- and posttreatment clinic observations were made by independent observers for each mother–child pair in the treatment group. Similar observations were made at the same intervals for the waiting-list control group. Significant increases in child compliance, parental positive statements, and parental use of verbal rewards contingent on compliance occurred from pre- to posttreatment assessment in both the clinic setting and in the home for the treatment group. In both settings, a decrease occurred in the number of parental commands to which there was no opportunity for child compliance because the commands were vague, were interrupted by parental verbage, or were complied to by the parent. The control group did not demonstrate changes in any of the target behaviors during their waiting-list period. Parent attitude measures were also administered to both the treatment and waiting-list control groups. From pre- to posttreatment, positive changes in the parents' perception of their children occurred for *both* groups, suggesting that parent attitude measures may show changes when, in fact, behavioral changes in either parent or child behavior have not occurred.

Forehand, Sturgis, Aguar, Beggs, Green, McMahon, and Wells (1976c) reported data for 10 mother–child pairs in an investigation of generality of treatment effects resulting from training parents to modify child noncompliance using the Hanf program. Independent observers assessed treatment effectiveness. At a 6-month follow-up, the mother and child behavior changes that occurred with treatment (see Peed *et al.* study reported above for the behaviors) were maintained in the home setting. Positive changes in parental attitudes toward children were also maintained. In addition, modification of child compliance in the clinic and home was not associated with any systematic changes in noncompliance and other inappropriate behaviors in the school for five children (for whom four school observations were made both prior to and after the parent training occurred). Finally, modification of child noncompliance was associated with a significant reduction in other inappropriate child behaviors, such as destruction, whining, and crying in the home.

Two other studies (Goocher & Grove, 1976; Reisinger, Frangia, & Hoffman, 1976) reported successful changes in child compliance in the home resulting from parent training in the clinic. Both these studies used independent observers to assess treatment outcome and both collected follow-up measures. Goocher and Grove (1976) trained one set of parents to modify noncompliance of their son by use of positive and negative consequences. The child complied to 37%, 82%, and 70% of the commands issued to him prior to treatment, after treatment, and at a 5-month follow-up, respectively. A similar increase occurred from pre- to posttreatment in positive consequences that the child received for compliance. This change was maintained at follow-up. Reisinger *et al.* (1976) reported that after six mothers were trained in a clinic setting in the use of differential reinforcement, they effectively used the procedures in the home setting to modify noncompliance as evaluated at a 12-month follow-up. These data are somewhat questionable since no pretreatment data were collected in the home. However, it is interesting to note that the three mothers who reported marital difficulties were less effective than the remaining three mothers in the use of differential reinforcement during the follow-up home observations.

Two studies (Brockway & Williams, 1976; Brown, Gamboa, Birkimer, & Brown, 1976) have appeared in which independent observers did not collect the home observational data. Both studies reported positive outcomes in the home resulting from training parents in a clinic setting to modify child noncompliance. However, only parent-recorded data, which have been shown by several investigators to be unreliable (for a review, see Patterson, Cobb, & Ray, 1973), were collected in the home and used to evaluate treatment effectiveness. Furthermore, Brockway and Williams trained only one family and achieved only a small percentage increase in compliance from baseline (mean of 79%) to treatment (mean of 85%). The high percentage of compliance during baseline in this study raises the question of whether noncompliance was even a behavior problem of the treated child.

Three investigators have failed to find changes in child compliance in the home after training individual parents to modify the behavior in a clinic setting. In two of the studies, instructions or parent retraining produced generality of results to the home, whereas in the third study the presence of the observer in the home inhibited a realistic assessment. Johnson and Green (1975, Experiment 2), reporting additional data for a mother–child pair described by Green *et al.* (1976), provided a mother with written instructions on the use of time-out. Instructions resulted in a marked reduction in the clinic in child negative verbal and physical responses that opposed parental requirements and in parental attention to such noncompliant behavior. However, negative responses failed to change in the home when the time-out program was implemented in the clinic. Subsequent instructions to the mother to use time-out in the home reduced noncompliance in that setting. The reduction was maintained at each of three follow-up checks over the next 3 months.

Sajwaj (1973) reported that training a mother in a clinic setting to modify her son's disobedience by praising compliance and ignoring noncompliance was ineffective in changing the child's behavior at home. The mother decreased her attention to the child's appropriate as well as inappropriate behaviors in the home, producing an increase in the child's noncompliant behavior. However, subsequent training of the mother in the use of time-out in the clinic did reduce disobedience in the home.

Finally, Moore and Bailey (1973) trained a mother to increase compliance in a clinic setting by the contingent use of social approval ("That's just great") and disapproval ("No, you're not doing what I asked you to do"). In the clinic setting, the mother was initially cued as to when and how to respond to the child and, subsequently, she responded without cueing. Under both cueing and no cueing conditions, the mother was effective in modifying compliance first to preacademic tasks and then to social requests. However, assessment of changes in child compliance in the home was not possible as the parents "never appeared to adapt to the observers and therefore never interacted normally" (p. 506).

These three studies (Johnson & Green, 1975; Moore & Bailey, 1973; Sajwaj, 1973) delineate several difficulties when modifying child compliance in a clinic setting and assessing generality to the home. First, generality to the home of changes in child compliance will not occur unless the parent implements his or her behavior management skills in the home. Second, the presence of an observer may well change the parent's and/or child's behavior.

In all the preceding studies reported in this section, individual parents or sets of parents were trained to modify child noncompliance. Several studies have utilized group procedures to convey behavior change techniques to parents of noncompliant children. In a recent description of a group parent training program designed to modify child noncompliance, Tams and Eyberg (1976) presented several advantages of group procedures over individual parent training procedures: (a) a decrease in cost in professional time; (b) a decrease in the waiting period for clients; (c) a sharing of experiences; and (d) an awareness that others are experiencing similar difficulties. In a study comparing group versus individual parent training procedures, Kovitz (1976) found that the two methodologies were equally effective. However, collection of only parent-recorded data in the home, use of a small sample of subjects, and the apparent absence of baseline data limit the conclusions of the study.

Mash, Lazere, Terdal, and Garner (1973) used modeling procedures to train a group of three parents. A fourth parent who had previously undergone behavioral training for modifying child noncompliance served as the model by interacting with her child during each session. This modeling procedure plus group discussion of behavior modification principles and their application to children were associated with an increase in child compliance in the clinic for all three children and in the home for two of the children. Unfortunately, only one brief pre- and posttreatment home observation was conducted.

Patterson and his colleagues (e.g., Patterson *et al.*, 1973) have also used group procedures to modify child behavior problems. As mentioned previously, in most of his papers, Patterson (e.g., Patterson, 1974; Patterson & Reid, 1973) has not analyzed noncompliance separately from other behavior problems. The group procedures used are described in detail by Patterson *et al.* (1973). In that contribution, an example of a procedure used to deal with noncompliance is described in which the effectiveness of time-out for noncompliance and parental attention contingent on less than two noncompliances per day is demonstrated.

In an attempt to replicate Patterson's work, Ferber, Keeley, and Shemberg (1974) presented, among other data, compliance to maternal and paternal commands for five children whose parents were trained with procedures utilized by Patterson. Ten baseline observations, two observations per week during treatment, and five follow-up observations were made on each family. Child compliance to maternal commands increased during treatment for all five children and continued above baseline for four of the five at a 2-month follow-up. Child compliance to paternal commands increased during treatment for two of four children for whom data were collected. Follow-up data for fathers were not reported. Based on both the behavioral data and several measurement and methodological difficulties (e.g., reactivity to the observer), the authors concluded their treatment was not successful.

Using lectures and discussions on behavior modification principles, staff demonstrations, and homework assignments, Brubakken, Derouin, and Greuter (1974) also examined the effectiveness of group procedures on training parents to modify child noncompliance. One 3-hour pre- and posttreatment home observation was conducted. One child demonstrated an increase in compliance from pre- to posttreatment assessment in the home, whereas one decreased in compliance and one failed to change. Use of parental reinforcement for compliance in the home did not appear to be associated with changes that occurred since the parents of the child who increased in compliance decreased in number of contingent reinforcements delivered for compliance, whereas parents of the child who decreased in compliance demonstrated a substantial increase in frequency of contingent reinforcement. These data support findings mentioned previously (Wahler *et al.*, 1965) in that positive reinforcement alone often is not sufficient to modify compliance of clinic-referred children. Brubakken *et al.* (1974) reported that they recorded parental use of punishment and time-out. However, no data regarding the use of these procedures were presented. The absence of such data suggests that after treatment the parents probably rarely employed these aversive consequences, which may account for the findings of the study.

The conclusions that can be reached when treatment of noncompliance occurs in a clinic and the measurement of such behavior occurs in the home are less clear-cut than those in which both treatment and measurement occur in the clinic. Some investigators (e.g., Brubakken *et al.*, 1974) have failed to produce systematic changes in child compliance in the home. Others have relied on parent reports of changes in child compliance in the home (e.g., Brockway & Williams, 1976) or have collected less than adequate home measures (Mash *et al.*, 1973). In one study (Ferber *et al.*, 1974), positive changes in child compliance were reported. However, these investigators were less than optimistic about the overall effectiveness of their treatment. In some studies (e.g., Peed *et al.*, 1977), increases in compliance in the home were reported as a result of treatment, whereas in others (Sajwaj, 1973) parent retraining was necessary in order to promote generality of behavior change to the home. Training of parents in a clinic is certainly efficient in terms of therapist time; however, unless it is also systematically effective, efficiency counts for little.

C. Home Treatment and Home Outcome Measures

In order to circumvent the problem of generalization of treatment effects from the clinic to the home, some investigators have directly intervened in the home. Zeilberger, Sampen, and Sloane (1968) reported cueing a mother in the home to reinforce compliance to instructions and to use time-out for disobedience. Relative to preceding baselines, this treatment procedure increased the percentage of instructions followed during each of two treatment conditions.

In another study, Wahler (1969a) taught each of two sets of

parents to modify noncompliance by the use of time-out for such behavior and positive reinforcement for compliance. Using reversal designs, the procedure effectively decreased each child's noncompliance to parental requests each time treatment was implemented. As a beneficial side effect, Wahler found that parental reinforcement value for the children was higher during treatment than during baseline.

In a subsequent study, Wahler and Nordquist (1973, Experiment 1) trained a parent in the home to use procedures similar to those described above (Wahler, 1969a) to effectively modify her child's noncompliance. In this case, the authors measured and found changes in the child's imitation of the parent: More imitation of the parent occurred during treatment periods than during baseline periods. Wahler and Nordquist concluded that compliance and imitation were members of a common response class in that changes in the frequency of child compliance were associated with concomitant changes in imitative behavior. In a more recent study, Wahler (1975) pursued the response class notion by training a set of parents to modify noncompliance in the home and by observing the changes in other behaviors of the child (e.g., social interaction with adults and sustained toy play). Treatment of the child's noncompliance was accompanied by changes in other behaviors. Only changes in noncompliance from baseline to treatment conditions were accompanied by systematic changes in parent responses, suggesting that generalization of parent behavior to nontreated responses was not the critical variable affecting these child behaviors. This suggests that treatment of noncompliance by parents may result in systematic changes in nontreated child behaviors.

Apparently, treatment of other deviant child behaviors can also affect noncompliance. Inspection of data collected by Barloon, Johnson, and Whitman (1975), who used treatment procedures similar to Wahler, suggests that deceleration by the mother and father of a child's bizarre vocalizations in the home was associated with decreases in child noncompliance. Similarly, Lavigueur (1976) reported that training a parent to treat negative verbalizations by ignoring and time-out was associated with decreases in noncompliance, even though inappropriate parental attention to noncompliance continued to occur. It would appear that child noncompliance in the home is a behavior that is functionally related to other child behaviors. At this stage, it is important to measure other child behaviors when training a parent to modify noncompliance. Hopefully, behaviors that systematically covary with noncompliance can be identified.

In addition to generalization of treatment from compliance to other behaviors, modification of noncompliance in the home may also result in generality of treatment effects across settings and across siblings. Wahler (1969b) monitored two children, their parents at home, and the teacher and children at school during baseline, home treatment, and treatment at both home and school. During treatment at home, each set of parents modified their child's noncompliance by the use of reinforcement and time-out. During this same phase, the teachers' attention to appropriate child behaviors remained at baseline levels. Each child's behavior at school did not change—that is, no setting generality was observed. When the teachers' responses to each child's behavior were modified in the final phase of treatment, the children's behavior at school also improved.

In a subsequent study, Wahler (1975) trained a set of parents to treat the behavior problems of their child and, subsequently, examined the covariation between the child's home and school behaviors across experimental phases. In each of two home treatment phases, the child's noncompliance in the home decreased from preceding baseline levels, whereas his noncompliance and peer interactions at school increased. No consistent changes in the school environment were found to account for the behavior changes in school. At 1- and 2-year follow-ups, noncompliance remained low at home. Peer interactions, but not increased noncompliance, were maintained at school.

Regarding generality of treatment effects across siblings, Resick, Forehand, and McWhorter (1976) trained a mother to use praise for compliance and time-out for noncompliance to modify the task completion times of her child. The effect on the task completion times of a sibling, who was present during treatment of his brother, was examined. Similarity of tasks assigned to siblings and the time at which the tasks occurred were important determinants of the effects on the untreated child. When the tasks were similar in terms of content, location of performance, and time of assignment, parental treatment of one child was associated with an immediate positive change (i.e., a decrease in task performance time) in the untreated child. When tasks differed in content and location of performance, but were assigned simultaneously, the untreated child's behavior change was neither immediate nor durable. Furthermore, when the content, location, and time of task assignment differed for the two children, parental treatment of the target child was associated with a negative behavior change (i.e., an increase in task performance time) by the untreated sibling.

Results of training parents in the home to treat noncompliance are positive in that all the studies reviewed indicated that time-out plus differential reinforcement are effective procedures for increasing compliance. Experimental designs also have been sufficiently rigorous to allow the systematic assessment of side effects that may occur when noncompliance is modified. It would appear, at least in some instances, that when noncompliance is modified in the home, systematic changes can occur in other behaviors of the child (Wahler, 1975), other settings (Wahler, 1975), and siblings of the child (Resick *et al.,* 1976). Furthermore, modification of other deviant child behaviors can result in changes in child compliance (Lavigueur, 1976).

Comparing across treatment and assessment settings, one would conclude that decreases in noncompliance in the home can best be affected by training parents in the home. Noncompliance can be modified in the clinic laboratory setting. However, in most studies in which generalization to the home was measured, adequate measurement of or changes in noncompliance failed to occur in the home.

VII. ETHICAL ISSUES

The studies reviewed in the two preceding sections indicate that noncompliance of children can be modified by parents. However, it should be noted that two ethical issues exist regarding compliance which should be considered. First, compliance is by no means a uniformly accepted positive quality of human beings. For example, while illustrating that obedience is a basic element in the structure of life, Milgram (1974) has found a level of compliance that he labels "disturbing." As he states, under certain conditions "good" people obey the demands of authority and perform actions that are callous and severe. Along a somewhat different line, Eisler, Miller, and Hersen (1973) have incorporated noncompliance as an important and positive component of assertive behavior in adults. These investigators, as well as most people in general, contend that the ability to say "no" to certain demands from others is a positive attribute. The relationship of child compliance to adult compliance is uncertain at this time.

Second, teaching parents to increase compliance should involve monitoring and training of parents by the therapists in regard to the kind of commands to be given, the proper use of contingencies, and parental expectations for percentage of child compliance. For example, although unlikely, it is conceivable that parents may use their behavior modification skills to obtain compliance to deviant or morally undesirable commands. Similarly, regarding the proper use of contingencies, parents may effectively reduce noncompliance by leaving a child in time-out most of the day. Regarding parental expectations, parents may expect 100% compliance from their children. The normative data that have been collected and the realistic concern of parents overcontrolling their children (Peterson, 1976) would make such a goal unrealistic and harmful. Hopefully, these examples rarely occur; however, the important issue is that therapists should be sensitive to their occurrence and incorporate didactic modeling and other instructional procedures into their training programs to prevent their occurrence. As Risley *et al.* (1976) have eloquently stated, our goal should not be to develop quiet, docile children, but rather to enhance the pleasure and significance of family interactions for all members of the family. Enhancing the pleasure of child as well as adult family members is an important goal. In addition, children's legal rights are receiving increasing attention, as evidenced by an upcoming Supreme Court decision (see APA Monitor, June, 1976) regarding the legal rights of children versus the prerogatives of their parents.

VIII. CONCLUDING COMMENTS

A number of areas have been described and discussed in this review of child noncompliance to parental commands. In general, noncompliance has been a child behavior problem that has been addressed by many investigators in many different ways. Obviously, it is difficult to draw conclusions across investigations, especially when the definition of the target behavior has varied. Nevertheless, one would seem justified in concluding that manipulation of parental antecedent and consequence behaviors is a sufficient condition to modify child noncompliance. Conclusions regarding norms for compliance and ethical guidelines in training parents to modify such behavior are less clear-cut. Not surprisingly, researchers using behavior modification with other problems and populations (e.g., retarded individuals) are facing similar difficulties regarding the establishment of ethical guidelines and normative data. Continual attempts to address such issues, as well as to expand and refine our modification procedures in the area of child noncompliance to parental commands hopefully will facilitate our understanding of both children and parent–child relationships and lead to improvements in the interactional systems of families.

ACKNOWLEDGMENTS

Appreciation is expressed to Beverly Atkeson and Karen Wells for their helpful comments on an earlier version of this chapter.

REFERENCES

Barloon, R., Johnson, M. R., & Whitman, T. L. *A home-based program for a pre-school aged behaviorally disturbed child with mother and father as therapist.* Paper read at the Midwestern Association of Behavior Analysis, Chicago, 1975.

Berkowitz, B. P., & Graziano, A. M. Training parents as behavior therapists: A review. *Behaviour Research and Therapy,* 1972, **10**, 297–317.

Bernal, M. E., Kreutzer, S. L., North, J. A., & Pelc, R. E. *Scoring system for home and school.* Paper read at the American Psychological Association. Montreal, August, 1973.

Bernhardt, A., & Forehand, R. The effects of labeled and unlabeled praise upon lower and middle class children. *Journal of Experimental Child Psychology,* 1975, **19**, 536–543.

Brockway, B. S., & Williams, W. W. Training in child management: A prevention-oriented model. In E. J. Mash, L. C. Handy & L. A. Hamerlynck (Eds.), *Behavior modification approaches to parenting.* New York: Brunner/Mazel, 1976. Pp. 19–35.

Brown, J. H., Gamboa, A. M., Birkimer, J., & Brown, R. Some positive effects of parent self-control training on parent-child interactions. In E. J. Mash, L. C. Handy, & L. A. Hamerlynck (Eds.), *Behavior modification approaches to parenting.* New York: Brunner/Mazel, 1976. Pp. 180–192.

Brubakken, D. M., Derouin, J., & Greuter, J. L. *Assessing parent training utilizing a behavioral index of parent-child interactions.* Paper read at the American Psychological Association, New Orleans, September, 1974.

Budd, K. S., Baer, D. M., & Green, D. R. *An analysis of multiple misplaced social contingencies in the mother of a preschool child.* Paper read at the American Psychological Association, New Orleans, September, 1974.

Christophersen, E. R., Barnard, J. D., Ford, D., & Wolf, M. M. The family training program: Improving parent-child interaction patterns. In E. J. Mash, L. C. Handy & L. A. Hamerlynck (Eds.), *Behavior modification approaches to parenting.* New York: Brunner/Mazel, 1976. Pp. 36–56.

Delfini, L. F., Bernal, M. E., & Rosen, P. M. Comparison of deviant and normal boys in home settings. In E. J. Mash, L. A. Hamerlynck, & L. C. Handy (Eds.), *Behavior modification and families.* New York: Brunner/Mazel, 1976. Pp. 228–248.

Doleys, D. M., Cartelli, L. M., & Doster, J. Comparison of patterns of mother-child interaction. *Journal of Learning Disabilities,* 1976, **9**, 42–46.

Eisler, R. M., Miller, P. M., & Hersen, M. Components of assertive behavior. *Journal of Clinical Psychology,* 1973, **29**, 295–299.

Eyberg, S. M., & Johnson, S. M. Multiple assessment of behavior modification with families: Effects of contingency contracting and order of treated problems. *Journal of Consulting and Clinical Psychology,* 1974, **42,** 594–606.

Ferber, H., Keeley, S. M., & Shemberg, K. M. Training parents in behavior modification: Outcome of and problems encountered in a program after Patterson's work. *Behavior Therapy,* 1974, **5,** 415–419.

Forehand, R., Cheney, T., & Yoder, P. Parent behavior training: Effects on the non-compliance of a deaf child. *Journal of Behavior Therapy and Experimental Psychiatry,* 1974, **5,** 281–283.

Forehand, R., & King, H. E. Pre-school children's noncompliance: Effects of short-term behavior therapy. *Journal of Community Psychology,* 1974, **2,** 42–44.

Forehand, R., & King, H. E. Noncompliant children: Effects of parent training on behavior and attitude change. *Behavior Modification,* 1977, **1,** 93–108.

Forehand, R., King, H. E., Peed, S., & Yoder, P. Mother-child interactions: Comparisons of a noncompliant clinic group and a non-clinic group. *Behaviour Research and Therapy,* 1975, **13,** 79–84. (a)

Forehand, R., Peed, S., & Roberts, M. *Coding manual for scoring mother-child interactions.* Unpublished manuscript, University of Georgia, 1975. (b)

Forehand, R., & MacDonough, T. S. Response contingent time out: An examination of outcome data. *European Journal of Behavioural Analysis and Modification,* 1975, **1,** 109–115.

Forehand, R., & Scarboro, M. E. An analysis of children's oppositional behavior. *Journal of Abnormal Child Psychology,* 1975, **3,** 27–31.

Forehand, R., Gardner, H. L., & Roberts, M. W. *Maternal response to child compliance and noncompliance: Some normative data.* Unpublished manuscript, University of Georgia, 1976. (a)

Forehand, R., Roberts, M. W., Doleys, D. M., Hobbs, S. A., & Resick, P. A. An examination of disciplinary procedures with children. *Journal of Experimental Child Psychology,* 1976, **21,** 109–120. (b)

Forehand, R., Sturgis, E., Aguar, D., Beggs, V., Green, K., McMahon, R., & Wells, K. *Generality of treatment effects resulting from a parent-training program to modify child noncompliance.* Paper read at the Association for Advancement of Behavior Therapy, New York, December, 1976. (c)

Forehand, R., Wells, K. C., & Sturgis, E. T. Predictors of child deviant behavior in the home. *Journal of Consulting and Clinical Psychology,* 1977, in press.

Gardner, H. L., Forehand, R., & Roberts, M. Timeout with children: Effects of an explanation and brief parent training on child and parent behaviors. *Journal of Abnormal Child Psychology,* 1976, **4,** 277–288.

Ginott, H. G. *Between parent and child.* New York: Avon, 1959.

Glogower, F., & Sloop, E. W. Two strategies of group training of parents as effective behavior modifiers. *Behavior Therapy,* 1976, **7,** 177–184.

Goetz, E. M., Holmberg, M. C., & LeBlanc, J. M. Differential reinforcement of other behavior and noncontingent reinforcement as control procedures during the modification of a proschooler's compliance. *Journal of Applied Behavior Analysis,* 1975, **8,** 77–82.

Goocher, B. E., & Grove, D. N. A model for training parents to manage their family systems using multiple data sources as measures of parent effectness. In E. J. Marh, L. C. Handy, & L. A. Hamerlynck (Eds.), *Behavior modification approaches to parenting.* New York: Brunner/Mazel, 1976. Pp. 57–74.

Green, D. R., Budd, K., Johnson, M., Lang, S., Pinkston, E., & Rudd, S. Training parents to modify child behaviors. In E. J. Mash, L. C. Handy, & L. A. Hamerlynck (Eds.), *Behavior modification approaches to parenting.* New York: Brunner/Mazel, 1976. Pp. 3–18.

Hanf, C. *Facilitating parent-child interaction: A two-stage procedure.* Unpublished manuscript, University of Oregon Medical School, 1972.

Hanf, C., & Kling, J. *Facilitating parent-child interaction: A two stage training model.* Unpublished manuscript, University of Oregon Medical School, 1973.

Hobbs, S. A., & Forehand, R. Effects of differential release from time-out on children's deviant behavior. *Journal of Behavior Therapy and Experimental Psychiatry,* 1975, **6**, 256–257.

Hobbs, S. A., Forehand, R., & Murray, R. G. Effects of various durations of timeout on the non-compliant behavior of children. *Behavior Therapy,* 1977, in press.

Holmes, R., The psychology of authority. In C. O. Rhodes (Ed.), *Authority in a changing society.* London: Constable Press, 1969. Pp. 16–27.

Johansson, S. *Compliance and noncompliance in young children.* Unpublished doctoral dissertation, University of Oregon, 1971.

Johnson, C. A., & Katz, R. C. Using parents as change agents for their children: A review. *Journal of Child Psychology and Psychiatry,* 1973, **14**, 181–200.

Johnson, M. R., & Green, D. R. *Effectiveness and durability of written instructions: Parental application of differential attention and time out for undesirable behaviors in children.* Unpublished manuscript, University of Notre Dame, 1975.

Johnson, S. M. Personal communication, August 5, 1975.

Johnson, S. M., & Lobitz, G. K. Parental manipulation of child behavior in home observations. *Journal of Applied Behavior Analysis,* 1974, **7**, 23–31.

Johnson, S. M., Wahl, G., Martin, S., & Johansson, S. How deviant is the normal child? A behavioral analysis of the preschool child and his family. In R. D. Rubin, J. P. Brady, & J. D. Henderson (Eds.), *Advances in behavior therapy* (Vol. 4). New York: Academic Press, 1973. Pp. 37–54.

Kagan, J., & Moss, H. A. *Birth to maturity, a study in psychological development.* New York: Wiley, 1962.

Kovitz, K. E. Comparing group and individual methods for training parents in child management techniques. In E. J. Mash, L. C. Handy, & L. A. Hamerlynck (Eds.), *Behavior modification approaches to parenting.* New York: Brunner/Mazel, 1976. Pp. 124–138.

Landauer, T. K., Carlsmith, J. M., & Lepper, M. Experimental analysis of the factors determining obedience of four-year-old children to adult females. *Child Development,* 1970, **41**, 601–611.

Lavigueur, H. The use of siblings as an adjunct to the behavioral treatment of children in the home with parents as therapists. *Behavior Therapy,* 1976, **7**, 602–613.

Lobitz, G. K., & Johnson, S. M. Normal versus deviant children: A multimethod comparison. *Journal of Abnormal Child Psychology,* 1977, in press.

MacDonough, T. S., & Forehand, R. Response-contingent time out: Important parameters in behavior modification with children. *Journal of Behavior Therapy and Experimental Psychiatry,* 1973, **4**, 231–236.

Mash, E. J., Lazere, R., Terdal, L., & Garner. A. Modification of mother-child interactions: A modeling approach for groups. *Child Study Journal,* 1973, **3**, 131–143.

Mash, E. J., & Terdal, L. Modification of mother-child interactions: Playing with children. *Mental Retardation,* 1973, **11**, 44–49.

Milgram, S. *Obedience to authority.* New York: Harper, 1974.

Moore, B. L., & Bailey, J. S. Social punishment in the modification of a preschool child's "autistic-like" behavior with mother as therapist. *Journal of Applied Behavior Analysis,* 1973, **6,** 497–507.

Nay, W. R. A systematic comparison of instructional techniques for parents. *Behavior Therapy,* 1975, **6,** 14–21.

O'Dell, S. Training parents in behavior modification: A review. *Psychological Bulletin,* 1974, **81,** 418–433.

Patterson, G. R. Interventions for boys with conduct problems: Multiple settings, treatments, and criteria. *Journal of Consulting and Clinical Psychology,* 1974, **42,** 471–481.

Patterson, G. R. The aggressive child: Victim and architect of a coercive system. In E. J. Mash, L. A. Hamerlynck, & L. C. Handy (Eds.), *Behavior modification and families.* New York: Brunner/Mazel, 1976. Pp. 267–316.

Patterson, G. R., Cobb, J. A., & Ray, R. S. A social engineering technology for retraining the families of aggressive boys. In H. E. Adams & I. P. Unikel (Eds.), *Issues and trends in behavior therapy.* Springfield, Illinois: Thomas, 1973. Pp. 139–210.

Patterson, G. R., Ray, R. S., Shaw, D. A., & Cobb, J. A. *Manual for coding of family interactions* (1969 revision). New York: Microfiche, 1969.

Patterson, G. R., & Reid, J. B. Intervention for families of aggressive boys: A replication study. *Behaviour Research and Therapy,* 1973, **11,** 383–394.

Peed, S., Roberts, M., & Forehand, R. Evaluation of the effectiveness of a standardized parent training program in altering the interaction of mothers and their noncompliant children. *Behavior Modification,* 1977, in press.

Peterson, R. F. Power, programming, and punishment: Could we be overcontrolling our children? In E. J. Mash, L. A. Hamerlynck, & L. C. Handy (Eds.), *Behavior modification and families.* New York: Brunner/Mazel, 1976. Pp. 338–352.

Reisinger, J. J., Frangia, G. W., & Hoffman, E. H. Toddler management training: Generalization and marital status. *Journal of Behavior Therapy and Experimental Psychiatry,* 1976, **7,** 335–340.

Resick, P. A., Forehand, R., & McWhorter, A. The effect of parent treatment with one child on an untreated sibling. *Behavior Therapy,* 1976, **7,** 544–548.

Risley, T. R., Clark, H. B., & Cataldo, M. F. Behavioral technology for the normal middle-class family. In E. J. Mash, L. A. Hamerlynck, & L. C. Handy (Eds.), *Behavior modification and families.* New York: Brunner/Mazel, 1976. Pp. 34–60.

Rosen, G. M. The development and use of nonprescription behavior therapies. *American Psychologist,* 1976, **31,** 139–141.

Rudestam, K. E., Fisher, R. H., & Fiester, A. R. Differential effectiveness of mother vs stranger in the control of children with behavior problems: An experiment in child swapping. *Psychological Reports,* 1974, **35,** 823–833.

Sajwaj, T. Difficulties in the use of behavioral techniques by parents in changing child behavior: Guides to success. *Journal of Nervous and Mental Disease,* 1973, **156,** 395–403.

Scarboro, M. E., & Forehand, R. Effects of two types of response-contingent time-out on compliance and oppositional behavior of children. *Journal of Experimental Child Psychology,* 1975, **19,** 252–264.

Simmons, H., & Schoggen, P. Mothers and fathers as sources of environmental pressure on children. In R. G. Barker (Ed.), *The stream of behavior.* New York: Appleton, 1963. Pp. 70–77.

Tams, V., & Eyberg, S. A group treatment program for parents. In E. J. Mash, L. C. Handy, & L. A. Hamerlynck (Eds.), *Behavior modification approaches to parenting.* New York: Brunner/Mazel, 1976. Pp. 101–123.

Taplin, P. S., & Reid, J. B. *Changes in parent consequation as a function of family intervention.* Unpublished manuscript, Oregon Research Institute, Eugene, Oregon, 1975.

Tavormina, J. B. Relative effectiveness of behavioral and reflective group counseling with parents of mentally retarded children. *Journal of Consulting and Clinical Psychology,* 1975, **43**, 22–31.

Tavormina, J. B., Henggeler, S. W., & Gayton, W. F. Age trends in parental assessments of behavior problems of their retarded children. *Mental Retardation,* 1976, **14**(1), 38–39.

Terdal, L., Jackson, R. H., & Garner, A. M. Mother-child interactions: A comparison between normal and developmentally delayed groups. In E. J. Mash, L. A. Hamerlynck, & L. C. Handy (Eds.), *Behavior modification and families.* New York: Brunner/Mazel, 1976. Pp. 249–264.

Toepfer, C., Reuter, J., & Maurer, C. Design and evaluation of an obedience training program for mothers of preschool children. *Journal of Consulting and Clinical Psychology,* 1972, **39**, 194–198.

Wahl, G., Johnson, S. M., Johansson, S., & Martin, S. An operant analysis of child-family interaction. *Behavior Therapy,* 1974, **5**, 64–78.

Wahler, R. G. Oppositional children: A quest for parental reinforcement control. *Journal of Applied Behavior Analysis,* 1969, **2**, 159–170. (a)

Wahler, R. G. Setting generality: Some specific and general effects of child behavior therapy. *Journal of Applied Behavior Analysis,* 1969, **2**, 239–246. (b)

Wahler, R. G. Some structural aspects of deviant child behavior. *Journal of Applied Behavior Analysis,* 1975, **8**, 27–42.

Wahler, R. G., House, A. E., & Stambaugh, E. E. *Ecological assessment of child problem behavior.* New York: Pergamon, 1976.

Wahler, R. G., & Nordquist, V. M. Adult discipline as a factor in childhood imitation. *Journal of Abnormal Child Psychology,* 1973, **1**, 40–56.

Wahler, R. G., Winkel, G. H., Peterson, R. F., & Morrison, D. C. Mothers as behavior therapists for their own children. *Behaviour Research and Therapy,* 1965, **3**, 113–124.

Weathers, L., & Liberman, R. P. Contingency contracting with families of delinquent adolescents. *Behavior Therapy,* 1975, **6**, 356–366.

Weinrott, M. *Rationale and procedure for standard score transformation of behavioral observation data.* Paper read at the Social Learning Conference, Eugene, Oregon, December, 1975.

Zegiob, L. E., & Forehand, R. Parent–child interactions: Observer effects and social class differences. *Behavior Therapy,* 1977, in press.

Zeilberger, J., Sampen, S. E., & Sloane, H. N. Modification of a child's problem behaviors in the home with the mother as therapist. *Journal of Applied Behavior Analysis,* 1968, **1**, 47–53.

BEHAVIORAL GROUP THERAPY: I. EMOTIONAL, AVOIDANCE, AND SOCIAL SKILLS PROBLEMS OF ADULTS

DENNIS UPPER
Veterans Administration Hospital
Brockton, Massachusetts

AND

STEVEN M. ROSS
Veterans Administration Hospital and University of Utah
Salt Lake City, Utah

I. INTRODUCTION

Although the uses of behavior therapy methods and techniques for the individual client have been covered extensively in the psychological literature of the past 15 years, it is only recently that applications of behavioral procedures in group therapy settings have been explored. Franks and Wilson (1973) find this situation all the more strange in light of their view that behavior therapy, with its emphasis on interindividual reinforcement schedules, should lend itself particularly well to group implementation, as well as facilitating this evaluation of treatment effectiveness.

In the present report (the second half of which will appear in Volume 6 of this series), a comprehensive review of behavioral group therapy approaches will be undertaken. Liberman (1971) has suggested that such a review should have two major thrusts or purposes: one theoretical and one practical. The theoretical thrust is designed to answer the question, "Is psychotherapy in general, and group psychotherapy in particular, a lawful, directive, and predictable process that can be understood from a behavioral point of view?" (p. 535). The practical thrust is directed to the question, "Can analyzing group therapy from a learning point of view suggest and direct our attention to practical improvements in the technical work that we carry out as group therapists, whatever our theoretical persuasions?" (p. 535). The present authors feel that the practical thrust of such a review should be directed toward answering a somewhat different question as well: "Which behavioral procedures have proved to be particularly amenable to implementation in group therapy situations and with what types of problem behaviors?"

It should be noted, before proceeding, that the focus of the present chapter will be on the application of behavioral procedures in *group therapy* settings, rather than upon the more general area of behavior modification with a group of patients (e.g., through the use of token economies). Also, although there is a substantial body of literature on the use of behavioral procedures in vocational counseling and training groups, space limitations make it necessary to delimit this review to those studies in which more "clinical" behavioral problems are the targets for change.

Goldstein, Heller, and Sechrest (1966) have differentiated between the process of doing therapy *in* groups and that of doing therapy *through* groups. In the former case, therapy is more therapist centered and individually oriented; in general, this approach is more directive, interpretive, and focused on the behaviors of individual group members, as in the case of group systematic desensitization. In the present context, many of the "in-group" studies that will be presented employ intervention techniques which were developed for use in individual therapy. They are employed in a group context primarily for the sake of efficiency of therapists' time. A good example of this is group systematic desensitization. As will be seen later, a limited amount of attention has been accorded to whether or not group interaction variables might enhance these individually developed therapies conducted in a group. The "through-groups" approach is more group centered; the therapist tends to be less overtly active, to promote member-to-member (rather than member-to-therapist) interactions and to be more oriented toward groupwide influences on individual patients. Viewed in this way, behavioral group therapy may be seen as a process in which the group leader trains the group members to become behavioral engineers for one another. As training progresses and the group members learn to appropriately reinforce, prompt, model, and shape each other's behavior, the leader gradually fades to a less active role. Ideally, the next step in the treatment process would be fading out the group itself, while programming generalization of new behavior outside the group and teaching members to engineer their own behavior. Rather than seeing the "in-groups" and "through-groups" orientations as dichotomous, one should view them as ends of a continuum, across which the studies reviewed in the present chapter will be distributed.

The present review will include: (1) a discussion of the advantages of treating patients or clients in a group rather than individually, (2) a brief review of the major theoretical positions and basic research from which much of the clinical work in this area was derived, and (3) a review of the literature on behavioral group therapy procedures which have proved effective in modifying the emotional, avoidance, and social skills problems of adults.

II. WHY CONDUCT BEHAVIOR THERAPY IN GROUPS?

The specific behavior therapy techniques used to help a client are similar in individual and group work; in fact, the majority of behavioral group therapy cases reported in the literature feature the direct transfer of individually oriented procedures, such as systematic desensitization, to a group of clients with homogeneous problems (e.g., phobic complaints, impotence or frigidity, problems with assertion). However, despite similarities among the behavioral methods used in individual and group therapy situations, communicating the techniques to the clients may require differences in timing and presentation, and the group therapist must assume the additional task of structuring the group experience in such a way as to enhance each client's chances of reaching his treatment goal (Frankel & Glasser, 1974). Specifically, this task may involve establishing group goals that create an atmosphere conducive to clients' helping each other. The therapist can establish these goals by attending carefully to the selection of clients, the specific problem areas to be dealt with in the group, and the means of reinforcing cohesiveness, cooperation among members, attendance, and other appropriate group-related behaviors.

Garvin and Glasser (1971) suggest that trying to structure and maintain group rules as a way of enhancing movement toward behavioral treatment goals can be seen as an indirect intervention technique in itself. As part of the *direct* intervention program, the therapist might teach each client the treatment method and techniques to be used in the group. This can be accomplished via the use of verbal instructions, contingency contracting, written information, and demonstrations. Later in the group experience, the clients may be able to initiate treatment for themselves and others.

There are a number of distinct advantages to implementing therapy in a group situation. In addition to saving the therapist's time and effort, the group therapy situation offers greater opportunities for behavioral rehearsal modeling. Systematic role-playing can be used to help clients practice new actions in a therapeutic atmosphere before testing the specified behaviors in their natural environment. Behavioral rehearsals provide the opportunity for vicarious learning by all the group members and may result in further savings in therapy time. The group situation offers unique opportunities to facilitate generalization through the use of these techniques because of the variety of participants with whom the client can practice new ways of behaving. The other group members also can provide controlled behavioral feedback, which can be more effective than a single therapist's feedback in helping the client to develop more appropriate behaviors. Frequently, a greater number of alternate solutions to problems can be generated from group discussion than from individual therapy.

Another advantage of the group approach is that group members can support and help each other in their attempts to achieve their treatment goals. One side benefit from this is that members may learn that their problems are not unique and that they are not alone in their unhappiness. In some studies (e.g., Rose, 1969), group members were encouraged to remind each other, outside of the therapy situation, to fulfill their behavioral assignments. This type of approach can be extended under controlled conditions so that group members can observe and reinforce each other in actual problem situations. For example, Packard (1970) reports a study in which one group member with appropriate assertive skills was paired with another member who was weak in this area, in order to help the latter perform a behavioral assignment. Further research of this type may demonstrate that pairing two differentially skilled group members in this manner will increase the probability that behavioral assignments will be completed by both.

Goldstein and Wolpe (1971) note that the group therapy setting offers the opportunity for a far more thorough behavioral analysis than does individual therapy. When dealing with a client on an individual session, the therapist is able to observe his behavior in relation to only one person, the therapist, which gives little information about the client's possible responses to other people. The client often is able to report a great deal about these interactions, but there may be certain behavior patterns of which he is hardly aware, either of the behavior itself or of the relationship between his behavior and the feelings, attitudes, and behavior of others in response to it. The group situation gives both the client and therapist (as well as the other group members) an opportunity to observe directly his behavior in a variety of interpersonal situations, thus providing information that can significantly enhance the formulation and implementation of treatment strategies.

Another benefit derived from the group approach is the increased opportunity for social reinforcement and motivational stimulation. For example, just as group pressure motivates the client to attempt new behaviors, group approval serves as a powerful reinforcer of those behaviors, further increasing the probability that it will be repeated and will generalize to other situations. Once a client begins to conform to group pressure, he not only receives reinforcement through direct statements of approval but, more importantly, is reinforced by being accepted for having tried, which makes him feel more a part of the group. The feeling of belonging that develops may further increase the motivational and reinforcing power of the group (Goldstein & Wolpe, 1971).

In addition to the general benefits deriving from the group approach, as noted above, there are a number of ways in which the group situation may serve to enhance the effectiveness of a particular treatment technique. For example, Paul and Shannon (1966) give several reasons why a group approach is valuable when applying systematic desensitization: (1) the construction of hierarchies through group discussion is particularly effective (hierarchies are set up to include the most common situational elements of all the clients in the group, with items geared to the most anxious members); (2) group desensitization goals are more effective than individual goals; (3) individuals can practice new skills in the group setting after a degree of relaxation has been achieved; and (4) there is immediate reinforcement from other members for changes in behavior and attitudes, which is not possible in individual systematic desensitization.

III. THEORETICAL INFLUENCES AND BASIC RESEARCH

Before reviewing studies in which behavioral group therapy procedures are used to treat specific clinical problems, it would be useful for us to review: (1) attempts to integrate findings from other areas relevant to the group therapy domain, and (2) to review those controlled studies that have been designed to explore lawful relationships between a number of variables in the group process.

One of the first attempts to examine group therapy from an empirical point of view was that of Goldstein *et al.* (1966). Since much of what they observed in the group therapy literature seemed to "... have remained at the earliest and most primitive level of observation and inquiry" (p. 319), Goldstein *et al.* attempted to generate research hypotheses from the individual psychotherapy and group dynamics literatures. Johnson (1975) also noted the absence of data concerning role-playing and behavior rehearsal in the behavioral group therapy literature, while pointing to more consistent findings in the social psychology literature. While the present authors agree that much of the nontherapy research examining such topics as attitude change, interpersonal attraction, memory, and learning are relevant for understanding therapy (cf. Frank, 1961), we feel it is obviously beyond the scope of this chapter to review what would amount to the entire field of psychology in order to draw conclusions for group interventions. Rather, in looking at the present status of behavioral group approaches (both theoretical and applied), we have attempted to limit our review to studies that seem to bear *directly* on conducting and evaluating this treatment. Our assumption is that behavioral group therapy is now, to some extent, and can be to a greater extent at some future date a lawful process (Johnson, 1975; Liberman, 1971; Shapiro & Birk, 1967), and that one or more learning paradigms can accommodate present and future data.

Jacobs (1974) has suggested a conceptual framework which may prove useful to our attempts to integrate data from diverse group "schools" and methodologies. He identifies three main therapeutic movements that appear to be converging with the increasing use of behavioral techniques to provide treatment and to investigate its effectiveness: (1) the operant conditioning approach of Skinner; (2) the systematic experiential learning of Truax and Carkhuff (especially in the use of modeling techniques, see Bandura, 1969); and (3) the cognitive behavioral rehearsal of Wolpe and Lazarus (1966).

A. Operant Conditioning

One of the earliest group studies demonstrating control of rate of talking as a function of reinforcement schedule was reported by McNair (1957), who employed a bell tone to signify approval. More recently, other reports have shown that, by using a tone to signify approval and a buzzer to indicate disapproval, the leadership role can be transferred within a group by increasing the verbal initiations of target members (Shapiro & Leiderman, 1964). In addition, members' sequence of speaking can be modified (Shapiro, 1964), and the amount of disagreement among members can be increased (Shapiro, 1963).

Similarly, a series of experiments by Oakes, Droge, and August (1960, 1961; Oakes, 1962a, 1962b) employed signal-light flashes visible to each subject in the group to provide individual reinforcement for various response classes. Oakes *et al.* (1960) demonstrated that the lights, which subjects had been instructed to regard as indicating the degree of "insight" or "lack of insight" of their remarks, exerted powerful control over their verbal behavior. Subsequently, Oakes and his co-workers (1961) demonstrated that conclusions reached by group subjects could be manipulated, that the prestige of the signaler exerted significant influence on the reinforcing properties of the light (Oakes, 1962a), and that a specific class of behavior (i.e., giving opinions) could be increased by means of signal-light reinforcement (Oakes, 1962b).

Hastorf (1965) modified Oakes' procedure by adding an additional colored light so that both positive (green) and negative (red) feedback could be provided each subject. He found that, when the target person (TP) was reinforced for talking and the other three group members (NTPs) were reinforced for decreased participation, TP's rate of speaking increased significantly, as did his sociometric status. Zdep and Oakes (1967) replicated these findings while controlling for positive reactivity of the sociometric questionnaire and the use of lights. A recent study by David (1972) employed similar methodology to investigate the generalization of effects; results indicated that, while TPs increased verbalizations in response to the light reinforcer, these gains did not generalize to other newly formed groups one week or even one day later.

Simkins and West (1966) report another modification of the signal-light technique. In order to control for possible nonverbal communication effects among the group members when they received signals, Simkins and West placed their subjects in isolation booths and dispensed reinforcement via counters on which points were accumulated (points could later be exchanged for small amounts of money). Results were similar to those cited earlier by Hastorf (1965) and by Bavelas, Hastorf, Gross, and Kite (1965), except for a lack of generalization to the no-feedback condition. This finding led Simkins and West to speculate that the nonverbal behavior of group members may serve to facilitate generalization. More recently, Fromme, Whisenant, Susky, and Tedesco (1974) demonstrated that effective verbalization could be induced with reinforcement and feedback from counters signaling reinforcement to each subject, as well as from a red light mounted on each subject's counter. Both the lights and the clicking of other subjects' counters were discriminable to all group members, with the expectation of enhanced motivation and modeling effects. Other groups featured a more traditionally oriented therapist, reinforcement plus therapist, or a no-reinforcement/no-therapist condition. Reinforcement-only and therapist-only conditions produced significant increments in affective verbalizations. While there was no significant interaction between factors, one group having both therapist and reinforcement conditions showed a rather large summation effect.

Using toys as a reinforcer with third- and fifth-grade subjects, Lott and Lott (1960) demonstrated that sociometric choices for participation in a group game could be altered in the direction of choosing those children in whose presence reinforcement was obtained in a prior game. Thus, cohesion of a group may be conceptualized as a function of the amount of reinforcement group members obtain in one another's presence.

Heckel, Wiggins, and Salzberg (1962) demonstrated that negative reinforcement could be used effectively to eliminate long silences in a therapy group; the procedure consisted of surreptitiously introducing a noxious noise whenever the group fell silent for more than 10 seconds and then turning off the noise as soon as a group member broke the silence.

While the preceding studies employed nonverbal reinforcers, similar effects have been obtained in groups by using verbal and social reinforcement. For example, Dinoff and his co-workers

(1960) used verbal elicitation and reinforcement techniques to increase "personal" and "group" references made by group therapy patients. Phillips (1969) used verbal reinforcement to increase the frequency with which group members used human nouns, and Bachrach, Candland, and Gibson (1961) showed general rate of talking to be a function of reinforcement (e.g., "yes," "good," "that's a good idea") and the sex of the experimenter. Shapiro and Birk (1967) demonstrated that the systematic, preplanned use of approval from the group therapist can serve effectively as a therapeutic tactic when dealing with patients' monopolizing the group's attention, using distancing maneuvers, and having an inability to express anger. Liberman (1970a) trained group therapists to use social reinforcement to facilitate the development of intermember cohesiveness (also termed intimacy, solidarity, and affection); results indicated that patients in the experimental group showed significantly more cohesiveness and earlier symptomatic improvement than those in the comparison group. In a related experiment (Liberman, 1970b), prompting and social reinforcement from the therapist proved effective in increasing the frequency of verbal expressions of hostility toward the therapist. Liberman argues that data from these studies indicate the potency of the therapist in shaping and modifying group dynamic behaviors and support the utility of a reinforcement or learning approach to the understanding of group therapy.

Several studies relevant to this section employed both verbal and nonverbal reinforcers. Tracey, Briddell, and Wilson (1974) used tokens, social reinforcement, a bell tone, and chalk marks to provide a rich schedule of reinforcement designed to increase two classes of verbal behavior in a group of 12 chronic hospitalized patients. Cross-class generalization occurred in that increased positive statements about activities were accompanied by actual participation outside the group; similar generalization did not occur, however, for the increase in positive verbal statements about people. Other studies have shown: (1) verbal prompts (questions) to be as effective as prompts plus verbal and nonverbal social reinforcement (smiles, nods, "mm-hmm") in increasing personal references among chronic patients (Rickard & Timmons, 1961), (2) points in combination with social and primary reinforcement to be effective in increasing group interaction and attention to tasks among hyperactive boys (Schofield, Hedland, & Worland, 1974), and (3) tokens plus social reinforcement to be effective in increasing patient-to-patient interactions (Flowers, Booraem, Brown, & Harris, 1974).

In summary, it can be seen that a variety of operant conditioning approaches, used singly or in combination, have proved effective in modifying rate of speech, speech content, duration of silences, group "cohesion," and a number of other variables relevant to the group therapy situation.

B. Systematic Experiential Learning and Modeling

Systematic experiential learning and modeling also have been effectively incorporated into the group process. Carkhuff (1971) has asserted that training clients and "significant others" in their environments, using systematic programs in interpersonal skills, can be more effective than unstructured experiential learning in producing lasting increases in adaptive behavior. As far as group therapy is concerned, the systematic experiential learning approach of Truax, Carkhuff, and their colleagues has emphasized such variables and techniques as role-playing, exercises, feedback, and the creation of empathy, warmth, and genuineness in a variety of populations of therapists and clients.

For example, vicarious therapy pretraining (VTP) has been proposed by Truax (1962a, 1962b) as a means of providing standard cognitive and experiential structuring of "how to be a good patient" and as a way of quickly engaging the patient in the process of group therapy. VTP simply involves presenting to prospective patients a 30-minute tape recording of excerpts of "good" patient in-therapy behavior. It provides a vicarious experience of how clients often explore their problems and feelings, as well as of how they can prove helpful to one another during group therapy. A study by Truax and Carkhuff (1965) indicated the therapeutic benefit of VTP aimed at teaching new group therapy patients those verbal behaviors deemed desirable in a therapeutic encounter. Truax and Wargo (1969) carried out a similar study with mildly disturbed neurotic outpatients and also found VTP to be highly facilitative in producing constructive behavioral changes.

The relative efficacy of modeling and instructional approaches in increasing interpersonal openness in a group setting was investigated in a study reported by Whalen (1969). Groups of subjects participated in a leaderless discussion session after exposure to one of four manipulations: a film model of interpersonal openness plus detailed exhortive and descriptive instructions, a film model plus minimal instructions, detailed instructions with no film, and minimal instructions only. It was found that subjects exposed to both the film and the detailed instructions tended to demonstrate more interpersonal openness, while groups in the other three conditions failed to do so, devoting most of their time to impersonal discussion.

Schwartz and Hawkins (1965), using two patients within a therapy group as models along with a therapist dispensing verbal reinforcers, succeeded in either increasing or decreasing other patients' verbal expressions of feeling. Using college student subjects, Marlatt, Jacobsen, Johnson, and Morrice (1966) modified the degree to which subjects admitted to having problems by means of a similar modeling–reinforcement procedure. Gutride, Goldstein, and Hunter (1973), employing acute and chronic schizophrenics as subjects, found that videotaped modeling, role-playing, and social reinforcement (i.e., structured learning therapy) produced similar significant effects on social interaction criteria.

In an effort to integrate what little data there are for conducting group treatment, Bednar, Weet, Evenson, Lanier, and Melnick (1974) discussed some of the pretherapy training, cohesion, and modeling literature in an attempt to establish some guidelines for practitioners. These three areas are not mutually exclusive and, as Bednar *et al.* pointed out, modeling may be useful not only during therapy for learning of new responses or new sets of responses, response facilitation, and inhibitory–disinhibitory effects, but also for facilitating group cohesion and for conducting pretherapy training by modeling appropriate group behavior.

Finally, Goldstein, Glassner, Greenberg, Gustin, Land, Liberman, and Streiner (1967) have discussed the advantages of using "planted" patients to enact those behaviors that would be most therapeutic for the other group members to emulate. During the course of two on-going therapy groups, a wide variety of potentially therapeutic plant roles were developed, rehearsed, and enacted. When necessary, the plants reassured, attacked, befriended, argued, yielded, encouraged, or elaborated in detail on their own supposed psychopathology. The plants at times aided in quieting monopolizers, permitted themselves to be "intimidated" by patients in need of assertiveness experiences, augmented feelings of cohesiveness, assisted in clique-busting and clique-formation, and encouraged other patients to bring material revealed to the plants during postsessions into the group session proper. Data from a posttherapy session sociometric questionnaire indicated that, while neither of the two planted patients was chosen as the most popular or best-liked group member, both were consistently seen—across sessions—as the most protherapeutic patient in their respective group.

C. Cognitive Behavioral Rehearsal

Cognitive behavioral rehearsal has also been effectively adapted for use in therapy groups. The potential for simultaneous group cognitive rehearsal by individuals with similar problems was demonstrated by the early impressive results of Lazarus (1961). Lazarus randomly assigned matched groups of phobic subjects to either a group desensitization or a group interpretation condition. In the desensitization groups, several individuals with the same phobia (e.g., claustrophobia) were treated simultaneously, and the therapist took an upward step in the hierarchy only when each patient in the group could endure a particular imagined scene without anxiety. The group desensitization procedures were found to be significantly more effective than the group interpretation methods in overcoming the phobic reactions. About two-thirds of the desensitization group subjects overcame their phobias in a mean of 20.4 sessions, as opposed to only 2 of 17 interpretation group subjects who were symptom-free after a mean of 22 sessions.

Lazarus extended this treatment procedure, with equally impressive results, to a group of four patients who had four different phobias. These patients, after participating in group relaxation training, received the items of their relevant anxiety hierarchies on slips of paper. Each group member was instructed to read the description of the scene, to close his eyes, and to try to imagine the situation with tranquility. Those who were able to imagine their scene without undue anxiety were then handed a more difficult anxiety situation. In this manner, each group member was able to proceed at his own pace.

Other group applications of cognitive behavioral rehearsal techniques of the type developed by Wolpe and Lazarus have included the implementation of assertiveness training groups (Lazarus, 1968), time-limited group approaches to the problems of impotence and frigidity (Lazarus, 1968), and implosive group therapy (Dawley & Wenrich, 1973). A more comprehensive review of the literature in this area will be included in Section IV of this chapter.

D. Other Relevant Theoretical Work

There have been a variety of other attempts to conceptualize the group therapy process in behavioral terms. Diamond (1974) discussed the use of a learning theory model in order to more fully understand encounter group behavior and the behavioral changes occurring following such groups. Lieberman, Yalom, and Miles (1973), in attempting to examine encounter group experiences and resulting changes, briefly note the importance of modeling and experimenting with new forms of behavior in the maintenance of change. In a book edited by Houts and Serber (1972), a group of behaviorists describe their reactions to a weekend encounter group experience; their accounts illustrate some translations of experiential techniques into behavioral terms, as well as areas of mutual concern and divergence. Similar behavioral translations have been offered for psychodrama (Sturm, 1970) and Synanon (Karen & Bower, 1968), and perhaps further theoretical work of this type will lead to the increased development and use of group treatment methods.

IV. CLINICAL APPLICATIONS FOR SPECIFIC BEHAVIORAL PROBLEMS

A. Emotional and Avoidance Behaviors

The literature on behavioral group treatment of maladaptive emotional and avoidance behaviors until very recently has focused primarily on applications of systematic desensitization (SD). This literature was first critically reviewed by Paul (1969) and recently summarized by Mayton and Atkinson (1974). While Paul's (1969) review included 75 papers, only ten were germane to group applications, and these ten consisted largely of studies demonstrating the effectiveness of SD applied in groups to several types of phobias. Mayton and Atkinson's (1974) review concentrated exclusively on group applications of SD. Forty-nine papers were cited, an increase of 490% in six years in papers dealing with group SD.

The present review, completed in mid-1976, covers approximately 80 papers. We will summarize, in the limited space available, papers dealing with reduction of maladaptive fear, including newer behavioral techniques in addition to SD. While 30 of the 80 papers encountered dealt with procedural and parametric questions of the type Paul (1969) suggested, the reader is cautioned against assuming that these studies comprise a representative or comprehensive review of this type of literature. On the contrary, the majority of these studies were excluded from the present review since experimental treatments were given *individually* and individuals were randomly assigned to "treatment groups" for statistical analyses. Because we do not wish to convey a distorted picture of this literature and because of the practical thrust of this chapter, our efforts will concentrate primarily on papers dealing with descriptions of effective or promising group interventions rather than on papers dealing with procedural and parametric issues.

1. STUDIES OF EFFECTIVENESS OF A SPECIFIC TECHNIQUE APPLIED IN A GROUP

A number of studies have demonstrated the effectiveness of SD in reducing fear and avoidance behavior when administered in a group setting. Using college students as subjects, Ihli and Garlington (1969), Scissons and Njaa (1973), Suinn (1968), Taylor (1971), and Werner (1972) demonstrated the effectiveness of group SD of test anxiety. Using elementary school children as subjects, Barabasz (1973) found that high-anxious subjects benefited from SD for test anxiety.

Goldfried and Trier (1974) found that group relaxation training, presented as an active self-control technique, resulted in significant within-group reductions in public-speaking anxiety with college students. Zemore (1975) tested Goldfried's (1971) earlier assertion that the SD package might be an active anxiety-reducing skill, but found no difference between standard SD and a modified active form. Both treatments significantly reduced two evaluation fears among college students.

Dawley and Wenrich (1973) tested the feasibility of using implosive therapy in groups while treating test-anxious college students. Subjects were recruited from introductory psychology classes and randomly assigned to an implosive therapy group, a placebo group, and a no-treatment group. All subjects had scored 66% or higher on the Test Anxiety Questionnaire (TAQ) (Mandler & Sarason, 1952). While subjects in the implosive group scored significantly lower on the TAQ both at posttreatment and at follow-up one month later, the results are only suggestive due to the failure of the implosive therapy subjects to differ significantly from placebo treatment subjects.

Stone (1971) compared the effectiveness of group versus individual implosive therapy for snake-phobic females. While individual treatment was more effective in reducing avoidance behavior than the individual control condition, group control subjects improved significantly more than group implosive subjects. Measures of fear indicated that implosion was ineffective in reducing the fear.

Viewed together, the evidence from the group SD studies suggests the efficacy of this procedure in reducing the test anxiety of students from grade school through the college level. However, methodological deficiencies in these studies (e.g., possible experimenter bias, lack of follow-up, exclusive use of self-report measures, and unequal durations of experimenter attention across treatment and control groups) do not permit firm conclusions. While the use of group relaxation training as an active self-control technique appears promising, the results thus far with group implosion do not appear encouraging.

It should be noted that the methodological deficiencies noted above are found to one degree or another in almost all the studies reported in subsequent subsections. Therefore, these deficiencies will not be reiterated for each group of studies.

In terms of other emotional behaviors treated by group behavioral methods, Lewinsohn (1974), Lewinsohn, Weinstein, and Alper (1970), and Lewinsohn, Weinstein, and Shaw (1969) describe the development of a group approach to depression which supplements individual therapy. Lewinsohn *et al.* (1970) define "depression" in terms of (1) low rates of behavior, (2) verbal statements of dysphoria, self-depreciation, guilt, material burden, fatigue, and (3) somatic complaints such as sleeplessness, loss of appetite, and headaches. Their assumption is that the depressed individual is on a lean schedule of positive reinforcement and that one way to increase this reinforcement is by teaching social skills. Social skill is defined as "the emission of behaviors which elicit reactions, particularly positive ones, from other people" (Lewinsohn *et al.*, 1970, p. 525).

Several measures of depression were employed as selection criteria: D scale of the MMPI greater than 70%, Grinker Feelings and Concerns Checklist (GFCC) (Grinker, Miller, Sabshin, Nunn, & Nunnally, 1961), Interpersonal Behavior Scale (IBS) (Dyer, 1967), Depression Adjective Checklists (DACL) (Lubin, 1965), and an individual interview. Four males and five females of a group of 60 university undergraduates were selected to serve as subjects. Interpersonal behavior within the group was coded by two observers and included categories related to the initiator of various classes of verbal behavior, as well as to the reaction of the group member to whom the message was directed. Interrater reliabilities for number of actions and reactions emitted by each group member were .97 and .99, respectively. By placing the number and kinds of behaviors emitted by each group member and toward whom they were directed in columns, and placing the numbers and kinds of behaviors directed toward each member in rows, an interactional matrix was formed.

Specifically, four measures that operationally defined social skill were obtained: total amount of behavior emitted by and directed toward each individual, use of positive and negative reactions, range of interactions, and the interpersonal efficiency ratio, which is the number of behaviors directed toward the individual divided by the number of behaviors emitted by him.

The group met for 15 1-hour and three 2-hour sessions, during which time the coleaders focused on the various types of interactions occurring. In addition, individual sessions were held between group meetings. In three sessions, considerable emphasis was placed on social skill behaviors. These individual meetings also were used to examine graphs and data of group behavior and to select treatment goals that would result in attaining a higher rate of positive social reinforcement.

While changes from pre- to posttreatment on the D scale, GFCC, and IBS were reported, their significance was not tested statistically. Graphs of individual changes in rates of positive and negative reactions and range of interaction in early, middle, and late group sessions indicated that changes in desired directions had occurred. The correlations between numbers of behaviors emitted and elicited were presented for each subject, and all were significant and ranged from .59 to .98.

Several other novel applications of behavioral techniques applied in group settings have been reported. Kass, Silvers, and Abroms (1972) provide a description of a pilot ward-level program for treatment of hysteria. A subgroup of five women on a 20-bed psychiatric unit employing a therapeutic community approach was given additional responsibilities for specifying each other's inappropriate hysterical behaviors, appropriate assertive alternatives, and negative and positive consequences for emission of those behaviors. While only an anecdotal study of five cases, the paper presents an interesting methodology which should be tested more rigorously. Four of the five patients were reported to have shown symptomatic improvement at discharge and at an 18-month follow-up.

Reich (1972) examined the effects of group SD for primary dysmenorrhea. Subjects treated by SD showed significant reductions in symptoms of dysmenorrhea and anxiety compared to a no-treatment control group. Significant correlations were found between level of anxiety and degree of dysmenorrhea or change in dysmenorrhea.

Kondas and Scetnidia (1972) compared the use of systematic desensitization with "psychoprophylactic" methods in reducing fear of childbirth. Two groups of subjects with an average age of 27 years were matched in regard to parity, age, education, and level of anxiety on the Manifest Anxiety Scale (MAS) and a special fear schedule, the KSAT. Only pregnancies that were expected to be normal (according to obstetric and gynecological examinations) were included. Both groups showed significant reduction in MAS and KSAT scores from pre- to posttreatment. In addition, duration of labor was significantly less for the desensitization group. Independent judges' ratings of pain and movement for the desensitization group were also lower. No reliability data are reported for judges, however, and the absence of no-treatment and placebo controls allows for alternative explanations of the results.

2. STUDIES OF COMBINATIONS OF GROUP INTERVENTIONS

Several studies have been reported in which behavioral group therapy was used in conjunction with other techniques, such as traditional counseling or individual retraining approaches, to treat test anxiety, agoraphobia, sexual dysfunction, and depression.

Burnett and Ryan (1964) anecdotally described the successful use of group systematic desensitization for mixed phobias of 100 day-care patients within a hospital setting. An unknown number of patients also received a variety of other treatments simultaneously (e.g., assertion training, reeducation, insulin coma, and electroshock).

Lazarus (1961) reported the successful use of desensitization combined with instructions in sexual technique for a group of impotent males and a group of frigid females ($N = 3$ per group). Follow-up information was obtained at six months for the females, all of whom reported maintenance of treatment gains. Only one male and his spouse were contacted from the impotence group at more than 2 years posttreatment. Both partners reported sustained treatment gains.

Test anxiety has been reported to be significantly reduced by study counseling plus relaxation and by relaxation alone (Allen, 1973), group discussion of study techniques in combination with group desensitization (McManus, 1971), and either combinations of desensitization and counseling within sessions or in a series over a number of sessions (Mitchell & Ng, 1972).

Katahn, Strenger, and Cherry (1966) combined SD with bibliotherapy and study skills discussion in treating two groups of test-anxious college students. The SD subjects improved significantly compared with volunteer and nonvolunteer control subjects on both grade point average (GPA) and Sarason's (1958) Test Anxiety Scale. Follow-up on 7 of 14 treatment subjects one semester later showed GPAs were still higher than pretreatment levels.

Crighton and Jehu (1969) treated 17 test-anxious college students in either an SD group or a nondirective therapy plus relaxation group. At posttreatment, significantly less distress was reported on the Affect Adjective Checklist (Zuckerman, 1960) and on a sleep questionnaire. In addition, significantly fewer psychotropic drugs were prescribed compared to the corresponding period the previous year. Pre- to posttreatment comparisons between experimental and control subjects matched on the basis of examination marks did not reach significance.

In treating agoraphobic subjects, Gelder and Marks (1966) found that systematic desensitization plus gradual retraining proved superior to brief reeducative group therapy in improving work ability. However, the reeducation therapy resulted in more improvement in social relationships. Watson, Mullet, and Pillay (1973) investigated the combination of imaginal treatment of agoraphobia with *in vivo* treatment. *In vivo* treatment proved superior to imaginal treatment regardless of order of administration. There was also an order effect, with the first treatment given on a particular day proving to be more effective than the second. While group discussion appeared to increase camaraderie, it did not increase the effectiveness of treatment in reducing fear. Emmelkamp and Emmelkamp-Benner (1975) compared self-observation of agoraphobic behavior carried out individually and in groups, in combination with videotaped modeling of the same procedures. Both group and individually treated subjects improved significantly in terms of client and observer ratings of anxiety, phobic anxiety and phobic avoidance (Watson & Marks, 1971), duration of time spent in a street, and scores on the Self-Rating Depression Scale (Zung, 1965). There were no significant differences in the effectiveness of group versus individual treatment, and videotaped modeling did not enhance group or individual treatment.

3. STUDIES COMPARING "TRADITIONAL" AND BEHAVIORAL GROUP INTERVENTION

Of the five studies reported in this category, the majority focused on some aspect of test anxiety. The two exceptions were the study cited earlier by Kondas and Scetnidia (1972) in which a psychoprophylactic method was compared to SD in reducing fear of childbirth, and a report by Solyom (1973) in treating fear of flying. In the study reported by Solyom, 16 airplane seats were arranged in front of a screen for behavioral treatments (SD, habituation, and aversion relief), which were found to be equally and significantly more effective than group therapy. Differences were not significant on a questionnaire follow-up 50 weeks later.

Louks (1972) compared the effectiveness of taped SD with taped lectures on test-taking skills in reducing test anxiety. Systematic desensitization proved effective in reducing the "emotionality" and "worry" components of the TAQ, and the lecture approach was effective in reducing response to an anxiety hierarchy. However, neither approach significantly improved the GPA of treated subjects compared to untreated controls.

Lomont and Sherman (1971) compared the effectiveness of a group insight approach with group SD for treating test-anxious college students. The SD group met for eight 50-minute sessions, while the insight-oriented group met for eight 90-minute sessions. There was no significant improvement in test anxiety on two paper-and-pencil and two performance measures of test anxiety between treatment groups or between either group and the control group.

Doctor, Aponte, Burry, and Welch (1970) compared the effectiveness of group counseling versus SD in treating college underachievement. Underachievement was defined as a predicted GPA greater than 2.0 and an actual GPA of less than 2.0. Both treatment groups combined demonstrated significant improvement in underachievement compared to volunteer and nonvolunteer control groups, but there were no significant quantitative differences between treatment groups. Qualitatively, the SD group seemed to generalize fear reduction to nonacademic settings. The counseling group showed an increase in interpersonal anxiety but decreased Fear Survey Schedule scores.

4. COMPARISONS OF DIFFERENT BEHAVIORAL GROUP INTERVENTIONS

Several studies have attempted to compare SD with other behavioral interventions, using subjects with test anxiety or interpersonal performance anxiety. In reducing test anxiety, SD proved equally and significantly as effective as reactive inhibition (cf. Graff, MacLean, & Loving, 1971) in reducing Achievement Anxiety Test (AAT) scores (Alpert & Haber, 1960), but inferior to both covert reinforcement and a control group in raising performance scores on an anagrams test (Kostka & Galassi, 1974). Systematic desensitization was equally and significantly as effective as relaxation alone or relaxation plus simulation of test taking in reducing test anxiety, according to a report by Laxer and Walker (1970). Mulder (1971) compared SD, implosion, and "classical" group counseling in reducing test anxiety among college students. All three treatments significantly reduced scores on Sarason's Test Anxiety Scale and the Emery Test Anxiety Scale. There were no significant differences between treatments.

In terms of interpersonal performance anxiety, Stark (1970) compared the relative effectiveness of SD, assertiveness training (A), and symbolic modeling (M) with relaxation (R) and no-treatment control groups. Eleven pre- and posttreatment measures were obtained of male subjects' reactions to close interpersonal contact with an attractive female peer. While there were some inconsistencies across measures, the results generally supported the hypotheses that A, SD, and M could significantly reduce interpersonal anxiety in a few sessions.

Calef and MacLean (1970) compared the effectiveness of group SD and reactive inhibition (or a form of flooding) in reducing speech anxiety. Two self-report measures, the Personal Report of Confidence as a Speaker (Gilkenson, 1942) and the MAS (Taylor, 1953), were used. Both treatment groups demonstrated significant improvement compared to no-treatment control group subjects at the end of treatment. More recently, Calef, Calef, Sundstrom, Jarrett, and Davis (1974) found that a tone, previously paired with relaxation, significantly enhanced SD of test anxiety, as compared to conventional SD and control conditions.

Meichenbaum, Gilmore, and Fedoravicius (1971) compared group insight, SD, and insight plus SD in reducing speech anxiety. In this study, insight consisted of (1) teaching subjects, in a group setting, to attend to self-verbalizations that produced anxiety, and (2) having subjects practice other incompatible self-verbalizations and behavior. A variety of assessments were conducted, including judges' ratings of speech characteristics in a test speech situation, and four self-report speech anxiety measures. Interrater reliability ranged from .78 to .93 for all measures of speech characteristics. The group insight treatment was as effective as group SD in significantly reducing speech anxiety, as reflected on all measures. The combination of SD plus insight resulted in significant reductions in speech anxiety, but these were less consistent across measures. These results were maintained at a 3-month follow-up. The authors speculate that there was insufficient time to fully explore incompatible self-verbalizations in the last four sessions of the SD-plus-insight group. A more recent study by Meichenbaum (1972) permitted a more equitable comparison between SD and SD plus insight (termed cognitive modification in this study). The procedures were similar to those in the Meichenbaum *et al.* (1971) study, except that test-anxious subjects were used and the cognitive modification group devoted time to cognitive rehearsal of coping strategies while practicing slow, deep breathing if they became anxious during the imagining of hierarchy items. Results indicated that the cognitive modification and SD groups were effective in reducing test anxiety compared to control subjects, and that the cognitive group displayed a greater increase in facilitating anxiety and in GPA than the SD group. These results were maintained at a 1-month follow-up.

A recent study by Kirsh, Wolpin, and Knutson (1975) compared the *in vivo* use of flooding, implosion, and successive approximations in a college classroom to reduce speech anxiety (stage fright). All three treatments were significantly better than no treatment, but flooding was significantly more effective than implosion and successive approximations.

Litvak (1969) compared very brief SD and *in vivo* contact desensitization in groups in reducing snake avoidance. Only the contact desensitization group showed significant reduction in avoidance behavior compared to no-treatment control subjects and SD subjects.

The group interventions compared in these studies were primarily SD, implosion, flooding, modeling, cognitive modification, a form of traditional group counseling, and *in vivo* applications of shaping, implosion, flooding, and contact SD. As was noted in previous sections of this chapter, groups were used here primarily for the sake of efficiency in generating sufficient numbers of subjects to compare the interventions rather than for examining group process variables per se. Nonetheless, it appears from the studies cited that no clear-cut superiority of one intervention over another emerged. However, *in vivo* flooding, contact SD, and cognitive modification groups appear promising compared to the standard SD package.

5. STUDIES EXAMINING INTERACTIONS WITH PERSONALITY VARIABLES

Several studies have attempted to examine other subject characteristics, in addition to the primary emotional or avoidance behavior, in order to determine if certain personality characteristics are predictive of differential responses to treatments.

Osterhouse (1972) compared the effectiveness of SD and study skills training groups for two types of test-anxious college students. One type was high in preexamination cognitive worry and the other was high in automatic arousal during exams, according to scores on the Inventory of Test Anxiety (Osterhouse, 1969). Systematic desensitization subjects reported significantly less anxiety before the final exam than no-treatment control subjects. High-arousal control subjects scored higher on the final examination than study skills trained and SD subjects. The hypotheses that cognitive worry subjects would benefit more from study skills training and subjects reporting high arousal during examinations would benefit more from SD were not supported.

McMillan and Osterhouse (1972) sought to determine if specific versus generalized anxiety might be a significant factor in subjects' response to SD of test anxiety. Highly test-anxious college students were divided into high and low general anxiety groups and given group SD with emphasis on relaxation during the last two sessions. Both groups were significantly more relaxed after treatment, but low general anxiety subjects scored significantly higher on their final examinations.

Mitchell and Ingham (1970) also compared the outcome of SD with high versus low general anxiety subjects who were being treated for test anxiety. Subjects were screened with the general anxiety scale of the IPAT and the debilitating and facilitating scales of the AAT. Group SD was equally effective in significantly reducing test anxiety for both high and low general anxiety subjects, as compared to motivated and no-treatment controls.

Mitchell (1971) examined intratreatment changes of subjects classified as having high and low neuroticism and anxiety. The neuroticism scale of Eysenck's Personality Inventory was used along with the debilitating scale of the AAT and the Fear Thermometer. There was a significant reduction in AAT scores for all treatment groups. The high anxiety/high neuroticism group required significantly less exposure time to complete each item in the hierarchy.

Weinstein (1968) hypothesized that test-anxious introverts would benefit more from group SD than extroverts and that extroverts would benefit more from a structured group interaction consisting of practice exams, role-playing, and self-control exercises. Introversion–extroversion was determined by the Eysenck Personality Inventory. Test anxiety was measured with three self-report measures. Both treatment groups demonstrated significant reductions in test anxiety compared to no-treatment and no-contact control groups. As predicted, there was no significant interaction between treatment modality and personality type, although the structured group interaction was described as "somewhat" more effective with extroverts than introverts.

Curran (1975) distinguished between reactive and conditioned anxiety in subjects with dating anxiety. As conceptualized, reactive anxiety was probably more realistic since there may have been actual deficits in skill, whereas conditioned anxiety may have been due to previous unpleasant experiences which may then have resulted in an irrational, phobic response. Subjects were randomly assigned to each of two treatment and two control groups. Interrater reliabilities for the role-plays of dates were .70 for anxiety and .76 for skill. Results indicated that both treatment approaches, SD and skills training, resulted in significant improvement compared to waiting-list controls and attention-placebo controls.

In the study cited earlier by Meichenbaum *et al.* (1971), one of the post hoc findings was that subjects who suffered from high school distress in a variety of situations were helped most by the insight-oriented group. On the other hand, SD was more effective with subjects who had low general social distress and whose speech anxiety was confined to more formal public speaking situations.

In sum, seven studies examined personality characteristics. The efforts were focused on specific versus general anxiety, introversion versus extroversion, cognitive versus autonomic fear components, and high versus low neuroticism and anxiety. In each case some form of evaluative anxiety was the primary problem while treatments consisted of either SD, structured skills training, or cognitive modification. For the most part, SD resulted in equal or superior reductions in evaluative anxiety regardless of personality factors. The one exception was the significant treatment × patient interaction reported by Meichenbaum *et al.* (1971) in which subjects having more circumscribed speech anxiety benefited more from cognitive modification. None of these studies examined group process variables, fears other than evaluative fears, or personality variables other than some aspect of anxiety or introversion–extroversion.

6. REPORTS OF PROCEDURAL VARIATIONS

Several studies have examined group SD with regard to observational learning processes in reducing fear. Shannon and Wolff (1966) report that group SD was as effective as group SD plus a stooge modeling a high treatment expectancy condition for reducing snake phobia. Zupnick (1971) found a significant reduction in snake phobia, especially when the appropriate behavior was modeled in a group rather than in an individual setting. Ritter (1968) employed vicarious and contact SD to reduce snake phobia in children. Both treatments resulted in significant improvement, with contact SD being superior to vicarious SD in reducing avoidance behavior. A second study by Ritter (1969) examined the effects of therapist contact per se on treatment of acrophobia with contact desensitization. Only the therapist contact group showed significant reductions in height avoidance compared to contact desensitization and no-treatment groups.

In comparing a group receiving SD for test anxiety with a similar group observing only the SD procedure, Mann and Rosenthal (1969) found significant improvement in both groups. More recently, Mann (1972) found that three procedures—imitation of videotaped SD, observation (without imitation), or observation (without imitation) of SD excluding relaxation—all resulted in significant reductions in test anxiety relative to control subjects. Similarly, Hall and Hinkle (1972) demonstrated that SD, whether massed or distributed, given in customary form or vicariously, was significantly more effective than no treatment in reducing test anxiety and that there were no differences between groups.

While several additional studies have examined temporal and relaxation parameters, these have largely been for the purpose of examining the SD process per se rather than group applications. These have therefore been omitted from the present review (cf. Richardson & Suinn, 1974; Russell, Miller, & June, 1975).

A number of studies have investigated group hierarchy variables. Group hierarchies have been demonstrated to be effective (Donner, 1970; Donner & Guerney, 1969; Fishman & Nawas, 1971; Nawas, Fishman, & Pucel, 1970) in reducing phobic behavior, whether printed, read, presented verbally (Lutker, Tasto, & Jorgensen, 1972), imagined viewed on a screen, witnessed *in vivo* (O'Neil & Howell, 1969), given simultaneously with relaxation or noncontiguously (Aponte & Aponte, 1971), with instructions to be calm (Marshall, Strawbridge, & Keltner, 1972), or whether the hierarchy is group-developed, individually developed, or is a prior standard hierarchy (Fitzsimmons, 1971). Denholtz and Mann (1974) describe an audio-visual program employing a standard hierarchy for fear of flying. Ross and Proctor (1970) describe a psychometrically constructed hierarchy later used to successfully reduce snake phobia (Ross & Proctor, 1973).

Three studies incorporated group interaction and group SD. Paul and Shannon (1966) report the efficacy and efficiency of a group SD procedure combined with group discussion which was aimed at teaching confidence and interpersonal skills in reducing social-evaluative anxiety. Additional apparent advantages to utilizing a group approach were also discussed, although a direct comparison between individual and group SD was not made. Cohen (1969) found that group interaction enhanced attraction toward treatment for a group exposed to the top of a hierarchy only and that there was a significant relationship between attraction and outcome. Hand, Lamontagne, and Marks (1974) found that increased group cohesion enhanced treatment effects at follow-up for *in vivo* flooding with agoraphobics. Akin and Kunzman (1974) found that an *in vivo* variation of SD significantly reduced speech anxiety scores.

The three studies reporting group interaction with SD are significant for several reasons. First, these studies represent a link between an individually developed technique most frequently applied *in* a group (i.e., SD) and techniques employing therapy *through* the group (i.e., group discussion, sharing ideas and feelings, mutual feedback among members). Second, there is a surprising lack of attention paid to the combination of SD and group interaction in the literature despite the promise shown in these and other studies (e.g., Katahn *et al.*, 1966). It would appear that further systematic research is warranted by these encouraging results in order to better operationalize and measure concepts such as cohesion, group interaction, and attraction, as well as to determine optimal group procedures to use for specific emotional and avoidance behavior, clients, and settings.

B. Behaviors of Psychiatric Inpatients

Surprisingly, few studies in the behavioral group therapy literature have employed patients in psychiatric hospitals as subjects. In two prototypical studies, Dinoff, Horner, Kurpiewski, and Timmons (1960) and Dinoff, Horner, Kurpiewski, Rickard, and Timmons (1960) attempted to modify either self- or group-referent statements of patients in a Veterans Administration Hospital. In the first study, operant levels of these statements were determined in a leaderless discussion-group setting. Patients were then divided into two experimental groups, in each of which the experimenter actively prompted and reinforced statements which referred either to the patient himself or to the group. The effects of this procedure were assessed in the original, larger group. The operant and extinction phases each consisted of three 50-minute sessions, with the experimental phase being conducted during six 50-minute meetings. The results were somewhat disappointing in that the mean differences in the frequencies of behaviors did not reach significance. However, sign tests did show a significant trend in the expected direction. The authors conducted an interesting additional manipulation, referred to as "counterconditioning." After the posttreatment assessments, subjects were returned to their smaller groups, where the experimenter reinforced that class of reference statements which had not been reinforced earlier (i.e., subjects initially reinforced for group-referent statements now were rewarded for self-referent statements, and vice versa). Here, again, suggestive trends were found with the sign test.

Since (in the first study) the groups in which effects were measured were different from the groups during which reinforcement had occurred, Dinoff and his colleagues (1960) conducted a similar study in an attempt to decrease the effects of generalization from group to group upon observed verbal frequencies. Essentially the design was the same, except that (1) the assessments and manipulations all occurred within the same group setting, and (2) the experimenter was absent during the assessment meetings. As predicted, statistically significant changes were found in this study.

Davison (1969) points out that, before regarding these studies as contributing significantly to the fruitful relationship between verbal conditioning and group therapy, it should be noted that the subjects were reinforced in a group therapy-like setting only to the extent that the experimenter conditioned each individual patient in the presence of fellow patients. No direct attempt was made to manipulate *interpersonal* behavior, and the assessments of change (during a leaderless group discussion) likewise were directed to individual responding. In addition, the authors of these studies gave little consideration to the role that modeling may have played in altering patients' verbal behavior.

O'Brien, Azrin, and Henson (1969) investigated the effects of reinforcement and response priming on the frequency with which chronic psychiatric patients suggested feasible improvements in their treatment. Priming consisted of requiring that patients attend a structured daily meeting, during which they were prompted to make suggestions; this procedure was compared to the more usual practice of "welcoming" patient attendance and suggestions. It was found that more suggestions were made when attendance was required, rather than optional, an effect which occurred in both group and private meetings (with the ward psychologist). An attempt then was made to analyze the probable reinforcer for the suggestions by experimentally varying the percentage of suggestions which actually were followed. Different staff members served as the discriminative stimuli within a multiple schedule design, and it was found that the number of suggestions made by the patients was a direct function of the percentage of suggestions which actually were followed by the staff. When one staff member followed the suggestions and a second one did not, a high frequency of suggestions occurred in the presence of the member who did reinforce and a low frequency in the presence of the one who did not. The priming procedure was complementary to the reinforcement procedure in that few suggestions were made when priming was used without reinforcement, or when reinforcement was used without priming.

O'Donnell (1972) reports a group therapy study in which chronic female psychiatric patients met weekly in small groups to complete a structured, four-step program centered around discharge planning. Step 1 involved writing a statement of the reasons the patient had come to the hospital; Step 2 consisted of discussing (in the group) what the patient was doing at the hospital to help herself improve; Step 3 involved writing out specific plans for the future; and Step 4 required the patient to list the necessary steps toward implementing future plans. At each 30-minute group meeting, members were individually requested to inform the group of their progress on the assignment of the preceding week, and other members then advanced their comments, questions, and suggestions. Members who did not complete their assignments for the week were not permitted to talk about themselves but were told to complete the same assignment for the next week. At the end of 23 weeks (at which point the program was discontinued for administrative reasons), 20 patients had completed the group activities. Sixteen graduates from the group had either been discharged ($N = 9$) or were awaiting discharge ($N = 7$), three were suspended from their group for failing to complete their assignments, and the behavior of one patient had deteriorated prior to discharge, necessitating her transfer to another ward. The 16 subjects who graduated from the group did so in an average of 6.2 sessions. Three comparisons of subjects functioning prior to and following the initiation of the structured group procedure indicated that group participation had significant effects in terms of facilitating discharge.

Olson and Greenberg (1972) conducted a study designed to assess the effectiveness of treatment-planning groups in enhancing patients' performance in a psychiatric hospital. In this study, 74 institutionalized male psychiatric patients were placed in one of three treatment conditions for a 4-month period. The subjects in the milieu condition received the customary hospital treatment; subjects in the interaction condition received the same treatment as milieu subjects but participated in 2 hours of additional group therapy per week; subjects in the incentive condition were placed in groups responsible for making decisions concerning the treatment program for group members. The concrete target for the incentive therapy groups was to produce a progress report on one of its members, selected by the group, including recommendations for his treatment in the hospital. Recommendations ranged from changes in work assignments or roommates to town passes, discharge, and plans for community placement. Progress reports were presented by each group leader once a week at patient government meetings, during which the staff decided whether to accept or reject the group leader's proposals. Access to personal funds, vacations from work assignments, and passes were used as additional reinforcers of appropriate behavior for subjects in the incentive condition.

After 4 months, patients in the incentive groups were found to be significantly different from patients in both the milieu and interaction conditions on four outcome measures: (1) number of patients spending days out of the hospital, (2) number of town passes, (3) percentage attendance at work details, and (4) Social Adjustment Behavior Rating Scale scores. The direction of differences on the first three of these measures indicated that the incentive treatment was more effective in modifying patients' behavior during the 4-month treatment period; these significant differences still were observed upon 4-month posttreatment follow-up. On the other hand, nurses' ratings indicated that the incentive patients' behavior actually had deteriorated relative to the other two conditions. The authors offer two possible explanations for this latter finding: (1) nursing personnel may have been responding less to actual patient behaviors than to their own feelings of resentment about having to carry out such a structured program, and (2) the treatment staff may have negatively interpreted the changes in the behavior of some formerly passive and apathetic patients who became more assertive and demanding of their rights as a result of the incentive program.

DiScipio and Trudeau (1972) report a study in which state hospital psychiatric inpatients, each of whom had been diagnosed as psychotic, were reinforced systematically during group psychotherapy meetings for appropriate personal appearance. Group leaders provided positive verbal reinforcement for improvements in appearance, personal hygiene, and general attractiveness; experimental subjects also were encouraged throughout the day to perform behaviors related to appropriate grooming (e.g., showering) and were reinforced verbally for doing so. Control subjects spent an equivalent amount of time participating in "supportive, reality-oriented" group discussions and had equal access to grooming-related services and activities. In addition to reporting improvement in grooming and self-care behaviors on the part of the experimental subjects (as reflected in daily nurses' notes), the authors report that experimental subjects made significantly fewer negative statements about themselves, on a self-esteem rating scale, than the control subjects following treatment. Experimental subjects also showed a significant decline in their scores on the Paranoid Belligerence scale of the Psychotic Reaction Profile, while control subjects demonstrated a slight increase in their scores on this scale. The authors discuss the possibility that enhancement of positive self-esteem through reinforcement of grooming may have served as a mediating process in bringing about a reduction in anxiety and accompanying psychotic symptoms such as paranoid belligerence.

A study conducted by Robinson and Jacobs (1970) investigated the effects of providing mental hospital patients in group psychotherapy an opportunity to view videotape recordings (VTR) of their performance in the group. Six groups met six times in 2 weeks for 1-hour videotaped therapy sessions with a therapist and cotherapist. Each group contained six or seven patients, and the total number of subjects participating was 40. One hour of videotaped feedback was given to the three experimental groups immediately following each therapy session. During these feedback sessions, each subject was asked to express his response to seeing himself, then the group was urged to comment upon what was seen on the tape, and finally the therapist made her observations, comments, and interpretations. The therapist commented upon maladaptive behavior which had occurred and pointed out and verbally reinforced specific adaptive responses exhibited by the participants. For the three control groups, a therapist-led discussion period of 1 hour was substituted for focused feedback and VTR following therapy sessions.

Results were evaluated in terms of (1) changes in the frequency of occurrence of patients' adaptive and maladaptive behaviors across sessions, and (2) changes in patients' self-ratings of the frequency of those adaptive behaviors for which feedback had been presented. Results indicated that subjects in the videotaped feedback groups made significantly greater increases in the frequency of adaptive behavior than did discussion group subjects. No differences, however, were found in patients' self-ratings of adaptive change, which the authors feel may have been due to the possibility that attitudinal changes of this type appeared more slowly than changes in overt behavior, perhaps as a result of the individual having a chance to experience the beneficial consequences of his changed behavior.

Rimm, Keyson, and Huziker (cited in Rimm & Masters, 1973) employed group assertion training procedures to modify antisocial aggressive behaviors in a group of adult male psychiatric inpatients. Treatment was conducted over six 1-hour sessions. Subjects in an attention-placebo group also received 6 hours of group treatment, consisting of reflection and advice-giving bearing upon the expression of anger. In terms of objective laboratory ratings of the subjects' assertiveness (as opposed to verbal aggressiveness or timidity), the assertiveness training group showed significantly greater increases in assertion than did the controls. Informal follow-up observations by ward personnel and patients' relatives tended to support the view that the assertiveness training resulted in less hostility and aggression.

C. Miscellaneous Target Behaviors and Techniques

1. ASSERTIVENESS TRAINING

While only a fraction of the growing assertiveness training (AT) literature describes the use of group treatments, those that do fall roughly into three areas: reports of the efficacy of AT with various populations and varieties of assertive responses, comparisons with other approaches, and effects of other techniques on AT outcome.

In terms of the first category, several studies report the successful use of group AT with college students in reducing inappropriate anger (Rimm, Hill, Brown, & Stuart, 1974) and increasing assertiveness while decreasing fear in social interactions (Galassi, Galassi, & Litz, 1974; Rathus, 1972; Roszell, 1971; Sansbury, 1974; Sansbury & McCarthy, 1972).

Rimm *et al.* (1974) examined the effectiveness of group AT in reducing inappropriate anger among college student volunteers. Subjects were 13 male undergraduates who responded to a student newspaper advertisement for male volunteers who had difficulty controlling their tempers. Seven subjects were randomly assigned to the AT group and six to a placebo-control group. Subjects were asked to respond to eight situations as they ordinarily would. The situations had previously been obtained from 12 male introductory psychology students as typically giving rise to intense anger. Two independent "blind" judges rated each response on a 7-point scale. Subjects also rated themselves on a 10-point scale in each of three areas: confidence, degree of anger, and degree of anxiety. In addition, two questionnaire measures—the Lawrence Assertive Inventory (Lawrence, 1970) and the Internal–External Scale (Rotter, 1966)—were used.

Treatment for the AT and placebo-control groups was carried out by the same therapists for equal amounts of time, although it is not clear if the groups ran concurrently or sequentially. An attempt was also made to provide the same expectation of success for both groups. Results indicated a significant increase in ratings of appropriate assertiveness by raters, as well as in all self-report measures except confidence. The two questionnaires did not show significant change. While an 8-month follow-up was attempted, only two subjects from each group could be found. These subjects all indicated some lasting improvements from their respective groups. The authors concluded that AT may be an effective tool in helping individuals deal with anger. Nonsignificant questionnaire results were interpreted to mean that the effects of AT were highly situation-specific and consistent with results obtained by Lawrence (1970).

Galassi and Litz (1974) also used group AT with college students. A total of 16 males and 16 females were randomly assigned to two experimental and two control groups. Subjects were preselected on the basis of low scores on the College Self-Expression Scale (CSES) (Galassi, DeLo, Galassi, & Bastein, 1974) and were paid for participation. Two male–female coleader teams alternated among groups to control for therapist effects. In addition to CSES scores, self-reports of anxiety and ratings of pre- and posttreatment performances were obtained. Average interrater reliabilities on the performance were .95 for content, .94 for latency of response, and .98 for eye contact. Significantly better performance was obtained at posttreatment testing for experimental groups on the CSES, self-reports of anxiety, eye contact, length of scene and assertiveness content. A possible pretesting effect was noted for anxiety and assertiveness content in that controls who were pretaped gave better assertive responses than those who were not.

Using female college students as subjects, Rathus (1972) examined the efficacy of group AT for shaping assertive behavior and reducing fear in social interactions. Fifty-seven subjects were selected (presumably) based on their scores on a self-reporting assertiveness schedule (Rathus, 1973) and were randomly assigned to AT groups (N = 18), discussion groups (N = 18), and no treatment (N = 21). Nine types of assertive tasks were assigned for AT subjects to practice within and between sessions. Discussion group subjects met for an equivalent amount of time to discuss the nature of fear and child-rearing practices that led to guilt and dependency, and to observe their acquaintances and apply their new knowledge in "character sketches." Five subjects from each condition were randomly selected to answer 10 questions concerning situations in which assertion was needed. Two raters (interrater r = .86) viewed the taped question-and-answer session and scored the responses for "assertiveness shown" and "knowledge shown." Assertiveness training subjects showed significantly higher assertion scores than control subjects. However, discussion and AT subjects did not differ significantly. The same results occurred for both the assertiveness schedule and the self-report measure of fear in interpersonal confrontations, that is, the total score of the Temple Fear Survey Inventory (TFSI). The two subscales of the TFSI measuring fear of social criticism and competence, which were considered most relevant in the context of the study, failed to show significant differences between any of the groups.

Several reports discuss the efficacy of AT with clinical populations, including psychiatric outpatients (Bloomfield, 1973; Percell, Berwick, & Beigel, 1974), drug addicts in residential treatment (Callner & Ross, 1973), and psychiatric inpatients (Booraem & Flowers, 1972; Lomont, Gilner, Spector, & Skinner, 1969). In addition, Fensterheim (1972) and Lazarus (1968) describe group AT procedures, exercises, and so on, based upon their clinical experience. More recently, Lazarus (1974) describes the use of cognitive techniques (identifying "shoulds" and "oughts") enabling group members to contain their aggressive feelings and to engage in appropriate assertive behavior.

Percell *et al.* (1974) hypothesized that assertion is positively correlated with self-acceptance and negatively correlated with general anxiety. This hypothesized relationship was supported with 100 psychiatric outpatients (50 males and 50 females with a mean age of 29.4 years and a variety of diagnoses) using the Lawrence Interpersonal Behavior Test (IBT) (Lawrence, 1970), the self-acceptance scales of the CPI (Gough, 1957), and the MAS (Taylor, 1953).

Pearson *r*s between the IBT and the SA scale of the CPI were .49 for men and .51 for women (both $p < .001$). The correlations between the IBT and the MAS were −.04 for men (NS) and −.88 for women ($p < .001$). To further test these relationships, the IBT, MAS, and Breger self-acceptance (SA) scale (Breger, 1952) were given to seven male and five psychiatric outpatients before and after group AT and to a similar group after the relationship-control therapy. As predicted, the AT group showed significant changes in the desired direction on all measures while controls did not. In addition, blind interviewers rated AT subjects as being significantly more assertive, aggressive, emphatic, spontaneous, outgoing, and less anxious ($p < .05$ for each comparison). No interrater reliability is reported, however.

The report by Callner and Ross (1973) describes the use of AT with hospitalized drug addicts on a rehabilitation ward. Eight addicts were randomly assigned to a treatment or a no-treatment control group. Both groups participated in other ongoing ward activities. Three measures of assertion in a variety of areas (e.g., turning down drug offers, expressing opinions to authority figures) were obtained: self-report, raters' scores of performance, and questionnaire scores. Interrater reliabilities were .83 for affect and .89 for fluency. The AT subjects showed significant improvement in self-report and in raters' evaluations of assertiveness, specifically in the areas of turning down drugs and giving and receiving positive and negative feedback.

Booraem and Flowers (1972) hypothesized that AT would decrease self-reported anxiety and the amount of personal space required by psychiatric inpatients. Fourteen males were randomly assigned to either a control group which participated in ongoing ward milieu therapy or an AT group which, in addition, met twice a week for 6 weeks. Subjects were referred by the ward psychiatrist, who felt they would benefit from being less passive. Personal space was measured by the distance at which subjects asked an unknown hospital employee to stop as he approached them. Both verbal and nonverbal stop requests were recorded. The anxiety measure consisted of the Speilberger Self-Evaluation Questionnaire. Results indicated that the AT group showed significant changes in predicted directions but did not differ significantly from the control group. Rho correlations between anxiety and verbal and nonverbal personal space were insignificant. While no follow-up was reported, the authors note that all AT group members were discharged within 3 weeks of posttesting, while six of seven control subjects were still hospitalized from 6 to 8 weeks after posttesting. These results are suggestive but are confounded by additional therapy time, expectation, and placebo-suggestion effects for AT subjects.

Several studies have compared different types of AT procedures. Lawrence (1970) compared a behavior rehearsal group with a "logical directive" group which listened to a discussion of the development of nonassertive behavior and the disadvantages of behaving nonassertively. An attention control group heard the same statements as the behavior rehearsal group, and their responses were paraphrased by the experimenter. A no-treatment group received only pre- and posttesting. Subjects were chosen from 54 undergraduate females who were assessed by means of an assertive inventory and social issue opinion test, developed as part of the research. Results indicated that the behavior rehearsal group was the most efficient procedure for increasing assertiveness over time and across issues. There was no support for the assumption that assertiveness was a general personality trait.

Lomont, Gilner, Spector, and Skinner (1969) compared group AT with group insight therapy in decreasing MMPI scale scores. Subjects were inpatients selected on the basis of judged social anxiety, at least average intelligence, and no evidence of brain damage or thought disorder. While results indicated significant decreases on the D and Pt scales of the MMPI for AT subjects, it was not clear how this might relate to change in actual assertive behavior.

A study by Hedquist and Weinhold (1970) compared two behavioral approaches in increasing assertiveness: "social learning" of problem-solving behavior and behavior rehearsal of assertive responses. Forty undergraduates who had been identified as unassertive and socially anxious according to scores on the S-R Inventory of Anxiousness and the -S scale of the Guilford–Zimmerman Temperament Survey were randomly assigned to one of three groups: rehearsal, social learning, and a control group consisting of "traditional discussion." Subjects were asked to keep diaries of their assertive responses outside the groups. Twelve validity checks were made of the diary data, with no false reports found. Both treatment groups produced significantly more assertive responses than controls at posttreatment. However, at follow-up 6 weeks later, the differences were no longer significant.

Only one study was found which sought to determine the effects of another technique on AT. Loo (1971) examined the effects of what he termed "projected consequences," or *in situ* reactions to the behavior rehearsal of assertive responses. Both treatment groups (rehearsal only or rehearsal plus projected consequences) improved on assertive measures compared to control subjects. The projected consequences group also showed significantly more refusals than the rehearsal only group. This difference was lost at follow-up some 3 months later.

2. GROUP TREATMENT OF CHRONIC PAIN

While a number of reports have begun to appear over the past several years which describe behavioral treatment of chronic pain (cf. Fordyce, 1971), little has thus far been done employing group methods per se. Scott (1972) compared the effectiveness of a behavioral and an existential group approach in the reduction of pain apperception. The dependent variables were scores on the Pain Apperception Test and the Semantic Differential Test. A total of 16 males and 16 females were randomly chosen from a population experiencing low back pain and were randomly assigned to either a behavioral, existential, placebo, or control group. Significantly fewer negative evaluations were found between both treatment groups and the control group on concepts of meaning for pain and intensity of pain. Only the behavioral group reported significantly less felt sensation of pain. Scott questioned the validity of the Pain Apperception Test in measuring pain apperception and suggested that the test may actually be measuring anxious reactions to pain rather than apperceptive tolerances to pain. More clear-cut differences among groups may have emerged if more direct observation of pain-incompatible behaviors had been used.

3. GROUP TREATMENT OF STUTTERING

While a substantial literature has been growing for some time in the area of verbal behavior, including speech dysfunction, little has been done in behavioral group settings to treat disorders such as stuttering. Only two papers were found employing a behavioral group approach. The most recent is by Leith and Uhlemann (1972) and consisted of an attempt to develop a "shaping group" to increase fluency. The report is descriptive rather than experimental. Subjects were asked to list their goals for change, which included increasing fluency, decreasing secondary mannerisms, increasing verbal participation in social settings, and reducing defensiveness. A combination of self, group, judges', and significant others' ratings were used, but reliabilities and intercorrelations of these ratings were not computed. While the group consisted of 10 members, only four were stutterers and the other six had "personal problems." A rationale for combining stutterers and nonstutterers, as well as for the use of marathon meetings, was not provided.

Results indicated that three of the four stutterers showed consistent improvement across ratings. However, only one set of ratings, pre- and posttreatment comparisons of stuttering severity made by a graduate class in stuttering, were analyzed statistically. These confirmed the impression of significant improvement.

The use of the term "shaping group" is probably a misnomer, since it is not apparent that approximations to the desired goals were identified and explicitly reinforced by either coleaders or other group members. The authors acknowledge that the procedures are in a developmental state and cite the need for further research to evaluate the effectiveness of the shaping group.

Eglof, Shames, and Seltzer (1971) attempted to use a time-out (TO) contingency for members of a therapy group each time they stuttered. Ten males, ranging in age from 22 to 52 years, met weekly for a 90-minute session. Each was permitted to speak until he stuttered, at which time he was not permitted to speak again for an indeterminate period. Sessions in which this contingency was in effect alternated with control meetings having no contingencies, in a ABABA format. Unfortunately, only one data point for each dependent variable (number of words and speaking duration means for the group) was obtained for each condition. While the TO contingency yielded significant increases in number of words and duration of talking, there were large individual variations and a trend toward improved functioning in the noncontingent condition. It is also doubtful that a true TO condition prevailed, since subjects remained in the group and probably were exposed to nonverbal reinforcement and vicarious learning by observing other group members.

4. GROUP TREATMENT OF INSOMNIA

Three papers were found in which insomnia was treated in groups employing relaxation (Haynes, Woodward, Moran, & Alexander, 1974), relaxation or SD (Gershman & Clouser, 1974), or relaxation or single-item SD under two demand conditions (Steinmark & Borkovec, 1974).

The study by Haynes *et al.* (1974) demonstrated significant improvement in both relaxation and placebo treatment groups for 14 insomniac college students. However, the relaxation group showed significantly greater improvement than the placebo group in both latency to fall asleep and number of times awake during the night. The authors caution against expectation and demand characteristics, especially when the data are of the self-report variety. While the results of the study by Gershman and Clouser (1974) are consistent with those of Haynes and co-workers in that relaxation and SD were both significantly effective in reducing self-rated latencies to sleep onset, ability to fall asleep, and how rested subjects felt in the morning, placebo-expectancy effects were not controlled.

The study by Steinmark and Borkovec (1974) also obtained results for reducing insomnia which were consistent with those obtained when employing relaxation alone or as part of SD. In addition, their procedure permitted an estimate of placebo effects. Moderately insomniac (31 minutes or more sleep latency) college students were grouped according to severity and randomly assigned to either a relaxation group, single-item SD group, placebo group, or no-treatment group. All treatment subjects were told that no improvement would occur until after the fourth session. Both relaxation and SD groups showed significant improvement in latency of sleep onset by the end of the third therapy session, and the subjects in all treatment groups, including the placebo group, reported significantly greater improvement than no-treatment subjects after the fourth session. In addition, significant improvement in rated difficulty to fall asleep and rated restfulness was obtained for treated subjects, with no differences between groups during the initial four sessions. After session four, all treatment subjects showed significant improvement in latency, difficulty in falling asleep, restfulness, number of times awakened, and difficulty in falling back to sleep. A 5-month follow-up was conducted via telephone on 10 subjects from the relaxation and SD groups and on eight from the placebo group. The interviewer, blind to the treatment provided, asked how long it took subjects to fall asleep. Relaxation and SD subjects reported significant improvement since posttreatment. The authors conclude that relaxation alone is probably an effective treatment for moderate insomniacs but that SD may be required for more severe cases. They caution against drawing conclusions of improvement for any group, including placebo subjects, particularly in the absence of EEG studies of sleep behavior.

V. DISCUSSION AND CONCLUSIONS

This chapter, the first of two, has attempted to provide an overview of the behavioral treatment of emotional, avoidance, and social skills problems in a group therapy context. In addition, some of the important theoretical influences and basic psychological research underlying the development of behavioral group therapy procedures have been explored.

One of the primary conclusions that can be drawn from the present review is that, despite the advantages to both clinicians and clients of conducting behavioral treatment in groups, clinical developments and research in this area are still at a relatively rudimentary level. The majority of behavioral group therapy studies in the current literature feature the direct transfer of individually oriented procedures, such as systematic desensitization, to a group of clients with homogeneous problems. Only a limited amount of attention has been accorded to whether or not group interaction variables (such as group discussion, sharing ideas and feelings, and mutual feedback among members) might enhance individually developed therapies conducted in a group. Groups were used in many studies primarily for the sake of efficiency in generating sufficient numbers of subjects to allow the comparison of various types of interventions, rather than for examining group process variables per se. Few attempts were made to manipulate interpersonal behavior, and the assessments of change were directed to individual responding. It would appear that future research could profitably be directed along the lines indicated by Paul and Shannon (1966), Cohen (1969), and Hand *et al.* (1974). These studies employed a combination of group interaction and group desensitization, and they represent a link between an individually developed technique that is applied *in* a group and techniques emphasizing the application of therapy *through* a group. Future studies could be directed, for example, toward assessing the degree to which the effectiveness of assertiveness training or of covert conditioning procedures could be enhanced by manipulating group process variables in a programmed way.

Another conclusion that can be drawn at this time is that a number of methodological deficiencies occurred again and again across studies, and these often make it difficult to reach substantive conclusions about the procedure used. Among these were: possible experimenter bias, unequal durations of experimenter attention across studies, and these often make it difficult to reach substantive port measures as dependent variables, and lack of adequate follow-up evaluations. Future research on behavioral group therapy not only should be directed toward correcting these deficiencies but should be extended into the following areas: (1) testing the limits of various techniques through comparative factorial studies across different sets of clients, therapists, problematic behaviors, and treatment environments; (2) appropriate "process studies" (including outcome measures) to determine the mechanisms of operation; (3) parametric studies to standardize and operationalize the most efficient procedures for individuals and groups; and (4) the development of standardized assessment procedures with adequate reliability and validity for use in conjunction with behavioral group interventions (cf. Paul, 1969).

There were two general areas of problematic behavior—social-dating anxiety and marital problems—that were not covered in the present review because most of the current behavioral treatment in these areas has been conducted with individuals and/or couples (e.g., Gambrill, 1973; Liberman, 1970c; McGovern, 1972; Stuart, 1969). Many of the individually developed techniques in these studies—behavioral rehearsal, self-reinforcement, mutual feedback, and desensitization—have been used effectively with groups whose members have other types of problems, and it would appear that extension of these procedures to larger groups of socially anxious or maritally troubled clients may be a fruitful area of future research.

In the second half of this review, to appear in Volume 6 of this series, behavioral group therapy with children, adolescents, and clients showing habitual and addictive behaviors will be reviewed. At the end of that chapter, further conclusions, probable future trends, and recommendations for additional research will be presented.

REFERENCES

Akin, D., & Kunzman, G. G. A group desensitization approach to public speaking anxiety. *Canadian Counsellor*, 1974, **8**, 106–111.

Allen, G. J. Treatment of test anxiety by group-administered and self-administered relaxation and study counseling. *Behavior Therapy*, 1973, **4**, 349–360.

Alpert, R., & Haber, R. N. Anxiety in academic achievement situations. *Journal of Abnormal and Social Psychology*, 1960, **61**, 207–215.

Aponte, J. F., & Aponte, C. F. Group preprogrammed systematic desensitization without the simultaneous presentation of aversive scenes with relaxation training. *Behaviour Research and Therapy*, 1971, **9**, 337–346.

Bachrach, A. J., Candland, D. K., & Gibson, J. T. Group reinforcement of individual response: Experiments in verbal behavior. In I. A. Berg & B. M. Bass (Eds.), *Conformity and deviation.* New York: Harper, 1961. Pp. 258–285.

Bandura, A. *Principles of behavior modification.* New York: Holt, 1969.

Barabasz, A. Group desensitization of test anxiety in elementary school. *Journal of Psychology,* 1973, **83**, 295–301.

Bavelas, A., Hastorf, A., Gross, A., & Kite, W. Experiments on the alteration of group structure. *Journal of Experimental and Social Psychology,* 1965, **1**, 55–70.

Bednar, R. L., Weet, C., Evenson, P., Lanier, D., & Melnick, J. Empirical guidelines for group therapy: Pretraining, cohesion, and modeling. *Journal of Applied Behavioral Science,* 1974, **10**, 149–165.

Bloomfield, H. H. Assertive training in an outpatient group of chronic schizophrenics: A preliminary report. *Behavior Therapy,* 1973, **4**, 277–381.

Booraem, C. D., & Flowers, J. V. Reduction of anxiety and personal space as a function of assertion training with severely disturbed neuropsychiatric inpatients. *Psychological Reports,* 1972, **30**, 923–929.

Breger, E. M. The relation between the expressed acceptance of self and the expressed acceptance of others. *Journal of Abnormal and Social Psychology,* 1952, **47**, 778–782.

Burnett, A., & Ryan, E. Conditioning techniques in psychotherapy. *Canadian Psychiatric Association Journal,* 1964, **9**, 140–146.

Calef, R. A., Calef, R. S., Sundstrom, P., Jarrett, J., & Davis, B. Facilitation of group desensitization of test anxiety. *Psychological Reports,* 1974, **35**, 1285–1286.

Calef, R. A., & MacLean, G. D. A comparison of reciprocal inhibition and reactive inhibition therapies in the treatment of speech anxiety. *Behavior Therapy,* 1970, **1**, 51–58.

Callner, D. A., & Ross, S. M. *The assessment and training of assertive skills with drug addicts: a preliminary study.* Paper read at the American Psychological Association, Montreal, September, 1973.

Carkhuff, R. Training as a systematic experiential learning preference mode of treatment. *Journal of Counseling Psychology,* 1971, **18**, 123–131.

Cohen, R. The effects of group interaction and progressive hierarchy presentation on desensitization of test anxiety. *Behaviour Research and Therapy,* 1969, **7**, 15–26.

Crighton, J., & Jehu, D. Treatment of examination anxiety by systematic desensitization or psychotherapy in groups. *Behaviour Research and Therapy,* 1969, **7**, 245–248.

Curran, J. P. Social skills training and systematic desensitization in reducing dating anxiety. *Behaviour Research and Therapy,* 1975, **13**, 65–68.

David, K. H. Generalization of operant conditioning of verbal output in three-man discussion groups. *Journal of Social Psychology,* 1972, **87**, 243–249.

Davison, G. C. Appraisal of behavior modification techniques with adults in institutional settings. In C. M. Franks (Ed.), *Behavior therapy: appraisal and status.* New York: McGraw-Hill, 1969. Pp. 220–278.

Dawley, H., & Wenrich, W. W. Implosive group therapy in the treatment of test anxiety. *Behavior Therapy,* 1973, **4**, 261–263.

Denholtz, M. S., & Mann, E. T. An individual program for group desensitization. *Journal of Behavior Therapy and Experimental Psychiatry,* 1974, **5**, 27–29.

Diamond, M. J. From Skinner to Satori? Toward a social learning analysis of encounter group behavior change. *Journal of Applied Behavioral Science,* 1974, **10**, 133–148.

Dinoff, M., Horner, R. F., Kurpiewski, B. S., Rickard, R. C., & Timmons, E. O. Conditioning verbal behavior of a psychiatric population in a group therapy-like-situation. *Journal of Clinical Psychology,* 1960, **16**, 371–372.

Dinoff, M., Horner, R. F., Kurpiewski, B. S., & Timmons, E. O. Conditioning verbal behavior of schizophrenics in a group therapy-like situation. *Journal of Clinical Psychology,* 1960, **16,** 367–370.

DiScipio, W. J., & Trudeau, P. F. Symptom changes and self-esteem as correlates of positive conditioning of grooming in hospitalized psychotics. *Journal of Abnormal Psychology,* 1972, **80,** 244–248.

Doctor, R. M., Aponte, J., Burry, A., & Welch, R. Group counseling versus behavior therapy in treatment of college underachievement. *Behaviour Research and Therapy,* 1970, **8,** 87–89.

Donner, L. Automated group desensitization. A follow-up report. *Behaviour Research and Therapy,* 1970, **8,** 241–247.

Donner, L., & Guerney, B. G. Automated group desensitization for test anxiety. *Behaviour Research and Therapy,* 1969, **7,** 1–13.

Dyer, R. *The effects of human relations training on the interpersonal behavior of college students.* Unpublished doctoral dissertation, University of Oregon, 1967.

Eglof, A. B., Shames, G. H., & Seltzer, H. N. The effects of time-out on the fluency of stutterers in group therapy. *Journal of Communication Disorders,* 1971, **4,** 111–118.

Emmelkamp, P. M. G., & Emmelkamp-Benner, B. A. Effects of historically portrayed modeling and group treatment on self-observation: a comparison with agoraphobics. *Behaviour Research and Therapy,* 1975, **13,** 135–139.

Fensterheim, H. Behavior therapy: assertive training in groups. In C. J. Sager & H. S. Kaplan (Eds.), *Progress in group and family therapy.* New York: Brunner/Mazel, 1972. Pp. 13–18.

Fishman, S. T., & Nawas, M. M. Standardized desensitization method in group treatment. *Journal of Counseling Psychology,* 1971, **18,** 520–523.

Fitzsimmons, B. L. *A comparative study of the effectiveness on three types of hierarchies in the group systematic desensitization of test anxiety.* Unpublished doctoral dissertation, Fordham University, 1971.

Flowers, J. V., Booraem, C. D., Brown, T. R., & Harris, A. E. An investigation of a technique for facilitating patient to patient therapeutic interactions in group therapy. *Journal of Community Psychology,* 1974, **2,** 39–42.

Fordyce, W. E. Behavioral methods in rehabilitation. In W. S. Neff (Ed.), *Rehabilitation psychology.* Washington, D.C.: American Psychological Association, 1971.

Frank, G. H. On the history of the objective investigation of the process of psychotherapy. *Journal of Psychology,* 1961, **51,** 89–95.

Frankel, A. J., & Glasser, P. H. Behavioral approaches to group work. *Social Work,* 1974, **19,** 163–175.

Franks, C. M., & Wilson, G. T. (Eds.). *Annual review of behavior therapy theory and practice.* New York: Brunner/Mazel, 1973.

Fromme, D. K., Whisenant, W. F., Susky, H. H., & Tedesco, J. F. Group modification of affective verbalizations. *Journal of Consulting and Clinical Psychology,* 1974, **42,** 866–871.

Galassi, J. P., DeLo, J. S., Galassi, M. D., & Bastein, S. The college self-expression scale: a measure of assertiveness. *Behavior Therapy,* 1974, **5,** 165–171.

Galassi, J. P., Galassi, M. D., & Litz, M. C. Assertive training in groups using video feedback. *Journal of Counseling Psychology,* 1974, **21,** 390–394.

Gambrill, E. D. *A behavioral program for increasing social interaction.* Paper read at the Association for the Advancement of Behavior Therapy, Miami, December, 1973.

Garvin, C. D., & Glasser, P. H. Social group work: the prevention and rehabilitative approach. In R. Morris (Ed.), *Encyclopedia of social work, 1971.* New York: National Association of Social Workers, 1971. Pp. 1263–1272.

Gelder, M. G., & Marks, I. M. Severe agoraphobia: A controlled prospective trial of behaviour therapy. *British Journal of Psychiatry,* 1966, **112,** 309–319.

Gershman, L., & Clouser, R. A. Treating insomnia with relaxation and desensitization in a group setting by an automated approach. *Journal of Behavior Therapy and Experimental Psychiatry,* 1974, **5,** 31–35.

Gilkenson, H. Social fear as reported by students in college speech classes. *Speech Monographs,* 1942, **9,** 141–150.

Goldfried, M. R. Systematic desensitization training in self-control. *Journal of Consulting and Clinical Psychology,* 1971, **37,** 228–236.

Goldfried, M. R., & Trier, C. S. Effectiveness of relaxation as an active coping skill. *Journal of Abnormal Psychology,* 1974, **83,** 348–355.

Goldstein, A. P., Gassner, S., Greenberg, R., Gustin, A., Land, J., Liberman, B., & Streiner, D. The use of planted patients in group psychotherapy. *American Journal of Psychotherapy,* 1967, **21,** 767–773.

Goldstein, A. P., Heller, K., & Sechrest, L. B. *Psychotherapy and the psychology of behavior change.* New York: Wiley, 1966.

Goldstein, A. P., & Wolpe, J. Behavior therapy in groups. In H. I. Kaplan & B. J. Sadock (Eds.), *Comprehensive group psychotherapy.* Baltimore: Williams & Wilkins, 1971. Pp. 292–327.

Gough, H. C. *Manual for the California Psychological Inventory.* Palo Alto, Calif.: Consulting Psychologists Press, 1975.

Graff, R. W., MacLean, G. A., & Loving, A. Group reactive inhibition and reciprocal inhibition therapies with anxious college students. *Journal of Counseling Psychology,* 1971, **18,** 431–436.

Greenhoot, J. H., & Sternbach, R. A. Conjoint treatment of chronic pain. In J. L. Bonica (Ed.), *Advances in neurology: International symposium on pain.* New York: Raven, 1974.

Grinker, R. R., Miller, I., Sabshin, M., Nunn, R. J., & Nunnally, I. C. *The phenomena of depressions.* New York: Harper, 1961.

Gutride, M. E., Goldstein, A. P., & Hunter, G. F. The use of modeling and role playing to increase social interaction among asocial psychiatric patients. *Journal of Consulting and Clinical Psychology,* 1973, **40,** 408–415.

Hall, R. A., & Hinkle, J. B. Vicarious desensitization of test anxiety. *Behaviour Research and Therapy,* 1972, **10,** 107–110.

Hand, I., Lamontagne, Y., & Marks, I. M. Group exposure (flooding) *in vivo* for agoraphobics. *British Journal of Psychiatry,* 1974, **124,** 588–602.

Hastorf, A. H. The "reinforcement" of individual actions in a group situation. In L. Krasner & L. P. Ullmann (Eds.), *Research in behavior modification.* New York: Holt, 1965. Pp. 268–284.

Haynes, S. N., Woodward, S., Moran, R., & Alexander, D. Relaxation treatment of insomnia. *Behavior Therapy,* 1974, **5,** 554–558.

Heckel, R. V., Wiggins, S. L., & Salzberg, H. C. Conditioning against silences in group therapy. *Journal of Clinical Psychology,* 1962, **28,** 216–217.

Hedquist, F. T., & Weinhold, B. K. Behavioral group counseling with socially anxious and unassertive college students. *Journal of Counseling Psychology,* 1970, **17,** 237–242.

Houts, P. S., & Serber, M. (Eds.). *After the turn on, what? Learning perspective on humanistic groups.* Champaign, Ill.: Research Press, 1972.

Ihli, K. L., & Garlington, W. K. A comparison of group vs. individual desensitization of test anxiety. *Behaviour Research and Therapy,* 1969, **7,** 207–209.

Jacobs, A. Learning-oriented and training-oriented approaches to the modification of emotional behavior in groups. In A. Jacobs & W. W. Spradlin (Eds.), *The group as agent of change.* New York: Behavioral Publications, 1974. Pp. 365–407.

Johnson, W. G. Group therapy: A behavioral perspective. *Behavior Therapy,* 1975, **6**, 30–38.

Karen, R. L., & Bower, R. C. A behavioral analysis of a social control agency–Syananon. *Journal of Research on Crime on Delinquency,* 1968, **5**, 18–34.

Kass, D. J., Silvers, F. M., & Abroms, G. M. Behavioral group treatment of hysteria. *Archives of General Psychiatry,* 1972, **26**, 42–50.

Katahn, M., Strenger, S., & Cherry, N. Group counseling and behavior therapy with test anxious college students. *Journal of Consulting Psychology,* 1966, **30**, 544–549.

Kirsh, I., Wolpin, M., & Knutson, J. L. A comparison of *in vivo* methods for rapid reduction of "stage-fright" in the college classroom: A field experiment. *Behavior Therapy,* 1975, **6**, 167–171.

Kondas, O., & Scetnidia, B. Systematic desensitization as a method of preparation for childbirth. *Journal of Behavior Therapy and Experimental Psychiatry,* 1972, **3**, 51–54.

Kostka, M. P., & Galassi, J. P. Group systematic desensitization versus covert positive reinforcement in the reduction of test anxiety. *Journal of Counseling Psychology,* 1974, **21**, 464–468.

Lawrence, P. S. *The assessment and modification of assertive behavior.* Unpublished doctoral dissertation, Arizona State University, 1970.

Laxer, R. M., & Walker, K. Counterconditioning versus relaxation in the desensitization of test anxiety. *Journal of Counseling Psychology,* 1970, **17**, 431–436.

Lazarus, A. A. Group therapy of phobic disorders by systematic desensitization. *Journal of Abnormal and Social Psychology,* 1961, **63**, 505–510.

Lazarus, A. A. Behavior therapy in groups. In G. M. Gazda (Ed.), *Basic approaches to group psychotherapy and group counseling.* Springfield, Ill.: Thomas, 1968. Pp. 149–175.

Lazarus, A. A. Understanding and modifying aggression in behavioral groups. In A. Jacobs & W. W. Spradlin (Eds.), *The group as agent of change.* New York: Behavioral Publications, 1974. Pp. 87–99.

Leith, W. R., & Uhlemann, M. R. The shaping group approach to stuttering: A pilot study. *Comparative Group Studies,* 1972, **3**, 175–199.

Lewinsohn, P. M. Clinical and theoretical aspects of depression. In K. S. Calhoun, H. E. Adams, & I. K. M. Mitchell (Eds.), *Innovative treatment methods in psychopathology.* New York: Wiley, 1974. Pp. 63–119.

Lewinsohn, P. M., Weinstein, M. S., & Alper, T. A behaviorally oriented approach to the group treatment of depressed persons: A methodological contribution. *Journal of Clinical Psychology,* 1970, **4**, 525–532.

Lewinsohn, P. M., Weinstein, M. S., & Shaw, D. S. Depression: a clinical-research approach. In R. D. Rubin & J. M. Franks (Eds.), *Advances in behavior therapy, 1968.* New York: Academic Press, 1969. Pp. 231–240.

Liberman, R. P. A behavioral approach to group dynamics. I. Reinforcement and prompting of cohesiveness in group therapy. *Behavior Therapy,* 1970, **1**, 141–175. (a)

Liberman, R. P. A behavioral approach to group dynamics. II. Reinforcing and prompting hostility-to-the-therapist in group therapy. *Behavior Therapy,* 1970, **1**, 312–327. (b)

Liberman, R. P. Behavioral approaches to family and couple therapy. *American Journal of Orthopsychiatry,* 1970, **40**, 106–118. (c)

Liberman, R. P. Behavioral group therapy: A controlled clinical study. *British Journal of Psychiatry,* 1971, **119**, 535–544.

Lieberman, M. A., Yalom, I. D., & Miles, M. B. *Encounter groups: First facts.* New York: Basic Books, 1973.

Litvak, S. B. A comparison of two brief group behavior therapy techniques in the reduction of avoidance behavior. *Psychological Record,* 1969, **19**, 329–334.

Lomont, J. F., Gilner, F. H., Spector, N. J., & Skinner, K. K. Group assertion training and group insight therapies. *Psychological Reports,* 1969, **25**, 463–470.

Lomont, J. F., & Sherman, L. J. Group systematic desensitization and group insight for test anxiety. *Behavior Therapy,* 1971, **2**, 511–518.

Loo, R. M. Y. *The effects of projected consequences and overt behavior rehearsal on assertive behavior.* Unpublished doctoral dissertation, University of Illinois, 1971.

Lott, B. E., & Lott, A. J. The formation of positive attitudes toward group members. *Journal of Abnormal and Social Psychology,* 1960, **61**, 297–300.

Louks, J. *Group systematic desensitization vs. test-wiseness training in reducing test anxiety.* Unpublished doctoral dissertation, University of Minnesota, 1972.

Lubin, B. Adjective check lists for the measurement of depression. *Archives of General Psychiatry,* 1965, **12**, 57–62.

Lutker, E. R., Tasto, D. L., & Jorgensen, G. A brief note on multihierarchy desensitization. *Behavior Therapy,* 1972, **3**, 619–621.

Mandler, G., & Sarason, S. B. A study of anxiety and learning. *Journal of Abnormal and Social Psychology,* 1952, **47**, 166–172.

Mann, J. Vicarious desensitization of test anxiety through observation of videotaped treatment. *Journal of Counseling Psychology,* 1972, **19**, 1–7.

Mann, J., & Rosenthal, T. L. Vicarious and direct counterconditioning of test anxiety through individual and group desensitization. *Behaviour Research and Therapy,* 1969, **7**, 359–367.

Marlatt, G. A., Jacobsen, E. A., Johnson, D. L., & Morrice, D. J. *Effect of exposure to a model receiving varied informational feedback upon consequent behavior in an interview.* Paper read at the Midwestern Psychological Association, Chicago, May 1966.

Marshall, W. L., Strawbridge, H., & Keltner, A. The role of mental relaxation in experimental desensitization. *Behaviour Research and Therapy,* 1972, **10**, 355–366.

Mayton, D. M., & Atkinson, D. R. Systematic desensitization in group counseling settings: an overview. *Journal of College Student Personnel,* 1974, **15**, 83–88.

McGovern, K. *The development and evaluation of a social skills training program.* Unpublished doctoral dissertation, University of Oregon, 1972.

McManus, M. Group desensitization of test anxiety. *Behaviour Research and Therapy,* 1971, **9**, 51–56.

McMillan, J. R., & Osterhouse, R. A. Specific and generalized anxiety as determinants of outcome with desensitization of test anxiety. *Journal of Counseling Psychology,* 1972, **19**, 518–521.

McNair, D. M. Reinforcement of verbal behavior. *Journal of Experimental Psychology,* 1957, **53**, 40–46.

Meichenbaum, D. H. Cognitive modification of test anxious college students. *Journal of Consulting and Clinical Psychology,* 1972, **39**, 370–380.

Meichenbaum, D. H., Gilmore, J., & Fedoravicius, A. Group insight versus group desensitization in treating speech anxiety. *Journal of Consulting and Clinical Psychology,* 1971, **36**, 310–481.

Mitchell, K. R. Effect of neuroticism on intra-treatment responsivity to group desensitization of test anxiety. *Behaviour Research and Therapy,* 1971, **9**, 371–374.

Mitchell, K. R., & Ingham, R. J. The effects of general anxiety on group desensitization of test anxiety. *Behaviour Research and Therapy,* 1970, **8**, 69–78.

Mitchell, K. R., & Ng, K. T. Effects of group counseling and behavior therapy on the academic achievement of test-anxious students. *Journal of Counseling Psychology*, 1972, **19**, 491–497.

Mulder, G. *A comparison of implosion and desensitization in group treatment of test anxiety*. Unpublished doctoral dissertation, University of Southern California, 1971.

Nawas, M. M., Fishman, S. T., & Pucel, J. C. A standardized desensitization program applicable to group and individual treatments. *Behaviour Research and Therapy*, 1970, **8**, 49–56.

Oakes, W. F. Effectiveness of signal light reinforcers given various meanings on participation in group discussions. *Psychological Reports*, 1962, **11**, 469–470. (a)

Oakes, W. F. Reinforcement of Bale's categories in group discussion. *Psychological Reports*, 1962, **11**, 427–435. (b)

Oakes, W. F., Droge, A. E., & August, B. Reinforcement effects on participation in group discussion. *Psychological Reports*, 1960, **7**, 503–514.

Oakes, W. F., Droge, A. E., & August, B. Reinforcement effects on conclusions reached in group discussion. *Psychological Reports*, 1961, **9**, 27–34.

O'Brien, F., Azrin, N. H., & Henson, K. Increased communications of chronic mental patients by reinforcement and by response priming. *Journal of Applied Behavior Analysis*, 1969, **2**, 23–29.

O'Donnell, C. Group behavior modification with chronic inpatients: A case study. *Psychotherapy: Theory, Research and Practice*, 1972, **9**, 120–122.

Olson, R. P., & Greenberg, D. J. Effects of contingency contracting and decision-making groups with chronic mental patients. *Journal of Consulting and Clinical Psychology*, 1972, **38**, 376–383.

O'Neil, D. G., & Howell, R. J. Three modes of hierarchy presentation in systematic desensitization therapy. *Behaviour Research and Therapy*, 1969, **7**, 280–294.

Osterhouse, R. A. *A comparison of desensitization and study skills training for the treatment of two kinds of test-anxious students.* Unpublished doctoral dissertation, Ohio State University, 1969.

Osterhouse, R. A. Desensitization and study-skills training as treatment for two types of test anxious students. *Journal of Counseling Psychology*, 1972, **19**, 301–307.

Packard, R. G. The control of classroom attention: A group contingency for complex behavior. *Journal of Applied Psychology*, 1970, **3**, 13–28.

Paul, G. L. Outcome of systematic desensitization. II: Controlled investigation of individual treatment technique variations, and current status. In C. M. Franks (Ed.), *Behavior therapy: Appraisal and status.* New York: McGraw-Hill, 1969. Pp. 105–159.

Paul, G. L., & Shannon, D. T. Treatment of anxiety through systematic desensitization in therapy groups. *Journal of Abnormal Psychology*, 1966, **71**, 124–135.

Percell, L. P., Berwick, P. T., & Beigel, A. The effects of assertive training on self-concept and anxiety. *Archives of General Psychiatry*, 1974, **31**, 502–504.

Phillips, R. E. Effect of noncontingent vicarious reinforcement on verbal learning in a group situation. *Psychological Reports*, 1969, **25**, 7–10.

Rathus, S. A. An experimental investigation of assertive training in a group setting. *Journal of Behavior Therapy and Experimental Psychiatry*, 1972, **3**, 81–86.

Rathus, S. A. A 30-item schedule for assessing assertive behavior. *Behavior Therapy*, 1973, **4**, 398–406.

Reich, S. K. *Effects of group systematic desensitization on the symptoms of primary dysmennorhea.* Unpublished doctoral dissertation, University of New Mexico, 1972.

Richardson, F. C., & Suinn, R. M. Effects of two short-term desensitization methods in the treatment of test anxiety. *Journal of Counseling Psychology*, 1974, **21**, 457–458.

Rickard, H. C., & Timmons, E. O. Manipulating verbal behavior in groups: a comparison of three intervention techniques. *Psychological Reports,* 1961, **9**, 729–736.

Rimm, D. C., Keyson, M., & Hunziker, J. *Group assertive training in the treatment of antisocial aggression.* Unpublished manuscript, Arizona State University, 1971.

Rimm, D. C., & Masters, J. C. *Behavior therapy: Techniques and empirical findings.* New York: Academic Press, 1973.

Ritter, B. The group desensitization of children's snake phobias using contact desensitization procedures. *Behaviour Research and Therapy,* 1968, **6**, 1–6.

Ritter, B. The treatment of acrophobia with contact desensitization. *Behaviour Research and Therapy,* 1969, **7**, 41–45.

Robinson, C., & Suinn, R. M. Group desensitization of a phobia in massed sessions. *Behaviour Research and Therapy,* 1969, **7**, 319–321.

Robinson, M., & Jacobs, A. Focused video-tape feedback and behavior change in group psychotherapy. *Psychotherapy: Theory, Research and Practice,* 1970, **7**, 169–172.

Rose, S. A behavioral approach to the group treatment of parents. *Social Work,* 1969, **14**, 21–30.

Ross, S. M., & Proctor, S. *A procedure for constructing a standardized group hierarchy.* Paper read at the Rocky Mountain Psychological Association, Salt Lake City, May, 1970.

Ross, S. M., & Proctor, S. Frequency and duration of hierarchy item exposure in a systematic desensitization analogue. *Behaviour Research and Therapy,* 1973, **11**, 303–312.

Roszell, B. L. *Pretraining awareness and behavioral group therapy approaches to assertive behavior.* Unpublished doctoral dissertation, University of Minnesota, 1971.

Rotter, J. Generalized expectancies for internal vs. external control of reinforcement. *Psychological Monographs,* 1966, **80** (1, Whole No. 609), 1–28.

Russell, R. P., Miller, D. E., & June, L. N. A comparison between group systematic desensitization and cue-controlled relaxation in the treatment of test anxiety. *Behavior Therapy,* 1975, **6**, 172–177.

Sansbury, D. L. Assertive training in groups. *Personnel and Guidance Journal,* 1974, **53**, 117–122.

Sansbury, D. L., & McCarthy, B. W. Behavioral groups in a college setting. Unpublished manuscript, American University, Washington, D.C., 1972.

Sarason, I. G. Interrelationships among individual difference variables, behavior in psychotherapy and verbal conditioning. *Journal of Abnormal and Social Psychology,* 1958, **56**, 339–351.

Schofield, L. J., Jr., Hedland, C., & Worland, J. Operant approaches to group therapy and effects on sociometric status. *Psychological Reports,* 1974, **35**, 83–90.

Schwartz, A. N., & Hawkins, H. L. Patient models and affect statements in group therapy. *Proceedings of the 73rd Annual Convention of the American Psychological Association,* 1965, **1**, 265–266.

Scissons, E. H., & Njaa, L. J. Systematic desensitization of test anxiety: A comparison of group and individual treatment. *Journal of Consulting and Clinical Psychology,* 1973, **41**, 470.

Scott, E. D. *Comparative effectiveness of existential and behavioral group counseling in reducing pain apperception in individuals experiencing chronic low back pain.* Unpublished doctoral dissertation, University of Southern California, 1972.

Shannon, D. T., & Wolff, M. E. *The effects of modeling in reduction of snake phobia by systematic desensitization.* Urbana: University of Illinois, 1966.

Shapiro, D. The reinforcement of disagreement in a small group. *Behaviour Research and Therapy,* 1963, **1**, 267–272.

Shapiro, D. Group learning of speech sequences without awareness. *Science,* 1964, **144,** 74–76.

Shapiro, D., & Birk, L. Group therapy in experimental perspective. *International Journal of Group Psychotherapy,* 1967, **17,** 211–224.

Shapiro, D., & Leiderman, P. H. Acts and activation: a psychophysiological study of social interaction. In P. H. Leiderman & D. Shapiro (Eds.), *Psychobiological approaches to social behavior.* Stanford: Stanford University Press, 1964. Pp. 110–126.

Simkins, L., & West, J. Reinforcement of duration of talking in trial groups. *Psychological Reports,* 1966, **18,** 231–236.

Solyom, L. Treatment of fear of flying. *American Journal of Psychiatry,* 1973, **130,** 423–427.

Stark, E. *The comparative efficacy of three behavior modification techniques in the treatment of interpersonal anxiety.* Unpublished doctoral dissertation, University of Georgia, 1970.

Steinmark, S. W., & Borkovec, T. D. Active and placebo treatment effects on moderate insomnia under counterdemand and positive demand instructions. *Journal of Abnormal Psychology,* 1974, **83,** 157–163.

Stone, W. R. *Individual and group implosive therapy: Fear and behavior change.* Unpublished doctoral dissertation, University of South Dakota, 1971.

Stuart, R. B. Operant-interpersonal treatment for marital discord. *Journal of Consulting and Clinical Psychology,* 1969, **33,** 675–682.

Sturm, I. E. A behavioral outline of psychodrama. *Psychotherapy: Theory, Research and Practice,* 1970, **7,** 245–247.

Suinn, R. M. The desensitization of test anxiety by group and individual treatment. *Behaviour Research and Therapy,* 1968, **6,** 385–387.

Taylor, D. W. A comparison group desensitization with two control procedures in the treatment of test anxiety. *Behaviour Research and Therapy,* 1971, **9,** 281–284.

Taylor, J. A personality scale of manifest anxiety. *Journal of Abnormal and Social Psychology,* 1953, **48,** 285–290.

Tracey, D. A., Briddell, D. W., & Wilson, G. T. Generalization of verbal conditioning to verbal and nonverbal behavior: Group therapy with chronic psychiatric patients. *Journal of Applied Behavior Analysis,* 1974, **7,** 391–402.

Truax, C. B. *Client-centered group psychotherapy.* Workshop presented at the American Group Psychotherapy Association Meeting, New York, January 1962. (a)

Truax, C. B. *The therapeutic process in group psychotherapy: A research investigation.* Madison: Wisconsin Psychiatric Institute, University of Wisconsin, 1962. (Mimeo) (b)

Truax, C. B., & Carkhuff, R. R. Personality change in hospitalized mental patients during group psychotherapy as a function of alternate sessions and vicarious therapy pretraining. *Journal of Clinical Psychology,* 1965, **21,** 225–228.

Truax, C. B., & Wargo, D. G. Effects of vicarious therapy pretraining and alternate sessions on outcome in group psychotherapy with outpatients. *Journal of Consulting and Clinical Psychology,* 1969, **33,** 440–447.

Watson, J. P., & Marks, I. M. Relevant and irrelevant fear in flooding: a cross-over study of phobic patients. *Behavior Therapy,* 1971, **2,** 275–295.

Watson, J. P., Mullet, G. E., & Pillay. H. The efforts of prolonged exposure to phobic situations upon agoraphobic patients treated in groups. *Behaviour Research and Therapy,* 1973, **11,** 531–545.

Weinstein, F. T. *The effect of personality type on systematic desensitization and structured group interaction in reducing examination anxiety.* Unpublished doctoral dissertation, Michigan State University, 1968.

Werner, J. A. *Group systematic desensitization of test anxiety in relation to measured changes in scholastic probation students.* Unpublished doctoral dissertation, Texas A&M University, 1972.

Whalen, C. Effects of a model and instructions on group verbal behaviors. *Journal of Consulting and Clinical Psychology,* 1969, **33**, 509–521.

Wolpe, J., & Lazarus, A. A. *Behavior therapy techniques: A guide to the treatment of neurosis.* Oxford: Pergamon, 1966.

Zdep, S. M., & Oakes, W. F. Reinforcement of leadership behavior in group discussion. *Journal of Experimental Social Psychology,* 1967, **3**, 310–320.

Zemore, R. Systematic desensitization as a method of teaching a general anxiety-reducing skill. *Journal of Consulting and Clinical Psychology,* 1975, **43**, 157–161.

Zuckerman, M. The development of an affect adjective check list for the measurement of anxiety. *Journal of Consulting Psychology,* 1960, **24**, 457–462.

Zung, W. W. K. A self-rating depression scale. *Archives of General Psychiatry,* 1965, **12**, 63–70.

Zupnick, S. Effects of varying degrees of a peer model's performance on extinction of a phobic response in an individual or group setting. *Proceedings of the 79th Annual Convention of the American Psychological Association,* 1971, **6**, 433–434.

BEHAVIORAL SELF-MANAGEMENT IN CHILDREN: CONCEPTS, METHODS, ISSUES, AND DIRECTIONS

PAUL KAROLY
Department of Psychology
University of Cincinnati
Cincinnati, Ohio

Young people have to be trained, in part by what we tell them, mostly by how we treat them, to think of themselves as irresponsible. ignorant, foolish, no-account.

John Holt
Escape from Childhood (1974)

I. INTRODUCTION

The behavioral analysis of adult dysfunction has, in recent years, evolved beyond its emphasis on change, control, and the extension of laboratory paradigms toward a concern for maintenance of change, the proper use of control, and the incorporation of meditational constructs. The goals of treatment now include the expansion of a client's cognitive as well as instrumental repertoire in an effort to establish the grounds for self-sufficiency and further growth. Behavioral self-control and self-regulation (together termed *self-management*) have become increasingly focal directions, giving behavior therapy a greater client-centeredness (as opposed to technique centeredness), at least insofar as adult psychopathology and psychotherapy are concerned. Behavioral analysis of children, however, has failed to demonstrate similar sophistication, with the behavioral psychologist, to a large extent, miniaturizing, simplifying, and externalizing his treatment approaches, as in years past. The path of self-management's rising star seems to have begun in mid-trajectory. The ascending branch (childhood) is all but invisible.

Perhaps the relative neglect of self-management in children is a function of the clinical appeal of adult "disorders" of self-control (such as alcoholism, drug abuse, obesity, excessive smoking, etc.). Or, it may be that American philosophies of the growing child preclude serious consideration of the possibilities of self-management, since the child is traditionally seen as a fragile, unfinished, helpless, reactive creature who, if biology and environment so dictate, will much later be permitted to partake of the culturally mandated pursuit of autonomy and self-enhancement.

Whatever the causes, the results are these: naturalistic, normative, and comparative data on the development of children's self-control and self-regulatory repertoires are virtually nonexistent; treatment studies with children are eclipsed by ever increasing adult applications; assessment and therapeutic practices with children are largely (though not entirely) downward extensions of adult procedures; a probabilistic, relativistic, and "living systems" orientation to the domain of behavioral self-management is often espoused (cf. Kanfer & Karoly, 1972a, 1972b). Yet, the clinical marketplace still elicits packaged treatments (deterministic and monolithic) that seem to blithely overlook individual differences; the resources of developmental psychology are rarely tapped, and the interface with general psychology remains extremely limited.

The author's goals in writing this chapter are to review and critique the conceptual underpinnings of research in children's self-management, to propose a working model as a guide to assessment and intervention, and to examine current treatment strategies in light of an expanded general perspective. It is hoped that such an appraisal will be timely and provocative.

II. THE EXPERIMENTAL BASES OF SELF-MANAGEMENT

An operant model, with cognitive social learning elaborations, has thus far provided an effective empirical scaffold for the delineation of behavioral self-management (e.g., Bandura, 1969; Franks & Wilson, 1973–1975; Kanfer & Phillips, 1970; Thoresen & Mahoney, 1974). In *Science and Human Behavior,* Skinner (1953) conceptualized self-determination as a class of actions requiring no new laws beyond those that serve to explicate the interdependence of behavior (organism) and environment. The response of controlling one's behavior is simply a response (not the product of an arcane, intrapsychic agency) whose probability is the joint function of history, genetic prewiring, and the immediate antecedent and consequent environmental stimulus conditions.

Safely delivered into the scientific arena, the process of self-direction requires some further clarification. The locus of determination has shifted from the experimenter-clinician to the subject-client. Thus, the observation of ongoing activity, the judgment of whether behavior satisfies preset contingency rules, and the dispensation of contingent reinforcements are operations to be taken over by the individual. Self-monitoring, self-evaluation, and self-reinforcement represent a three-step sequence whose empirical investigation has been championed by Bandura, Ferster, Kanfer, Marston, Mischel, and others, with the provision that these typically covert operations either be transformed to overt actions or anchored in observable events to permit the assessment of their functional significance.

Two explicit applications of self-directed behavior control have been considered: maintenance and change. First (regarding maintenance), an individual might find him- or herself in a situation where external rewards are either absent, lower in amount than anticipated, under a capricious schedule of delivery, impoverished in quality, or available only for behavior that is incompatible with current goal-directed activity. The three-stage sequence provides a useful framework for conceptualizing the process of self-maintenance, often called *self-regulation* (Kanfer, 1971, 1975; Kanfer & Karoly, 1972a, 1972b). Second, the special case of self-regulation that involves changing one's behavioral direction is called *self-control.* While some writers define as self-control any self-initiated change in behavior (any habit reversal or any "therapeutic" maneuver that is started, evaluated, assisted, or largely administered by the client), such an undifferentiated view only tends to overburden and dilute a concept already liable for the sins of 2,000 years of naive psychology (not to mention theology, economics, and philosophy). Self-control here refers to a complex of specific responses called self-controlling responses (SCRs), not under immediate or explicit external direction, initiated in order to alter the probability of a target response, called a to-be-controlled response (TBCR). A TBCR is problematic because of the conflicting temporal contingencies with which it is inherently associated (Kanfer, 1975; Thoresen & Mahoney, 1974). For example, a TBCR that elicits immediate reward, but eventual punishment (such as excessive drinking or smoking) requires SCRs that have decelerative, suppressive, interruptive, or aversive properties. However, a TBCR with short-range unpleasant but long-range positive consequences (such as studying or visiting the dentist) is potentially controlled by SCRs with facilitative, supportive, persuasive, or response-enhancing properties. The term self-control is often limited to cases of behavioral restraint or the elimination of maladaptive approach responses. But SCRs are also appropriately applied to the establishment of adaptive approach responses that aid in the tolerance of unpleasant, strenuous, or difficult situations which carry a long-term "promise" of reward.

For an extended discussion of the varieties of SCRs that have been found to be of clinical value and the complex issues involved in the design, implementation, and maintenance of self-regulatory and self-control projects, the reader is referred to Kanfer and Phillips (1970), Kanfer (1975, 1976), Thoresen and Mahoney (1974), and Thoresen and Coates (1976).

The following assertions are fundamental to the main thesis of the present chapter: (1) the operant-social learning model has demonstrated its heuristic value in spurring the experimental and clinical study of self-control and self-regulation (which, for the sake of convenience, are hereafter called *self-management* methods); and (2) the assumption of reciprocal interaction between person and environment plus the incorporation of "mediational" constructs from social psychology, cognitive psychology, and personality have augmented the descriptive, predictive, and therapeutic effectiveness of the streamlined S-O-R paradigm (consult the references listed in the previous paragraph for supportive evidence; see also M. J. Mahoney, 1974, for a discussion of issues in theory-building and theory-testing). In all likelihood, recent calls for further broadening or expansion of the conceptual bases of self-management (Kanfer, 1976; Thoresen & Coates, 1976) will contribute to the construction of a more fully integrated, systematic model (cf. also Staats, 1975).

Social learning theory provides a broad, general framework for the analysis of the role of modeling and of direct reinforcement and punishment in the acquisition of discriminative self-control and self-regulatory behavior (Aronfreed, 1968; Bandura & Walters, 1963). Specific mediation through the child's use of language and imagery and the adult's application of reasoning has also been investigated (e.g., Cheyne & Walters, 1970; LaVoie, 1974; Meichenbaum, 1975b; Mischel & Baker, 1975; Staats, 1975; Underwood, Moore, & Rosenhan, 1973). Still, a developmentally buttressed applied psychology of self-management is not yet a reality.

To establish an adequate theoretical and empirical base for self-management applications to children, it is proposed that: (1) the assessment and modification of children's self-management problems be conducted in the same spirit of continuity and integration with general psychology that now characterizes the study of adult self-management; (2) researchers carefully observe Kantor's (1970) injunction against transforming original events (in this case, the *in situ* display of self-management or dysfunctions in self-management by children) into qualitatively different events so as to fit them into restricted definitions and conventions of laboratory research; (3) the pitting of traditional willpower versions of self-management against a unitary, functional behavioral position be recognized as obscuring potentially fertile conceptual dimensions, issues, and parameters around which an integrative model might be erected; (4) children's learning be viewed as active, purposive, self-regulating, and organized rather than passive, in the *tabula rasa* sense. Young children can, for example, make causal inferences (Kuhn & Phelps, 1976), direct their attention in a planful, deliberate, and efficient manner (Pick, Frankel, & Hess, 1975), engage in nonegocentric role-taking (Shatz & Gelman, 1973), and reliably deliver contingent self-reinforcement (Masters & Mokros, 1974). Thus, children's attitudes, values, interpretations, and preferences should be given serious consideration in the design of intervention programs, especially "self-guided" programs. A fifth point is that the cumulative and hierarchical nature of children's learning be acknowledged (Staats, 1975); that is, we can expect that "wherever there is a progression in learning—where one learned skill is basic to the learning of another—*age-related limits* to learning will occur" (Staats, 1975, p. 356, italics added). A thorough skills assessment prior to behavioral training, taking age and/or experiential limits into account, is suggested. Similarly, attitudinal, motivational, and skill components of children's self-management should not be expected to be functionally equivalent to their adult counterparts.

The developmental psychology of self-management requires that its proponents adopt what George Kelly called an open or "invitational" mood regarding conceptualization and data gathering. In the next section, six relatively distinct personality models will be reviewed. The unique or unheralded potential contributions of each to a broad, social learning analysis of self-control and self-regulation will be underscored. The limitations of each position (conceptually or methodologically) will also be treated.

III. SUPPLEMENTAL MODELS

A. Trait Conceptions

Although the trait approach to personality is associated with concepts that have shown an unenviable tendency toward circularity, surplus meaning, and predictive fallibility, its methodologies are grounded in a time-honored psychometric tradition. Isolated behaviors are arranged into molar categories according to similarities of organization (covariation), stability, structure, and causal influence (Wiggins, Renner, Clore, & Rose, 1971). In a like manner, attempts to characterize the psychosocial impact of environmental settings (Moos, 1973), and analyses of functionally related response classes in children's behavioral repertoires (Gewirtz & Stingle, 1968; Lovaas, Koegel, Simmons, & Long, 1973; Sajwaj, Twardosz, & Burke, 1972; Wahler, 1975) reflect a concern among contemporary behavioral investigators for the ordering of observations and for the determination of factors relevant to the persistence and generalizability of their interventions. Self-control and self-regulatory operations are especially valued as prime contributors to the maintenance (over time) and transfer (across settings) of behavior change efforts (Conway & Bucher, 1976). Yet, the search for consistencies in the display of self-control and self-regulation, the detection of interrelationships among various self-management skills, and attempts to characterize behavior settings with respect to their facilitative or disruptive effects on the self-management efforts of children (or adults) are, at best, disjointed undertakings. Before asking self-management to provide a solution to the critical "maintenance gap" in behavior modification, we may first need to inquire into the ecological and structural networks within which are embedded the component activities of self-monitoring, standard-setting, self-reward, internal versus external control attributions, plans for the sequencing of complex behavior chains, and facilitative self-instructions, all of which have demonstrated their short-range utility, but on a small scale.

The specific trait (multidimensional) conceptualization that most closely dovetails with the operational domain of behavioral self-management is that of *morality.* In a recent edited collection of writings on the subject (Lickona, 1976), Aronfreed, Mischel, Eysenck, Liebert, and other experimentalists considered such topics as the manner by which children learn to make judgments of right and wrong, the relation between moral judgment and self-controlling actions, the role of cognitive representations of parental socialization practices, the importance of modeling, and of the wide-ranging effects of television as a teacher of rule obedience, tolerance of delay, persistence, and other self-management skills. Bypassing its religious connotations and recognizing its situationality, the concept of morality nevertheless reminds us that children appraise, evaluate, and order their world in accordance with "higher order" principles of social conduct, and that these processes influence behavior directly and indirectly. In training children in self-management, attention to the establishment of transsituational, internally consistent, and inter-behaviorally organized social conditions, value systems, and decision-making styles in the service of self-control should reap benefits in the form of long-range maintenance and generalization. Some efforts in this direction will be reviewed later in this chapter.

B. Psychodynamic Considerations

Within a psychoanalytic framework, the search for intraindividual consistencies in self-management leads to the examination of adaptive, self-preservative, and mastery motives, patterns of conflict between ideals or reality constraints and hostile urges or sexual temptations, dependency and its management, and the role of the family in the transmission of gender-appropriate patterns of adaptation. Unfortunately, such global concepts as "id," "ego," "super-ego," and "identification," or Freud's drive theory do not hold up well under empirical scrutiny. Similarly, the emphasis in psychoanalytic theory and research has been on aspects of "conscience" that are not necessarily related to the instrumental skills of self-control, namely, guilt feelings and guilt-relieving (posttransgression) maneuvers. Yet, the extraction of meaningful material from the works of Freud and other analytic thinkers should not be ruled out, especially in light of their contribution to early social learning theory (cf. Baldwin, 1967).

Recasting the dynamic notions of drive, conflict, and defense within an adaptational perspective, White (1974) has suggested that the organism is capable of compromise, as opposed to constant struggle, and achieves general self-management (1) by obtaining adequate information about the environment, (2) by maintaining an internal balance such that reason and deliberate action are not precluded by disorganizing affect, and (3) by maintaining freedom, within the system, to use its repertoire in a flexible, self-determined fashion. Many of these essential conditions outlined by White are mirrored in the concept of behavioral self-regulation (Kanfer, 1970). Self-monitoring is a special case of the securing of information from the environment, including one's own behavior. Self-evaluation, planning, and self-instructional control maintain the individual's goal directedness, even in the face of opposing contingencies. And, self-reward and self-punishment provide the motivational fuel to direct and redirect approach and avoidance responses under the guidance of internalized standards.

Because the dynamic study of adaptation originated in the clinic, as opposed to the laboratory, it has engendered considerable study (mostly speculative) of adaptive failures (Wachtel, 1973). The most devastating form of ego disruption is said to be that which follows the emergence of affect (biological urges translated into sexual or aggressive wishes) for which defensive strategies are effective, but at the cost of "symptom formation."

Psychodynamic formulations highlight the potentially disruptive effects of excessive emotionality in self-management systems (whereas emotional deficits are more often discussed by learning theorists, e.g., Staats, 1971). Only recently have social learning-based investigations of mood states in children been initiated. An interesting curvilinear relationship between affect and self-reward has been reported (Rosenhan, Underwood, & Moore, 1974; Underwood *et al.*, 1973) wherein both positive and negative affective states have resulted in heightened levels of noncontingent self-reward, relative to that displayed by nonaroused control children. Negative mood has also been shown to reduce voluntary delay of gratification in preschoolers (Moore, Clyburn, & Underwood, 1976), and in 7- and 8-year-olds (Fry, 1975). Finally, in a series of studies, Masters and Santrock (1976) have shown that contingently verbalized or imagined affective responses can significantly influence behavioral persistence (self-regulated performance). Children talking about how much fun a task was (contingent upon working at the task) showed greater task persistence than those verbalizing a task-irrelevant phrase (controls), who, in turn, performed longer than those asked to talk about how little fun the task was. However, even nontask-related happy thoughts had response-maintenance effects. In almost all the studies relating mood and children's self-management, sex differences have been reported. In general, girls seem more influenced by the emotional concomitants of goal-directed behavior than are boys.

If emotions can disrupt self-regulation, then perhaps the strategies or control mechanisms discussed by psychoanalytic writers might be taught, after the necessary operationalization, as self-management aids. Highlighting this possibility, Miller and Karniol (1976) recently investigated the Freudian prediction that "time-binding" in an externally imposed delay of gratification situation would be facilitated by ideation about the absent rewards. Using the child's time estimate to assess the aversiveness of the imposed delay, these authors found support for the efficacy of the analytic "hallucinatory image" coping mechanism.

In addition to focusing on adaptation and adaptive complications, the psychodynamic model highlights the child-rearing determinants of self-management skills and motives. While there has been no dearth of laboratory simulations of parenting styles (based upon not only Freudian but Piagetian and social learning constructs), little naturalistic observation data exist upon which to expand our appreciation of how self-control and self-management repertoires are built.

C. Cognitive-Developmental Viewpoints

The guiding assumptions of cognitive-developmental theorists (Werner, Piaget, Bruner, Kohlberg, *et al.*) are that children structure the environment via internal experiencing and that cognitive structures and functions unfold in a regular developmental sequence. This theoretical perspective is not simply cognitive or developmental, it is interactional. Important and lasting behavioral tendencies are the product of "the interaction of certain structuring tendencies within the organism and the structure of the external world" (Wiggins *et al.*, 1971, p. 526). Some implications of this viewpoint will be considered next.

First, one need not accept the validity of a Piagetian invariant-stage model of cognitive (and personality) development to appreciate the logic of what Staats (1975) has called "cumulative-hierarchical learning." Learning of self-management or any other complex skill does not occur in separate disconnected pieces or as uniform blocks piled one upon another. Typically, one skill is prerequisite to another; the progressive nature of learning implies that often a younger child will appear to be unable to perform what an older (more experienced) child finds easy. The establishment of effective self-management is an objective of far greater dimension than that usually attained in behavior modification studies with children. Self-management is a type of interpersonal and intrapersonal competence that is more like the skilled playing of a musical instrument than the isolated production of a single note or the rote memorization of a simple tune.

The varieties of cognitive growth associated with self-mastery appear, especially in the works of Piaget and Bruner, to involve some common dimensions: an increased capacity to differentiate, store, and represent experience, and the ability to act in accordance with an "internal" frame of reference (as opposed to being dominated by the salience of stimuli or by the power of socializing agents). A look at some of the major components of behavioral self-management, for example, decision-making, standard setting, self-evaluation, symbolic self-reinforcement, self-labeling, planning, and directive self-instruction, may well reveal that the functional effectiveness of each is likewise built upon the gradually developing capacities of (a) selective attention, (b) long-term memory, (c) time perception, and (d) the coordination of internal and external perspectives. The expanded study of self-management in children should therefore include these variables (and others such as achievement striving, causal attribution, etc.) whose delayed or deficient development might be remediated early, thereby permitting the prevention as well as the reduction of clinical disorders.

A study conducted by Reppucci (1970) illustrates how the relation between behavioral and cognitive components of self-management might be explored in young children. Measures of sustained involvement with toys in a playroom were collected along with data on 2-year-olds' response latencies in a conflict (two-choice, approach-approach, discrimination) task. Positive correlations between motor persistence in the playroom and decision time in the uncertainty task (of the order of .50) were reported. Reppucci suggested that stylistic regularities in the conflictful decision task and deliberateness in behavioral self-regulation which were reliably observed in preschoolers might serve as a basis for individual differences in impulse control later in childhood. An inverse relation between behavioral mobility (open field movements) in the playroom and sustained involvement with toys suggested "a possible biological influence" as well.

Comparing 7- to 11-year-old boys described as "emotionally disturbed" with a normal group, Davids (1969) reported a *differential* pattern of intercorrelations among measures of motor inhibition (a tracing task), time estimation, level of aspiration, and delay of gratification (a choice measure). Orderly developmental trends characterized the normal group, while inconsistent relationships and generally poorer performance were found in the behavior-disordered children. Future research is needed to address the association between multiple indices of cognitive, motivational and instrumental skill components in children's competence, and to clarify the role of family, school, peer group, social class, and ethnic determinants.

Basic to all of the psychological processes cited is the emergent language capability of the child. The act of naming orients the child to selected portions of reality, including important attributes of himself or herself—such as pleasant and unpleasant affective states (Church, 1961). Language assists young children in acquiring temporal discriminations and in retaining such learning. And, with language, the child is able to approach and solve problems in a manner whose efficiency exceeds that of the sensorimotor system (Blank, 1974). Regarding self-management, the most conspicuous function of language is the supposedly progressive (age-related) shift from external to inner speech control of motor behavior (Luria, 1961). While a major clinical thrust in the treatment of self-management disorders has involved the sequential establishment of covert language cue control (Meichenbaum, 1975a), the role of language as an aid to attentional control, problem solving, memory, and the extraction of "meaning" from a complex world should not be overlooked, as these functions are presumably related to the exercise of self-control and self-regulation, albeit indirectly.

Before proceeding, a word of clarification is in order. I should like to forestall any reader's interpreting what has been presented in this and previous sections as implying that self-management should be equated with *general intelligence* or any such molar "trait" construct. The available literature (admittedly scanty) suggests that self-control and self-regulation skills are widely applicable, yet specific (analogous to a computer program). Differences among children (and among adults) in the execution of successful self-management are therefore best conceived as stemming from differences in their "arsenal of modularized skills" or differences in their "local competencies" (cf. Carey, 1974).

D. Self Theory

Neither the conceptual nor empirical status of the concept of self in general psychology can be adjudged certain and imperishable (Wylie, 1974). Its confusion value for the area of behavioral self-management prompted Kanfer and Karoly (1972a, 1972b) to suggest that inert prefixes (alpha and beta) be substituted for the term self. Yet, the term is widely used in broad spectrum behavior theory (albeit in hyphenated form) and is well ingrained in current writings on child socialization (McCandless, 1976). To be incorporated into a cognitive social learning model, the concept of self needs only to occupy a hypothetical as opposed to a substantive position. The measurable influences of self-attribution and self-perception on behavioral consistency and instrumental effectiveness are not only legitimate, but central concerns of contemporary behavioral investigators (Bem & Allen, 1974; Mischel, 1973; Rotter, 1966).

Self theorists and behavioral theorists are converging, for example, in their analysis of the critical role of awareness in human adaptation (Bandura, 1969; Kanfer & Phillips, 1970; M. J. Mahoney, 1974). Yet, very little is currently known about the development of accurate self-observation, consistent and contingent self-evaluation, and effective self-reinforcement—all of which involve the awareness of one's own behavior, the impact of environmental contingencies, and the reciprocity of action and environmental reaction.

Specific self-referenced thoughts might be viewed as a subclass of coverants (Homme, 1965) whose directive influence over behavior can be assessed empirically. If a child is an accurate perceiver of his or her physical and social stimulus value, it is likely that a "set" of consistent self-appraisals will emerge, subject to both situational and motivational input, which can be useful in predicting the child's short- and long-term success at self-management (cf. Eisen, 1972; Kanfer, Karoly, & Newman, 1975; Lepper, 1973). Duval and Wicklund (1972) have outlined a model for the development of objective self-awareness, with interesting implications both for training and assessment.

Since self-theorists are "sociological and learning theorists" (McCandless, 1976, p. 193), structured perceptions about behavior appropriateness are said to be acquired through the social interaction process, and are considered to be highly influential determinants of human response topography. While the imitation of specific action has been of central concern to behaviorists (e.g., Bandura, 1969), the acquisition of higher order values, expectancies, and broad behavior repertoires called *roles* has occupied the attention of social theorists such as Goffman (1959), Mead (1934), and Sullivan (1953). The compatibility between the two approaches lies in their mutual contextual emphasis and in their concern for delimiting the consistency and specificity of behavior. Is it therefore not possible that some proportion of the variance in self-managed behavior can be accounted for, not only by instrumental skill, motivation, situational cues, and contingencies, but by role perceptions? Certainly the *absence* of self-management, globally described by the term juvenile delinquency, has often been attributed to deviant socialization of roles (cf. Ross, 1974). Unfortunately, little has been written of the normative role enactments of self-control and self-regulatory behaviors, or of their possible demographic and developmental antecedents.

E. Learning Variations

The cognitive social learning perspective on self-management is built upon an essentially Skinnerian substructure. But it would be a mistake to assume that mediational positions have superseded their S-R predecessors. In fact, a variety of learning positions may be located along a continuum from strict environmental to higher order interactional.

There are those who allow for the introduction of a finite number of nonphysical concepts. Blackwood's (1972) "mediated self-control" model is one requiring but "a limited relaxation of the radical empiricist approach" (p. 17). Essentially, this position entails a recognition (1) of the role of externally managed verbal stimuli (functioning as cues or conditioned reinforcers) in the chain of overt responses leading to a specifiable self-control response, and (2) of the possibility of covert verbal mediation (self-cueing and self-reinforcement) in behavioral self-management. The work of Cautela, Dollard, Miller, Ellis, Homme, Kanfer, Meichenbaum, and the other like-minded conceptualizers is not mentioned; nor does Blackwood's mediational position venture far beyond the assumption of continuity between overt and covert learning principles. Mediation training consists first of teaching children to emit specific, vivid, and concrete descriptions of the ultimate consequences of failing either to resist temptation or to display tolerance of unpleasant stimulation. Second, Blackwood advocates improving children's knowledge of the response-contingency relationships operative in their environment. While a major strength of this position is the requirement that all change operations be anchored in observables, a formal weakness is the failure to recognize "hidden" and possibly instructive mediational assumptions, the cognitive forest, for the pristine procedural trees.

However, there are those who will not relax (assumptions, that is). Hyphenated constructs and nonhedonic systems appear to do violence to parsimony and to the laws of learning (Gewirtz, 1971). The effective cause of all behavior is localized in the environment. Behavior appearing to be under self-reinforcement control will, when analyzed further (i.e., when all possible, nonobvious contextual influences and reinforcement history are closely examined), be shown to be caused, as Rachlin (1974) put it, "more directly than anything else" by near and distant environmental contingencies.

The importance of the radical position lies in its tightening of the data language of self-management. We are reminded that self-controlling responses are acquired and maintained in the environment and that only a measured change in the probability of an overt response, while external contingencies remain the same, can be used as evidence for successful self-control. For self-regulation to occur, behavior must be shown to be maintained over time and across different situational contexts in the relative absence of external supports. Otherwise, self-control and self-regulation are mere attributions, "projections" of the observer rather than measurable aspects of ongoing performance. Unfortunately, the radical position also incorporates a kind of "transempirical validation" (Bolles, 1967) which assumes only one true path to behavioral change and behavioral persistence–environmental control. The possibility that the observable change is even partially due to internal events (Kanfer & Karoly, 1972a, 1972b) or that "covert contingencies" can transcend the overt is ruled out by definition. The danger of a "constrained scientific horizon" (Kantor, 1970) should be painfully apparent.

The sole intervening variable in the Rachlin-Ainslie (Ainslie, 1975; Rachlin & Green, 1972) analysis of impulse control is *choice.* But the selection, by an animal or a human, of a delayed larger reward over a smaller, immediate one requires no complex network of inferred culturally mediated skills, attitudes, or expectancies. Neither does the choice of the immediate reward imply behavioral or moral deficiencies, or the operation of a unique psychodynamic system (the pleasure principle; primary process). A simple matching formula (or choice function) explains how larger delayed rewards naturally lose their effectiveness over shorter time spans while gaining the choice advantage over longer intervals. The fact that pigeons as well as people can learn to constrain their choices, so that the smaller (specious) reward is never a temptation to them suggests that no higher functions need be invoked to explain impulse control (Ainslie, 1975; Azrin & Powell, 1968; Rachlin, 1974).

The strength of this position is that it does provide a parsimonious explanation of some forms of self-control and is supported by laboratory and field experiences. The problems with this appealing conception, however, are: (1) that it incorrectly assumes that change in, or reversal of, preferences constitutes the sole criterion of self-control in a choice situation. Other necessary ingredients are that the choice be self-initiated, the rewards be personally relevant, the temporal conflict be recognized as in need of resolution, and the option (or possibility) of reassigning priorities be continuously available; (2) it focuses on decisional self-control (cf. Mischel, 1973) while ignoring the more problematic and clinically meaningful area of protracted self-control (Kanfer, 1976). The continued struggle with conflicting alternatives and the persistent use of SCRs characterizes protracted self-control, a process which typically follows, but is in no way equivalent to the initial decision; (3) it assumes a static internal and external environment (where reward values and expectancies remain the same), and a one-way flow of information and influence (cf. Brigham, 1977; Kanfer & Karoly, 1972a, 1972b); and (4) it doesn't always predict accurately (e.g., Burns and Powers (1975) found that as the temporal delay preceding a choice was increased, their two 9- and 10-year-old human subjects preferred the more immediate reward, almost exclusively).

F. Incentive and Intrinsic Motivation

Self-control and self-regulatory problems are emotional and motivational in nature. Self-control begins with the recognition of a conflict, and is maintained by the persistent use of controlling mechanisms *under stress.* A child who, for example, must study at home to insure his promotion may focus on future rewards and current "challenges" in order to reduce the impact of the temptation to go out and play with friends. There is also the need to control attention to academic material which, owing to its difficulty, may arouse affect associated with uncertainty or the outright fear of failure. Self-regulation requires the establishment of a goal, the evaluation of progress toward that goal, and the self-selection and self-administration of various rewards on a contingent basis, often in the face of inconsistent or contradictory situational demands.

The social learning models of self-management, with their heavily cognitive constituents, may be aptly criticized for their "bloodless" appearance (cf. Kopel, 1972; Marston & Feldman, 1972; Premack, 1970). Relatively little attention has been paid to affective arousal processes, short of considering the sustaining power of self-reinforcement operations and some recent studies of disruptive or inhibitory factors in self-regulation (cf. Bandura & Perloff, 1967; Kirschenbaum & Karoly, 1976; Masters & Santrock, 1976).

Motivational systems that serve to balance the Skinnerian and Freudian emphasis on disorganizing emotions will be briefly considered. A number of humanists and experimentalists have, over the years, contributed to the study of the energizing function of affect. Only two of the most prominent positions will be reviewed here: (1) the self-control drive and incentive concepts of Logan (1973), and (2) theories of intrinsic motivation.

By stating that his concern is with "how organisms make decisions," Logan (1973) is clearly addressing the initial phases of the self-control sequence and is implicating choice as a motivational element. He notes that while the principles of reinforcement may be applied by an individual to control some behaviors, there is a class of TBCRs that present some unique problems—namely, consummatory (primary drive-reducing) responses (such as eating and drinking) which are purportedly rewarding *by nature,* but which may be undesirable over the long run to the individual or to society.

To overcome powerful motivations, a self-control drive and a self-control incentive are postulated by Logan; the first, a conditioned avoidance response learned over the course of socialization in response to parental displeasure or punishment, and the second, a "set" or expectancy that reward will result from the display of self-control (or that punishment will result from the failure to display self-control). Bear in mind that Logan is not playing the drive-naming game or postulating any new intervening mechanisms to explain self-management. Rather, his emphasis upon the study of original learning conditions, and of individual differences and awareness seems thoroughly consistent with current positions on complex social learning (Bandura, 1974; Grings, 1973; Kanfer & Phillips, 1970; Rotter, Chance, & Phares, 1972), and his introduction (or reintroduction) of a value-expectancy (or reinforcer anticipation) factor when approached psychometrically and developmentally may provide a useful adjunct in the design of workable self-management programs with children.

Another conceptual approach, likewise stressing the positive role of affect as an antecedent to and energizer of goal-directed self-management behavior, provides for self-determination its own independent, central nervous system-based justification. We refer to those theories that presuppose an innate "basic and undifferentiated need for feeling competent and self-determining" (Deci, 1975, p. 65). Whether this inborn incentive is called "effectance" or "competence" (White, 1959), "exploratory drive" (Montgomery, 1954), or the seeking after "optimal incongruity" (Hunt, 1965), the central premise is that self-management striving is not just another pretty face in the individual's repertoire of instrumental skills. Rather, intrinsically motivated behaviors are independent of tissue needs; they supposedly explain (but are not explained by) reinforcement operations (cf. Deci, 1975, for an extended presentation).

At first glance, the intrinsic motivation position gives little comfort to the behavioral clinician. What are its implications for treatment or individual difference measurement? Explaining (circularly) why reinforcement should work does not help when reinforcement is not working. Shall we rewire the organism? But, like some of the other theoretical views discussed here, the intrinsic motivation position may prove useful despite its apparent explanatory inadequacy (i.e., the position may score higher as a generative than as a descriptive instrument, cf. Rychlak, 1968).

Intrinsic motivation theorists have observed that, because even infants seem to work toward mastery or show intense curiosity, learning cannot be a plausible explanation of these behaviors. However, if we refer to neonatal patterns as diffuse activity, and highlight the essential differences between gross motor movements and competent performance, we can undercut nativist objections to learning and proceed to explore the manner by which intrinsic motivation unfolds or differentiates via interaction with the environment. We can also assess individual differences in children's tendencies to seek specific forms of stimulation, and relate variations in motivational orientation to success and failure of self-management.

Switzky and Haywood (1974), for example, measured the intrinsic versus extrinsic orientation of children 8 to 11 years old via a forced-choice vocational interest test. Children's reasons for selecting an activity were scored as either intrinsic (IM) (the challenge, personal satisfaction, etc.) or extrinsic (EM) (easy, safe, high salary, etc.). These authors then assigned IM and EM children to either a self-reinforcement, external reinforcement, incentive (noncontingent receipt of all rewards prior to performance), or a no-token control condition, and assessed performance on a Bandura-Perloff type wheel-turning (self-regulation) task. The interaction between motiva-

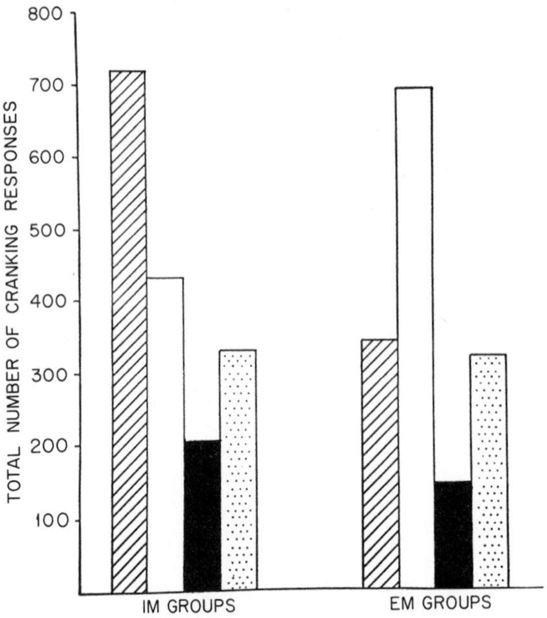

Fig. 1. Total number of cranking responses (self-regulated performance) as a function of motivational orientation and reinforcement conditions. IM = intrinsically motivated; EM = extrinsically motivated. ▨, *Self-reinforcement;* □, *external reinforcement;* ■, *incentive control;* ▦, *no token control. From Switzky and Haywood,* Journal of Personality and Social Psychology, *1974,* **30**, *360–366. Copyright 1974 by the American Psychological Association. Reprinted by permission.*

tional orientation and the reinforcement condition was significant (see Fig. 1). The intrinsically motivated children worked harder under self-reinforcement than did externally motivated children who, in turn, worked harder under external reinforcement conditions. Intrinsically motivated children also set a leaner schedule of self-reward than did EM children.

IV. A SYNTHESIS

If the various perspectives thus far reviewed were all taking off in different directions and at cross-purposes, precipitating endless debates and impeding the treatment enterprise, then the present author would advocate a purely pragmatic approach to the solution of self-management problems (cf. London, 1972). Or, if self-management was a field within which investigators were groping for relevance or relatedness, then the possibility of mindless theoretical "fusionism" (Wolpe, 1976) would make one wary of synthesizing efforts. But, in fact, the field is alive and growing, under the banner of an expanded social learning theory. And, the accumulated clinical and empirical knowledge of diverse groups is thematic and compatible. The absurd claim that we must sample from all known universes of discourse (in essence, know everything) before we can effect change must be distinguished from the evolutionary "principle of progression" enunciated by Staats. In his test *Social Behaviorism,* Staats (1975) points out:

> . . . that where the science involves hierarchically related sets of events, progression in dealing with the various levels is *required*. . . The movement must be in the direction of continually extending the elementary principles in a progressive way, to the more and more complex events. . . . Moreover, the principle indicates that separation between areas so related is not justified. [pp. 583–584]

At least three other factors can serve as justifications for the integration and extension of our conceptual and operational perspectives. First, it should be clear to anyone closely examining the literature on children's self-management that our knowledge is heavily paradigm-specific. Factors influencing children's choice of delayed versus immediate rewards, for example, are not necessarily the same as those affecting actual self-controlling behavior in a voluntary delay situation (Mischel, 1974). The decision itself also varies as a function of the social context in which it is made (Nisan, 1976), the relevance of the incentives (Dmitruk, 1974), and a number of individual difference and historical variables. Second, it is apparent that self-management is not a unitary process, but a multidimensional one involving situational, perceptual, cognitive, behavioral, attitudinal, and emotional components (Burton, 1971; Grim, Kohlberg, & White, 1968; Hogan, 1973; McReynolds, 1972). Third, with the growing trend toward the use of empirical strategies emphasizing person–situation interaction (Ekehammar, 1974), the potential of a social-learning position may be more completely realized, provided that the field is willing to acknowledge content from domains such as personality and developmental psychology, and is able to incorporate a complex reciprocity, which according to M. J. Mahoney (1974), may press S-R functional analyses to the wall, and force a major renovation in the assumptive worlds of behavioral psychologists.

Kimble (1973) has commented favorably on the trend in psychology toward more general theorizing. We have sought thus far to build a rationale, based both upon speculative and empirical literature, for the model to be presented next. Its main feature is a broadened scope; that is, it focuses on the extended display of self-management, incorporating perceptual, decisional, and behavioral manifestations. Readers are asked to view it as a first approximation in need of refinement, and to anticipate (as we do) the excitement of empirically based "remodeling."

The following four stages are seen as descriptive of self-change and self-regulatory efforts:

(1) Problem recognition and appraisal → ← (2) Commitment → ← (3) Extended self-management → (4) Habit reorganization

The bidirectional arrows separating the first three stages are to remind us that self-management exists within an open system, and that complex behavior is mutually corresponsive rather than emissive (Kantor, 1970). The importance of this oft-neglected view, particularly for the assessment enterprise, will be stressed often in the following discussion.

To initiate self-control, the individual must first become aware of the temporal conflict associated with current, problematic behavior. If other people recognize the implications, but the individual does not, then it cannot be said that a self-control process exists. For self-regulation to occur, the person's "feedback circuitry" must be activated by novel circumstances such as a dramatic change in the quality or quantity of external guidance, unanticipated consequences of his own actions, or other motivational operations (see Kanfer, 1971). Automatic chains of response become deautomated, and the system shifts to "manual control."

Recognition of the possibility of system change and personal responsibility is an invariant initial component of self-management. Although occasionally addressed, the recognition stage has remained largely implicit[1]—neglected by researchers, theorists, and child clinicians (cf. however, D'Zurilla & Goldfried, 1971; Mischel, 1973; Miller, Galanter, & Pribram, 1960).

Therapists dealing with adult clients (or research subjects) may understandably disregard the self-diagnosis phase. Adult, voluntary

[1] Although self-control theorists assert that the individual must recognize the environmental variables determining behavior, what is often neglected is the equally important recognition that contingencies are likewise a function of behavior. As Powers (1973) has stated, "Only a system that senses the consequences of its behavior can suffer true conflict, and that conflict arises directly from opposition to the outputs of the system" (p. 254).

patients have obviously traversed the recognition and decision stages by the time they appear at the doctor's office. Similarly, research subjects self-select for smoking, obesity, or study skills research projects. But children are typically nonvoluntary clients (or at least they are not often consulted), and failure to ascertain their perceptions of the relevance of the procedures they are about to undergo amounts to tacit repudiation of their rights as citizens, and may be an invitation to therapeutic ineffectiveness. There are several other reasons for questioning this implicit devaluation of children's judgments, reasons applicable to adults as well as children.

First, Bem and Allen (1974) have aptly debunked the nomothetic fallacy of assuming that people vary along fixed dimensions and that they necessarily share the psychologist's definition of a response class, while ordering specific instances of that class along the same scale of intensity. When, for example, is a child's response merely opportunistic as opposed to impulsive? When is a stimulus distracting as opposed to stimulating (cf. Doleys, 1976)? Unnecessarily poor behavioral prediction and the appearance of inconsistency are the typical sequelae of the nomothetic fallacy. Thinking in terms of absolutes is unfortunately more likely to be viewed as justified when young children are the objects of study, raising another issue—that of overcontrol.

According to Peterson (1976), overcontrol involves the external specification of desirable behavior, repeatedly, arbitrarily, and noncollaboratively, followed by the manipulation by the controller of the target's reinforcers. The most blatant response by children is *countercontrol,* the spiteful reappearance or worsening of problem behavior. It is our contention that children can and will resist inappropriate attempts to instill even self-controlling or self-regulatory repertoires. Should children perceive the relevance of self-management training in one setting, they may not evidence transfer to contexts which, to them, do not warrant a similar appreciation. When, for example, is self-reinforcement a poor substitute for parental approval?

Finally, there is a justification for attention to the recognition phase, which rests upon a fundamental assumption about self-management, namely, that it exists in an open system. Specifically, self-management is not a continuous preprogrammed process. The long-term maintenance of self-controlling and self-regulating behaviors requires periodic reappraisal of a fluctuating internal and external milieu. Though we may have a clear idea of a person's initial perception of the existence of a conflict and the need for instituting self-management, transitional events may alter the initial formulation sufficiently as well as the incentives and contingencies associated with the problem behavior to bring the process back to "Go." For example, when a child decides to study, come home on time, or control his or her eagerness to purchase the first attractive toy seen, there is a characteristic vacillation that accompanies the making of a risky decision which involves ends with conflicting payoffs (Dollard & Miller, 1950). Similarly, once a partially successful self-management program is put into effect, the success alters the original appraisal, motive, or decision—a fact to which anyone who has ever been on a diet will attest. Thus, the possibility of the child tuning out the self-management problem before it is solved is ever present, and requires careful and recurring assessment of affective, behavioral, and cognitive reactions over the course of treatment.

Table I presents a partial listing of factors, suggested by an expanded theoretical perspective, which would influence the child's initial problem recognition. Note the inclusion of factors that are presumed capable of terminating the process. These will serve to remind us that self-management failure can result not only from misapplications, but from active counterchange elements as well.

The next stage in our description of self-change and self-regulation is labeled commitment, and reflects an important distinction between knowing and wanting. The child *must prefer self-management over the perceived alternatives,* and this decision is determined, in part, by the manner with which the alternatives are construed (assuming they are construed at all). Thus, Stage 1 and Stage 2 are closely related. Operating from a problem-solving model, D'Zurilla and Goldfried (1971) have proposed a general outline of behavior modification practice that similarly highlights the importance of choice among self-generated alternatives and the dependence of decision-making upon earlier problem definition and formulation. They discuss a set or "general orientation" toward problem recognition (an interesting premise, especially if its development can be understood) which can facilitate decision-making.

In addition to the nature of problem appraisal, other more or less immediate determinants of the choice to engage in self-management (more precisely, self-control) have been discussed by Kanfer and Karoly (1972a, 1972b) and Kanfer (1975). These include the individual's reaction to the aversive aspects of the problem behavior (e.g., the delinquent child detained in the assistant principal's office; the obese child unable to engage in physical exercise) and possible

TABLE I

Hypothetical Facilitative and Nonfacilitative Influences at Each Stage of the Self-Management Process

Problem recognition and appraisal

Facilitative

Direct social and proprioceptive feedback; increased salience of the consequences associated with the behavior to be changed; emergent age- and experience-specific capabilities for recall perception, labeling, causal attribution, and verbalization of temporal conflict; heightened arousal leading to increased self-monitoring; change in role, status, or duties within family, school, peer group emphasizing the self-management process

Nonfacilitative

Metatheories about the causes and consequences of action which preclude recognition of self-determination; externalizing attributions or denial of responsibility supported by significant adults

Commitment (choice)

Facilitative

Intention statements rewarded; expectancies for successful self-management; availability of self-evaluative standards; history of promise-keeping; mobilization of achievement strivings; interpersonal trust; value of ultimate consequences is disproportionately high; the persistence of aversive consequences of failure to engage in self-management

Nonfacilitative

Counterchange social norms; history of failure to carry through intentions; nonspecific, rigid, unrealistic self-evaluative criteria; self-management incentives low; inadequate problem formulation

Extended self-management

Facilitative

Availability of component skills; adequacy of contract (formal/informal); thoroughness of training in stimulus, cognitive, and reinforcement control of TBCR; planning and problem-solving incorporated into therapeutic program; involvement of "significant others" in self-management program; success in program execution

Nonfacilitative

Specific skill deficiencies; disorganizing affect; emergence of psychological "reactance" or countercontrol motives; change in the value of immediate or long-term payoff associated with self-management

Habit reorganization[a]

Depends on the success of preceding elements

[a]Potential for the emergence of "new" self-management disorders presumably reduced.

positive and/or negative reinforcement for statements of intention to change.

Historical determinants of self-control choices have also been extensively investigated. Among the variables found to be related to choice for delayed versus immediate rewards are age and intelligence (Mischel & Metzner, 1962), affective state (Seeman & Schwarz, 1974), perceived value of the delayed reward (also a function of age) (Nisan, 1974, 1975), expectations about probable reward (Mischel & Grusec, 1967), trust (Mahrer, 1956), and various cognitive and imaginal abilities (Klineberg, 1968; Looft, 1972; Mischel & Ebbesen, 1970). No single theoretical perspective has yet proved sufficient to explain the total variance in self-management choice (see Table I).

The extended self-management of behavior (Stage 3) has received the most attention from behavioral clinicians. The assessment and inculcation of specific skills in self-observation, in stimulus control, and in the self-presentation of directive and motivational (reinforcing) cues are the legacy of learning theory to self-management. This is not surprising, for the control and maintenance of goal-directed behaviors are the foci of convenience of learning conceptions, despite the inconvenience of having to deal with private events along the way.

A review of recent learning applications to children's problems will be presented later. For now, only one point will be raised. Specifically, if we were to examine where therapeutic efforts have been directed, keeping our multiprocess model in mind, we would find anything but proportional attention. Stage 3 training, via modeling, role-playing, and direct instruction in the component and adjunctive (e.g., relaxation, assertion) skills of self-management, along with contracting for their continued application, has dominated the field (although there is a growing interest in teaching decisional skills). Systematic pretreatment assessment and multilevel intervention are relatively rare.

The end point in self-management is reached when, in the case of self-control, the probability of the TBCR is high in the absence of both SCRs and powerful external control. When a child chooses to study for an exam and former temptations are relatively unappealing, then self-control need not be implicated—rather, habit reorganization has occurred. Self-regulation becomes irrelevant as an explanatory construct when it can be demonstrated that a behavior chain is primarily under discriminative or reinforcement control and that deliberate self-monitoring, self-evaluative, and self-reinforcing operations are no longer operating. This habit reorganization phase is perhaps the most neglected of all—for few, if any, clinical case or experimental group studies of self-management have attempted an assessment of the eventual disuse of mechanisms in favor of "natural" contingencies. This procedural issue is but a special case of the more general problem in self-management methodology—that of incomplete assessment; and it serves as an apt bridge into our consideration of measurement. The reader is asked to ponder whether it might be instructive to be able to distinguish individuals (or individuals-in-situations) who fail to learn self-management methods from those for whom the probability of the targeted response can be continuously and successfully managed, but not altered.

V. TOWARD SYSTEMATIC ASSESSMENT

Suggestions and tentative guidelines are offered next for the measurement of children's self-management. Based upon converging conceptualizations, clinical experience, research trends, and the tenets of modern behavioral assessment, the prescriptive statements may also be read as an outline for future research, since standardized and validated procedures with clear-cut treatment implications are not yet available.

A. Problem Specification

As is true for any clinical disorder, assessment begins with the detection and specification of a problem. However, deciding whether to label the problem at hand a matter of self-management is not a simple process. If a teacher wishes her pupils to be better able to work independently, can we not assume a mass self-regulatory problem? If a young child is diagnosed by a physician as "hyperactive," is self-control training not clearly indicated? If parents complain about their son's negative attitude toward himself and his unresponsiveness to the demands of authorities, does not the covert nature of the problem and its insensitivity to external remediation call for a cognitively oriented, self-directed program? The answer to all these questions: a definite maybe!

A distinction can be made between a self-management problem and a problem for which self-management methods would be feasible and appropriate. Instances of the latter are self-administered treatment programs designed either as primary therapeutic modes or faded into use to maximize behavioral persistence as contact with the therapist diminishes. As a maintenance strategy, training in self-management is nearly always appropriate, since the component skills of self-monitoring (problem awareness) of self-evaluation (standard setting, contracting, knowledge of results) and of self-reinforcement should prove transferable to varied and changing extratherapy settings.

The concern here, however, is not with self-management as an adjunct to therapy, but with the deficiencies in children's repertoires that contribute to failures of self-control or self-regulation. To begin, how do we identify a self-control problem? Judgments about the existence of a behavior with conflicting immediate and long-range consequences are usually made in the absence of an extended contingency analysis. It is usually assumed that overeating, smoking two packs of cigarettes a day, chronic drug and alcoholic ingestion, excessive scratching, nail biting, hair pulling, and so on, involve positive short-term outcomes for the individual but damaging results over the long run. Similarly, studying (concentrating on difficult material and denying oneself alternate, available pleasures), exercising, undergoing medical or dental treatment, or engaging in some forms of social interaction are presumed to be aversive actions when performed, but involve ultimate benefits to the individual.

Self-regulatory dysfunctions are likewise defined inferentially. Moreover, the supposed presence of other forms of psychopathology forms the basis for assuming a causal role for self-regulatory components. Delinquency is said to stem from deviant standards and from contingent self-reward for skillful "criminal" performance. Low achievement may follow inconsistent or poorly articulated self-evaluative responses. Austere systems of self-reinforcement (usually owing to unrealistically high standards) may be causally linked to depression, feelings of despair, aimlessness, self-injury, or suicide (Bandura, 1971).

In essence, the initial phase of self-management diagnosis involves the framing of a plausible hypothesis in light of the client's observable behavior and self-reports, and the observer's theoretical predilections. External observation (by parents, teacher, or peers) may provide supportive evidence, especially when a child is unable or unwilling to provide data useful for the functional analysis phase of assessment. However, the decision to view the problem as one of self-management is always somewhat tentative, arbitrary, and subject to revision. Yet it is a necessary *first* step (see Yates, 1975).

B. Functional, Criterion, and Component Analysis

The assessor's next step is to delimit the impact of situational and historical antecedents, environmental consequences, organismic factors (especially seeking to rule out biochemical, nutritional, or central nervous system determinants), and the frequency, intensity, duration, and (in)appropriateness of the identified target response (Goldfried & Sprafkin, 1974; Kanfer & Saslow, 1969). From a comprehensive analysis, one should be able to extract information that will "flesh out" the initial hypothesis and permit answers to the following questions: (1) Does the child recognize a causal relationship between current behavior and distant contingencies and does he or she acknowledge the desirability of altering current activities? (2) Is self-management or some form of externally administered treatment most appropriate for this child? (3) If self-management is appropriate, are remedial training steps necessary to bring the child to a point of readiness for a comprehensive program of self-management? (4) Do specific forms of self-management intervention suggest themselves as particularly fitting, owing to the child's unique patterns of preexisting skills and attitudes? (5) How will the child's efforts at self-management affect significant others (family, friends, etc.)? Are the efforts likely to be supported after contact with the therapist has ceased? How will the use of self-management skills influence the child over the long run?

It should be obvious that a functional assessment based solely on observational data, collected in a limited number of behavior settings, will not supply the answers to these questions. First, a good portion of the target response system is hidden from view. Internal mediating events (self-generated stimuli and responses), sometimes called symbolic regulators (Bandura, 1969), coverants, value systems, and implicit language responses (Rotter, 1954) play a significant role in the stimulus and consequential control of the child's behavior. Second, as Bellack and Schwartz (1976) have noted, treatment-oriented assessment for self-control (and we will add for self-regulation) requires the evaluation of some *unique* and *specific* sources of data not likely to be observed unless one is explicitly looking for them. The social-learning model previously outlined can help guide us in the delineation of relevant foci of assessment. As such, the model acts to fill a conceptual and practical vacuum, which results from the general rejection by behaviorally oriented clinicians of what Kanfer (1972) has labeled "critical content elements in individual functioning." These are elements whose existence may be indirectly assessed and whose potential contribution to the success of self-management has been empirically and/or logically demonstrated (cf. M. J. Mahoney, 1974; Meichenbaum, 1976).

The analytic approach to assessment, first articulated by Stern, Stein, and Bloom (1956) and more recently adapted by Goldfried and D'Zurilla (1969) in their study of adult behavioral competence, permits the translation of our cognitive social learning heuristic, especially its covert and theoretically derived components, into concrete operational steps. Assessment in self-management should involve a great deal more than the measurement of rate or intensity of behavior and the evaluation of intervention strategies (see Mahoney & Thoresen, 1974, chapter 3), although such steps are necessary. Given a behavioral formulation of the self-management process, it should be possible to identify criterion performances and describe specific testing instruments or modes to gauge the underlying components. Data gathered in this systematic manner should aid in predicting (and improving) the success of individual and group self-management programs (cf. Wiggins, 1973).

Several characteristics of the analytic approach should be emphasized. First, the methodology depends on the assumption that behavior is a function of "the transactional relationship between the individual and his environment," an epistemological justification for including social, psychological, and biological subsystems (Ambrosino, 1974) as well as the traditional functional analysis of immediate antecedents and consequences. Second, although a child's frame of reference defines a behavior as self-controlling or self-reinforcing, parents and teachers are significant others whose view of the criterion performance cannot be ignored in the final prediction equation. Stern *et al.* (1956) suggest that the *shared expectancies* of the person and significant others be considered when formulating the criterion. They also point out the importance of explicitness in arriving at the criterion. Finally, by suggesting that "psychological job requirements, stated in psychological terms, are the true criterion," they mirror the present view that a content-free S-R analysis alone will not capture the internal perspective of the actor in the self-management context.

Although developed primarily as a means for improving group prediction, personnel selection, and institutional evaluation, the analytic model of Stern and his colleagues can provide a useful four-step assessment guide for the individual case. Step 1 is called a *situational analysis.* In seeking to specify an appropriate training objective (criterion), it will be necessary to collect from the child, and from those others in whose presence self-control or self-regulatory performances will be displayed, a list of problematic situations. For example, where and in whose company does the child act in a reckless and impulsive manner? What is meant by the term *studying*? In other words, does the parent expect 3 solid hours of uninterrupted concentration? Is the child only producing 1 hour per night. Does the teacher feel that 2 hours is adequate? How does the subject matter determine the amount of requisite study time?

It is at this stage that the child's perspective on the so-called "problem" behavior is ascertained. Can the child understand, for example, the ultimate value of his or her learning to work without help or reassurance? Does the child realize that too much "clowning" in class may be responsible for his continued academic failure? Or, is he attributing failure elsewhere?

In summary, two kinds of information are essential: a comprehensive survey of contexts for target problem behavior emission, and an understanding of how the child and significant others view the problem (and any discrepancies in these perceptions).

Specifying the psychological role requirements is Step 2 of the assessment. Goldfried and D'Zurilla (1969) refer to this as *response enumeration,* wherein samples of acceptable as well as problematic responses to the relevant situations are gathered. For present purposes, the model suggests that informants be polled as to their views of what alternative behaviors should replace problematic ones. Careful surveillance of children will often reveal that the same child who is disruptive or overactive in one context is appropriately "controlled" in another. A thorough functional analysis may reveal the hidden regularities in each of the discrepant situations that account for the varied response topographies. But it is most essential that the desirable or "good" forms of response be delineated along with the "bad."

Psychological role requirements may be age- sex- and situation-specific. The importance of this assumption cannot be overstated. We make implicit formulations about an intact adult's capacity to tolerate the withdrawal of one pack of cigarettes a day or his ability to self-record daily caloric intake. Parents and teachers must be aware of the explicit cognitive, intellectual, physical, and emotional limitations enforced by age and inexperience on children's self-management repertoires, and set role requirements accordingly. In a classroom, the teacher is advised to find for the problem child an age- and sex-matched peer whose behavior comes closer to the desired performance level, rather than setting arbitrary standards.

Goldfried and D'Zurilla's recommendations for *response evaluation,* Step 3 of the assessment, are likewise pertinent. In an extension of the previous step, the goal here is to determine which of the various modes of available self-management response is most effective in each context. Are the specific self-controlling or self-regulating responses likely to "resolve the problematic nature of the situation and avoid possible negative consequences" (Goldfried & D'Zurilla, 1969, p. 166)? Opinions of the child and important adult monitors of the child's behavior should be solicited. However, trial-and-error is likely to be the primary source of effectiveness assessment. Attitudes or expectancies toward effective responding are only useful to the extent that they predict actual performance.

The greatest amount of attention to assessment issues has accrued at this point (without necessarily considering preceding steps). As Mahoney and Thoresen (1974) aptly put it, at this point, "The data tell the story." After a baseline period, the individual is usually required to monitor instances of problem behaviors (overt, such as instances of stealing, or covert, such as urges to steal) and to record in some fashion the use of various self-management maneuvers. External verification is desirable, but extremely rare in the individual case and group designs heretofore reported.

In many instances, assessment and treatment begin to merge at this stage. Having a child self-monitor informs the assessor whether a self-monitoring deficiency exists (e.g., when records are incomplete or inaccurate). If self-monitoring is carried out correctly, it may have therapeutically reactive effects (Kazdin, 1974; Romanczyk, 1974). Stimulus control, self-reward, planning techniques, and the like can not only be viewed as treatments, but as simulations in the service of pinpointing behavioral dysfunctions in the self-management system. This empirical approach to the evaluation of response effectiveness works best if the assessor has some a priori reason for focusing on specific self-management components. The basis for such judgments derives from a working knowledge of the self-management literature and from clinical acumen; there are no proven formulae yet available (but for enlightening discussions of these issues, see Bellack & Schwartz, 1976; Kanfer & Phillips, 1970; Thoresen & Mahoney, 1974).

The methods chosen for assessing component effectiveness need not be restricted to the naturalistic observation, self-report, or simulation (role-playing) modes—although these are currently the most powerful. Nor should self-monitoring, self-evaluation, and self-reward be the only variables measured. Our broad spectrum schema (what

Stern *et al.* would label a hypothetical personality model) has shaped the direction of the situational, role requirement, and response effectiveness analyses, and should likewise contribute to the stage of "psychodiagnostic testing" (Stern *et al.*, 1956) or the preparation of the empirical "measurement format" (Goldfried & D'Zurilla, 1969). While our goal is individual assessment, not the construction of a battery of tests, the use of multiple instruments (modes) tapping different aspects of the target dimension is nonetheless recommended. A list of self-management dimensions and types of assessment modality is presented in Table II.

Potentially, there are many more than 48 concept-by-method combinations (if subcategories are included). No one would realistically employ more than a handful in any time-limited clinical case application. However, the list is offered to suggest that the invitational mood that characterized the original theorizing about self-management be sustained here. Or, said slightly differently, a sense of certainty about appropriate methods of assessment should be ruled premature at this stage of our knowledge.

Indirect measures (fantasy, projective, and story completion formats) and physiological methods are accorded probationary status on the list. Conceptual and empirical grounds for their application are available (Burton, 1971; McClelland, 1972; McGuigan & Winstead, 1974), although the majority of data are inconclusive at best (Mischel, 1968, 1972; Scott & Johnson, 1972).

Personality scales of the traditional variety, that is, wherein an

TABLE II

Assessment Modes Potentially Applicable to Dimensions of Self-Management

Dimensions of self-management	Assessment modes
Task perception	Indirect measures
Decision-making (choice) and intentionality	Personality scales
Motivational, attributional, and attitudinal underpinnings	Self-report (S-R model)
	"Assisted" self-report
Self-management component skills (e.g., self-monitoring, self-evaluation, self-reward, and self-criticism)	Interview
	Physiological measures
	Naturalistic observation
Undifferentiated measures (e.g., resistance to temptation, tolerance of unpleasant stimulation, behavioral persistence)	Performance and role-playing tests
Environment factors (antecedents and consequences; behavior of significant others)	

explicit theoretical framework serves as a frame of reference for evaluating the *content* of self-reports (cf. Wiggins, 1973), are included since a number of substantive personality constructs have been useful in predicting individual differences in children's self-management. Generalized expectancy for internal versus external locus of control is an important attributional dimension for which a number of paper-and-pencil tests are available for use with young children (e.g., Bialer, 1961; Crandall, Crandall, & Katkovsky, 1965; Mischel, Zeiss, & Zeiss, 1974; Nowicki & Strickland, 1973). Measures of self-esteem (e.g., Coopersmith, 1959, 1967), motivational orientation (Haywood, 1968), introversion-extraversion (Eysenck & Eysenck, 1969), and reasoning about "moral behavior" (Stein, 1967), among others, have also been useful in accounting for some portion of the variance on self-managed behavior. In fact, Knudson and Golding (1974) have suggested that for predicting certain aspects of interpersonal behavior (using self and peer ratings as criteria) the traditional format may be superior to the more popular S-R inventory approach.

Self-report inventories calling for specific reactions to a limited set of stimuli are used as screening devices, dependent (change-sensitive) measures, and to assess the impact of currently acting environmental factors (Goldfried, 1976). Such devices can be readily adapted for the assessment of all dimensions, in accordance with the outcome of situational and response enumeration analyses. The paper-and-pencil format is sometimes more efficient than either teacher-, parent-, or psychologist-directed interviewing, especially for older children for whom multiple testing is anticipated.

The term *assisted self-report* is used here to refer to methods which include the concurrent acquisition of data on either the situational control of self-reports, or their behavioral correlates. As covert behaviors constitute the "core" of self-management, and the self-report mode is the principal means of tapping private experiences, it is essential that techniques be developed to corroborate their occurrence.

Mahoney, Thoresen, and Danaher (1972), for example, employed an ABAB design to test the effects of reward and punishment (response cost) on adult subjects' use of various procedures for memorization of noun pairs. Studies of mediation in paired-associate learning have shown that imagery facilitates recall performance, whereas a method such as repetition of pairs is much less potent. Given the apparent performance-enhancing effects of imagery, the authors were able to demonstrate, in tandem, that imagery could be reinforced and punished and that parallel changes in recall could be directly assessed, serving as a check on the self-reported use of imaginal mediation. Few attempts have been made to extend this approach.

Voluntary delay of gratification, perhaps the most important manifestation of self-control skill from the point of view of child socialization, has been shown to depend, in large measure, upon how the child visualizes or represents reward objects, instrumental acts, and temporal distance, and how he or she cognitively transforms these in order to facilitate waiting (e.g., Mischel & Baker, 1975; Mischel & Moore, 1973). The development of assisted self-report methodologies to assess such covert activities is one of the most pressing needs in a field where the paucity of reliable measurement operations is no longer justifiable (as it once was) by claims of scientific immaturity.

The bulk of the recent innovation in behavioral assessment has occurred in the three remaining areas: the interview, naturalistic observation, and performance tests. For our purposes only the final format requires discussion (see Gelfand & Hartmann, 1975; Goldfried & Sprafkin, 1974; Hersen & Bellack, 1976; Patterson, Reid, Jones, & Conger, 1975; Wahler, House, & Stambaugh, 1976, for up-to-date presentations of issues and methods in child behavior analysis).

Self-control, self-regulation, and their essential elements are most often assayed by "confronting the subject with situations likely to elicit the type of behavior toward which the assessment is specifically directed" (Goldfried, 1976, p. 295) or by placing the individual in an analogous context (performance and role-simulation techniques, respectively).

Undifferentiated performance measures of self-control or self-regulation are those which, rather than seeking to concretize component processes, require the individual to achieve a discernible goal, either altering the probability of a conflictful response (self-control) or maintaining performance under nonreinforcing conditions (self-regulation). Typically, the behavioral process is unobtrusively observed and appropriately coded. In the clinic (if not in the laboratory) the situational test should be followed by an interview with the child to determine subjective impressions, extent of self-observation, causal attributions, and so on.

Among the difficulties in studying self-management in the clinic, school, or home is the relative lack of control over extraneous factors. The prime deficiency of laboratory simulations, however, is lack of generalizability. A practical compromise would involve collecting data on undifferentiated performance in both settings. To create a self-management simulation in the clinical, home, or school environment in order to more easily quantify and to lay the groundwork for component analyses, the psychologist can adopt any of a number of popular analogs.

The resistance-to-temptation paradigm is the most common form of self-control simulation. The child is typically presented with a variety of manipulable or edible reinforcers and asked to rank-order them according to current preference. Next, the child is asked to wait or to work for an unspecified interval, after which the adult promises to deliver the highest ranked item. The child is then left alone and knows that he or she will not be intruded upon during the delay interval. If for any reason the child cannot wait, he or she has been shown how to recall the adult (by sounding a bell, for example), whose return under this arrangement signals the delivery of the *least* preferred reward. The amount of elapsed time before the sounding of the bell is taken as an indicant of the child's ability to self-impose a frustrative delay (cf. Mischel & Ebbesen, 1970). A variation of this procedure is to leave the child alone with several preferred toys, request that he or she not touch or play with them in any way (the child might be assigned a repetitive task to perform to occupy his or her time), and measure the latency to the first "transgression," the total number of prohibited acts, and the duration per deviation as multiple indicators of self-control failure (e.g., LaVoie, 1974). If, in the latter case, the child also has to contend with a Satan-like temptation in the form of a "Clown Box" loudspeaker over which is heard the Siren call of an adult or child, seeking to distract the child from work, the analog becomes even more challenging (Patterson & Mischel, 1975). Such tasks are enjoyable, relatively simple to arrange, and can be used to measure the effectiveness of any self-control training program to which the child is exposed. For older children or adolescents, a hypothetical delay situation may be presented orally, for example, "If I gave you 25¢, what would you do with it? If I gave you $10, what would you do with it?" Children's responses to a variety of amounts can be assigned to mutually exclusive categories such as no delay, short delay, and relatively long postponement of gratification (Davids, 1969). Actual self-control performance of older subjects, for whom toys or marshmallows are irrelevant rewards, may be assessed using any of the cheating paradigms described in the classic Hartshorne and May (1928) experiments. Since different amounts of cheating may attend differential arousal of achievement motivation, assessment of situational demands and individual susceptibility to achievement cues is suggested.

Tolerance of immediate, unpleasant experiences in the anticipation of ultimate gain is a form of self-control about which much less is known. A natural reluctance to subject youngsters to "aversive" stimuli undoubtedly accounts for the relative neglect of this aspect of self-management. However, both natural and simulated performance measures are available. A "scarecrow game" (Karoly & Dirks, in press; Karoly & Kanfer, 1974) has been used successfully to measure the self-control performance of pre- and primary grade school children. Children are offered a friendly challenge to see if they can imitate a scarecrow by holding their arms out at shoulder level for as long as possible (preschool children tested by us worked for a minute or less; our 7- to 9-year-olds for 3–5 minutes). Arm extension time is taken as a rough index of children's tolerance of noxious stimulation. The task is reliable (when children are allowed practice trials), sensitive to various training maneuvers, and can be used to assess the differential stimulus control properties of socialization agents, that is, in whose presence, for whose approval, or in response to whose instructions will the child perform the longest? Finally, a naturally occurring tolerance situation for many children is classroom participation, especially oral recitation. Teachers can arrange for observers to not only record the duration of children's public speaking but to evaluate overt signs of anxiety and discomfort by employing a rating scale similar to that used by Paul (1966) in his well-known study of systematic desensitization (cf. also Thorpe, Amatu, Blakey, & Burns, 1976).

The measurement of the various component aspects of children's self-management requires somewhat greater theoretical sophistication, particularly in the pinpointing of probable areas of deficiency. Assuming a plausible rationale, the assessor can zero in on a component by adapting techniques from the experimental laboratory, as follows.

1. *Self-monitoring.* Older children can be required to keep diaries or data cards detailing the occurrence of target responses (e.g., Broden, Hall, & Mitts, 1971), while younger children may find mechanical counters easier to use (e.g., K. Mahoney, 1974).

2. *Self-evaluation.* Standard-setting and self-appraisal propensities in skill and chance situations may be assessed by way of a level of aspiration paradigm (e.g., Diggory, 1966; Rotter, 1954). By controlling the feedback, an assessor can gauge the sensitivity of children's goal-setting to "success" and "failure" experiences.

3. *Self-reward and self-punishment.* Children can be asked to

assign themselves points, take redeemable tokens, or award themselves candy contingent upon self-evaluated performance on simple (copying, tracing) or complex (maze-working, mathematical problem-solving) tasks. Self-imposed fines (return of reinforcers) can be levied by children when they fail to reach their stated objectives (Humphrey, Karoly, & Kirschenbaum, 1977). Absolute levels of self-reward and self-punishment (prior to training), consistency of self-administered reinforcement, whether rewards are, in fact, presented contingently, and the effects on children's self-reinforcement of such variables as adult modeling, peer coperformance, success and failure, and social comparison feedback all represent potentially useful kinds of clinical information.

4. *Verbal self-regulation.* Young children may be evaluated with regard to the frequency and effectiveness of self-directed instructions, questions, intention statements, evaluations, and approvals or disapprovals, after first assessing their responsivity to adult directives and their mastery of age-appropriate vocabulary (using the Stanford-Binet, McCarthy Scales, WISC, or other such standardized instruments). Task content is, of course, critical to such an assessment. Depending upon the role requirements, the child's verbal controlling skills might be tested for their inhibitory or facilitative power over simple or gross motor movements, fine motor movements, a series of coordinated actions, behaviors requiring the modulation of such attributes as latency, amplitude, consistency, and accuracy, and behaviors emitted in the context of conflict or uncertainty. As the task requirements increase in complexity, the directive power of overt (or covert) speech signals may be expected to vary as a function of such factors as the child's age, sex, semantic comprehension, development of temporal concepts, motivational state, and problem-solving style (cf. Blank, 1974; Kagan, Moss, & Sigel, 1963; Kanfer & Duerfeldt, 1968; Maccoby, 1966; Van Duyne, 1974).

5. *Cognitive control.* Discriminative attention to relevant task dimensions and requirements is a prerequisite of effective self-management at the stage(s) of problem recognition and throughout the course of extended self-management. Kagan's Matching Familiar Figures Test (Kagan, Rosman, Day, Albert, & Phillips, 1964) is the most widely used instrument for assessing school-age children's cognitive control of decision time in a response uncertainty situation. Children's performance on the Embedded Figures Test (see Reppucci, 1970) or on a simple reaction time test (Grim *et al.*, 1968) has also been used to infer information-processing style. The so-called reflective child is one who typically has a longer decision time in the

matching-to-sample task, and who is presumed to be thinking over alternative solutions, scanning the alternatives in a deliberate fashion and preferring to be right rather than quick. Although a number of performance correlates of reflection–impulsivity have been reported consistent with the view that it is tapping a general cognitive control dimension, its "microstructure is insufficiently understood" (Siegelman, 1969) and its clinical relevance incompletely assessed. It is preferable to be able to assess in context and with greater specificity a child's information-processing abilities and to relate the data to measured differences in self-management.

Siegelman (1969) tested 9-year-old boys' *observing behavior* on the MFFT by placing each of the choice pictures and the standard into wooden panels mounted on Masonite boards. Over each opening was a square of ground, light-diffusing Lucite which could be brought closer to the picture until, by making contact, the picture was clearly distinguishable. The children were required to depress a button to look at each picture and keep the button depressed lest the Lucite move forward and obscure the view. The frequency, duration, and sequence of scanning were thus directly measured. As expected, the children previously labeled as impulsive on the standard MFFT showed a greater biasing of attention, that is, focusing on the alternates less, ignoring some alternatives, favoring others, and looking for shorter durations, while less frequently comparing the standard and the alternatives.

The important implication of this study is that children's search strategies differed qualitatively or stylistically. In the absence of such an assessment, it might have appeared reasonable to try instructing impulsive problem-solvers to slow down (indeed, the short response latency is the most popular indicant of impulsivity in so-called "clinical studies" of children). However, "simply forcing impulsives to delay . . . should not be expected to reduce their errors in a multichoice problem" (Siegelman, 1969, p. 1221) because it is the pattern of the search that apparently determines success rather than processing time per se. Thus, a minimal requirement for the use of the MFFT as an index of cognitive or behavioral dysfunction is to establish, for the population under study, that it predicts criterion performance.

How well the child is able to generate alternatives in an open-ended problem-solving situation is another potentially important "cognitive construction competency" (Mischel, 1973; Mischel & Mischel, 1976). A children's version of the Means-Ends Problem-Solving Procedure (MEPS), developed by Shure and Spivack (1972), is recommended for the measurement of planning ability in preschoolers. This procedure, called the Preschool Interpersonal Problem-Solving Test (PIPS) involves the presentation of stories simulating real-life problems, requiring the child to fill in the details between an aroused need (the child wants to play with a toy) and the outcome (the child possesses the toy). Protocols are scored as to the number and types of alternate solutions created.

6. *Task perception and choice.* This critical component of self-management may be assessed through a semistructured interview built around the data gathered as part of the situational analysis (e.g., "How often do you do homework? Do you ever forget? What happens if you don't turn in your homework on time?"). Various self-management situations can also be simulated in a gamelike fashion for younger children whose spontaneous task-relevant comments can be recorded for later analysis (cf. Patterson & Mischel, 1975). Finally, in addition to tapping the child's awareness of the conflicting contingencies and their association with his or her actions, the value of near and distant contingencies can be assessed. It is often presumed that the distant rewards or punishers, when recognized, can become powerful enough cues to counteract current environmental pressures. To test this assumption, children might be presented with paired outcomes and asked to choose one, while holding the temporal delay factor constant. If a child greatly prefers to obtain peer approval immediately over a grade of A+ immediately, can we expect him to want to give up the former (and stop clowning in class) in order to possibly gain the latter in a month, when report card time comes? Because incentive values fluctuate, measurements, as earlier stated, should be taken periodically.

7. *Aspects of motivation and attribution.* It has been proposed that self-management is not just a matter of executing skilled behaviors. Along with appraisal and value components, motivation for change is another key element, subject to both current and long-term situational influences. To repeat a point, self-management does not occur in a nonaroused organism. More specifically, it was suggested that acquired general and situation-specific expectancies about the relationship of behavior to incentives serve to activate action. Therefore, in addition to measures of the child's orientation toward challenge, mastery, or control (e.g., internal–external locus of control; Haywood's, 1968, Choice Motivator scale and Harter & Zigler's, 1974, effectance motivation battery), the assessor is advised to examine children's specific task-relevant intentions and expectancies. Via interview or a self-report inventory, children can communicate

what they understand, want, and expect from a self-management program. Following Rotter (1954), children can be asked to provide data about the behavior potential of self-management (a function of expectancy × reward value) (cf. also Mausner & Platt, 1971).

8. *Parent and teacher perceptions, expectancies, values, and behaviors.* No assessment is complete without a thorough understanding of environmental support or nonsupport for self-management. These are basic ecological parameters affecting the initiation and maintenance of treatment. For example, Forehand, King, Peed, and Yoder (1975) report that parents of noncompliant children expect more noncompliance and are more critical of their children than are parents of nonclinic children. Similarly, Nakamura and Rogers (1969) found that parents' expectations of "assertive autonomy" predicted nursery school children's ability to separate from parents (measured via a behavior rating scale). The first study made use of the Parent Attitude Test (Cowen, Huser, Beach, & Rappaport, 1970) and the second a 70-item Parent's Expectancy Inventory (available from the authors). Even more important than expressed attitudes, however, is the behavior of significant others. Based on the pioneering work of Patterson and his colleagues, it is suggested that parent–child or teacher–child interaction sequences (either in the home, school, or via semistructured simulations) be observed and coded, and the conditional probabilities linking children's self-management and adult antecedent and consequent behaviors be assessed.

VI. STRATEGIES FOR THE REMEDIATION OF CHILDREN'S SELF-CONTROL DEFICIENCIES

In this and the following section, a number of intervention studies will be reviewed (self-control efforts in the present section and self-regulatory procedures in the next). Since most of what has been said thus far represents an idealized conceptualization of theory and assessment, the material that follows may appear to be comparatively imprecise, modest, and provisional. In truth, it is; but so too is much of the developing cognitive social learning product—ideal as well as actual.

Under the best of circumstances a theory of personality should underlie a theory of pathology which, in turn, should provide the basis for a theory of assessment and behavior change. However, eschewing issues relating to personality and its development, and sidestepping systematic assessment, behavioral intervention efforts have thus far been built largely upon specialized paradigms, such as observational learning, verbal self-instruction, and Kanfer's elaboration of the Skinnerian perspective (incorporating self-monitoring, self-evaluation, and self-reinforcement operations). To avoid seeming too hindsightful, we will offer only a brief, general critique of the extant research (in light of our expanded model), and then provide the reader with a positive overview of the often painstaking and innovative treatment formats currently being developed.

First it is probably a fair characterization of the field to assert that self-control training has: (1) been conducted mainly in laboratory settings, (2) employed nonclinical populations, (3) neglected individual differences and cognitive-developmental variables, (4) failed to apply systematic pretreatment assessment, (5) operated under the assumption of a general skills deficiency (as opposed to possible perceptual, decisional, or motivational deficiencies), (6) attempted to demonstrate the efficacy of a singluar (or limited) intervention strategy, (7) focused on a narrow range of self-control responses (where the frequent use of quotation marks around terms like hyperactive, impulsive, overactive, distractible, learning disabled, delinquent, excitable, aggressive, and disruptive has served to absolve investigators of the responsibility for delineating topographic boundaries and for blasting the patient homogeneity myth), and (8) failed to pay sufficient attention to issues of maintenance and transfer. Self-management researchers will have their work cut out for them in the late 1970s. Of this there can be no doubt.

However, valuable studies have appeared in the last few years, employing a variety of intervention strategies targeted to a host of locally defined and measured aspects of self-control, often summarized under the heading of impulsivity. Studies relying on external management of self-control problems or self-regulation of other target problems will not concern us here. What is needed, however, is a taxonomy of self-control disorders that will permit a meaningful comparative analysis of treatment outcomes. Etiologically, self-control disorders can all be viewed as stemming from a systems deficiency, wherein faulty perceptual, decisional, motivational, or skill components yield maladaptive approach or avoidance responses that involve a loss to the actor, either immediately or over the long run. However, in the absence of component assessment and with the increasing use of broad, all-inclusive treatment programs, such a causal analysis may be of little practical utility. Perhaps the best approach is a descriptive format, focusing on: (1) the personality system affected [Staats postulates three interacting systems, including the cognitive-language, emotional-motivational, and instrumental-motor (Staats, 1975, chapter 8)], (2) the topography of the maladaptive response (including such attributes as timing, frequency, intensity, accuracy, and variability), and (3) the context in which the behavior is emitted (conflict, distraction, uncertainty, differential reward, or no discernible consequences).

Cheating, for example, may be viewed as an ill-timed instrumental act emitted in a conflict and/or uncertainty situation. Touching a "forbidden toy" in a resistance to temptation experiment constitutes a short latency instrumental act in a conflict situation. The aggressive behavior of boys toward their peers represents high-intensity instrumental responses for which immediate reward but eventual punishment usually accrues. Because each of these examples includes temporal conflict, each is classed as a self-control problem. The errors made by children on the MFFT can be viewed as information-processing (cognitive-language) inaccuracies on a task involving response uncertainty. Strictly speaking, this kind of problem is a self-regulatory one, although many authors use the term self-control to describe its treatment.

With this brief introduction, let us examine some promising therapeutic approaches.

A. Modeling

Assumptions regarding the observational learning of self-control skills and attitudes in children are tied to modern theories of socialization. For the "well-being of society," the child, it is reasoned, must acquire the ability to discriminate circumstances that permit or proscribe the expression of sexuality, aggression, competition, dependency, and other forms of self-indulgence. Primarily through early training and parental example, the groundwork is established for mature self-control or for patterns of rule violation, disobedience to authority, and nonreflective action (Bandura & Walters, 1963; Freud, 1915/1957).

The empirical relation (in the laboratory) between modeling and various aspects of self-control has been moderately well-established. Children's display of self-imposed delay of reward can be instilled and maintained for short durations through exposure to high-delay adult models (e.g., Bandura & Mischel, 1965), although the power of models to produce disinhibitory effects appears greater than their power to promote inhibition (Rosenkoetter, 1973; Stein, 1967). If modeled behavior is accompanied by task-relevant verbalizations (Wolf, 1973) and persuasive arguments supportive of delay (Staub, 1972), and if the child is permitted to practice requisite responses (White, 1972), then self-control performance is augmented. The potential for model-induced alterations of other aspects of self-control such as delay choice, conceptual tempo (i.e., performance on Kagan's MFFT), and adoption of self-evaluative standards has also been demonstrated (Allen & Liebert, 1969; Debus, 1970; Denney, 1972; Mischel, 1966). In general, laboratory studies tend to confirm social learning hypotheses regarding the acquisition of self-control-related skills and attitudes. However, the translation from basic developmental and/or socialization research to clinical or child-rearing application has not been extensive.

The use of modeling procedures as therapeutic tools is itself a recent occurrence, and has been confined primarily to the disinhibition of fears and the acquisition of social behaviors (typically in autistic or retarded children) (cf. Rachman, 1972; Rimm & Masters, 1974). However, if we assume that some of the deficiencies underlying self-control disorders result from lack of knowledge, an inappropriate set, or ineffective controls over affect and attention, then the acquisition of information (rules) and vicarious emotional extinction effects associated with the typical phobia treatment experiment may have implications for self-control treatments. One way to prevent a child from cheating on tests is to teach (to model) alternative, acceptable behaviors that are scholastically effective. And one way to get the child to visit the dentist is to overcome his fear of the drill.

Perhaps the most direct attack on disorders of self-control via modeling has been taken by investigators working with adolescent delinquents. Stumphauzer (1972) sought to alter the delay choices of youthful offenders, who tended to show immediate gratification orientations, by exposing them to older prestigious inmates who modeled preference for delayed rewards. Choice of delayed rewards increased, and the gains were maintained at a 1-month follow-up. Unfortunately, the same experimenter conducted all tests, and this may account for persistence of the modeling effect. In addition, evidence for generalization was meager.

Fry (1972) attempted a similar kind of intervention with high school dropouts in an actual job-seeking context. Subjects were required to choose either a low-paying job ($1.50/hour) "beginning tomorrow" or a slightly better paying job ($1.65/hour) "in two weeks" after seeing a 5-minute film depicting either high- or low-status (employer vs. peer) models advising immediate or delayed choices. High-status models, as expected, induced a greater number of delay choices.

Moral judgments, rather than delay choices, were the targets of a modeling intervention designed by Prentice (1972), whose subjects were 13-year-old Mexican-American delinquent children. Experimental subjects viewed graduate students making, and being reinforced for, judgments about fictitious events that reflected a recognition of subjective responsibility (that a person's motives rather than the amount of damage done by a "deviant" act should determine the evaluation of its rightness or wrongness). In addition, children were directly rewarded for imitating model choices. Both live and symbolic modeling raised the moral orientation of Prentice's experimental subjects, who did not differ from controls, however, on the number of offenses committed at 9-month follow-up.

The association between choice (intention) and actual self-control behavior is complex (Kanfer & Karoly, 1972a, 1972b). Unless the target of a modeling treatment is an observable self-control behavior as well as component attitudes, values, and choices, the intervention is likely to be short-lived. However, lack of persistence may also attend treatments that are restricted solely to behaviors.

Any comprehensive training program for the remediation of self-control disorders should count modeling procedures among its most important ingredients (see below). While approach or avoidance tendencies can clearly be taught or disinhibited, a modeling display (instructional and/or demonstrative) can also convey abstract and novel concepts, styles of information-processing, decision-making, attitudes, and knowledge about behavior-incentive relationships in particular settings. In short, the components of self-management that have been proposed under the general rubric of an expanded social learning model can be incorporated into sequential modeling displays, modified by "amount of client handicap and response to provisional regimens" (Rosenthal, 1976, p. 62).

A particularly appealing characteristic of modeling as a therapeutic framework for children's self-management problems is the existence of a body of potentially instructive empirical research relating observational learning to age, and its cognitive-developmental correlates, such as perspective-taking, sex-role learning, symbolization ability, memory for extended temporal sequences, use of spontaneous task-relevant verbalizations, and the ability to understand the motivations and feelings of models (Coates & Hartup, 1969; Flanders, 1968; Hicks, 1968; Joslin, Coates, & McKown, 1973; Liefer, Collins, Gross, Taylor, Andrews, & Blackmer, 1971; Maccoby, 1959).

B. Self-Instructional Training

Another treatment strategy, with roots in child development research, is self-instructional training. Beginning with the stage theory of Soviet psychologists Vygotsky and Luria, behavioral investigators, most notably Meichenbaum and his colleagues (cf. Meichenbaum, 1975a, 1975b; Meichenbaum & Goodman, 1971), have been developing multicomponent programs for bringing various self-control disorders (including high-frequency, short-latency, and high-amplitude reponses) under verbal self-direction.

In constructing a model of the emergence of voluntary control of behavior, Luria (1961)[2] assumes that functions of the "second signal system" (language) come to transcend the laws of stimulus-response conditioning. Language alters perception, acts to concretize temporal relationships, and underlies intelligent interaction with the world. At age 2 or 3, words directed at children act as conditioned stimuli, impelling action, but without significative meaning. Prior to that time, behavior is not regulated by speech. Next, a stage is reached when the child's own self-directed speech becomes capable of initiating behavior. By age 4 or 5 the child's speech moves into an analytic mode of significative connections—the child can direct himself or herself to initiate *and* inhibit action. In addition, speech becomes internalized. By age 6 or 7, private (silent, inner) speech is dominant.

Although the time line laid down by Luria has been challenged by American investigators (Bem, 1967; Jarvis, 1968; Meichenbaum, 1975b), the sequence has proved useful as a guide to the design of verbal self-control training programs. Comprised of various combinations of modeling, overt and covert rehearsal, prompts, feedback, and reinforcement, self-instructional "packages" have been used successfully to establish inner speech control over the disruptive or nonproductive classroom activity of 4-year-olds (Bornstein & Quevillon, 1976), cheating behavior in kindergartners and first graders (Monahan & O'Leary, 1971), normal children's latency and errors on

[2] Other theorists whose views of verbal self-control in children have been influential in stimulating research are Dulany (1968) and S. H. White (1965).

the MFFT (Bender, 1975; Meichenbaum & Goodman, 1971), the Porteus Maze performance of hyperactive boys (Palkes, Stewart, & Freedman, 1972; Palkes, Stewart, & Kahana, 1968), the conceptual tempo (MFFT performance) of emotionally disturbed boys (Finch, Wilkinson, Nelson, & Montgomery, 1975), tolerance for prolonged exposure to total darkness in 5- and 6-year-olds (Kanfer *et al.*, 1975), and children's transgression latencies in a resistance to temptation situation (Hartig & Kanfer, 1973).

A number of treatment considerations have been proposed to facilitate the process of self-instructional training. Some of the suggestions offered by Meichenbaum (1975a; Meichenbaum & Cameron, 1974) include: (1) using the child's own medium—play—to initiate and model self-talk, (2) using tasks with which the child is already somewhat proficient, but which have high "pull" (appropriateness) for cognitive strategies, (3) having the child verbally instruct another child in the performance of a complex task, (4) moving through the program at the child's rate, (5) supplementing the training with imagery practice, such as the "Turtle Technique" (Schneider & Robin, 1976), (6) guarding against the child's mechanical droning of self-instructions which implies noninvolvement with the procedure, and (7) insuring that the content of self-instructions is not limited to simple "start" and "stop" instructions, but includes self-talk of a problem-solving variety (questioning, answering one's questions, making an intention statement, formulating a plan of action, guiding oneself in that plan, and self-reinforcement).

The last point is especially important in light of the four-stage model discussed earlier. It has been suggested that the persistence and generalization of self-control efforts may depend upon attention to problem discrimination and appraisal as well as to specific controlling mechanisms. Many self-instructional programs (and other therapeutic endeavors) have been initiated following an adult's recognition of the self-control problem and an adult's decision that change is necessary. Self-directed instructions that force the child's attention to the conflictual nature of his or her behavior may be as important as instructions that expedite performance of the TBCR.

C. Component Skills Training

In contrast to research on the effects of a specific technique on a single dimension of self-control (choice, response latency, etc.) are those investigations in which a multicomponent treatment package is directed at establishing a set of conceptually or empirically related self-control skills. Components have been identified within Kanfer's (1970, 1975) three-stage model, Mischel's (1973) discussion of cognitive and behavioral construction competencies, expectancies, and self-regulatory plans, D'Zurilla and Goldfried's (1971) and Spivack and Shure's (1974) emphasis on problem solving. In addition, developmental research on the correlates of impulsivity and hyperactivity in children, and the fact that clinical work often "demands sequential or simultaneous intervention on many problems or several aspects of the same problem" (Thoresen & Coates, 1976, p. 320) provide a kind of convergent justification for systematic treatment efforts.

Kanfer (1975) offers a useful guideline for training self-monitoring skills, with the emphasis upon direct instruction and role-playing of carefully selected and easily recordable behaviors. The establishment of reliable self-evaluation is typically approached via a combination of instruction and modeling, followed by children's attempts at matching the criterion that has been set by the adult. External reward and eventually self-reinforcement for performance and accurate self-assessment are the final links in the chain designed to teach children to be their own contingency managers. Gradual fading of tangible backup reinforcers and of contact with (dependence on) the teacher helps strengthen or internalize the skills of self-guidance and contributes to persistence of learning (Johnson & Martin, 1973; Masters & Mokros, 1974; Turkewitz, O'Leary, & Ironsmith, 1975).

At least one group of children may present special problems that will make training of the three components of Kanfer's model something other than routine. Children diagnosed, behaviorally, as hyperactive (hyperkinetic) tend to show a cluster of behaviors indicative of limited attention span and attentional control (in sustained performance tasks), rapid judgment speeds (and reaction times), motor restlessness, field dependence, and aggressiveness (Douglas, 1972; Lambert, Windmiller, Sandoval, & Moore, 1976). For such children, attentional training is a prerequisite to higher order skills development. The work of Palkes and her colleagues (e.g., Palkes *et al.,* 1972) on self-instructional training, Santostefano and Stayton (1967), who used a parent training format, and Simpson and Nelson (1974), who obtained interesting preliminary findings on a breathing control training procedure, all represent promising avenues for the behavioral solution of a significant clinical disorder of self-control. Although drugs (e.g., Ritalin, Dexedrine) have been used to control hyperactivity, their overuse and negative side effects have prompted the development of contingency management programs (e.g., O'Leary, Pelham, Rosenbaum, & Price, 1976; Stableford, Butz, Hasazi, Leitenberg, & Peyser, 1976). An obvious question is whether self-management programs might not work as well as externally managed ones or ultimately prove capable of establishing behaviors that are more generalizable and resistant to extinction.

Planning is one general skills component that has received recent research attention, but has not been incorporated into clinical self-control treatment packages. Preschoolers' resistance to temptation in a setting containing an active distraction (a Clown Box with a tape-recorded message enjoining the child to "Just come over and push my nose and see what happens") was aided by training in plans to resist distraction (Patterson & Mischel, 1975). Children rehearsed such tactics as imagining a brick wall between them and the Clown Box, self-instructions to continue working, and assertive statements indicating refusal to be tempted. In a clinical context, children should be able to learn to generate their own plans, and practice them for extended periods across a variety of problematic situations (simulated and *in vivo*). Patterson and Mischel's plans were restricted to relatively specific SCRs. An alternative approach is to provide children with general problem-solving skills applicable to situations varying in complexity, stressfulness, and in the amount of external impediments to goal-directed activity.

Russell and Thoresen (1976), following the D'Zurilla and Goldfried's (1971) problem-solving rationale, have, for example, sought to teach decision-making to "acting out" preadolescents in a residential treatment home. Self-controlling behaviors emphasizing stimulus control as well as modification of thoughts, perceptions, and images are the teaching objectives of the program, along with specific attention to enlarging the adaptive capacity of the residents. A *Decision-Making Book for Children* containing written and audiotape programmed materials appropriate for 8- to 12-year-olds is the nexus of the decision-making training program. Moving at his own rate, a child is taught to identify problems, generate alternatives, collect information, recognize personal values, make a decision, and review the decision at a later time. Controlled evaluations of this promising therapeutic modality are in progress. Particularly noteworthy is the possibility of employing such a program to address deficiencies in the neglected problem appraisal phase of self-control.

Another broad-based intervention program designed for young (6- to 8-year-old) boys with aggressive histories has been described by

Camp and her associates (Camp, Blom, Hebert, & van Doorninck, 1976). Camp determined that aggressive boys possess adequate verbal ability, but typically fail to use verbal mediation to either inhibit first responses or to evaluate and plan solutions, but rather use speech in a self-stimulatory way. Therefore, Camp and her colleagues developed the "Think Aloud" program. Seven program objectives included teaching children how to (1) slow down, (2) inhibit first associations, (3) increase verbal mediation, (4) inhibit immature, irrelevant speech, (5) develop alternative responses, (6) build planning skills, and (7) transfer their skill acquisitions to life situations (Camp & Bash, 1975). Self-instructional methods (following Meichenbaum) were used to establish the first three objectives. Signaling for an incompatible activity was used to make children aware of their irrelevant speech and to disrupt irrelevant speech control of behavior. Modeling of problem-solving and frustration-coping strategies along with problem simulations were employed to increase the child's repertoire of adaptive responses. A game format and performance practice with feedback were used to assist children in recognizing the relation of their actions to environmental consequences (an aspect of problem appraisal as here conceptualized). Finally, transfer was sought by means of role-playing of real-life situations and open discussions of alternative strategies, while the need for cooperativeness, empathy, and self-awareness was continuously stressed. Preliminary outcome data are encouraging, although program refinements are clearly indicated (Camp *et al.*, 1976). Camp's approach is appealing because, unlike many training endeavors, hers was based upon thorough multidimensional assessment of her target population (Camp, 1975) and a multicomponent treatment approach targeted to a set of interrelated cognitive and instrumental response deficiencies.

A necessary component of self-control learning is motivation for change. The more the child is involved with the program, the easier it will be to relate to the materials and to retain and practice what has been learned. When motivational deficiencies result from skill deficiencies ("I won't because I can't"), a well-balanced and graduated program can often overcome the child's reluctance to perform. However, when the child feels manipulated to someone else's ends, or when implicit counterchange attitudes, attributions, or (mis)-conceptions exist, then preprogram motivational upgrading is required. In such cases the quality of the interpersonal relationship between therapist and child may prove to be the most important factor (Goldstein, 1975). The use of negotiated contracts based upon the exchange of positive reinforcers is desirable (Kanfer, 1975) as are any and all attempts to understand the child's perspective on his or her behavior.

VII. SELF-REGULATION IN THE CLASSROOM

Self-management applications are not confined to the remediation of impulsive, disruptive, or deficient performance or to laboratory demonstrations. Self-regulation is a classroom fixture (or it should be); for whether pedagogic philosophies are "open" or traditional, the stated or implicit goals of primary and secondary education include the imparting of independent scholarship, a sense of involvement with the learning process, self-pacing, and the ability to use basic skills in the service of continued growth and development (Lovitt, 1973; Winett, 1973). Although these goals have taken a back seat to interventions designed to achieve teacher-defined objectives (typically for classroom order and pupil compliance), a body of literature is emerging in which self-management theory and technology are applied toward the mutual enhancement of both pupil and teacher. It is perhaps the preventive implications of early self-management training, however, that mark the area as potentially the most important laboratory for the application of behavioral principles to children (Graziano, 1975).

Historically, the earliest concern of school-based research was to gauge the effectiveness and feasibility of student-assisted scholastic management via self-reward. A trend-setting study was that of Lovitt and Curtiss (1969), whose subject was a 12-year-old behavior-disordered child. After a baseline period, the student next performed under a teacher-determined contingency. Work done (correct answers) in various content areas earned points redeemable for free time (the terms *contract* and *agreement* were used inappropriately to describe these unilateral contingency arrangements). The child evidenced an increase in academic response rate, but only when he was permitted to specify verbally and record his own payoff ratios. The authors demonstrated, further, that the fact of self-scheduling rather than the child's generous payoff rate accounted for the increase (e.g., no improvement was observed when the teacher dispensed the rewards according to the child's schedule).

In addition to providing an impetus to the study of the self-reward component of self-regulation, the Lovitt and Curtiss experiment also raised the possibility that choice might be viewed as a response facilitator. This finding has since been replicated and extended by others (e.g., Brigham & Bushell, 1973; Brigham & Sherman, 1973; Brigham & Stoerzinger, 1976). However, the role of choice in children's learning and self-management is both intriguing and complex: because the act of choosing may involve various uncontrolled collateral covert events (M. J. Mahoney, 1974), the thing chosen may include type or unit amount of reward, specific schedule of reward delivery, and self versus other reward selection or administration, while all of these factors may enter into a higher order interaction with the target response and with various individual difference, history, and demographic factors. Why self-reinforcement works may be of less concern to clinicians than the fact that it does have behavioral maintenance properties. Yet, ultimately, the most effective clinical application will derive, not simply from naked empirical relationships, but from a thorough knowledge of children's emergent growth requirements and the demands placed upon them by a rapidly changing environment.

The work of Glynn and his associates (Ballard & Glynn, 1975; Glynn & Thomas, 1974; Glynn, Thomas, & Shee, 1973) exemplifies the current programmatic approach to self-regulation training in the normal classroom setting–including not only self-reward, but the self-monitoring and self-evaluation components as well. While the study of specific subprocesses remains an important enterprise (cf. Broden *et al.,* 1971; Drabman, Spitalnik, & O'Leary, 1973; Glynn, 1970; Gottman, & McFall, 1972; Kaufman & O'Leary, 1972; Winett, Richards, & Krasner, 1971), the field is advancing in the direction of comprehensive multicomponent skills training with its potential for instilling general and enduring behavioral competencies.

For example, Glynn *et al.* (1973) reasoned that children trained to emit "on-task" behavior (e.g., looking at the teacher, reading or writing at their desks, etc.) under an external reinforcement program would be capable of maintaining their performance levels through the use of self-recording, self-assessment (self-evaluation), and both self-determined and self-administered rewards. Working in a "typical" New Zealand second-grade classroom (mean age = 6 years 11 months), the investigators randomly selected 8 of a total of 37 children for observation. The study took place over 85 days and was conducted in 10 phases. A series of baselines and class contingency procedures constituted the first 6 phases, by the end of which the classwide mean daily percentage on-task behavior was 88% (compared to the 58% level at first baseline). Behavioral self-control (or, in keeping with the present usage, behavioral self-regulation) procedures were then introduced. Children were provided with self-monitoring cards on which they were to indicate when their on-task behavior corresponded with randomly presented auditory signals. Children could obtain free time plus access to other backup reinforcers of their choosing on the basis of 1 minute for every check mark recorded (redeemable prior to their normal morning recess). As the authors point out, this procedure involves self-monitoring, partial self-evaluation, as the standard of conduct was teacher-determined, and partial self-determination of reinforcement, as the types and amounts of reinforcement were also experimenter-determined.

These self-regulation procedures not only successfully maintained children's performances (an intervening return to baseline saw levels decline by about 15%), but, during the three self-control periods, behavioral variances were noticeably smaller. This bonus of greater performance stability has important implications for classroom management. In addition to saving teacher time, self-regulatory procedures appear to hold the promise of recruiting more consistent involvement with the tasks at hand (perhaps because they involve the added reinforcing value of choice, self-perceptions of acting in a more grown up fashion, or heightened predictability of behavior-reinforcer relationships in the classroom).

In their follow-up, Glynn and Thomas (1974) not only extended the earlier study to 7- and 8-year-olds designated as management problems, but also introduced noteworthy procedural changes. Most important was their immediate introduction of self-regulatory operations after a single baseline period (an ABAB design). Could the children self-regulate without extensive experimenter-controlled discrimination training and fading periods? This question was asked in the knowledge that even when training procedures were included in other studies, children sometimes failed to match the performance levels obtained under teacher-administered regimens (cf. Drabman *et al.*, 1973; Santogrossi, O'Leary, Romanczyk, & Kaufman, 1973). Second, a "behavioral cueing procedure" was introduced to correct for the tendency for classroom requirements to conflict with experimental design considerations. Specifically, the teacher often called children off the task at which they were working in order to make a point, clarify an example, or otherwise engage in requisite instructional activity. In such cases, children were observed to lose points for not sustaining on-task behavior because the cue for self-recording came during a teacher interruption period. Also, after diverting attention to a new task, the teacher often failed to provide a return-to-task instruction. To overcome these problems, the teacher used a color-coded behavior specification chart to continuously cue children as to which behavior, teacher-directed or work-directed, would be considered on-task. The children awarded themselves points for "doing what the chart says."

Results indicated that self-regulatory operations could indeed be put into effect without prior external reinforcement, and that the combination of self-regulatory operations and cueing proved most powerful (an average of 91% on-task as compared to 50% during the baselines and 70% during the uncued self-regulation phase). Unfortunately, along with the cueing chart the experimenters also introduced another procedural variation, that of providing more opportunities for self-reward. Thus, the effects of cueing per se could not be seperately assessed.

It is worth bearing in mind that in each of the Glynn *et al.* experiments, the teacher was cooperative, the classroom structure was largely unaltered, and the children were working toward valued activity reinforcers. These seemingly "incidental" components may eventually prove to be essential to the success of such programs. Moreover, the relative ease and rapidity with which the regulatory components were adopted may be partly attributable to task structuring provided by the self-assessment auditory signals, the self-monitoring cards, the continued presence of the teacher, and the fact that the entire class was involved in the program. These comments, far from intending criticism, are offered (1) to console investigators whose self-regulatory projects will be undertaken in less than ideal conditions, and (2) to suggest that persistence and generalization of effects may be sacrificed for the benefits of efficient instigation of relatively specific responses.

An alternate approach to training would involve instruction in the self-assessment of self-regulatory disorders, the presentation of the general social learning model, and remedial training in areas in which the child is deficient or unpracticed. The objective would be to provide the child with a set of cognitive and instrumental skills capable of facilitating behavioral persistence in the face of multiple external deterrants (including nonreward, punishment, conflict, etc.). Among the didactic strategies that could be used are formal information-giving (via lecture, film, and written materials), simulation "games," group discussion, programmed materials, and guided practice (cf. Krumboltz & Thoresen, 1976), all tailored to meet age, motivational, and relevant individual difference requirements.

While no systematic self-regulation training of the sort mentioned is currently available for children, attempts to teach more abstract principles relevant to self-management have been reported. Specifically, programs aimed at establishing skills in decision-making (Russell & Thoresen, 1976), means–end thinking (Spivack & Shure, 1974), verbal–motor regulation (Meichenbaum, 1975a), contracting (Homme, Csanyi, Gonzales, & Rechs, 1970), and planning (Patterson & Mischel, 1975) may, when integrated, serve as models for future innovative classroom operations. An example of a practical, inexpensive, multicomponent self-management course for sixth graders has recently been described by Niemann and Brigham (1976). The course incorporates lectures and laboratory experiences with operant conditioning and self-management methods and research. Children select an individualized self-management project, design an intervention plan (with assistance from the experimenter), record their progress, and write a final summary report. Children participating in this course, when compared to a group of children assigned to a general psychology course and to a no-training control group drawn from a different classroom, showed improved performance on a self-management questionnaire and evidenced some transfer of learning to a "good behavior game" (Barrish, Saunders, & Wolf, 1969). Although potential artifacts were uncontrolled, and long-term maintenance and transfer were unassessed, the Niemann and Brigham generalized skills approach merits detailed parametric analysis and extension, laterally, to the family and peer group, and intrapersonally to incorporate the idiosyncratic perceptions and incentives of individual children.[3]

VIII. THE FUTURE

A broad-spectrum conceptual framework for the study of children's self-management has been outlined. Emphasizing the need (1) to overcome prejudices which formalize the dependent position of children, (2) to incorporate knowledge from diverse sources, especially child development, (3) to engage in thorough pretreatment assessment of relevant skills, attitudes, cognitions, and reinforcement

[3] The author only recently became aware of the work of Fagan, Long, and Stevens (1975) who have developed a broadly based, multicomponent "psychoeducational curriculum" for teaching self-management to elementary school children. The book, *Teaching Children Self-Control* (Columbus, Ohio: Charles E. Merrill, 1975), by Fagan *et al.* is recommended to the interested reader.

systems, and (4) to accord to children and their caretakers the status of cotherapist, the ideals presented in this chapter are well within the realm of possibility. Nevertheless, there is much unfinished as well as unstarted business.

The following are among the most critical needs in the domain of children's self-management:

1. Further development of methodologies consistent with the interactional perspective on behavior. Such an enterprise would include better specification of appropriate units of analysis, greater emphasis on assessment of supportive and disruptive environmental forces, study of naturally occurring episodes of self-management, and measurement of the dimensions of children's situational and self-perceptions.

2. Increased stress with "high-risk" children upon preventative applications of self-management.

3. Greater attention to individual differences in the design of children's self-management programs. Age, sex, ethnic background, cognitive styles, causal attributions, and motivational orientation have all been found to be differentially predictive of success at self-control or self-regulation.

4. Clarification of the determinants of children's tolerance of unpleasant stimulation, a neglected form of self-control. Unlike many delay-of-gratification situations, wherein inevitable negative consequences follow upon approach to or indulgence in the immediately reinforcing activity, the delayed payoff for engaging in behavior with short-term aversive elements is decidedly more probabilistic. What if a child studies, but fails the exam anyway? What if adults do not reward altruistic self-sacrifice? Specific training for as well as parental socialization practices to instill tolerance motivation may involve relatively unique problems and processes.

5. Increased study of self-regulatory dysfunctions in children. While the clinical implications of self-control deficiencies in children are recognized, the self-regulatory insufficiencies of everyday life have less often been the subject of conceptual or empirical investigation. Why are some children better independent decision-makers and plan-implementers than others? Why can some youngsters persist in the face of ridicule, nonsupport, or contradictory messages, whereas others seem unable or unwilling to shed their apparent need for social validation? Can we identify social systems that differentially generate self-management dysfunctions in children?

6. Expanded cognitive social learning analysis of children's active

role in behavioral persistence and transfer of therapeutic learning. Investigations of the emergence of such abilities as causal reasoning, constructive memory, and cognitive control over emotional responses, as well as generalized expectancies regarding situational and behavioral covariation are likely to yield increased appreciation of the importance of children's cognitive competencies (Mischel, 1973) and to spur innovations in the design and implementation of multicomponent treatment and transfer training programs.

We can think of no better "set" to impart to clinicians and researchers working in the field of self-management than that contained in these words of William Powers (1973): "What is necessary," he argues, "is not to avoid attributing human properties to human beings, but to avoid attributing such properties arbitrarily" (Preface, p. x). Our efforts may be judged by how well we achieve systemization and objectivity, on the one hand, and clinical and developmental relevance on the other.

ACKNOWLEDGMENTS

I am indebted to Wes Allinsmith, Dan Kirschenbaum, Bob Stutz, Ron Bale, and Larry Cox for their helpful comments on an earlier version of this manuscript. I also wish to acknowledge the extraordinary display of self-control (of the tolerance variety) by Ms. Diane Kopriwa and Ms. Jacqueline Joseph who typed various portions of the manuscript. Both persevered in the face of the same noxious stimulus—me!

REFERENCES

Ainslie, G. Specious reward: A behavioral theory of impulsiveness and impulse control. *Psychological Bulletin,* 1975, **82,** 463–496.

Allen, M. K., & Liebert, R. M. Effects of live and symbolic deviant-modeling cues on adoption of a previously learned standard. *Journal of Personality and Social Psychology,* 1969, **11,** 253–260.

Ambrosino, S. V. Epistemological assumptions for a psychoeducational methodology. *Psychotherapy and Psychosomatics,* 1974, **24,** 98–101.

Aronfreed, J. *Conduct and conscience.* New York: Academic Press, 1968.

Azrin, N. H., & Powell, J. Behavioral engineering: The reduction of smoking behavior by a conditioning apparatus and procedure. *Journal of Applied Behavior Analysis,* 1968, **1,** 193–200.

Baldwin, A. L. *Theories of child development.* New York: Wiley, 1967.

Ballard, K. D., & Glynn, T. Behavioral self-management in story writing with elementary school children. *Journal of Applied Behavior Analysis,* 1975, **8,** 61–72.

Bandura, A. *Principles of behavior modification.* New York: Holt, 1969.

Bandura, A. Vicarious- and self-reinforcement processes. In R. Glaser (Ed.), *The nature of reinforcement.* New York: Academic Press, 1971. Pp. 228–278.

Bandura, A. Behavior theory and the models of man. *American Psychologist,* 1974, **29,** 859–869.

Bandura, A., & Mischel, W. Modification of self-imposed delay of reward through exposure to live and symbolic models. *Journal of Personality and Social Psychology,* 1965, **2,** 698–705.

Bandura, A., & Perloff, B. Relative efficacy of self-monitored and externally imposed reinforcement systems. *Journal of Personality and Social Psychology,* 1967, **7,** 111–116.

Bandura, A., & Walters, R. H. *Social learning and personality.* New York: Holt, 1963.

Barrish, H., Saunders, M., & Wolf, M. Good behavior game: Effects of individual contingencies for group consequences on disruptive behavior in a classroom. *Journal of Applied Behavior Analysis,* 1969, **2,** 119–124.

Bellack, A. S., & Schwartz, J. S. Assessment for self-control programs. In M. Hersen & A. S. Bellack (Eds.), *Behavioral assessment: A practical handbook.* New York: Pergamon, 1976.

Bem, D. J., & Allen, A. On predicting some of the people some of the time: The search for cross-situational consistencies in behavior. *Psychological Review,* 1974, **81,** 506–520.

Bem, S. L. Verbal self-control: The establishment of effective self-instruction. *Journal of Experimental Psychology,* 1967, **74,** 485–491.

Bender, N. N. *Self-verbalization versus strategy training: The immediate effects of verbal self-instruction training on impulsive first grade children.* Paper read at the American Education Research Association, Washington, D.C., April 1975.

Bialer, I. Conceptualization of success and failure in mentally retarded and normal children. *Journal of Personality,* 1961, **29,** 303–320.

Blackwood, R. O. *Mediated self-control: An operant model of rational behavior.* Akron, Ohio: Exordium Press, 1972.

Blank, M. Cognitive functions of langauge in the preschool years. *Developmental Psychology,* 1974, **10,** 229–245.

Bolles, R. C. *Theory of motivation.* New York: Harper, 1967.

Bornstein, P. H., & Quevillon, R. D. The effects of a self-instructional package with overactive pre-school boys. *Journal of Applied Behavior Analysis,* 1976, **9,** 179–188.

Brigham, T. A. Some speculations about self-control. In T. A. Brigham & A. C. Catania (Eds.), *The handbook of applied behavior research: Social and instructional processes.* New York: Irvington Press, 1977. In press.

Brigham, T. A., & Bushell, D. Notes on autonomous environments: Effects of student-selected and teacher-selected rewards on academic performance. *Educational Technology,* 1973, **13,** 19–22.

Brigham, T. A., & Sherman, J. A. Effects of choice and immediacy of reinforcement on single response and switching behavior of children. *Journal of the Experimental Analysis of Behavior,* 1973, **19,** 425–435.

Brigham, T. A., & Stoerzinger, A. An experimental analysis of children's preference for self-selected rewards. In T. A. Brigham, R. Hawkins, J. Scott, & T. F. McLaughlin (Eds.), *Behavioral analysis in education: Self-control and reading.* Dubuque, Iowa: Kendall/Hunt, 1976. Pp. 47–55.

Broden, M., Hall, R. V., & Mitts, B. The effect of self-recording on the classroom behavior of two eighth-grade students. *Journal of Applied Behavior Analysis,* 1971, **4,** 191–199.

Burns, D. J., & Powers, R. B. Choice and self-control in children: A test of Rachlin's model. *Bulletin of the Psychonomic Society,* 1975, **5**, 156–158.
Burton, R. V. Correspondence between behavioral and doll-play measures of conscience. *Developmental Psychology,* 1971, **5**, 320–332.
Camp, B. *Verbal mediation in young aggressive boys.* Unpublished manuscript, University of Colorado School of Medicine, 1975.
Camp, B., & Bash, M. A. S. *Think Aloud Program: Group manual.* Unpublished manual, University of Colorado School of Medicine, 1975.
Camp, B., Blom, G. E., Hebert, F., & van Doorninck, W. J. *"Think aloud": A program for developing self-control in young aggressive boys.* Unpublished manuscript, University of Colorado School of Medicine, 1976.
Carey, S. Cognitive competence. In K. Connolly & J. Bruner (Eds.), *The growth of competence.* New York: Academic Press, 1974. Pp. 169–193.
Cheyne, J. A., & Walters, R. H. Punishment and prohibition: Some origins of self-control. *New directions in psychology.* New York: Holt, 1970. Pp. 281–366.
Church, J. *Language and the discovery of reality.* New York: Vintage Books, 1961.
Coates, B., & Hartup, W. W. Age and verbalization in observational learning. *Developmental Psychology,* 1969, **5**, 556–562.
Conway, J. B., & Bucher, B. D. Transfer and maintenance of behavior change in children: A Review and suggestions. In E. J. Mash, L. A. Hammerlynck, & L. C. Handy (Eds.), *Behavior modification and families.* New York: Brunner/Mazel, 1976. Pp. 119–159.
Coopersmith, S. A method of determining types of self-esteem. *Journal of Abnormal and Social Psychology,* 1959, **59**, 87–94.
Coopersmith, S. *The antecedents of self-esteem.* San Francisco: Freeman, 1967.
Cowen, E. L., Huser, J., Beach, D. R., & Rappaport, J. Parental perceptions of young children and their relation to indexes of adjustment. *Journal of Consulting and Clinical Psychology,* 1970, **34**, 97–103.
Crandall, V. C., Crandall, V. J., & Katkovsky, W. A. Children's social desirability questionnaire. *Journal of Consulting Psychology,* 1965, **29**, 27–36.
Davids, A. Ego functions in disturbed and normal children: Aspiration, inhibition, time estimation, and delayed gratification. *Journal of Consulting and Clinical Psychology,* 1969, **33**, 61–70.
Debus, R. Effects of brief observation of model behavior on conceptual tempo of impulsive children. *Developmental Psychology,* 1970, **2**, 22–32.
Deci, E. L. *Intrinsic motivation.* New York: Plenum, 1975.
Denney, D. Modeling effects upon conceptual style and cognitive tempo. *Child Development,* 1972, **43**, 105–119.
Diggory, J. C. *Self-evaluation: Concepts and studies.* New York: Wiley (Krieger), 1966.
Dmitruk, V. M. Delay of gratification as a function of incentive preference and race of experimenter. *Developmental Psychology,* 1974, **10**, 302.
Doleys, D. M. Distractibility and distracting stimuli: Inconsistent and contradictory results. *Psychological Record,* 1976, **26**, 279–287.
Dollard, J., & Miller, N. E. *Personality and psychotherapy.* New York: McGraw-Hill, 1950.
Douglas, V. I. Stop, look, and listen: The problem of sustained attention and impulse control in hyperactive and normal children. *Canadian Journal of Behavioral Science,* 1972, **4**, 259–282.
Drabman, R. S., Spitalnik, R., & O'Leary, K. D. Teaching self-control to disruptive children. *Journal of Abnormal Psychology,* 1972, **82**, 10–16.
Dulany, D. E. Awareness, rules, and propositional control: A confrontation with S-R

behavior theory. In T. Dixon & D. Horton (Eds.), *Verbal behavior and general behavior theory.* Englewood Cliffs, N.J.: Prentice-Hall, 1968. Pp. 340–387.

Duval, S., & Wicklund, R. A. *A theory of objective self awareness.* New York: Academic Press, 1972.

D'Zurilla, T. J., & Goldfried, M. R. Problem solving and behavior modification. *Journal of Abnormal Psychology,* 1971, **78,** 107–126.

Eisen, M. Characteristic self-esteem, sex, and resistance to temptation. *Journal of Personality and Social Psychology,* 1972, **24,** 68–72.

Ekehammar, B. Interactionism in personality from a historical perspective. *Psychological Bulletin,* 1974, **81,** 1026–1048.

Eysenck, H. J., & Eysenck, S. B. G. *Personality structure and measurement.* San Diego, Calif.: Knapp, 1969.

Finch, A. J., Wilkinson, M. D., Nelson, W. M., & Montgomery, L. E. Modification of an impulsive cognitive tempo in emotionally disturbed boys. *Journal of Abnormal Child Psychology,* 1975, **3,** 49–52.

Flanders, J. P. A review of research on imitative behavior. *Psychological Bulletin,* 1968, **5,** 316–337.

Forehand, R., King, H. E., Peed, S., & Yoder, P. Mother-child interactions: Comparison of a noncompliant clinic group and a non-clinic group. *Behaviour Research and Therapy,* 1975, **13,** 79–84.

Franks, C. M., & Wilson, G. T. (Eds.). *Annual review of behavior therapy, theory, and practice* (Vols. 1, 2, 3). New York: Brunner/Mazel, 1973–1975.

Freud, S. Instincts and their vicissitudes. *Standard edition* (Vol. 14). London: Hogarth, 1957. (Originally published, 1915.)

Fry, P. S. Self-imposed delay of gratification as a function of modeling. *Journal of Counseling Psychology,* 1972, **19,** 234–237.

Fry, P. S. Affect and resistance to temptation. *Developmental Psychology,* 1975, **11,** 466–472.

Gelfand, D. M., & Hartmann, D. P. *Child behavior analysis and therapy.* New York: Pergamon, 1975.

Gewirtz, J. L. The roles of overt responding and extrinsic reinforcement in "self"- and "vicarious-reinforcement" and in "observational learning" and imitation. In R. Glaser (Ed.), *The nature of reinforcement.* New York: Academic Press, 1971. Pp. 279–309.

Gewirtz, J. L., & Stingle, K. G. The learning of generalized imitation as the basis for identification. *Psychological Review,* 1968, **75,** 374–397.

Glynn, E. L. Classroom applications of self-determined reinforcement. *Journal of Applied Behavior Analysis,* 1970, **3,** 123–132.

Glynn, E. L., & Thomas, J. D. Effect of cueing on self-control of classroom behavior. *Journal of Applied Behavior Analysis,* 1974, **7,** 299–306.

Glynn, E. L., Thomas, J. D., & Shee, S. K. Behavioral self-control of on-task behavior in an elementary classroom. *Journal of Applied Behavior Analysis,* 1973, **6,** 105–118.

Goffman, E. *The presentation of self in everyday life.* Garden City, N.Y.: Doubleday, 1959.

Goldfried, M. R. Behavioral assessment. In I. B. Weiner (Ed.), *Clinical methods in psychology.* New York: Wiley, 1976. Pp. 281–330.

Goldfried, M. R., & D'Zurilla, T. J. A behavioral-analytic model for assessing competence. In C. D. Spielberger (Ed.), *Current topics in clinical and community psychology* (Vol. 1). New York: Academic Press, 1969. Pp. 151–196.

Goldfried, M. R., & Sprafkin, J. N. *Behavioral personality assessment.* Morristown, N.J.: General Learning Press, 1974.

Goldstein, A. P. Relationship enhancement methods. In F. H. Kanfer & A. P. Goldstein (Eds.), *Helping people change.* New York: Pergamon, 1975. Pp. 15–49.

Gottman, J. M., & McFall, R. M. Self-monitoring effects in a program for potential high school dropouts: A time-series analysis. *Journal of Consulting and Clinical Psychology,* 1972, **39**, 273–281.

Graziano, A. M. *Behavior therapy with children* (Vol. 2). Chicago: Aldine, 1975.

Grim, P. F., Kohlberg, L., & White, S. H. Some relationships between conscience and attentional processes. *Journal of Personality and Social Psychology,* 1968, **8**, 239–252.

Grings, W. W. The role of consciousness and cognition in autonomic behavior change. In F. J. McGuigan & R. Schoonover (Eds.), *The psychophysiology of thinking.* New York: Academic Press, 1973. Pp. 233–262.

Harter, S., & Zigler, E. The assessment of effectance motivation in normal and retarded children. *Developmental Psychology,* 1974, **10**, 169–180.

Hartig, M., & Kanfer, F. H. The role of verbal self-instructions in children's resistance to temptation. *Journal of Personality and Social Psychology,* 1973, **25**, 259–267.

Hartshorne, H., & May, M. A. *Studies in deceit.* New York: Macmillan, 1928.

Haywood, H. C. Motivational orientation of overachieving and underachieving elementary school children. *American Journal of Mental Deficiency,* 1968, **72**, 662–667.

Hersen, M., & Bellack, A. S. (Eds.). *Behavioral assessment: A practical handbook.* New York: Pergamon, 1976.

Hicks, D. J. Short- and long-term retention of affectively varied modeled behavior. *Psychonomic Science,* 1968, **11**, 369–370.

Hogan, R. Moral conduct and moral character. *Psychology Bulletin,* 1973, **79**, 217–232.

Homme, L. Perspectives in psychology—XXIV. Control of coverants, the operants of the mind. *Psychological Record,* 1965, **15**, 501–511.

Homme, L., Csanyi, A. P., Gonzales, M. A., & Rechs, J. R. *How to use contingency contracting in the classroom.* Champaign, Ill.: Research Press, 1970.

Humphrey, L., Karoly, P., & Kirschenbaum, D. Self-reward versus self-imposed response cost in classroom behavior management. Paper presented at the Midwestern Psychological Association Meetings, Chicago, May, 1977.

Hunt, J. McV. Intrinsic motivation and its role in psychological development. In D. Levine (Ed.), *Nebraska Symposium on Motivation* (Vol. 13). Lincoln: University of Nebraska Press, 1965. Pp. 189–282.

Jarvis, P. E. Verbal control of sensory-motor performance: A test of Luria's hypothesis. *Human Development,* 1968, **11**, 172–183.

Johnson, S. M., & Martin, S. Developing self-evaluation as a conditioned reinforcer. In B. Ashem & E. G. Poser (Eds.), *Adaptive learning: Behavior modification with children.* New York: Pergamon. 1973. Pp. 69–78.

Joslin, D., Coates, B., & McKown, A. Age of child and rewardingness of adult model in observational learning. *Child Study Journal,* 1973, **3**, 115–124.

Kagan, J., Moss, H. A., & Sigel, I. E. Psychological significance of styles of conceptualization. *Monographs of the Society for Research in Child Development,* 1963, **28**(2, Serial No. 86).

Kagan, J., Rosman, B. C., Day, D., Albert, J., & Phillips, W. Information processing in the child: Significance of analytic and reflective attitudes. *Psychological Monographs,* 1964, **78**(1, Whole No. 578).

Kanfer, F. H. Self-regulation: Research, issues, and speculation. In C. Neuringer & J. L. Michael (Eds.), *Behavior modification in clinical psychology.* New York: Appleton, 1970. Pp. 178–220.

Kanfer, F. H. The maintenance of behavior by self-generated stimuli and reinforcement. In A. Jacobs & L. B. Sachs (Eds.), *The psychology of private events.* New York: Academic Press, 1971. Pp. 39–59.

Kanfer, F. H. Assessment for behavior modification. *Journal of Personality Assessment,* 1972, **36,** 418–423.

Kanfer, F. H. Self-management methods. In F. H. Kanfer & A. P. Goldstein (Eds.), *Helping people change.* New York: Pergamon, 1975. Pp. 309–355.

Kanfer, F. H. *The many faces of self-control, or behavior modification changes its focus.* Paper read at the eighth International Banff Conference, March 1976.

Kanfer, F. H., & Duerfeldt, P. H. Age, class standing, and commitment as determinants of cheating in children. *Child Development,* 1968, **39,** 545–557.

Kanfer, F. H., & Karoly, P. Self-control: A behavioristic exursion into the lion's den. *Behavior Therapy,* 1972, **3,** 398–416. (a)

Kanfer, F. H., & Karoly, P. Self-regulation and its clinical applications: Some additional considerations. In R. C. Johnson, P. R. Dokecki, & O. H. Mowrer (Eds.), *Conscience, contract, and social reality.* New York: Holt, 1972. Pp. 428–437. (b)

Kanfer, F. H., Karoly, P., & Newman, A. Reduction of children's fear of the dark by competence-related and situational threat-related verbal cues. *Journal of Consulting and Clinical Psychology,* 1975, **43,** 251–258.

Kanfer, F. H., & Phillips, J. S. *Learning foundations of behavior therapy.* New York: Wiley, 1970.

Kanfer, F. H., & Saslow, G. Behavioral diagnosis. In C. M. Franks (Ed.), *Behavior therapy: Appraisal and status.* New York: McGraw-Hill, 1969. Pp. 417–444.

Kantor, J. R. An analysis of the experimental analysis of behavior (TEAB). *Journal of the Experimental Analysis of Behavior,* 1970, **13,** 101–108.

Karoly, P., & Dirks, M. Developing self-control in preschool children through correspondence training. *Behavior Therapy,* in press.

Karoly, P., & Kanfer, F. H. Effects of prior contractual experiences on self-control in children. *Developmental Psychology,* 1974, **10,** 459–460.

Kaufman, K. F., & O'Leary, K. D. Reward, cost, and self-evaluation procedures for disruptive adolescents in a psychiatric hospital school. *Journal of Applied Behavior Analysis,* 1972, **5,** 293–309.

Kazdin, A. E. Self-monitoring and behavior change. In M. J. Mahoney & C. E. Thoresen (Eds.), *Self-control: Power to the person.* Monterey, Calif.: Brooks-Cole, 1974. Pp. 218–246.

Kimble, G. A. Scientific psychology in transition. In F. J. McGuigan & D. B. Lumsden (Eds.), *Contemporary approaches to conditioning and learning.* Washington, D.C.: Winston, 1973.

Kirschenbaum, D., & Karoly, P. *When self-regulation fails: Tests of some preliminary hypotheses.* Unpublished manuscript, University of Cincinnati, 1976.

Klineberg, S. L. Future time perspective and the preference for delayed reward. *Journal of Personality and Social Psychology,* 1968, **8,** 253–257.

Knudson, R. M., & Golding, S. L. Comparative validity of traditional versus S-R format inventories of interpersonal behavior. *Journal of Research in Personality,* 1974, **8,** 111–127.

Kopel, S. *Behavioral self-control: A reconceptualization and new perspectives.* Paper read at the Northwest Chapter, Association for Advancement of Behavior Therapy, Renton, Washington, May 1972.

Krumboltz, J. D., & Thoresen, C. E. (Eds.). *Counseling methods.* New York: Holt, 1976.

Kuhn, D., & Phelps, H. The development of children's comprehension of causal direction. *Child Development,* 1976, **47,** 248–251.

Lambert, N. M., Windmiller, M., Sandoval, J., & Moore, B. Hyperactive children and the efficacy of psychoactive drugs as a treatment intervention. *American Journal of Orthopsychiatry,* 1976, **46,** 335–352.

LaVoie, J. C. Cognitive determinants of resistance to deviation in seven-, nine-, and eleven-year old children of low and high maturity of moral judgment. *Developmental Psychology,* 1974, **10,** 393–403.

Leifer, A. D., Collins, W. A., Gross, B. M., Taylor, P. H., Andrews, L., & Blackmer. Developmental aspects of variables relevant to observational learning. *Child Development,* 1971, **42,** 1509–1516.

Lepper, M. Dissonance, self-perception, and honesty in children. *Journal of Personality and Social Psychology,* 1973, **25,** 65–74.

Lickona, T. (Ed.). *Moral development and behavior.* New York: Holt, 1976.

Logan, F. A. Self-control as habit, drive, and incentive. *Journal of Abnormal Psychology,* 1973, **81,** 127–136.

London, P. The end of ideology in behavior modification. *American Psychologist,* 1972, **27,** 913–920.

Looft, W. R. Egocentrism and social interaction across the life-span. *Psychological Bulletin,* 1972, **78,** 73–92.

Lovaas, O. I., Koegel, R., Simmons, J. A., & Long, J. S. Some generalizations and follow-up measures on autistic children in behavior therapy. *Journal of Applied Behavior Analysis,* 1973, **6,** 131–166.

Lovitt, T. C. Self-management projects with children with behavioral disabilities. *Journal of Learning Disabilities,* 1973, **6,** 138–150.

Lovitt, T. C., & Curtiss, K. Academic response rate as a function of teacher and self-imposed contingencies. *Journal of Applied Behavior Analysis,* 1969, **2,** 49–53.

Luria, A. R. *The role of speech in the regulation of normal and abnormal behavior.* New York: Liveright, 1961.

Maccoby, E. E. Role-taking in childhood and its consequences for social learning. *Child Development,* 1959, **30,** 239–252.

Maccoby, E. E. (Ed.). *The development of sex differences.* Stanford: Stanford University Press, 1966.

Mahoney, K. Count on it: A simple self-monitoring device. *Behavior Therapy,* 1974, **5,** 701–703.

Mahoney, M. J. *Cognition and behavior modification.* Boston: Ballinger, 1974.

Mahoney, M. J., & Thoresen, C. E. (Eds.). *Self-control: Power to the person.* Monterey, Calif.: Brooks-Cole, 1974.

Mahoney, M. J., Thoresen, C. E., & Danaher, B. G. Covert behavior modification: An experimental analogue. *Journal of Behavior Therapy and Experimental Psychiatry,* 1972, **3,** 7–14.

Mahrer, A. R. The role of expectancy in delayed reinforcement. *Journal of Experimental Psychology,* 1956, **52,** 101–105.

Marston, A. R., & Feldman, S. E. Toward the use of self-control in behavior modification. *Journal of Consulting and Clinical Psychology,* 1972, **39,** 429–433.

Masters, J. C., & Mokros, J. R. Self-reinforcement processes in children. In H. W. Reese (Ed.), *Advances in child development and behavior* (Vol. 9). New York: Academic Press, 1974.

Masters, J. C., & Santrock, J. W. Studies in the self-regulation of behavior: Effects of contingent cognitive and affective events. *Developmental Psychology,* 1976, **12,** 334–348.

Mausner, B., & Platt, E. S. *Smoking: A behavioral analysis.* New York: Pergamon, 1971.

McCandless, B. R. The socialization of the individual. In E. Schopler & R. J. Reichler (Eds.), *Psychopathology and child development.* New York: Plenum, 1976. Pp. 185–202.

McClelland, D. C. Opinions about opinions: So what else is new? *Journal of Consulting and Clinical Psychology,* 1972, **38,** 325–326.

McGuigan, F. J., & Winstead, C. L. Discriminative relationship between covert oral behavior and the phonemic system in internal information processing. *Journal of Experimental Psychology,* 1974, **103,** 885–890.

McReynolds, P. *Theoretical basis of self regulation.* Paper read at the Conference on Developmental Aspects of Self-Regulation, LaJolla, California, February 1972.

Mead, G. H. *Mind, self, and society.* Chicago, Ill.: University of Chicago Press, 1934.

Meichenbaum, D. Self-instructional methods. In F. H. Kanfer & A. P. Goldstein (Eds.), *Helping people change.* New York: Pergamon, 1975. Pp. 357–391. (a)

Meichenbaum, D. Theoretical and treatment implications of developmental research on verbal control of behavior. *Canadian Psychological Review,* 1975, **16,** 22–27. (b)

Meichenbaum, D. Toward a cognitive theory of self-control. In G. E. Schwartz & D. Shapiro (Eds.), *Consciousness and self-regulation: Advances in research* (Vol. 1). New York: Plenum, 1976. Pp. 223–260.

Meichenbaum, D., & Cameron, R. The clinical potential of modifying what clients say to themselves. In M. J. Mahoney & C. E. Thoresen (Eds.), *Self-control: Power to the person.* Monterey, Calif.: Brooks-Cole, 1974. Pp. 263–290.

Meichenbaum, D., & Goodman, J. Training impulsive children to talk to themselves: A means of developing self-control. *Journal of Abnormal Psychology,* 1971, **77,** 115–126.

Miller, D. T., & Karniol, R. The role of rewards in externally and self-imposed delay of gratification. *Journal of Personality and Social Psychology,* 1976, **33,** 594–600.

Miller, G.A., Galanter, E., & Pribram, K. *Plans and the structure of behavior.* New York: Holt, 1960.

Mischel, W. Theory and research on the antecedents of self-imposed delay of reward. In B. A. Maher (Ed.), *Progress in experimental personality* (Vol. 3). New York: Academic Press, 1966. Pp. 85–132.

Mischel, W. *Personality and assessment.* New York: Wiley, 1968.

Mischel, W. Direct versus indirect personality assessment: Evidence and implications. *Journal of Consulting and Clinical Psychology,* 1972, **38,** 319–324.

Mischel, W. Toward a cognitive social learning reconceptualization of personality. *Psychological Review,* 1973, **80,** 252–283.

Mischel, W. Processes in delay of gratification. In L. Berkowitz (Ed.), *Advances in experimental social psychology* (Vol. 7). New York: Academic Press, 1974. Pp. 249–292.

Mischel, W. *Introduction to personality.* New York: Holt, 1976.

Mischel, W., & Baker, N. Cognitive transformations of reward objects through instructions. *Journal of Personality and Social Psychology,* 1975, **31,** 254–261.

Mischel, W., & Ebbesen, E. B. Attention in delay of gratification. *Journal of Personality and Social Psychology,* 1970, **16,** 329–337.

Mischel, W., & Grusec, J. Waiting for rewards and punishments: Effects of time and probability on choice. *Journal of Personality and Social Psychology,* 1967, **5,** 24–31.

Mischel, W., & Metzner, R. Preference for delayed reward as a function of age, intelligence, and length of delay interval. *Journal of Abnormal and Social Psychology,* 1962, **64,** 425–431.

Mischel, W., & Mischel, H. N. A cognitive social-learning approach to morality and self-regulation. In T. Lickona (Ed.), *Moral development and behavior.* New York: Holt, 1976. Pp. 84–107.

Mischel, W., & Moore, B. Effects of attention to symbolically presented rewards upon self-control. *Journal of Personality and Social Personality,* 1973, **28,** 172–179.

Mischel, W., Zeiss, R., & Zeiss, A. R. Internal–external control and persistence: Validation and implications of the Stanford Preschool Internal–External Scale. *Journal of Personality and Social Psychology,* 1974, **29,** 265–278.

Monahan, J., & O'Leary, K. D. Effects of self-instruction on rule-breaking behavior. *Psychological Reports,* 1971, **29,** 1059–1066.

Montgomery, K. C. The role of exploratory drive in learning. *Journal of Comparative and Physiological Psychology,* 1954, **47,** 60–64.

Moore, B. S., Clyburn, A., & Underwood, B. The role of affect in delay of gratification. *Child Development,* 1976, **47,** 273–276.

Moos, R. H. Conceptualizations of human environments. *American Psychologist,* 1973, **28,** 652–665.

Nakamura, C. Y., & Rogers, M. M. Parent's expectations of autonomous behavior and children's autonomy. *Developmental Psychology,* 1969, **1,** 613–617.

Niemann, J. E., & Brigham, T. A. *The development and experimental validation of a course in self-management for sixth graders.* Unpublished manuscript, Washington State University, 1976.

Nisan, M. Exposure to rewards and the delay of gratification. *Developmental Psychology,* 1974, **10,** 376–380.

Nisan, M. Children's evaluations of temporally distant outcomes. *Journal of Genetic Psychology,* 1975, **126,** 53–60.

Nisan, M. Delay of gratification in children: Personal versus group choices. *Child Development,* 1976, **47,** 195–200.

Nowicki, S., & Strickland, B. A locus of control scale for children. *Journal of Consulting and Clinical Psychology,* 1973, **40,** 148–154.

O'Leary, K. D., Pelham, W. E., Rosenbaum, A., & Price, G. H. Behavioral treatment of hyperkinetic children. *Clinical Pediatrics,* 1976, **15,** 510–515.

Palkes, H., Stewart, M. S., & Freeman, J. Improvements in maze performance of hyperactive boys as a function of verbal-training procedures. *Journal of Special Education,* 1972, **5,** 337–342.

Palkes, H., Stewart, M., & Kahana, B. Porteus maze performance of hyperactive boys after training in self-directed verbal commands. *Child Development,* 1968, **39,** 817–826.

Patterson, C. J., & Mischel, W. Plans to resist distraction. *Developmental Psychology,* 1975, **11,** 369–378.

Patterson, G. R., Reid, J. B., Jones, R. R., & Conger, R. E. *A social learning approach to family intervention.* Eugene, Ore: Castalia Publishing, 1975.

Paul, G. L. *Insight versus desensitization in psychotherapy.* Stanford: Stanford University, 1966.

Peterson, R. F. Power, programming, and punishment: Could we be overcontrolling our children? In E. J. Mash *et al.* (Eds.), *Behavior modification and families.* New York: Brunner/Mazel, 1976. Pp. 338–352.

Pick, A. D., Frankel, D. G., & Hess, V. L. *Children's attention: The development of selectivity.* Chicago: University of Chicago Press, 1975.

Powers, W. T. *Behavior: The control of perception.* Chicago: Aldine, 1973.

Premack, D. Mechanisms of self-control. In W. Hunt (Ed.), *Learning and mechanisms of control in smoking.* Chicago: Aldine, 1970. Pp. 107–123.

Prentice, N. M. The influence of live and symbolic modeling on promoting moral judgment of adolescent delinquents. *Journal of Abnormal Psychology,* 1972, **80,** 157–161.

Rachlin, H. Self-control. *Behaviorism,* 1974, **2,** 94–107.

Rachlin, H., & Green, L. Commitment, choice, and self-control. *Journal of the Experimental Analysis of Behavior,* 1972, **17,** 15–22.

Rachman, S. Clinical applications of observational learning, imitation and modeling. *Behavior Therapy,* 1972, **3,** 379–397.

Reppucci, N. D. Individual differences in the consideration of information among two-year-old children. *Developmental Psychology,* 1970, **2,** 240–246.

Rimm, D. C., & Masters, J. C. *Behavior therapy: Techniques and empirical findings.* New York: Academic Press, 1974.

Romancyzk, R. G. Self-monitoring in the treatment of obesity: Parameters of reactivity. *Behavior Therapy,* 1974, **5,** 531–540.

Rosenhan, D. L., Underwood, B., & Moore, B. S. Affect moderates self-gratification and altruism. *Journal of Personality and Social Psychology,* 1974, **30,** 546–552.

Rosenkoetter, L. I. Resistance to temptation: Inhibitory and disinhibitory effects of models. *Developmental Psychology,* 1973, **8,** 80–84.

Rosenthal, T. L. Modeling therapies. In M. Hersen, R. Eisler, & P. M. Miller (Eds.), *Progress in behavior modification* (Vol. 2). New York: Academic Press, 1976. Pp. 53–97.

Ross, A. O. *Psychological disorders of children.* New York: McGraw-Hill, 1974.

Rotter, J. B. *Social learning and clinical psychology.* Englewood Cliffs, Prentice-Hall, 1954.

Rotter, J. B. Generalized expectancies for internal versus external control of reinforcement. *Psychological Monographs,* 1966, **80** (No. 1, Whole No. 609).

Rotter, J. B., Chance, J. E., & Phares, E. J. (Eds.),. *Applications of a social learning theory of personality.* New York: Holt, 1972.

Russell, M. L., & Thoresen, C. E. Teaching decision-making skills to children. In J. D. Krumboltz & C. E. Thoresen (Eds.), *Counseling methods.* New York: Holt, 1976. Pp. 377–383.

Rychlak, J. F. *A philosophy of science for personality theory.* Boston: Houghton, 1968.

Sajwaj, T., Twardosz, S., & Burke, M. Side effects of extinction procedures in a remedial preschool. *Journal of Applied Behavior Analysis,* 1972, **5,** 163–175.

Santogrossi, D. A., O'Leary, K. D., Romanczyk, R. G., & Kaufman, K. F. Self-evaluation by adolescents in a psychiatric hospital program. *Journal of Applied Behavior Analysis,* 1973, **6,** 277–287.

Santostefano, S., & Stayton, S. Training the preschool retarded child in focusing attention: A program for parents. *American Journal of Orthopsychiatry,* 1967, **37,** 732–743.

Schneider, M., & Robin, A. The turtle technique: A method for the self-control of impulsive behavior. In J. D. Krumboltz & C. E. Thoresen (Eds.), *Counseling methods.* New York: Holt, 1976. Pp. 157–163.

Scott, W. A., & Johnson, R. C. Comparative validities of direct and indirect personality tests. *Journal of Consulting and Clinical Psychology,* 1972, **38,** 301–318.

Seeman, G., & Schwarz, J. C. Affective state and preference for immediate versus delayed reward. *Journal of Personality,* 1974, **7,** 384–394.

Shatz, M., & Gelman, R. The development of communication skills: Modifications in the speech of young children as a function of listener. *Monographs of the Society for Research in Child Development,* 1973, **38**(5, Serial No. 152).

Shure, M., & Spivack, G. Means—ends thinking, adjustment and social class among elementary school-aged children. *Journal of Consulting and Clinical Psychology,* 1972, **38,** 348–353.

Siegelman, E. Reflective and impulsive observing behavior. *Child Development,* 1969, **40,** 1213–1222.

Simpson, D. D., & Nelson, A. E. Attention training through breathing control to modify hyperactivity. *Journal of Learning Disabilities,* 1974, **7,** 274–283.

Skinner, B. F. *Science and human behavior.* New York: Macmillan, 1953.

Spivack, G., & Shure, M. B. *Social adjustment of young children: A cognitive approach to solving real-life problems.* San Francisco: Jossey-Bass, 1974.

Staats, A. W. *Child learning, intelligence, and personality.* New York: Harper, 1971.

Staats, A. W. *Social behaviorism.* Homewood, Ill.: Dorsey, 1975.

Stableford, W., Butz, R., Hasazi, J., Leitenberg, H., & Peyser, J. Sequential withdrawal of stimulant drugs and use of behavior therapy with two hyperactive boys. *American Journal of Orthopsychiatry,* 1976, **46,** 302–312.

Staub, E. Effects of persuasion and modeling on delay of gratification. *Developmental Psychology,* 1972, **6,** 166–177.

Stein, A. H. Imitation of resistance to temptation. *Child Development,* 1967, **38,** 157–169.

Stern, G. G., Stein, M. I., & Bloom, B. S. *Methods in personality assessment.* Glencoe, Ill.: Free Press, 1956.

Stumphauzer, J. S. Increased delay of gratification in young prison inmates through imitation of high delay peer models. *Journal of Personality and Social Psychology,* 1972, **21,** 10–17.

Sullivan, H. S. *The interpersonal theory of psychiatry.* New York: Norton, 1953.

Switzky, H. N., & Haywood, H. C. Motivational orientation and the relative efficacy of self-monitored and externally imposed reinforcement systems in children. *Journal of Personality and Social Psychology,* 1974, **30,** 360–366.

Thoresen, C. E., & Coates, T. J. Behavioral self-control: Some clinical concerns. In M. Hersen, R. M. Eisler, & P. M. Miller (Eds.), *Progress in behavior modification* (Vol. 2). New York: Academic Press, 1976. Pp. 307–352.

Thoresen, C. E., & Mahoney, M. J. *Behavioral self-control.* New York: Holt, 1974.

Thorpe, G. L., Amatu, H. I., Blakey, R. S., & Burns, L. E. Contributions of overt instructional rehearsal and "specific insight" to the effectiveness of self-instructional training: A preliminary study. *Behavior Therapy,* 1976, **7,** 504–511.

Turkewitz, H., O'Leary, K. D., & Ironsmith, M. Generalization and maintenance of appropriate behavior through self-control. *Journal of Consulting and Clinical Psychology,* 1975, **43,** 577–583.

Underwood, B., Moore, B. S., & Rosenhan, D. L. Affect and self-gratification. *Developmental Psychology,* 1973, **8,** 209–214.

Van Duyne, H. J. Age and intelligence factors as predictors of the development of verbal control of nonverbal behavior. *Journal of Genetic Psychology,* 1974, **124,** 321–331.

Wachtel, P. Psychodynamics, behavior therapy, and the implacable experimenter. *Journal of Abnormal Psychology,* 1973, **82,** 323–334.

Wahler, R. G. Some structural aspects of deviant child behavior. *Journal of Applied Behavior Analysis,* 1975, **8,** 27–42.

Wahler, R. G., House, A. E., & Stambaugh, E. E. *Ecological assessment of child problem behavior.* New York: Pergamon, 1976.

White, G. M. Immediate and deferred effects of model observation and guided and unguided rehearsal of donating and stealing. *Journal of Personality and Social Psychology,* 1972, **21,** 139–148.

White, R. W. Motivation reconsidered: The concept of competence. *Psychological Review,* 1959, **66,** 297–333.

White, R. W. Strategies of adaptation: An attempt at systematic description. In G. V. Coelho, D. A. Hamburg, & J. E. Adams (Eds.), *Coping and adaptation.* New York: Basic Books, 1974. Pp. 47–68.

White, S. H. Evidence for a hierarchical arrangement of learning processes. In L. P. Lipsitt & C. C. Spiker (Eds.), *Advances in child development and behavior.* Vol. 2. New York: Academic Press, 1965.

Wiggins, J. S. *Personality and prediction: Principles of personality assessment.* Reading, Mass.: Addison-Wesley, 1973.

Wiggins, J. S., Renner, K. E., Clore, G. L., & Rose, R. J. *The psychology of personality.* Reading, Mass.: Addison-Wesley, 1971.

Winett, R. A. Behavior modification and open education. *Journal of School Psychology,* 1973, **11**, 207–214.

Winett, R. A., Richards, C. S., Krasner, L., & Krasner, M. Child-monitored token reading program. *Psychology in the Schools,* 1971, **8**, 259–262.

Wolf, T. M. Effects of televised modeled verbalizations and behavior on resistance to deviation. *Developmental Psychology,* 1973, **8**, 51–56.

Wolpe, J. Behavior therapy and its malcontents—I. Denial of its bases and psychodynamic fusionism. *Journal of Behavior Therapy and Experimental Psychiatry,* 1976, **7**, 1–5.

Wylie, R. *The self-concept: Review of methodological considerations and measuring instruments* (Rev. ed., Vol. 1). Lincoln: University of Nebraska Press, 1974.

Yates, A. J. *Theory and practice in behavior therapy.* New York: Wiley, 1975.

ASSESSMENT AND THERAPEUTIC FUNCTIONS OF SELF-MONITORING

ROSEMERY O. NELSON
Department of Psychology
University of North Carolina at Greensboro
Greensboro, North Carolina

I. THE SELF-MONITORING PROCEDURE

A. Overview

Self-monitoring or self-recording refers to an individual noticing and recording the occurrences of his or her own target behaviors. Self-monitoring is used for both assessment and therapeutic purposes. When data are collected by self-recording, their accuracy is an important issue. A portion of this chapter provides examples of the mutable accuracy of self-recorders, and discusses research-based procedures to enhance this accuracy. When self-recording is used for therapeutic purposes, its reactivity is also important. Another portion of this chapter describes variables which enhance this reactivity.

B. Definition of Self-Monitoring

Self-monitoring or self-recording is a two-stage process. First, the subject or client must notice or discriminate aspects of his or her own behavior; that is, determine that the target behavior has indeed occurred. Second, he or she must make the self-recording response; that is, use the procedure that records the occurrence of the target behavior. The self-recorder must perform both of these behaviors in order to produce accurate self-recordings. However, performing even the first of these behaviors may result in reactive behavior changes (see Section III,E). It is worthwhile for clinical, theoretical, and research purposes to recall that self-recording involves two discrete stages (Simkins, 1971).

C. Popularity of Self-Monitoring

In the last 6 or 7 years, the clinical popularity of self-monitoring has increased enormously. This popularity is congruent with other trends in contemporary behavior therapy. A hallmark of behavior therapy has been its emphasis on empiricism. One primary source of noninferential data is observations by trained, independent observers. In many situations, however, the use of observers is impractical because of unavailability, cost, or inconvenience. This is especially true when the target behavior is private, such as sexual behavior. An alternative to data collection by observers is data collection by the subject (i.e., self-recording). In theory, self-recorders may be able to provide more complete data than observers because they witness the entire population of their target behaviors, as compared with the sample usually witnessed by observers (Kazdin, 1974b). Another aspect of recent behavior therapy has been an emphasis on self-control programs, with a corresponding deemphasis on externally managed controls. Self-recording has played an integral role in many self-control programs, either as a means of data collection or as a therapeutic strategy in its own right. A final contemporary characteristic of behavior therapy is its interest in cognitive behaviors. Given current technology, these covert events are public to an audience of only one person, the self-recorder. If data are to be collected on covert events, self-recording is at present the only feasible technique.

D. Functions of Self-Monitoring

Self-monitoring is useful for both assessment and therapeutic purposes. With reference to assessment, self-recording may be employed to collect data during two phases of therapeutic contact. During the earlier phase, it is useful in determining the target behaviors and their controlling variables. The client usually keeps a behavioral diary, noting problematic events and the circumstances that surround them. From this information, consistent patterns may be ascertained which lead to the selection of the target behaviors and possible treatment techniques. In the subsequent phase of therapeutic contact, self-recording is again used during baseline and intervention to monitor the frequency of selected target behaviors in order to evaluate the success or failure of the treatment strategy.

In addition to assessment functions, self-monitoring has a therapeutic function. When it is used for data collection, it not only provides a count of the target behavior, but also may produce reactive changes in the rate of the target behavior. In other words, the very act of self-recording a behavior often causes the frequency of that behavior to change. This reactivity proves to be therapeutic because the behavior changes that occur are generally in desirable directions. Through self-recording, positively evaluated behaviors increase and, conversely, negatively evaluated behaviors decrease (Broden, Hall, & Mitts, 1971; Cavior & Marabotto, 1976; Kazdin, 1974a; Nelson, Lipinski, & Black, 1976a; Sieck & McFall, 1976). Given the desirability of these reactive behavior changes, self-monitoring has been employed for primarily therapeutic purposes (i.e., to alter the rate of a target behavior). While the reactivity of self-monitoring may be therapeutically useful, this same reactivity is a liability when self-monitoring is used for data collection purposes. It becomes very difficult to collect stable baseline data when the frequency of the target behavior is changing. Similarly, it is difficult to evaluate the effectiveness of a treatment technique when both the treatment technique and the means of data collection are contributing to the behavior change. These two functions of self-recording, assessment and therapeutic functions, are examined in greater detail in the remainder of this chapter.

E. Self-Recording Devices and Procedures

Almost no research has been conducted to provide guidelines for the most useful self-recording devices and procedures. The discussion that follows is based on current common practices and on thoughtful speculation. Research validation, however, is yet to come.

One of the most important considerations in selecting a self-recording procedure is that it fits the target behavior being recorded. If, for example, a client is requested to self-monitor a high-frequency or nearly continuous behavior by means of a frequency count, he may cease to self-record, simply because of the tedium of the assigned self-recording procedure. However, if a time-sampling procedure had been suggested, the client may have continued to self-monitor. Similarly, an obese client who is asked to self-record only daily weight may become discouraged because of typical fluctuations and slow progress. Caloric intake may be a more suitable behavior for obese clients to record (Romanczyk, 1974).

Other factors to consider in the choice of a self-monitoring procedure are ease and accessibility. As noted above (Section I,B), self-recording involves two stages (i.e., discriminating and recording the occurrences of the target behavior). If the self-monitoring procedure is too difficult, the client may discriminate occurrences of the target behavior, but fail to make the self-recording response, resulting in poor accuracy of self-recorded data. Alternatively, the client may "store up" occurrences of the target behavior and record them only aperiodically. Frederiksen, Epstein, and Kosevsky (1975) found that immediate self-recordings of cigarettes smoked was preferable to nightly or weekly recordings. Immediate recordings were more accurate and also effected greater reductions in smoking.

Final factors to consider in selecting a self-monitoring procedure are cost and device obtrusiveness. Most self-monitoring devices are quite inexpensive. Some of the mechanical devices, however, are more costly. There are differences of opinion regarding the merits of obtrusive self-recording devices. Thoresen and Mahoney (1974, p. 48) generally recommend small unobtrusive devices. However, an obtrusive device may be a discriminative stimulus to cue both accurate self-recording and reactive behavior changes. Maletzky (1974), for example, reported that the rate of self-recorded undesirable behaviors began to increase in frequency when the wrist counters used for self-recording were removed. A similar phenomenon was noted by Broden *et al.* (1971); the presence of slips of paper used to self-record study behavior seemed to cause increased studying, even when the subject did not engage in the self-recording response. In an attempt to evaluate the effects of device obtrusiveness on the accuracy and reactivity of self-monitoring, Nelson, Lipinski, and Boykin (in press, c) compared a hand-held with a belt-worn counter, both used by adolescent retarded subjects to self-record appropriate classroom verbalizations. Although the differences were not statistically significant, the hand-held counter tended to produce a greater number of appropriate verbalizations (5.44 per 15 minutes, compared with 4.46 for the belt-worn counter) and more accurate self-recordings (.845, compared with .820 for the belt-worn counter). In this particular study, the differences in obtrusiveness between the hand-held and the belt-worn counter may have been minimal, attenuating differences in results. Further research on device obtrusiveness is needed to determine if obtrusive devices do indeed produce more reactive and more accurate self-recordings.

As noted above, one requirement for a self-recording procedure is that it fits the target behavior being self-monitored. The next few pages describe several self-recording procedures which suit target behaviors measured, respectively, by narrations, by frequency counts, by duration, by time sampling, by ratings, and by mechanical means.

1. NARRATIONS

One goal of the early stages of behavioral assessment is not only to select the target behaviors, but also to determine the variables controlling their occurrence. Hence, one of the most popular forms of self-monitoring, especially during the early stages of assessment, is the behavioral diary. Instances of hypothesized target behaviors or fluctuations in feelings or thoughts are self-recorded. In addition, circumstances surrounding these events, namely, antecedents and consequences, are also recorded. Behavioral diaries may be unstructured or, alternatively, structured guidelines may be provided. Examples of more structured behavioral diaries include Knox's charts to record marital interactions (Knox, 1972, Charts 7 and 8), and Stuart and Davis' charts to record the circumstances surrounding eating behaviors (Stuart & Davis, 1972, Fig. 3). A structured self-recording diary for children is Kunzelmann's *countoon* (1970), as described in detail by Thoresen and Mahoney (1974). The countoon utilizes a pictorial sequence so that the child may record not only instances of the target behavior, but also its consequences. Even when structured diaries are used, Mahoney (in press) suggests leaving an open-ended column for clients to self-record their additional thoughts or comments. The reason for this suggestion is the importance accorded the entertaining of new or additional hypotheses about potential target behaviors and their controlling variables, especially during the early stages of behavioral assessment.

Diaries, as described above, involve written responses on the part of the self-recorder. Alternatively, the client may verbally narrate diary materials either by using a tape recorder or by using a telephone answering service (Mahoney, in press).

In conclusion, the purpose of these diaries is to select target behaviors and to determine their controlling variables, thereby facilitating choice of treatment strategies. Once the target behaviors have been selected and a treatment strategy proposed, the target behaviors will continue to be monitored during baseline and intervention to evaluate the success or failure of the treatment program.

2. FREQUENCY COUNTS

A frequency count is an appropriate recording procedure when the target behavior is discrete (i.e., when the durations of separate occurrences of the target behavior do not vary a great deal). The same unit of time must be used to record frequencies of any specific behavior so that one frequency count can be compared with another. One common way of self-recording frequency counts is to make tallies on a piece of paper, for example, a paper tucked into the cellophane of a cigarette package on which the frequency of cigarettes smoked per day is self-recorded. Watson and Tharp (1972) reported some novel but simple self-recording procedures. One client moved a toothpick from one compartment of her purse to another each time the target behavior occurred. Another person transferred pennies from one pocket to another, each penny representing one occurrence of the target behavior. Behavioral frequencies have also been self-recorded on a variety of counters: Lindsley's (1968) wrist gold counter; K. Mahoney's (1974) hand-crafted leather jewelry that disguises counting devices; Sheehan and Casey's (1974) knit tally; and Mattos' (1968) hand-held digital counter for recording frequencies of several target behaviors. This latter counter may be useful in self-recording discriminated operants. A discriminated operant is a behavior that occurs only in the presence of a clearly specified antecedent. If a multiple-channel counter is available, one channel may be used to self-record the occurrence of the antecedents (e.g., provocations to argue), while another channel records the occurrence of the target behavior (e.g., keeping one's temper). Discriminated operants are reported as a percentage: frequency of the target behavior divided by the frequency of the antecedent.

3. DURATION MEASURES

While frequency counts are used to self-record discrete target behaviors, the time consumed by each occurrence of other target behaviors may vary considerably. A duration measure is more sensitive to these varying time intervals. Duration may be self-recorded by means of a stopwatch. Several commercially available wrist watches have a stopwatch accessory, called an elapsed time indicator. Mahoney and Thoresen (1974) describe a switch that may be used with an electric clock which can be used to self-record, for example, the duration of television watching or study time; when the target behavior is occurring, the switch remains in the "on" position, permitting the self-recording clock to accumulate the duration measure.

4. TIME SAMPLING

As an alternative to self-recording duration, time sampling may be used to self-record nondiscrete behaviors whose occurrences vary in duration. Time sampling is also used to self-record high-frequency discrete behaviors when recording each instance of the behavior would be tedious. In time sampling, a longer unit of time, for example, a day, is subdivided into smaller units, for example, half-hour intervals. The self-recorder simply notes whether the target behavior occurred or not during this shorter time interval. Mahoney and Thoresen (1974) label this procedure an all-or-none method because only binary information is recorded. Although time sampling is convenient, its disadvantage is that each interval scored as positive may not contain comparable frequencies or intensities of the target behavior. A more refined form of time sampling is described by Stumphauzer (1974). A 4-point rating scale is used, where each interval is rated 0, 1, 2, or 3, depending on whether the behavior never occurred, or occurred occasionally, often, or very frequently within that interval.

Another form of time sampling is spot-checking (Kubany & Sloggett, 1973). A timing device is set for varying time intervals. When the timer sounds, the self-recorder simply notes whether the target behavior is or is not occurring at that instance. Spot-checking is reported as a percentage: the number of spot-checks during which the target behavior was occurring divided by the total number of spot-checks made. Timing devices accessible to self-recorders include alarm clocks, wrist watch alarms, kitchen timers, and parking meter reminders (Foxx & Martin, 1971). It is important for the subject or confederate to set the timing device on a variable interval schedule. An example using a parking meter timer was provided by Sirota and Mahoney (1974). An asthmatic client set the timer on a variable interval 30-minute schedule. When the timer signaled, she monitored her level of muscular tension.

5. RATINGS

The example above points to another form of self-monitoring, self-ratings of mood or emotional states. For example, daily levels of depression or anxiety can be measured by self-ratings. These ratings can be temporally cued, as was done with Sirota and Mahoney's subject (1974), or cued by specific environmental stimuli, previously identified as being related to target feelings. Examples of self-ratings of depression include a 10-point daily rating scale (Jackson, 1972), and daily completions of the Depressed Adjective Checklist (Hammen & Glass, 1975; Lewinsohn, 1974; Lubin, 1965). However, self-ratings of moods may not produce the reactive behavior changes often found with self-monitoring of motor activities (Section IV,C).

6. PASSIVE AND/OR MECHANICAL SELF-MONITORING PROCEDURES

Several mechanical self-recording procedures involve no response from the self-recorder except a commitment to use the self-recording device. For example, Azrin and Powell (1968) have developed a cigarette case that automatically records the number of times it is opened. If a subject takes only one cigarette at a time, and takes cigarettes only from this cigarette case, an automatic recording of the number of cigarettes smoked is produced. Similarly, Azrin, Rubin, O'Brien, Ayllon, and Roll (1968) developed an apparatus that automatically counts the number of times a subject assumes an inappropriate posture, given that the subject is wearing the apparatus. Schwitzgebel and Kolb (1974) describe a variety of other automated devices that, given the subject's cooperation, record specific aspects of his or her behavior. Some of their examples include: radio telemetry to record conversations (Soskin & John, 1963); ultrasonic speakers worn by the individual to measure body movements (Goldman, 1961); and a gravity-sensitive watch to measure hyperactivity (Schulmann & Reisman, 1959).

Another form of passive self-monitoring is the use of residual records (McFall, 1976; Webb, Campbell, Schwartz, & Sechrest, 1966), or other by-product or product measures. For example, an individual can count the number of cigarettes that have been smoked by counting the number of butts in the ashtray. In weight control studies, changes in body weight indirectly measure changes in eating behaviors (Mahoney, Moura, & Wade, 1973b). Similarly, fingernail length may be used as a measure of nail biting (McNamara, 1972), hair length as a measure of hair pulling (McLaughlin & Nay, 1975), and grades as an outcome of study behaviors (Johnson & White, 1971). Physiological outcome measures may also be used, for example, blood-alcohol level as a measure of drinking alcohol (Miller, Hersen, Eisler, & Watts, 1974), urine analysis to detect drug usage (Goldstein & Brown, 1970), and carbon monoxide in the breath to measure smoking (Lando, 1975).

McFall (1976) suggested that another form of passive self-monitoring might be archival records (e.g., telephone bills, and checking or charge account statements).

All of these forms of self-monitoring, mechanical procedures, residual records, product measures, and archival records, are passive in the sense that the subject need not make a self-recording response after each occurrence of the target behavior. It is not yet known whether such passive procedures produce reactive behavior changes. It may be hypothesized, however, that less reactivity would occur than with active self-monitoring. Another characteristic the passive procedures have in common is that feedback may be delayed. A considerable time lag may occur between the target behavior and the record of its occurrence. This delay may also attenuate the reactivity sometimes produced by self-monitoring.

One form of delayed self-monitoring has produced reactive behavior changes. Subjects' behaviors were recorded on videotape and the subjects were subsequently asked to self-monitor from them. As a result, changes in the rate of target behavior occurred in the criterion situation (Cavior & Marabotto, 1976; Thomas, 1971). Self-recording from videotape may be reactive since the self-recorder has no competing responses to make while watching the videotape, as compared with self-recording in the criterion situation itself.

7. COMMUNICATION OF SELF-MONITORED DATA

One convenient way to summarize self-recorded data is a behavioral graph. The abscissa generally consists of days, or other units of time. The ordinate consists of a unit of measurement of the self-recorded behavior (e.g., frequency, percentage, or time). No evaluative data of the relative effects of graphing one's self-recorded data by oneself as compared with graphing with one's therapist, has yet been collected. Other parameters of graphing that merit investigation are daily versus weekly graphing, and public display versus private access to the graphed data.

8. SUMMARY

Self-monitoring may be useful during both stages of behavioral assessment. In the first stage, when a target behavior and its controlling variables are being determined, the most useful form of self-monitoring seems to be the behavioral diary or narration. During this time, not only are instances of the hypothesized target behavior being recorded, but also environmental circumstances. After the target behavior and the treatment strategy are selected, self-monitoring of the target behavior continues during the second stage of assessment (baseline and intervention) in order to evaluate the effects of the treatment strategy. A large variety of self-recording procedures are available. One factor in selecting among these procedures is the suitability of each for the particular behavior. Different self-recording devices are available to record frequency counts, durations, time samplings, or ratings.

II. ASSESSMENT FUNCTIONS OF SELF-MONITORING

A. Methodological Issues in Evaluating Self-Monitored Data

1. PROCEDURES TO DETERMINE THE ACCURACY OF SELF-MONITORED DATA

The accuracy of self-recorded data is usually determined in one of three ways. The first procedure, and the most commonly used, is to compare the simultaneous recordings made by self-recorders and other observers. For example, Herbert and Baer (1972) compared an observer's data with that of two mothers to determine the accuracy of their self-recordings of attention to appropriate child behaviors. The second procedure is to compare the simultaneous recordings made by self-recorders and by mechanical recording devices. For example, a teaching machine used by Mahoney, Moore, Wade, and Moura (1973a) automatically recorded the students' answers while the students were also self-recording their correct answers. The accuracy of the students' self-monitoring was determined by comparing their self-recorded responses with the machine's recordings. The third procedure is to compare self-recordings with a by-product, believed to be related to the self-recorded target behavior. For example, changes in body weight indirectly reflect changes in eating habits. When eating habits are self-monitored, body weight can be used as an accuracy check (Mahoney *et al.,* 1973b). Other examples described above (Section I,E,6) include hair length as a measure of accuracy of self-monitored hair pulling (McLaughlin & Nay, 1975).

2. ACCURACY VERSUS INTEROBSERVER AGREEMENT

Procedures parallel to establishing the accuracy of self-recorded data have been used to evaluate external observers' data. With reference to external observers, Johnson and Bolstad (1973) have distinguished between observer accuracy and observer agreement. If the recordings of observers are compared with a previously established criterion for coding the behaviors, observer accuracy is measured. However, if the recordings of two observers are compared with each other, observer agreement is measured. Two observers may be in agreement with each other, yet neither of their recordings may truly reflect the actual occurrences of the target behavior (Lipinski & Nelson, 1974a).

A parallel phenomenon exists with procedures used to assess the accuracy of self-recorded data. Only when self-recorded data are compared with mechanical or criterion recordings is the *accuracy* of self-monitored data being evaluated. The usual procedure involves comparing self-recorded data with simultaneous recordings made by other observers and produces only a measure of observer *agreement.*

The quality of self-recorded data is usually evaluated by comparing the self-recorder's data with the observer's data. Because two observers are usually employed and interobserver agreement is assessed between them, the observers' data are generally taken as the criterion against which to judge the self-recorder's data. Limited research, however, has been conducted to determine if the observers' data are more accurate than the self-recorder's data. Perhaps the self-recorder more carefully observes and records his or her own behavior than external observers do.

This question of the relative accuracy of self-recorders and external observers was raised by McFall (1970). A correlation of .61 was reported between smokers' self-recordings of the number of cigarettes smoked and observers' recordings of their smoking frequency. A closer examination of the data revealed that generally the observers counted fewer cigarettes than the subjects, raising the question of the relative accuracy of the subjects and the observers. By examining other data, McFall (1970) concluded that observers were probably more accurate than the subjects. Further research on this topic is needed, especially since the usual procedure to evaluate the accuracy of self-monitored data considers the observers' data as a criterion.

The distinction between observer accuracy and observer agreement is made based on the data of Fixsen, Phillips, and Wolf (1974). Self-reports made by boys on the cleanliness of their rooms agreed 76% with peer reports. However, their self-reports and reports on their peers' rooms agreed with adult observers' recordings 50%. Thus, conclusions about the quality of the self-monitored data depend on the specific observer whose ratings are being compared.

In summary, observer accuracy and observer agreement refer to two different phenomena. With current methodology, the agreement of self-recorded data is assessed much more often than its accuracy. Throughout this chapter, however, the term accuracy will be used to refer to both accuracy and agreement. In the studies described below, an assumption is usually made that observers' data are more accurate than self-recorders' data, a notion that merits further experimental investigation.

3. ACCURACY OF COVERT SELF-RECORDED BEHAVIORS

Self-recording is the usual procedure employed to collect data on the frequency of covert events. As a result of the increasing popularity of cognitive behavior modification (M. J. Mahoney, 1974a), self-monitoring is frequently used for recording coverants (Homme, 1965). In some studies, coverants are self-monitored during baseline and implementation of a treatment procedure designed to modify the frequency of coverants. For example, to evaluate the effectiveness of coverant control procedures (Homme, 1965), Mahoney's subject (1971) self-monitored obsessions and positive self thoughts; Jackson's subject (1972) self-recorded depression ratings; and Hannum, Thoresen, and Hubbard's (1974) teachers self-recorded positive and negative self thoughts. Particular sexual and drug-related urges were self-recorded to evaluate, respectively, the effectiveness of covert sensitization (Barlow, Leitenberg, & Agras, 1969) and of aversive counterconditioning (Spevack, Pihl, & Rowan, 1973). Similarly, Zimmerman (1975) had subjects self-monitor their aversive feelings to assess the effectiveness of "self-implosion." Because of the reactivity of self-monitoring, self-recording was used as both the coverant data collection method and the therapeutic strategy to reduce the frequency of hallucinations (Rutner & Bugle, 1969), ruminative thinking (Frederiksen, 1975), and paranoid thoughts (Williams, 1976). Self-recording of coverants has grown in popularity to the point that attempts have been made to train subjects to more accurately discriminate and self-record the occurrence of covert events (Meyers, Mercatoris, & Artz, 1976).

Two main problems exist regarding the use of self-monitoring to collect data on the frequency of coverants. The first relates to its reactivity. Reactivity makes it difficult to establish a stable baseline of coverant frequency. Also, effectiveness of the treatment technique alone cannot be established. Even if the self-recorded coverants change in frequency, this modification may only be attributed to the interaction of the treatment technique and self-monitoring. These issues are discussed in greater detail below (Section II,G).

The second main problem is establishing the accuracy of the self-recording of covert events. Given their nature and current technology, covert events are directly observable only to the subject. However, two attempts have been made to indirectly corroborate their self-recording. Danaher and Thoresen (1972) attempted to establish the validity of self-reports of imagery by employing a number of indirect behavioral measures. They concluded that further evaluation was necessary to establish the convergent and discriminant validity of these behavioral measures. The second attempt, suggested by Kanfer (1970), was to correlate the self-recorded frequency of the covert event with the frequency of a related observable event. Several studies that correlated the frequencies of covert and seemingly related overt events produced a variety of outcomes. A rather good correspondence was reported by Williams (1976) between self-recordings of paranoid thoughts and esophagitis episodes, and by Barlow *et al.* (1969) between self-recordings of specific sexual urges and a card-sort measure. An expected inverse relationship between self-reported depression and self-reinforcement was found by Jackson (1972). However, low correlations were reported between other coverants and their seemingly related overt behaviors. Hannum *et al.* (1974) found only a minimal relationship between teachers' self-monitored positive and negative self statements and their classroom behavior as recorded by observers. Horan and Johnson (1971) reported a correlation of .27 between weight loss and frequency of weight-related coverants. Nelson, Hay, and Hay (in press, a) found only a moderate relationship, $r = .48$, between self-recorded study thoughts and self-recorded study time. McFall (1970) found only a weak relationship ($r = .25$) between subjects' reported decisions *not* to smoke and the observers' recordings of their actual smoking frequency.

Several explanations are possible for low correlations between frequency of self-reported coverants and frequency of observable events that were supposedly related. One is that the relationship between the two is weak. For example, Lewinsohn's theory of depression (1974), that depressed feelings and activity level are inversely related, has been challenged by Hammen and Glass (1975). Given Lang's formulation (1968) of the relative independence of covert, autonomic, and overt behaviors, weak relationships between covert and overt behaviors are not surprising. Nelson and McReynolds (1971) had previously warned that overt behaviors may not be a viable index of the accuracy of self-recorded covert behaviors. A second explanation for the low correlations is that the behaviors in fact are highly correlated, but that the self-recorders' frequency counts of their covert behaviors are inexact, thus creating the low correlation. In conclusion, a high correlation between the self-recorded frequency of a covert event and the observed frequency of an overt event may lend some credence to the self-recorded data. However, a low correlation cannot be taken as evidence of inaccurate self-recording since the two sets of behavior may have been only minimally related.

B. Accuracy of Self-Monitored Data

As noted above, comparisons of simultaneous observations by self-recorders and observers are used to evaluate accuracy of self-monitored data in most studies. Given this methodology, some studies found self-recorders to be very accurate, whereas others found them to be relatively inaccurate.

Kazdin (1974b) has tentatively suggested that adult subjects may be more accurate self-recorders than children. In their study, McKenzie and Rushall (1974) found that swimmers' and experimenters' counts of the number of laps completed in a swimming pool agreed 100%. Azrin and Powell (1969) reported a 98% agreement between self-reported pill-taking and hospital employees' records. Ober (1968) found a .94 agreement between self-reports and friends' reports of subjects' smoking. Mahoney *et al.* (1973a) found a high degree of agreement (.938) between subjects' self-monitored study responses and simultaneous mechanical recordings of their responses. Aides' reports of behavior modification training sessions for retarded clients were found to agree well with other measures of the occurrence of these sessions (Shaw, Peterson, & Cone, 1974).

In contrast to these studies demonstrating accurate adult self-recordings are others reporting relatively low agreement between self-recordings and independent observations. For instance, agreement for two mothers' self-recordings and observers' recordings in Herbert and Baer's (1972) study was 46% and 42%, respectively. College students' records of their smoking rates and simultaneous records taken by their classmates correlated .61 (McFall, 1970). Cavior and Marabotto (1976) found a .37 agreement between trained observers and college students who self-monitored their verbal behavior in a dyadic situation. Hendricks, Thoresen, and Hubbard (1973) reported that the agreement rate between self-monitoring teachers and external observers ranged from 41% to 87.8%.

As Kazdin (1974b) has observed, children have generally been found to be inaccurate self-recorders. Fixsen *et al.* (1972) reported that boys' self-reports on the cleanliness of their own rooms agreed with peer reports 76%, but agreement with adult observers decreased to 50%. Broden *et al.* (1971) found that there were large day-to-day discrepancies in a student's self-recording of her studying and observers' recordings. Risley and Hart (1968) found low correspondence between children's self-reports of nonverbal behaviors and the frequency of these behaviors as measured by observers.

C. Patterns of Self-Recorders' and Observers' Recordings

The accuracy of self-recording as reported in the above studies varied from acceptable to poor. The methodology generally used to obtain these evaluations was to compare self-recorders' and observers' simultaneous reports. When self-recorders' and observers' data are examined more closely, the pattern of their relationship may be ascertained. Kazdin (1974b) concluded that subjects as compared with observers tended to underestimate their performance of undesirable behaviors (Bolstad & Johnson, 1972; Thomas, Abrams, & Johnson, 1971), and to overestimate their desirable ones (Fixsen *et al.*, 1972; Risley & Hart, 1968). This particular pattern was not evidenced by six teachers who self-monitored their positive and/or negative classroom verbalizations (Nelson, Hay, Hay, & Carstens, in press, b). Particular teachers seemed to be accurate self-recorders, underestimators, or overestimators regardless of the valence of the target behavior. Nelson *et al.* (in press, c) requested nine retarded adolescents to self-record their appropriate classroom verbalizations. Despite the positive valence of this target behavior, no subject's self-recordings were consistently higher than the observer's.

Regardless of the specific pattern of self-recorders' and observers' data, Simkins (1971) proposed several reasons for the discrepancies between two sets of recordings. Differences in motivation and/or in response criteria utilized may exist between the self-recorders and the observers. Self-recorders may have other behaviors to perform that compete with the behavior of self-recording.

Comparisons of self-recorders' and observers' data have produced variable results and varying patterns of relationship. The next section, therefore, examines some of the variables that have been determined to influence the accuracy of self-monitored data.

D. Variables Affecting the Accuracy of Self-Monitoring

1. AWARENESS OF ACCURACY ASSESSMENT

One variable which has been repeatedly shown to influence the accuracy of self-recording is awareness of accuracy assessment. Self-recording is more accurate when self-observers are aware that their accuracy is being monitored than when their accuracy is monitored covertly. This finding has been replicated in three analog studies in which the target behavior was classroom face touching. Lipinski and Nelson (1974b) found that the agreement between self-recorders and trained observers was .86 when the subjects were aware of reliability checks, as compared with .52 when accuracy checks were made covertly. In two similar studies, Nelson, Lipinski, and Black (1975) found that awareness of reliability checks increased the accuracy of self-recorded face touching from .554 to .810, and Lipinski, Black, Nelson, and Ciminero (1975) reported a comparable increase from .46 to .67. This influence of awareness of accuracy checks was replicated with verbal responses by Bailey and Peterson (1977). Awareness of accuracy estimates increased agreement for self-recordings and external recordings of praise words from 37.7% to 51.6%. Similarly, Santogrossi (1974) reported that discrepancies between children's self-recordings of correct reading responses and external observers' recordings were decreased when either a teacher or a peer also monitored children's reading responses. Comparable effects were obtained by peer and teacher monitors.

2. REINFORCEMENT CONTINGENT ON ACCURATE SELF-RECORDED DATA

Another variable consistently found to influence the accuracy of self-recorded data is reinforcement for accuracy. Risley and Hart (1968) found that the initially low correspondence between children's verbal and nonverbal behavior could be improved when reinforcement was made contingent on correspondence, as evaluated by external observers. Fixsen *et al.* (1972) found that the .76 level of agreement between peer and self-reports of room cleanliness could be enhanced to .86 through contingent reinforcement. Cheating behavior of a sixth-grade student was significantly reduced when her weekly grades were made contingent on daily accurate self-evaluation (Flowers, 1972). Nelson *et al.* (1976a) reinforced adult retarded subjects for increases in self-monitoring accuracy. Under this contingency, the accuracy of self-recording the touching of environmental objects increased from .70 to .92, and the accuracy of self-monitored face touching increased from .45 to .82. Lipinski *et al.* (1975) differentially reinforced some college students for increases in the accuracy of their self-recorded face touches, and other students for decreases in the frequency of self-recorded face touches. Compared with a baseline self-monitoring accuracy of .67, the former group increased their accuracy to .84 under differential reinforcement for accuracy, while the latter increased their accuracy to .72 under differential reinforcement for reductions in face touching. Peterson, House, and Alford (1975) similarly found that contingent reinforcement increased their subject's accuracy from 0% to 50.1% when self-recording the phrase "you know."

Just as positive reinforcement has been demonstrated to increase the accuracy of self-recorded data, punishment has also been reported to minimize discrepant self-recordings (Seymour & Stokes, 1976).

Given that contingent consequences may alter self-recording accuracy, a related question is whether these consequences can be gradually withdrawn while nonetheless maintaining high accuracy. Unsuccessful attempts to maintain high accuracy of self-ratings of classroom behavior while gradually withdrawing accuracy checks and reinforcement were reported by Drabman, Spitalnik, and O'Leary (1973) and by Turkewitz, O'Leary, and Ironsmith (1975). In these two studies, the number of children whose self-ratings were examined was gradually decreased. However, when the number of days on which accuracy of self-reporting was checked and consequently was reduced by using a variable ratio schedule, self-recording accuracy was maintained (Layne, Rickard, Jones, & Lyman, 1976).

3. NATURE OF THE TARGET BEHAVIOR

While awareness of accuracy assessment and reinforcement for self-recorded data have consistently been demonstrated to increase self-monitoring accuracy, the remaining variables that are discussed as influencing self-recording accuracy have much less empirical support. One of these variables is the nature of the target behavior being self-recorded. Bailey and Peterson (1977) proposed that verbal responses may be more difficult to self-record accurately than motor responses. This suggestion was based on a comparison of their self-recording accuracy for praise statements (51.6% and 37.7% in the aware and unaware conditions; Section II,D,1) with Lipinski and Nelson's self-recording accuracy (1974b) for face touching (.86 and .52 in the aware and unaware conditions). Peterson *et al.* (1975) provided further evidence that higher self-recording accuracies may be obtained for face touching (64.3% agreement) than for verbal responses (0% agreement for the phrase "you know," and 31.4% agreement for the phrase "and all that"). Cavior and Marabotto (1976) reported similar results (.37) for self-recorded verbal responses. Finally, Hayes and Cavior (in press) compared the agreement between self-recorders and observers for face touching (.87), value judgments (.40), and speech nonfluencies (.00). These results lend further credence to the notion that verbal responses may be more difficult to self-record accurately than motor responses. Further research is needed to determine the relative difficulty of self-recording other target behaviors.

4. CONCURRENT RESPONSE REQUIREMENTS

Although Cavior and Marabotto (1976) found the accuracy of self-recording to be .37 when the subjects attempted to self-monitor their verbal behaviors while engaging in a dyadic interaction, their accuracy increased to .89 when given the opportunity to self-record their verbal behaviors from videotapes. It is possible that subjects could not accurately self-record during dyadic interactions because concurrent responses interfered with their accuracy. The detrimental effects of concurrent responding on self-recording accuracy were confirmed in experiments by Epstein, Webster, and Miller (1975) and Epstein, Miller, and Webster (1976). Subjects made fewer errors in their self-monitoring of respiration when they engaged in self-recording alone (respective error rates of .28, .23, and 4%), than when they engaged in a concurrent operant task of lever pressing in addition to self-monitoring (respective error rates of .72, .49, and 9.5%).

5. SCHEDULE OF SELF-MONITORING

Frederiksen *et al.* (1975) reported that when subjects self-recorded each cigarette that was smoked, their accuracy of self-recording was greater (93.59%) than when they self-recorded the number of cigarettes smoked at the end of each day (85.77%) or at the end of each week (87.32%).

6. VALENCE OF TARGET BEHAVIOR

Kanfer (1976) suggested that subjects may self-record negatively valenced behaviors less accurately than positively valenced behaviors. Since attention to undesirable behaviors may produce negative self-evaluation, the subject may avoid negative self-evaluation by not attending to and/or not recording the occurrence of undesirable behaviors, thus producing inaccurate data. Kanfer's suggestion has received some empirical support. Nelson *et al.* (1976a) reported a higher agreement between adult retarded self-recorders and observers for the positive behavior of social conversation (.73) than for the negative behavior of face touching (.45). In two experiments in which teachers self-recorded their classroom verbalizations, their accuracy was greater for positive verbalizations (.582 and .533, respectively) than for negative verbalizations (.408 and .373, respectively) (Nelson *et al.*, in press, b). In another classroom experiment, children were also found to self-record their appropriate classroom verbalizations more accurately (.807) than their inappropriate classroom verbalizations (.569) (Nelson, Hay, & Koslow-Green, 1977a).

7. SOCIAL PSYCHOLOGY MANIPULATIONS

Bornstein, Hamilton, Miller, Quevillon, and Spitzform (in press) found that the accuracy of self-report was greater for subjects who received a "reliability enhancement" package than for control subjects. The reliability enhancement package consisted of three manipulations borrowed from social psychology: the foot-in-the-door technique, induced self-esteem, and guilt induction. In a related study (Bornstein, Hamilton, Carmody, Rychtarik, & Veraldi, in press), the components of the reliability enhancement package that also produced greater self-recording accuracy than the control condition were four other social psychology variables: cognitive consistency, consequence clarification, public commitment, and a cueing statement. In a third study, Hamilton and Bornstein (in press) found that with an easily discriminable verbal response, a reliability enhancement package consisting of bogus feedback on the "honesty" of the subject and of accuracy instructions improved self-monitoring accuracy more than a control condition.

8. TRAINING IN SELF-MONITORING

In an attempt to increase the very low accuracy with which their subject self-recorded the phrase "you know," Peterson *et al.* (1975) requested the subject to practice self-recording his own conversation from videotape. While this procedure was effective in raising his accuracy to 62% while self-recording from the videotape, training did not generalize to the criterion situation of *in vivo* conversation, where accuracy dropped to 20%. For the training of their retarded adolescent subjects, Nelson *et al.* (in press, c) used both videotape practice and practice in the criterion classroom situation. Four trained subjects more accurately self-recorded their appropriate classroom verbalizations (.914) than five less trained subjects (.784). Hamilton and Bornstein (in press) also found that practicing self-recording of speech nonfluencies from both audiotape and an *in vivo* speech produced greater self-recording accuracy than a control condition. Further research is needed, however, to delineate the components of efficient and efficacious training procedures.

9. CHARACTERISTICS OF THE SELF-MONITORING DEVICE

As described earlier (Section I,E), a great many self-recording devices are available. The characteristics of these devices which contribute to self-recording accuracy have received almost no empirical attention. Nelson *et al.* (in press, c) attempted to discriminate the effects on accuracy of the obtrusive hand-held counter from the less obtrusive belt-worn counter, but produced only minimal results (.845 in the former condition, .820 in the latter). Again, additional research is needed to provide experimentally based guidelines for the selection of self-recording devices to enhance the accuracy of the resultant data.

10. SUMMARY

The accuracy of self-monitored data varies from high to low. Several variables, however, have been delineated which enhance the accuracy of self-monitoring. Extensive empirical support exists for the utility of some of these variables (e.g., awareness of accuracy assessment and reinforcement for accuracy). Additional research is needed to strengthen the utility of proposed variables and to discover other variables that may also improve the accuracy of self-monitoring.

E. Limitations in Employing Self-Monitoring for Assessment

Self-monitoring is used for data collection in order to determine appropriate target behaviors and treatment strategy and to monitor the frequency of the target behavior during baseline and intervention. There are two limitations when self-monitoring is used for data collection. The first is the possibility that the self-recorded data are inaccurate. The second is the reactive nature of self-monitoring (i.e., the very process of self-recording the frequency of a target behavior sometimes alters that frequency).

In clinical situations, the first limitation is of more concern than the second. Because self-recording generally increases the frequency of desirable behaviors and decreases undesirable behaviors, reactivity of self-monitoring may actually enhance therapeutic intervention. However, it is important that the therapist be provided with accurate data so that effectiveness of the therapeutic program may be correctly evaluated. When self-monitoring is used to collect data in clinical situations, reactivity of self-monitoring is of less concern, but attention should be paid to maintaining and enhancing the accuracy of self-monitoring.

In research situations, the emphasis is not only on accuracy of data, but also on identification of controlling variables. In most research situations, even when data are collected by self-recorders, the data are usually validated by other observers, by mechanical monitoring devices, or through a by-product related to the self-monitored behavior. Even when the self-recorders are inaccurate, other data sources on which to rely may exist. The reactivity of self-monitoring presents a greater problem. First, it is difficult to establish a stable baseline if the frequency of the target behavior is changing. Second, it is difficult to discriminate behavior changes caused by the assessment technique (self-monitoring) from behavior changes caused by the intervention technique under investigation.

F. Procedures to Obtain Consistent and Accurate Self-Monitoring

An issue even more fundamental than inducing clients to produce accurate self-monitored data is persuading them to self-monitor at all. Some practical suggestions to ensure the consistent collection of self-monitored data have been provided by Mahoney (in press). One of his suggestions is to provide the client with a simple and reliable self-recording device that is also compatible with the target behavior. An ancillary idea is that the measuring procedure (i.e., frequency count vs. duration) should be suited to the target behavior. Thus, a client may terminate self-recording if either the measuring procedure is not appropriate for the target behavior or if the self-recording device does not suit the measuring procedure and the target behavior. A related notion is the possibility of using a tape recorder or a telephone answering service to promote self-monitoring in clients who dislike writing.

Another of Mahoney's (in press) suggestions is that the therapist must determine which clients are suitable for self-monitoring procedures. For example, it may be unwise to prescribe self-monitoring for clients who are suspicious of quantification. However, "obsessive-compulsive" clients may willingly engage in elaborate self-monitoring procedures. After determining that a particular client is a good candidate for self-monitoring, one should train the client to discriminate occurrences of the target behavior and to use the self-recording device. Mahoney (in press) provides some explicit suggested steps for this training: (1) give explicit definitions and examples of target behaviors; (2) give explicit self-monitoring instructions; (3) model the appropriate use of the self-monitoring device; (4) ask the client to repeat the target definitions and self-monitoring instructions; and (5) have the client self-monitor several occurrences of the target behavior as described by the therapist. Parenthetically, Nelson *et al.* (in press, c) found this training procedure to be effective with adolescent retarded self-recorders.

Mahoney (in press) also proposed that positive target behaviors be self-recorded rather than negative target behaviors; for example, the depressive should record positive self thoughts rather than negative ones. Kanfer (1976) provided theoretical support for this suggestion by noting that attention to undesirable target behaviors may produce negative self-evaluation and avoidance of self-monitoring. A client is more likely to continue self-recording if desirable behaviors whose self-recording produces positive self-evaluation are selected to self-monitor.

Finally, Mahoney (in press) proposed that the therapist prompt and reinforce the client for the production of self-monitored data. Therapist prompting may involve statements concerning the importance of self-monitoring or modeling by the therapist of his or her own uses of the strategy. Therapist consequences may include praise or fee reductions for the production of self-recorded data, or termination of therapeutic services for consistent failure to keep self-recorded data.

The above suggestions are offered to increase the probability of clients' engaging in consistent self-recording. Additional suggestions to increase the accuracy of these self-recorded data follow. These recommendations are based on research described earlier (Section II,D) which delineated some variables controlling the accuracy of self-monitoring. One of these variables was awareness of accuracy assessment. O'Leary and Kent (1973) suggested three procedures that include this awareness to maintain good accuracy in trained observers: (1) have interobserver agreement continuously checked; (2) have interobserver agreement assessed on a random basis; and (3) use mechanical recordings of target behaviors in order to permit calculation of interobserver agreement with these recordings. Parellel procedures may be applied with self-recorders to enhance their accuracy. With reference to the first suggestion, Rutner (1967) had someone else in the environment initial each self-recording of cigarettes smoked. Similarly, Nelson *et al.* (in press, a) required subjects to have someone else initial their self-recorded beginning and ending study times. Regarding the second suggestion, Tokarz and Lawrence (1974) requested insomniacs to self-record their time of falling asleep and awakening. After informing the insomniacs that they would be aware of accuracy assessment, Tokarz and Lawrence used roommates to assess periodically and covertly the insomniacs' accuracy. Regarding the third suggestion, clients were informed that their self-recording accuracy would be determined by checks such as weight (Mahoney *et al.,* 1973b), or grades (Johnson & White, 1971), or by other unobtrusive and/or mechanical devices (Mahoney *et al.,* 1973a; Schwitzgebel & Kolb, 1974; Webb *et al.,* 1966).

In addition to utilizing awareness of accuracy assessment to enhance the accuracy of self-recording, another procedure consists of rewarding clients for data that are congruent with these checks. Praise, fee reductions, or suggestions for self-reinforcement may be employed by the therapist to reinforce accurate self-recordings.

Other recommendations to enhance self-monitoring accuracy include having the client self-record each instance of low-frequency target behaviors, selecting desirable rather than undesirable target behaviors to self-record, providing the client with a suitable self-recording procedure, device, and training, and having the client self-record only when he or she is not overly busy with other behaviors.

G. Experimental Controls for Reactivity in Research Situations

When data are collected by means of self-monitoring in clinical situations, reactivity of self-recording may not be of concern and may in fact have some therapeutic values. However, since the only source of data is often the self-recorder, procedures should be utilized to enhance accuracy of the self-recorded data so that a correct evaluation of therapeutic progress can be made.

When data are collected by means of self-monitoring in research situations, an opposite emphasis is placed on the reactivity and accuracy issues. Even when data are collected through self-recording, these data are usually corroborated by other observers or by some measurable by-product. The self-recorders' data, in the final analysis, may not even be used. For example, although Lipinski and Nelson's college students (1974b) self-recorded face touching, the observers' data on the subjects' face touching were used to evaluate reactivity of self-monitoring. Similarly, although Bellack's (1976) subjects were required to self-monitor food intake, only their actual body weights were used in data analysis. Even when self-monitored data are reported, for example, the rate of hair pulling as self-recorded by McLaughlin and Nay's subject (1975), an independent check is also reported, that is, the measured length of hair. Because self-recorders' data are not the sole source in most research, their accuracy may not be of utmost concern.

Since the goal of research is to identify precisely the controlling variables, reactivity of self-monitoring is a much more crucial issue. If self-recording is initiated at the beginning of an experiment, no "true" baseline will be established because the very process of self-monitoring alters the frequency of target behavior. If self-monitoring is used concurrently with another therapeutic technique, behavior changes cannot be attributed solely to the technique. These problems related to reactivity exist even when data are also collected by observers or by mechanical means since the recorded behavior changes in frequency. Fortunately, several experimental procedures have been described that control for the reactive effects of self-monitoring.

When a within-subject experimental design is used, Jeffrey (1974) suggests the use of an ABCABC design in which A is an independently assessed baseline, B is self-monitoring, and C is self-monitoring plus an additional treatment technique. This concept may also be applied to multiple baseline designs in which the ABC procedure is applied sequentially to different subjects, behaviors, or situations (Hall, Christler, Cranston, & Tucker, 1970). The preself-monitoring baseline of Condition A may be assessed in several different ways. One procedure is to have the subject estimate the preself-recording occurrence of the target behavior. Berecz (1972), for example, had his subjects provide a prebaseline estimate of the number of cigarettes smoked per day prior to another baseline where subjects self-recorded their smoking rates. As might be expected, self-recorded levels of smoking were lower than the prebaseline estimates. An alternative procedure was to have independent observers collect data prior to initiation of subjects' self-recording. Lipinski *et al.* (1975), for example, utilized a two-stage baseline. Subjects who were college students in a classroom setting were observed by trained observers from behind a one-way mirror to obtain a baseline frequency of subjects' face touching. The subjects were then asked to self-record their own face touching. Additional manipulations were subsequently evaluated against the independent observers' and self-recorders' baselines. While an independently assessed preself-recording baseline may be ideal, in some situations this procedure may be impractical, and with some target behaviors, such as covert responses, impossible. Under these circumstances, initial self-monitored data may be utilized as an artificial baseline against which to evaluate further changes produced by additional intervention strategies.

When a between-subject experimental design is used, Nelson and McReynolds (1971) and Jeffrey (1974) suggested the inclusion of a self-monitoring only control group. In comparison with this and other control groups, the therapeutic effects of other treatment techniques may be assessed while still using self-recording to monitor the dependent variable. It must be cautioned, however, that independent effects of treatment techniques are not examined, but only interactive effects of these techniques and of self-monitoring.

III. THERAPEUTIC FUNCTIONS OF SELF-MONITORING

A. Demonstrations of Reactivity

Reactive effects of self-monitoring have been replicated numerous times by means of case studies, within-subject experimental designs, and between-subject experimental designs. The following behaviors have been altered in frequency by self-monitoring: reports of hallucinations (Rutner & Bugle, 1969), hair pulling (Bayer, 1972), lip and mouth biting (Ernst, 1973), alcoholic drinking (Sobell & Sobell, 1973), a variety of repetitive motor behaviors (Maletzky, 1974), reports of ruminative thinking (Frederiksen, 1975), insomniac sleeping patterns (Jason, 1975), reports of paranoid ideation (Williams, 1976), and amphetamine abuse and drug-related thoughts (Hay, Hay, & Angle, in press).

Within-subject experimental designs included Leitenberg, Agras, Thompson, and Wright's (1968) B-A-B demonstration in which a claustrophobic patient increased the time she spent in a small room when she used a stopwatch to determine elapsed time of each trial. Using a reversal design, Herbert and Baer (1972) found that self-recording increased contingent maternal attention and appropriate child behaviors. Two experiments were reported by McKenzie and Rushall (1974), one utilizing a multiple baseline design, and the other a reversal design. Both studies demonstrated that swimmers could utilize self-monitoring to improve various aspects of swimming practice. Using multiple baseline designs across several behaviors of two tiqueurs, Thomas *et al.* (1971) and Hutzell, Platzek, and Logue (1974) demonstrated that the frequency of tics was effectively reduced by self-recording. Finally, a multiple baseline design across settings was employed by Seymour and Stokes (1976) to demonstrate that self-monitoring increased the frequency of work behaviors in delinquent girls.

Between-subject experimental designs have also demonstrated the reactive effects of self-monitoring. College students who self-recorded their study activities earned better grades than control subjects and students who self-monitored their dating activities (Johnson & White, 1971). Vargas and Adesso (1976) measured longer nail lengths in nail-biters who self-monitored their nail biting than in those who did not self-monitor.

Finally, a series of studies has compared the reactive effects of self-monitoring with behavior changes produced by other therapeutic techniques. Nelson *et al.* (1976a) found that retarded adults' self-monitoring was more effective than a token economy in increasing the frequencies of three desirable target behaviors: social conversation, room tidiness, and recreational participation. In another between-subject design, self-recording by agoraphobic clients was found to produce as much time outside as differential reinforcement for longer excursions (Emmelkamp & Ultee, 1974) and as imaginal and *in vivo* flooding (Emmelkamp, 1974). Richards (1975) reported that a combined study skills and self-monitoring group earned better grades than a study skills group. However, a combination of self-monitoring and self-reinforcement produced greater weight loss than self-monitoring alone (Bellack, 1976; M.J. Mahoney, 1974b; Mahoney *et al.*, 1973b).

While all the above studies demonstrated the reactive effects of self-monitoring, self-monitoring did not produce reactive effects in other studies (Jackson, 1972; Mahoney, 1971; McNamara, 1972). The variable results effected by self-recording are typified by Zimmerman and Levitt (1975). Of 22 clients who were asked to self-record by 14 different therapists, reactive changes occurred in eight under the direction of seven different therapists. McFall (1976) commented that a box score approach (i.e., tallying the numbers of studies in which self-monitoring is or is not reactive) is probably minimally productive in terms of understanding inconsistent effects. A more fruitful approach is to examine the specific variables that seem to control the reactivity of self-monitoring.

B. Variables Controlling the Reactivity of Self-Monitoring

1. MOTIVATION FOR BEHAVIOR CHANGE

The suggestion that motivation for behavior change influences the reactivity of self-monitoring is based largely on several studies in which cigarette smoking was the target behavior. The subjects selected by McFall and Hammen (1971) were students who indicated they were motivated to stop smoking. Under these conditions, all four groups of subjects decreased their smoking, regardless of the specific self-recording procedure employed. In contrast, the subjects used by McFall (1970) were those in a class who happened to be smokers. When the subjects were not necessarily motivated to stop smoking, self-monitoring of the number of cigarettes smoked actually increased smoking rates, although self-recording of resisted urges decreased smoking frequency. A specific comparison of motivated and unmotivated smokers was reported by Lipinski *et al.* (1975). Self-recording decreased smoking only for the motivated smokers who signed up for an experiment designated to reduce smoking; self-recording did not decrease smoking for the unmotivated smokers who signed up for an experiment advertised for smokers. The influence of motivation on the reactivity of self-monitoring was verified with a different target behavior by Komaki and Dore-Boyce (in press); self-recording increased verbal participation only for students who had expressed an interest in modifying this behavior.

2. VALENCE OF TARGET BEHAVIOR

While the subject's motivation may determine whether reactive changes occur through self-recording, the valence of the target behavior may determine the direction of the reactive changes. Self-monitoring increases the frequency of desirable behaviors and decreases the frequency of undesirable ones. This conclusion was confirmed in two laboratory studies where positive or negative valences were assigned to the same target behavior. Self-recording increased self-reference statements when they had been assigned a positive valence, and decreased these statements when they had been assigned a negative valence (Kazdin, 1974a). Similar results were reported by Sieck and McFall (1976) when positive or negative valences were assigned to the rate of eye-blinking. Consistent findings were also reported in a third laboratory study by Cavior and Marabotto (1976) in which subjects themselves selected a verbal behavior that they regarded positively or negatively. In a naturalistic setting, Broden *et al.* (1971) found that self-recording increased the study behavior of an eighth-grade girl, and conversely decreased the inappropriate classroom verbalizations of her peer. Similarly, with adult retarded subjects, Nelson *et al.* (1976a) demonstrated that through self-recording, a positive behavior (social conversation) increased in frequency, and a negative behavior (face touching) decreased.

3. EXPERIMENTER INSTRUCTIONS

The class of experimenter instructions used in the above experiments, namely, the assignment of differential valences to the same target behavior, was effective in producing differential behavior change in the self-monitoring subjects. Two other types of experimenter instructions, expectancy regarding direction of behavior change and demand for differential behavior change, were unsuccessful in producing differential behavior change in self-monitoring subjects. Whether subjects were told that self-recording would decrease, increase, or not change their face-touching frequency, self-recording clearly decreased this frequency in all groups (Nelson *et al.*, 1975). Similarly, Hutzell (1977) found that all subjects decreased their self-monitored eye-blinking, even though the groups were given differential expectancies that self-monitoring would increase or decrease this behavior. Orne (1970) and Kazdin (1974b) suggested that implicit or explicit demand to produce differential behavior change may contribute to the differential reactivity of self-monitoring. After a baseline period of conversation, Nelson, Kapust, Dorsey, and Hayes (1977b) instructed college students to increase, decrease, or not change their rate of first-person personal pronouns. For the subjects who did not self-monitor, these instructions produced the requested rates. Conversely, the frequency of the target pronouns decreased for all groups of subjects who self-monitored, regardless of differential instructions. Of all the experimental instructions investigated thus far, only valence induction has been successful in producing differential behavior change during self-monitoring.

4. GOALS, REINFORCEMENT, AND FEEDBACK

Another set of variables contributing to the reactivity of self-recording is the setting of performance goals, and reinforcement or feedback contingent on the self-recorder's performance. In Kazdin's (1974a) study, subjects who were provided with a specific goal of the number of self-reference statements to make while self-monitoring produced more statements than a self-monitoring group that was not so instructed. Kazdin (1974a) also specifically manipulated the amount of feedback accorded his self-recording subjects. The self-recorders who were permitted to view the counter on which they self-monitored made more self-reference statements than self-recorders for whom the counter displays were covered. The importance of feedback in contributing to the reactivity of self-monitoring was also demonstrated by Richards, McReynolds, Holt, and Sexton (1976). Students who were relatively unaware of the amount of time they spent studying benefited more from feedback produced by self-recording of study time than students who were already aware of the extent of this time. Reinforcement contingent on behavior change also seems to enhance reactivity of self-monitoring. Kolb, Winter, and Berlew (1968) found that more behavior change was produced by self-recorders who met weekly to discuss their progress than by those who met weekly but did not discuss their individual projects. When adult retarded self-recorders believed edible reinforcers were contingent on changes in response frequency, they increased the frequency of talking and of touching environmental objects and generally decreased face touching (Nelson *et al.*, 1976a). Similarly, monetary reinforcement contingent on decreases in face touching produced decrements below baseline self-recording levels in college students (Lipinski *et al.*, 1975). Finally, Lyman, Rickard, and Elder (1975) found improvements in boys' self-recorded tent-cleaning when prompt access to breakfast was made contingent on increases in cleanliness.

5. NUMBER OF BEHAVIORS CONCURRENTLY SELF-MONITORED

Hayes and Cavior (in press) had subjects concurrently self-record one, two, or three target behaviors. Using a change ratio as a dependent measure, they found that the reactive effects of self-monitoring were greatest when only a single behavior was self-recorded. Self-monitoring of two or three behaviors did not produce significantly different results.

6. NATURE OF THE TARGET BEHAVIOR

Peterson *et al.* (1975) suggested that self-recording is more reactive when the target behavior is nonverbal rather than verbal. In their study, self-monitoring produced greater changes in the frequency of face touching than in the frequency of two verbal expressions. Similar results were reported by Hayes and Cavior (in press), who found that verbalizations containing value judgments changed least via self-monitoring, verbal nonfluencies changed more, and face touching was most reactive. Other studies have shown that reactivity depends on the specific target behavior assigned for self-recording. Romanczyk (1974) found that self-monitoring produced greater weight loss if both daily weight and caloric intake were monitored than if only weight was self-recorded. Gottman and McFall (1972) demonstrated that self-recording of instances of classroom participation increased their frequency, whereas self-recording of unfulfilled urges to participate decreased their frequency. Instructions to self-monitor resisted urges to smoke decreased smoking rates, whereas instructions to self-record number of cigarettes smoked increased smoking rates (McFall, 1970). However, Karoly and Doyle (1975) reported equal smoking reductions whether urges or completed cigarettes were self-monitored.

7. TIMING OF SELF-MONITORING

The reactivity of self-recording also seems to be affected by the timing of the self-recording response in relation to the occurrence of the target behavior. Kanfer (1970) proposed that self-monitoring prior to rather than after the occurrence of an undesirable behavior would produce greater reactivity because the self-recording response interrupts a behavior chain and provides an alternative to the target behavior. Although the timing conditions were confounded with sequence effects, Rozensky's subject (1974) reduced her smoking more when she self-recorded prior to rather than after smoking. These results were confirmed by Bellack, Rozensky, and Schwartz (1974), who reported greater weight loss by a group who self-recorded food intake information before rather than after eating. With young children, however, Nelson *et al.* (1977a) found that self-monitoring before or after classroom verbalizations did not differentially affect the reactivity of appropriate or inappropriate verbalizations.

8. SCHEDULE OF SELF-MONITORING

Mahoney *et al.* (1973a) found that continuous self-recording of correct answers produced longer study sessions than intermittent self-recording (e.g., recording after every third correct response). Similarly, Frederiksen *et al.* (1975) reported greater smoking reductions when each cigarette was self-recorded than when daily or weekly totals were kept.

9. NATURE OF THE SELF-RECORDING DEVICE

The device itself may serve as a discriminative stimulus controlling the frequency of the self-monitored response. The results presented by Nelson *et al.* (in press, c) suggested that a more obtrusive device may produce greater reactivity than a less obvious one.

C. Suggestions to Maximize the Reactivity of Self-Monitoring

Since self-monitoring produces behavior changes in desirable directions (Section III,B,2), the goal in therapeutic situations should be to maximize its reactivity. The following suggestions to enhance reactivity are based on research delineating variables controlling the reactivity of self-monitoring (Section III,B). Reactivity is more likely to occur when subjects are motivated for behavior change, and when they are given specific performance goals with feedback and reinforcement for meeting those goals. The self-recording device should be relatively obtrusive, and only one target behavior should be selected for self-recording during any time interval. Each instance of the target behavior should be recorded, and the recording of undesirable behavior should take place prior to the occurrence of the target behavior.

D. Explanations for the Reactivity of Self-Monitoring

The two major theories proposed to account for the reactivity of self-monitoring stress the consequences produced by the self-recorded target behavior. Kanfer (1970) proposed a three-stage mediational model to explain reactivity. The self-recorder first observes his or her own behavior, then evaluates the behavior in accordance with norms established during his or her learning history, and finally engages in self-reinforcement for positively evaluated behaviors and self-punishment for negatively evaluated behaviors. In contrast with Kanfer's mediational explanation is Rachlin's nonmediational approach (1974). According to Rachlin, self-monitoring serves to remind or cue the subject about the ultimate environmental consequences accorded the self-recorded behavior. To compare the two approaches, according to Kanfer, self-monitoring of smoking may decrease its frequency because the self-recorder punishes himself by self-verbalizations such as "I really should quit smoking" or by self-deprivation such as not watching television because of the smoking transgression. Conversely, according to Rachlin, self-monitoring of smoking may decrease its frequency because self-recording reminds the smoker of the negative environmental consequences produced by smoking, such as poor health or financial expenses. One point that the two theories have in common is emphasis on the consequences cued by self-monitoring, either self- or environmentally generated. Both theories also correctly predict that self-recording increases the frequency of desirable behaviors and decreases the frequency of undesirable ones. One problem with both of these theories is that they depend on occurrences of the target behavior to cue self-monitoring, self-evaluation, and/or environmental consequences. However, sometimes the reactivity of the self-recording of undesirable behaviors is so effective as to eliminate the occurrence of the target behaviors. An alternate interpretation for the reactivity of self-monitoring which would include reduced frequencies of target behavior was proposed by Hayes and Cavior (in press). They suggested that the entire self-monitoring procedure (training, the device, etc.) may exercise instructional control producing changes in the target behavior.

Similar to the reactivity of self-monitoring is the reactivity produced by other observations (e.g., Zegiob, Arnold, & Forehand, 1975). Mash and Hedley's explanation (1975) of differential observee reactivity also stresses the perceived consequences to the observee of the observation process. Several studies have compared the relative reactivity of self-monitoring and external observation, with inconsistent results. While neither Kazdin (1974a) nor Cavior and Marabotto (1976) found any difference between the reactive changes produced by self-monitoring versus observation by others, Ciminero, Graham, and Jackson (1975) and Nelson, Lipinski, and Black (1976b) reported greater reactive effects produced by self-recording than by another person's recording. These inconsistent findings may be due to the relative strength of the consequences attributed to the target behavior and/or the observation process in each of these studies.

E. Relationship between the Accuracy and Reactivity of Self-Monitoring

Nelson and McReynolds (1971) suggested that even though self-recording may be inaccurate, it may nonetheless produce consistent reactive effects. This suggestion was experimentally confirmed by Broden *et al.* (1971), Fixsen *et al.* (1972), Herbert and Baer (1972), and Lipinski and Nelson (1974b), all of whom demonstrated that self-recording produced reactive effects even though self-recording itself was inaccurate as compared with external observations. Hayes and Cavior (in press) concluded that the accuracy of self-recording was not correlated with the magnitude of its reactive effects. Very small correlations were found between individual subjects' accuracy scores and their ratio change scores: .01 for face touching, −.02 for nonfluencies, and .26 for value judgments.

A mechanism for reactive behavior change must be discovered, despite the inaccuracy of subjects in self-recording instances of the target behavior. Peterson *et al.* (1975) suggested that a minimal level of accuracy is necessary before reactivity occurs. In their study, when the self-monitoring accuracy of the phrase "you know" was .00, no reactivity occurred; only when training and reinforcement increased the level of accuracy did reactivity occur. However, Hayes and Cavior (in press) reported considerable reactivity for nonfluencies, even though agreement between self-recorders and observers on the occurrences of these nonfluencies was .00.

An alternative suggestion relates to the two components of the self-recording response: discriminating the occurrence of the target behavior, and recording this occurrence on the self-monitoring device (Section I,B). Reactivity may occur when the subject sufficiently discriminates occurrences of the target behavior, even if the subject produces inaccurate self-recordings by not recording these occurrences on the self-monitoring device.

With undesirable target behaviors, there may be no, or very few, occurrences of the target behavior to notice. For example, Lipinski *et al.* (1975) reported that during one experimental phase, self-recorders produced only .90 face touches per 5 minutes. As an alternative to occurrences of the target behavior cueing reactivity, Hayes and Cavior (in press) suggested that the entire self-monitoring procedure may act in the same way instructions do in prompting behavior change, regardless of whether the target behavior occurs, is noticed, and is recorded.

IV. FUTURE RESEARCH DIRECTIONS

A. Variables Influencing the Reactivity and Accuracy of Self-Monitoring

A large number of variables influence reactivity and/or accuracy of self-monitoring. The effects of all these variables on *both* reactivity and accuracy is not known. Unfortunately, researchers do not routinely measure and/or report both behavior changes produced by self-recording and the quality of self-recorded data. However, dual information could be obtained from each study on self-monitoring if both sets of measures were routinely reported.

Particular variables meriting additional investigation include the selection of self-recorded target behavior, choice of the self-monitoring device, effective training procedures for self-monitoring, and subject characteristics. Kanfer's (1976) and Mahoney's (in press) suggestion that desirable behaviors be selected for self-recording (Section II,D,6) merits further research. Very little data exist at present to guide the selection of the self-recording device (Section I,E). Although Mahoney's proposed method for training self-recorders was incorporated into the training procedure successfully used by Nelson *et al.* (in press, c), the components of the most efficient and effective training procedure have not been identified (Section II,D,8). Finally, subject characteristics of consistent and accurate self-recorders have not been identified. Nelson *et al.* (1976a) demonstrated that under certain conditions retarded self-recorders could be as accurate as college student self-recorders. McFall (1976) proposed that children, hospitalized psychiatric patients, and involuntary research subjects might be inaccurate self-recorders.

B. Longevity of Reactive Effects of Self-Monitoring

There are two research topics related to the longevity of reactive effects. One is the maintenance or extent of reactivity when a subject continues to self-record over a long period of time. It is not known if behavior change would continue or be maintained if self-recording persisted over months or years. A second topic is whether the reactive behavior changes produced by self-monitoring are maintained when self-monitoring is no longer employed. Several studies with reversal designs found the effects of self-monitoring to be ephemeral (Broden *et al.*, 1971; Herbert & Baer, 1972; Lipinski & Nelson, 1974b). Greater generalization to nonself-monitoring phases was produced when the self-monitoring device was gradually withdrawn (Maletzky, 1974) and when praise was paired with reactive behavior changes (Broden *et al.*, 1971).

Some variables that may influence the longevity of reactive effects produced by self-recording even when self-monitoring is terminated include: scheduling—intermittent self-recording may be more resistant to extinction than continuous self-recording; duration—self-recording over a longer period of time may produce more durable results than that over a shorter time period; and history of the target behavior—behaviors performed for many years may be more resistant to long-term reactive changes than relatively new behaviors.

C. Relative Reactivity of Ratings of Emotions

Kanfer (1976) raised the question of how arousal level associated with the monitored behavior affects the accuracy and reactivity of self-monitoring. A related issue is the accuracy and reactivity of self-ratings of emotions. Methodological problems, of course, exist in assessing the accuracy of emotional ratings because even physiological recordings may not be synonymous with perceived emotional reactions. Similar methodological problems exist in assessing the reactivity of emotional ratings because of difficulties in establishing a preself-monitoring baseline against which to evaluate reactivity. There is some suggestion, however, that self-ratings of moods may not produce reactive behavioral changes. Jackson (1972) and Lewinsohn (1974, Fig. 10) both reported that daily self-ratings of depression did not consistently alter these ratings. However, an improvement in depressive self-ratings occurred when subjects were instructed to self-monitor their participation in pleasant activities (Hammen & Glass, 1975). Further research is necessary to determine the reactivity and accuracy of self-monitoring of emotional self-ratings and other emotionally charged behaviors.

D. Accuracy versus Interobserver Agreement

The quality of self-recording is usually determined by comparing self-recordings with other observations. The assumption is usually made that the observer is more accurate than the self-recorder (Section II,A,1,2). Research is needed in which both the self-recorder's and the observer's data are evaluated against a mechanically obtained criterion. Not only would the relationship between self-recorder and observer agreement as well as self-recorder accuracy be ascertained, but also relative accuracy of observer and self-recorder would be determined.

E. The Importance of Accuracy in Self-Reinforcement Paradigms

Components of self-control programs may include both self-monitoring and self-reinforcement (Mahoney & Thoresen, 1974). Sometimes when behavior change is attempted through self-reinforcement, attempts are also made to increase the accuracy of self-evaluation or self-monitoring (Drabman *et al.*, 1973; Santogrossi, O'Leary, Romanczyk, & Kaufman, 1973; Turkewitz *et al.*, 1975). Accuracy of self-monitoring has been shown not to be crucial to obtain reactivity through self-monitoring (Section III,E). Similarly, it has not been demonstrated that accurate self-evaluation enhances the effectiveness of self-reinforcement programs. Kaufman and O'Leary (1972) reported low levels of disruptive behavior despite a poor relationship between pupils' evaluations and teachers' ratings. Additional research is needed to determine the role of accurate self-evaluation in the success of self-reinforcement programs.

F. Relationship between Self-Recording and External Observation

Several parallel phenomena exist between self-recording and external observation. For example, both self-monitoring and observation by others produce reactive behavior changes in the persons being observed (Section III,D). Similarly, awareness of accuracy checks has been shown to improve greatly the accuracy both of self-recorders (Section II,D,1) and of observers (Reid, 1970; Romanczyk, Kent, Diament, & O'Leary, 1973; Taplin & Reid, 1973). Given the wealth of research dealing with the observation process (e.g., Kent & Foster, 1977), it would be interesting to determine if these findings also hold true with self-recording. For example, quantitative behavioral observations are not influenced by inductions of bias, whereas qualitative ratings are susceptible to bias (Kent, O'Leary, Diament, & Dietz, 1974; Shuller & McNamara, 1976). It would be noteworthy to determine if self-recordings which are quantitative are not susceptible to the problems usually associated with more narrative self-report measures. Similarly, methodological findings, such as the fact that widely dispersed time samples produce the most representative data (Thomson, Holmberg, & Baer, 1974), have not been applied to self-recording procedures.

G. Conclusion

In the last few years, self-monitoring has been widely used to collect data in clinical and research situations, and has also been the topic in its own right of a great many empirical investigations. Much progress has been made not only in documenting the accuracy and reactivity of self-monitoring, but also in determining the variables that control this accuracy and reactivity. With the current emphasis on self-control and cognitive behavior modification programs, self-monitoring will most likely continue its present popularity. Hence, additional research as suggested above and otherwise generated will be most welcome.

REFERENCES

Azrin, N. H., & Powell, J. Behavioral engineering: The reduction of smoking behavior by a conditioning apparatus and procedure. *Journal of Applied Behavior Analysis,* **1968, 1,** 193–200.

Azrin, N. H., & Powell, J. Behavioral engineering: The use of response priming to improve self-medication. *Journal of Applied Behavior Analysis,* 1969, **2,** 39–42.

Azrin, N. H., Rubin, H., O'Brien, F., Ayllon, T., & Roll, D. Behavioral engineering: Postural control by a portable operant apparatus. *Journal of Applied Behavior Analysis,* 1968, **1,** 99–108.

Bailey, M. I., & Peterson, G. L. *Reactivity and accuracy of self-monitored verbal responses.* Manuscript submitted for publication, 1977.

Barlow, D. H., Leitenberg, H., & Agras, W. S. Experimental control of sexual deviation through manipulation of the noxious scene in covert sensitization. *Journal of Abnormal Psychology,* 1969, **74,** 596–601.

Bayer, C. A. Self-monitoring and mild aversion treatment by trichotillomania. *Journal of Behavior Therapy and Experimental Psychiatry,* 1972, **3,** 139–141.

Bellack, A. S. A comparison of self-reinforcement and self-monitoring in a weight reduction program. *Behavior Therapy,* 1976, **7,** 68–75.

Bellack, A. S., Rozensky, R., & Schwartz, J. A comparison of two forms of self-monitoring in a behavioral weight reduction program. *Behavior Therapy,* 1974, **5,** 523–530.

Berecz, J. Modification of smoking behavior through self-administered punishment of imagined behavior: A new approach to aversive therapy. *Journal of Consulting and Clinical Psychology,* 1972, **38,** 244–250.

Bolstad, O. D., & Johnson, S. M. Self-regulation in the modification of disruptive behavior. *Journal of Applied Behavior Analysis,* 1972, **5,** 443–454.

Bornstein, P. H., Hamilton, S. B., Carmody, T. P., Rychtarik, R. G., & Veraldi, D. M. Reliability enhancement: Increasing the accuracy of self-report through mediation based procedures. *Cognitive Therapy and Research,* in press.

Bornstein, P. H., Hamilton, S. B. Miller, R. K., Quevillon, R. P., & Spitzform, M. Reliability and validity enhancement: A treatment package for increasing fidelity of self-report. *Journal of Clinical Psychology,* in press.

Broden, M., Hall, R. V., & Mitts, B. The effect of self-recording on the classroom behavior of two eighth-grade students. *Journal of Applied Behavior Analysis,* 1971, **4,** 191–199.

Cavior, N., & Marabotto, C. M. Monitoring verbal behaviors in a dyadic interaction: Valence of target behaviors, type, timing, and reactivity to monitoring. *Journal of Consulting and Clinical Psychology,* 1976, **44,** 68–76.

Ciminero, A., Graham, L., & Jackson, J. *A comparison of obtrusive- and self-recording procedures.* Paper read at the Southeastern Psychological Association, Atlanta, March 1975.

Danaher, B. G., & Thoresen, C. E. Imagery assessment by self-report and behavioral measures. *Behaviour Research and Therapy,* 1972, **10,** 131–138.

Drabman, R. S., Spitalnik, R., & O'Leary, K. D. Teaching self-control to disruptive children. *Journal of Abnormal Psychology,* 1973, **82,** 10–16.

Emmelkamp, P. M. G. Self-observation versus flooding in the treatment of agoraphobia. *Behaviour Research and Therapy,* 1974, **12,** 229–237.

Emmelkamp, P. M. G., & Ultee, K. A. A comparison of "successive approximation" and "self-observation" in the treatment of agoraphobia. *Behavior Therapy,* 1974, **5,** 606–613.

Epstein, L. H., Miller, P. M., & Webster, J. S. The effects of reinforcing concurrent behavior on self-monitoring. *Behavior Therapy,* 1976, **7,** 89–95.

Epstein, L. H., Webster, J. S., & Miller, P. M. Accuracy and controlling effects of self-monitoring as a function of concurrent responding and reinforcement. *Behavior Therapy,* 1975, **6,** 654–666.

Ernst, F. Self-recording and counterconditioning of a self-mutilative compulsion. *Behavior Therapy,* 1973, **4,** 144–146.

Fixsen, D. L., Phillips, E. L., & Wolf, M. M. Achievement Place: The reliability of self-reporting and peer-reporting and their effects on behavior. *Journal of Applied Behavior Analysis,* 1972, **5,** 19–30.

Flowers, J. V. Behavior modification of cheating in an elementary school student: A brief note. *Behavior Therapy,* 1972, **3,** 311–312.

Foxx, R. M., & Martin, P. L. A useful portable timer. *Journal of Applied Behavior Analysis,* 1971, **4,** 60.

Frederiksen, L. W. Treatment of ruminative thinking by self-monitoring. *Journal of Behavior Therapy and Experimental Psychiatry,* 1975, **6,** 258–259.

Frederiksen, L. W., Epstein, L. H., & Kosevsky, B. P. Reliability and controlling effects of three procedures for self-monitoring smoking. *Psychological Record,* 1975, **25,** 255–264.

Goldman, J. A look at measurements in industry. In L. E. Slater (Ed.), *Interdisciplinary clinic on the instrumentation requirements for psychophysiological research.* New York: Fier, 1961.

Goldstein, A., & Brown, B. W. Urine testing schedules in methadone maintenance treatment of heroin addiction. *Journal of the American Medical Association,* 1970, **214,** 311–315.

Gottman, J. M., & McFall, R. M. Self-monitoring effects in a program for potential high school dropouts: A time-series analysis. *Journal of Consulting and Clinical Psychology,* 1972, 39, 273–281.

Hall, R. V., Christler, C., Cranston, S. S., & Tucker, B. Teachers and parents as researchers using multiple baseline designs. *Journal of Applied Behavior Analysis,* 1970, **3,** 247–255.

Hamilton, S. B., & Bornstein, P. H. Increasing the accuracy of self-recording in speech anxious undergraduates through the use of self-monitoring training and reliability enhancement procedures. *Journal of Consulting and Clinical Psychology,* in press.

Hammen, C. L., & Glass, D. R. Depression, activity, and evaluation of reinforcement. *Journal of Abnormal Psychology,* 1975, **84,** 718–721.

Hannum, J. W., Thoresen, C. E., & Hubbard, D. R. A behavioral study of self-esteem with elementary teachers. In M. J. Mahoney & C. E. Thoresen (Eds.), *Self-control: Power to the person.* Monterey, Calif.: Brooks-Cole, 1974. Pp. 144–155.

Hay, L. R., Hay, W. M., & Angle, H. V. The reactivity of self recording: A case report of a drug abuser. *Behavior Therapy,* in press.

Hayes, S. C., & Cavior, N. Multiple tracking and the reactivity of self monitoring: I. Negative behaviors. *Behavior Therapy,* in press.

Hendricks, C. G., Thoresen, C. E., & Hubbard, D. R. *Effects of behavioral self-observation on elementary teachers and students.* Unpublished manuscript, Stanford University, 1973.

Herbert, E. W., & Baer, D. M. Training parents as behavior modifier: Self recording of contingent attention *Journal of Applied Behavior Analysis,* 1972, **5,** 139–149.

Homme, L. E. Perspectives in psychology: XXIV. Control of coverants, the operants of the mind. *Psychological Record,* 1965, **4,** 501–511.

Horan, J. J., & Johnson, R. G. Coverant conditioning through a self-management application of the Premack principle: Its effect on weight reduction. *Journal of Behavior Therapy and Experimental Psychiatry,* 1971, **2,** 243–249.

Hutzell, R. R. *Effects of self-recording and expectancy on a neutral valued behavior.* Manuscript submitted for publication, 1977.

Hutzell, R. R., Platzek, D., & Logue, P. E. Control of symptoms of Giles de la Tourette's Syndrome by self-monitoring. *Journal of Behavior Therapy and Experimental Psychiatry,* 1974, **5,** 71–76.

Jackson, B. Treatment of depression by self-reinforcement. *Behavior Therapy,* 1972, **3,** 298–307.

Jason, L. Rapid improvement in insomnia following self-monitoring. *Journal of Behavior Therapy and Experimental Psychiatry,* 1975, **6,** 349–350.

Jeffrey, D. B. Self-control: Methodological issues and research trends. In M. J. Mahoney & C. E. Thoresen (Eds.), *Self-control: Power to the person.* Monterey, Calif.: Brooks-Cole, 1974. Pp. 166–199.

Johnson, S. M., & Bolstad, O. D. Methodological issues in naturalistic observation: Some problems and solutions for field research. In L. A. Hamerlynck, L. C. Handy, & E. J. Mash (Eds.), *Behavior change: Methodology, concepts, and practice.* Champaign, Ill.: Research Press, 1973. Pp. 7–67.

Johnson, S. M., & White, G. Self-observation as an agent of behavioral change. *Behavior Therapy,* 1971, **2,** 488–497.

Kanfer, F. H. Self-Monitoring: Methodological limitations and clinical applications. *Journal of Consulting and Clinical Psychology,* 1970, **35,** 148–152.

Kanfer, F. H. *The many faces of self-control, or behavior modification changes its focus.* Paper read at the eighth International Banff Conference, March, 1976.

Karoly, P., & Doyle, W. W. Effects of outcome expectancy and timing of self-monitoring on cigarette smoking. *Journal of Clinical Psychology,* 1975, **31,** 351–355.

Kaufman, K. F., & O'Leary, K. D. Reward, cost, and self-evaluation procedures for disruptive adolescents in a psychiatric hospital school. *Journal of Applied Behavior Analysis,* 1972, **5,** 293–309.

Kazdin, A. E. Reactive self-monitoring: The effects of response desirability, goal setting, and feedback. *Journal of Consulting and Clinical Psychology,* 1974, **42,** 704–716. (a)

Kazdin, A. E. Self-monitoring and behavior change. In M. J. Mahoney & C. E. Thoresen (Eds.), *Self-control: Power to the person.* Monterey, Calif.: Brooks-Cole, 1974. Pp. 218–246. (b)

Kent, R. N., & Foster, S. L. Direct observational procedures: Methodological issues in naturalistic settings. In A. Ciminero, K. Calhoun, & H. E. Adams (Eds.), *Handbook of behavioral assessment.* New York: Wiley, 1977.

Kent, R. N., O'Leary, K. D., Diament, C., & Dietz, A. Expectation biases in observational evaluation of therapeutic change. *Journal of Consulting and Clinical Psychology,* 1974, **42,** 774–780.

Knox, D. *Marriage Happiness.* Campaign, Ill.: Research Press, 1972.

Kolb, D. A., Winter, S. K., & Berlew, D. E. Self-directed behavior change: Two studies. *Journal of Applied Behavior Science,* 1968, **4,** 453–471.

Komaki, J., & Dore-Boyce, K. Self-recording: Its effects on individuals high and low in motivation. *Behavior Therapy,* in press.

Kubany, E. S., & Sloggett, B. B. Coding procedures for teachers. *Journal of Applied Behavior Analysis,* 1973, **6,** 339–344.

Kunzelmann, H. D. (Ed.), *Precision teaching.* Seattle: Special Child Publications, 1970.

Lando, H. A. An objective check upon self-reported smoking levels: A preliminary report. *Behavior Therapy,* 1975, **6,** 547–549.

Lang, P. J. Fear reduction and fear behavior: Problems in treating a construct. *Research in Psychotherapy,* 1968, **3,** 90–102.

Layne, C. C., Rickard, H. C., Jones, M. T., & Lyman, R. D. Accuracy of self-monitoring on a variable ratio schedule of observer verification. *Behavior Therapy,* 1976, **7,** 481–488.

Leitenberg, H., Agras, W. S., Thompson, L. E., & Wright, D. E. Feedback in behavior modification: An experimental analysis in two phobic cases. *Journal of Applied Behavior Analysis,* 1968, **1,** 131–137.

Lewinsohn, P. M. Clinical and theoretical aspects of depression. In K. S. Calhoun, H. E. Adams, & K. M. Mithcell (Eds.), *Innovative treatment methods in psychopathology.* New York: Wiley, 1974. Pp. 63–120.

Lindsley, O. R. A reliable wrist counter for recording behavior rates. *Journal of Applied Behavior Analysis,* 1968, **1,** 77–78.

Lipinski, D. P., Black, J. L., Nelson, R. O., & Ciminero, A. R. The influence of motivational variables on the reactivity and reliability of self-recording. *Journal of Consulting and Clinical Psychology,* 1975, **43,** 637–646.

Lipinski, D. P., & Nelson, R. O. Problems in the use of naturalistic observation as a means of behavioral assessment. *Behavior Therapy,* 1974, **5,** 341–351. (a)

Lipinski, D. P., & Nelson, R. O. The reactivity and unreliability of self-recording. *Journal of Consulting and Clinical Psychology,* 1974, **42,** 118–123. (b)

Lubin, G. Adjective checklists for the measurement of depression. *Archives of General Psychiatry,* 1965, **17,** 183–186.

Lyman, R. D., Rickard, H. C., & Elder, I. R. Contingency management of self-report and cleaning behavior. *Journal of Abnormal Child Psychology,* 1975, **3,** 155–162.

Mahoney, K. Count on it: A simple self-monitoring device. *Behavior Therapy,* 1974, **5,** 701–703.

Mahoney, M. J. The self-management of covert behavior: A case study. *Behavior Therapy,* 1971, **2,** 575–578.

Mahoney, M. J. *Cognition and behavior modification.* Cambridge, Mass.: Ballinger, 1974. (a)

Mahoney, M. J. Self-reward and self-monitoring techniques for weight control. *Behavior Therapy,* 1974, **5**, 48–57. (b)

Mahoney, M. J. Some applied issues in self-monitoring. In J. D. Cone & R. P. Hawkins (Eds.), *Behavioral assessment: New directions in clinical psychology.* New York: Brunner/Mazel, in press.

Mahoney, M. J., Moore, B. S., Wade, T. C., & Moura, N. G. M. The effects of continuous and intermittent self-monitoring on academic behavior. *Journal of Consulting and Clinical Psychology,* 1973, **41**, 65–69. (a)

Mahoney, M. J., Moura, N. G. M., & Wade, T. C. The relative efficacy of self-reward, self-punishment, and self-monitoring techniques for weight loss. *Journal of Consulting and Clinical Psychology,* 1973, **40**, 404–407. (b)

Mahoney, M. J., & Thoresen, C. E. (Eds.). *Self-control: Power to the person.* Monterey, Calif.: Brooks-Cole, 1974.

Maletzky, B. M. Behavior recording as treatment: A brief note. *Behavior Therapy,* 1974, **5**, 107–111.

Mash, E. J., & Hedley, J. Effect of observer as a function of prior history of social interaction. *Perceptual and Motor Skills,* 1975, **40**, 659–669.

Mattos, R. L. A manual counter for recording multiple behavior. *Journal of Applied Behavior Analysis,* 1968, **1**, 130.

McFall, R. M. Effects of self-monitoring on normal smoking behavior. *Journal of Consulting and Clinical Psychology,* 1970, **35**, 135–142.

McFall, R. M. *Parameters of self-monitoring.* Paper read at the eighth International Banff Conference on Behavior Modification, March 1976.

McFall, R. M., & Hammen, C. L. Motivation, structure, and self-monitoring: Role of nonspecific factors in smoking reduction. *Journal of Consulting and Clinical Psychology,* 1971, **37**, 80–86.

McKenzie, T. L., & Rushall, B. S. Effects of self-recording on attendance and performance in a competitive swimming training environment. *Journal of Applied Behavior Analysis,* 1974, **7**, 199–206.

McLaughlin, J. G., & Nay, W. R. Treatment of trichotillomania using positive coverants and response cost: A case report*Behavior Therapy,* 1975, **6**, 87–91.

McNamara, J. R. The use of self-monitoring techniques to treat nail biting. *Behaviour Research and Therapy,* 1972, **10**, 193–194.

Meyers, A. Mercatoris, M., & Artz, L. On the development of a cognitive self-monitoring skill. *Behavior Therapy,* 1976, **7**, 128–129.

Miller, P. M., Hersen, M., Eisler, R. M., & Watts, J. G. Contingent reinforcement of lowered blood alcohol levels in an outpatient chronic alcoholic. *Behaviour Research and Therapy,* 1974, **12**, 261–263.

Nelson, C. M., & McReynolds, W. T. Self-recording and control of behavior: A reply to Simkins. *Behavior Therapy,* 1971, **2**, 594–597.

Nelson, R. O., Hay, L. R., & Hay, W. M. Cue versus consequence functions of high probability behaviors in the modification of self-monitored study coverants and study time. *The Psychological Record,* in press. (a)

Nelson, R. O., Hay, L. R., Hay, W. M., & Carstens, C. B. The reactivity and accuracy of teachers' self-monitoring of positive and negative classroom verbalizations. *Behavior Therapy,* in press.(b)

Nelson, R. O., Hay, L. R., & Koslow-Green, L. *Cautions in the use of classroom self-monitoring with young children.* Manuscript submitted for publication. 1977. (a)

Nelson, R. O., Kapust, J. A., Dorsey, B. L., & Hayes, S. C. *Differential behavior change produced by instructions and by self-monitoring.* Manuscript submitted for publication, 1977. (b)

Nelson, R. O., Lipinski, D. P., & Black, J. L. The effects of expectancy on the reactivity of self-recording. *Behavior Therapy*, 1975, **6**, 337–349.

Nelson, R. O., Lipinski, D. P., & Black, J. L. The reactivity of adult retardates' self-monitoring: A comparison among behaviors of different valences, and a comparison with token reinforcement. *Psychological Record*, 1976, **26**, 189–201. (a)

Nelson, R. O., Lipinski, D. P., & Black, J. L. The relative reactivity of external observations and self-monitoring. *Behavior Therapy*, 1976, **7**, 314–321. (b)

Nelson, R. O., Lipinski, D. P., & Boykin, R. A. The effects of self-recorders' training and the obtrusiveness of the self-recording device on the accuracy and reactivity of self-monitoring. *Behavior Therapy*, in press. (c)

Ober, D. C. Modification of smoking behavior. *Journal of Consulting and Clinical Psychology*, 1968, **32**, 543–549.

O'Leary, K. D., & Kent, R. N. Behavior modification for social action: Research tactics and problems. In L. A. Hamerlynck, L. C. Handy, & E. J. Mach (Eds.), *Behavior change: Methodology, concepts, and practice.* Champaign, Ill.: Research Press, 1973. Pp. 69–96.

Orne, M. T. From the subject's point of view, when is behavior private and when is it public: Problems of inference. *Journal of Consulting and Clinical Psychology*, 1970, **35**, 143–147.

Peterson, G. L., House, A. E., & Alford, H. F. *Self-monitoring: Accuracy and reactivity in a patient's recording of three clinically targeted behaviors.* Paper read at the Southeastern Psychological Association, Atlanta, March 1975.

Rachlin, H. Self-control. *Behaviorism*, 1974, **2**, 94–107.

Reid, J. B. Reliability assessment of observation data: A possible methodological problem. *Child Development*, 1970, **41**, 1143–1150.

Richards, C. S. Behavior modification of studying through study skills advice and self-control procedures. *Journal of Counseling Psychology*, 1975, **22**, 431–436.

Richards, C. S., McReynolds, W. T., Holt, S., & Sexton, T. Effects of information feedback and self-administered consequences on self-monitoring study behavior. *Journal of Counseling Psychology*, 1976, **23**, 316–321.

Risley, T. R., & Hart, B. Developing correspondence between the non-verbal and verbal behavior of pre-school children. *Journal of Applied Behavior Analysis*, 1968, **1**, 267–281.

Romanczyk, R. G. Self-monitoring in the treatment of obesity: Parameters of reactivity. *Behavior Therapy*, 1974, **5**, 531–540.

Romanczyk, R. G., Kent, R. N., Diament, C., & O'Leary, K. D. Measuring the reliability of observational data: A reactive process. *Journal of Applied Behavior Analysis*, 1973, **6**, 175–184.

Rozensky, R. H. The effect of timing of self-monitoring behavior on reducing cigarette consumption. *Journal of Behavior Therapy and Experimental Psychiatry*, 1974, **5**, 301–303.

Rutner, I. T. *The modification of smoking behavior through techniques of self-control.* Unpublished master's thesis, Wichita State University, 1967.

Rutner, I. T., & Bugle, C. An experimental procedure for the modification of psychotic behavior. *Journal of Consulting and Clinical Psychology*, 1969, **33**, 651–653.

Santogrossi, D. A. *Self-reinforcement and external monitoring of performance on an academic task.* Paper read at the fifth annual Conference on Applied Behavior Analysis in Education, Kansas City, Kansas, October 1974.

Santogrossi, D. A., O'Leary, K. D., Romanczyk, R. G., & Kaufman, K. F. Self-evaluation by adolescents in a psychiatric hospital school token program. *Journal of Applied Behavior Analysis*, 1973, **6**, 277–287.

Schulmann, J. L., & Reisman, J. M. An objective measurement of hyperactivity. *American Journal of Mental Deficiency,* 1959, **64,** 455–456.

Schwitzgebel, R. K., & Kolb, D. A. *Changing human behavior: Principles of planned intervention.* New York: McGraw-Hill, 1974.

Seymour, F. W., & Stokes, T. F. Self-recording in training girls to increase work and evoke staff praise in an institution for offenders. *Journal of Applied Behavior Analysis,* 1976, **9,** 41–54.

Shaw, D. L., Peterson, G. L., & Cone, J. D. *Aides' reports of behavior modification training: Experimental analysis of their validity.* Paper read at the Southeastern Psychological Association, Hollywood, Florida, May 1974.

Sheehan, D. J., & Casey, B. Communication. *Journal of Applied Behavior Analysis,* 1974, **7,** 446.

Shuller, D. Y., & McNamara, J. R. Expectancy factors in behavioral observation. *Behavior Therapy,* 1976, **7,** 519–527.

Sieck, W. A., & McFall, R. M. Some determinants of self-monitoring effects. *Journal of Consulting and Clinical Psychology,* 1976, **44,** 958–965.

Simkins, L. The reliability of self-recorded behaviors. *Behavior Therapy,* 1971, **2,** 83–87.

Sirota, A. D., & Mahoney, M. J. Relaxing on cue: The self regulation of asthma. *Journal of Behavior Therapy and Experimental Psychiatry,* 1974, **5,** 65–66.

Sobell, L. C., & Sobell, M. B. A self-feedback technique to monitor drinking behavior in alcoholics. *Behaviour Research and Therapy,* 1973, **11,** 237–238.

Soskin, W. F., & John, V. The study of spontaneous talk. In R. Barker (Ed.), *The stream of behavior.* New York: Appleton, 1963.

Spevack, M., Pihl, R., & Rowan, T. Behavior therapies in the treatment of drug abuse: Some case studies. *Psychological Record,* 1973, **23,** 179–184.

Stuart, R. B., & Davis, B. *Slim chance in a fat world.* Champaign, Ill.: Research Press, 1972.

Stumphauzer, J. S. *Daily behavior card.* Venice, Calif.: Behaviometrics, 1974.

Taplin, P. S., & Reid, J. B. Effects of instructional set and experimenter influence on observer reliability. *Child Development,* 1973, **44,** 547–554.

Thomas, D. R. Preliminary findings on self-monitoring for modifying teaching behaviors. In E. A. Ramp & B. L. Hopkins (Eds.), *A new direction for education: Behavior analysis, 1971.* Lawrence: University of Kansas, 1971. Pp. 102–114.

Thomas, E. J., Abrams, K. S., & Johnson, J. B. Self-monitoring and reciprocal inhibition in the modification of multiple tics of Gilles de la Tourette's syndrome. *Journal of Behavior Therapy and Experimental Psychiatry,* 1971, **2,** 159–171.

Thomson, C., Holmberg, M., & Baer, D. M. A brief report on a comparison of time-sampling procedures. *Journal of Applied Behavior Analysis,* 1974, **7,** 623–626.

Thoresen, C. E., & Mahoney, M. J. *Behavioral self-control.* New York: Holt, 1974.

Tokarz, T., & Lawrence, P. S. *An analysis of temporal and stimulus factors in the treatment of insomnia.* Paper read at the Association for Advancement of Behavior Therapy, Chicago, November 1974.

Turkewitz, H., O'Leary, K. D., & Ironsmith, M. Generalization and maintenance of appropriate behavior through self-control. *Journal of Consulting and Clinical Psychology,* 1975, **43,** 577–583.

Vargas, J. M., & Adesso, V. J. A comparison of aversion therapies for nailbiting behavior. *Behavior Therapy,* 1976, **7,** 322–329.

Watson, D., & Tharp, R. *Self-directed behavior: Self-modification for personal adjustment.* Monterey: Brooks-Cole, 1972.

Webb, E. J., Campbell, D. T., Schwartz, R. D., & Sechrest, L. *Unobtrusive measures: Nonreactive research in the social sciences.* Chicago: Rand McNally, 1966.

Williams, J. E. Self-monitoring of paranoid behavior. *Behavior Therapy,* 1976. **7,** 562.

Zegiob, L. E., Arnold, S., & Forehand, R. An examination of observer effects in parent-child interactions. *Child Development*, 1975, **46**, 509–512.

Zimmerman, J. If it's what's inside that counts, why not count it? I: Self-recording of feelings and treatment by "self-implosion." *Psychological Record*, 1975, **25**, 3–16.

Zimmerman, J., & Levitt, E. E. Why not give your client a counter: A survey of what happened when we did. *Behaviour Research and Therapy*, 1975, **13**, 333–337.

BEHAVIORAL TREATMENT IN HOMOSEXUALITY

N. McCONAGHY
School of Psychiatry
University of New South Wales
Sydney, Australia

I. METHODOLOGICAL ISSUES

The most important aspect of treatment is, of course, its effect. A review of treatment procedures should therefore have as its major aim assessment of their efficacy; and secondarily, determination of the mechanisms whereby the treatments operate to produce their effects.

Though evaluation of behavioral forms of therapy appears to have been attempted much more intensively than evaluation of relationship forms of psychotherapy, this work has not yet resulted in conclusions generally accepted by the practitioners of behavior therapies, let alone by a wider body of psychotherapists.

The inability to reach generally accepted conclusions concerning the efficacy of treatments that modify behavior is clearly not entirely a function of the difficulty of assessing behavioral change, even when patterns of behavior are involved that are themselves ill-defined and the subject of dispute. Therapists using drugs in the treatment of schizophrenia and depression have achieved a satisfactory level of agreement as to the effects of the drugs. The conclusions of these therapists are gradually being accepted by workers outside their field despite the existence of marked ideological prejudices concerning both the use of drugs to modify behavior and the existence of schizophrenia and depression as entities warranting treatment.

The reason that consensus has been reached in regard to evaluation of behavioral change with drug therapy but not with psychotherapy and behavioral treatments would appear to be that research workers evaluating drugs have appreciated the *need for adequate replication of findings.* In the process of attempting to replicate findings these workers have learned to avoid the errors inherent in the *formalistic approach to methodology* which has continued to characterize research evaluating behavioral change with psychotherapies. Without clarification of the methodological issues involved, agreement will not be reached as to the value of behavioral treatment in homosexuality or, indeed, generally.

A. Methodological Formalism and Evaluation of Treatment

Methodological formalism in research consists of the uncritical adoption of certain procedures in collecting and analyzing data on the basis that the procedures will establish the validity of the findings reached. In fact, the procedures may result in distortion or apparent invalidation of the correct findings, which would have been reached had appropriate methods of collecting and analyzing the data been used. Only by reanalysis of the data of the experiment in light of data from subsequent experiments can the correct conclusions be revealed and the distortions introduced by methodological formalism understood.

If replicatory studies are not carried out, the errors resulting from methodological formalism will not be revealed and will remain in the literature as undisputed findings. In this situation, the dangers of methodological formalism also remain unrevealed.

1. STATISTICAL SIGNIFICANCE AND TYPE I AND TYPE II ERRORS

The commonest errors resulting from methodological formalism are Type I and Type II errors. In theory, every research worker is familiar with these errors and the reason for their occurrence. In practice, when the majority of research workers read that a finding is statistically significant, they do not automatically suspect that a Type I error has occurred and wait until the finding has been adequately replicated before accepting it. Nor when they read that a finding is not statistically significant do they automatically check to see that it is not a Type II error, but is based on an adequate number of observations to ensure that any effect of meaningful strength would have reached statistical significance.

For the benefit of those readers who have forgotten their introductory statistical training, Type I and Type II errors occur inevitably from time to time in analyses that use statistical significance as a criterion of validity. If a finding is statistically significant at, say, the 5% level, the possibility that it could have occurred by chance rather than be due to the experimental procedure is by definition 5%. Utilizing the convention concerning statistical significance, one dismisses this possibility and concludes that the finding was produced by the experimental procedure. On 5% of occasions, or, in other words, on 1 occasion in 20, one dismisses the possibility incorrectly—the finding was due to chance, and a Type I or false positive error has been made.

In published research the probability that findings reported to be significant at the 5% level are due to chance is in fact greater than 5%. Many research workers do not bother to report findings that do not reach statistical significance. Those reported therefore represent the visible tip of an iceberg of which the much vaster submerged portion consists of findings tested for significance, found wanting, and never reported. In addition, tests of significance are often applied to relationships not predicted prior to the experiment but which are discovered when, following the experiment, the data it provided are examined in detail; that is, relationships found in the data that look as if they might reach statistical significance are then tested, without the experimenter realizing he is ignoring and hence not testing many other relationships in the data because they clearly are not significant. Of every 20 relationships that could be found in the data and be tested for significance, one will be significant at the 5% level by chance.

Type II or false negative errors of importance are those made when a relationship is found which is of sufficient strength to be worthy of attention, but is based on too few observations to be statistically significant. As an example, a controlled trial is carried out with 20 subjects in the treatment and 20 in the control group. Ten (50%) of the experimental group show marked improvement. Five (25%) of the control group show similar improvement. This difference is not statistically significant. If this difference represents the actual response of the subjects to the treatment rather than a chance effect, the treatment clearly is worth using—of every 100 patients treated 25 will show marked improvement who, without the treatment, would not.

The appropriate procedure in this situation would be to repeat the experiment using a sufficient number of subjects such that if the treatment effect is of comparable strength in the replicatory study it will then be statistically significant. From the table provided by Clark and Downie (1966), it can be determined that 28 subjects need to be included in the treatment group and 28 in the control for a controlled trial to have a 50% chance of demonstrating a treatment effect that is statistically significant (i.e., if 50% of subjects respond to the treatment and 25% to the control procedure). Clearly, it would be preferable to use a larger number of subjects than 28 per group to increase the probability that treatment effect of this strength will be statistically significant.

In practice, when a study is reported investigating a small number of subjects and showing an important treatment effect that did not reach statistical significance, it is rare that the authors suggest replicating the study with a larger number of subjects. Usually they follow the conventional but astoundingly illogical procedure of concluding that because the effect found in their study failed to reach statistical significance it was produced by chance, not their treatment.

To demonstrate how fixation on statistical significance as the criterion establishing validity of findings has led to the commission of Type I and Type II errors in studies evaluating behavioral therapy, it is necessary to find studies that have been both carried out by workers who show this fixation and have been replicated. A study can be considered to have been replicated only if the procedure followed in the replication is sufficiently similar to that of the original such that if the findings of the second study differ from those of the original, the validity of the findings of the original can be called into question. Otherwise, the differences in the findings of the two studies can be attributed to differences in their procedures, and the findings of both can be claimed to be valid. Correct replications, as just specified, of studies evaluating therapies are rare except when the therapies involve the use of drugs.

2. DESENSITIZATION CONSIDERED MORE EFFECTIVE IN CIRCUMSCRIBED PHOBIAS: TYPE I ERROR

A series of correctly replicated studies was carried out at the Institute of Psychiatry, London, to evaluate desensitization in the treatment of phobias. Since systematic desensitization is one of the behavioral therapies used in homosexuality and these studies are the only *series* so far published that have evaluated desensitization in a patient group rather than in students with phobias, they are of particular relevance.

The initial study by Cooper (1963) reported the results presented in Table I.

Cooper *combined* the response of the much improved and improved groups to obtain a ratio of improvement to no change of 9:1 for systematic desensitization, and 5:5 for the control therapy. Presumably Cooper combined the two groups to obtain a response to systematic desensitization that as near as possible approached statistical significance. Combining the groups had the result that the ratio of response at one year was 6:3 for systematic desensitization and 5:4 for the control therapy. Cooper concluded, ". . . if behavior therapy is a worthwhile addition to other therapy in this type of patient, as seems likely, its effect is transient."

It can be seen from Table I that at 1 year following systematic densensitization, five (50%) patients were *much improved*, as against

TABLE I

Symptom Improvement in Agoraphobic Patients[a]

	Treated with desensitization		Controls	
At end of treatment:	(N = 10)		(N = 10)	
Much improved	4	9	1	5
Improved	5		4	
No change	1		5	
One year following treatment:	(N = 9)		(N = 9)	
Much improved	5	6	2	5
Improved	1		3	
No change	3		4	

[a] From Cooper (1963).

two (20%) of the control group. As stated above, with the number of patients investigated, a difference of this strength was not statistically significant. This difference was ignored by Cooper; however, if valid it indicated that a clinically worthwhile response to systematic desensitization did take place which was not transient.

The next study was reported by Marks and Gelder (1965) and their findings are presented in Table II.

Following treatment and at 1-year follow-up, 9 (approximately 50%) of the 20 agoraphobic patients treated with desensitization were *much improved* compared with 5 (25%) of the 20 controls. With the sample size the difference was not statistically significant and was ignored by Marks and Gelder. The similarity of response of the patients reported by their colleague Cooper was unnoticed.

It can be calculated from data jointly published by these workers (Cooper, Gelder, & Marks, 1965) that of the 10 phobic patients whose response to desensitization Cooper (1963) reported, 9 were agoraphobic. Marks and Gelder therefore failed to replicate Cooper's finding of which Cooper stated that it "just failed to reached the usually accepted level of significance" (i.e., that 9 of 10 patients were *improved or much improved* with desensitization compared with 5 of the 10 controls). In Marks and Gelder's study, only 12 of 20 agoraphobic patients showed this degree of improvement with desensitization compared with 11 of 20 controls.

Marks and Gelder's failure to replicate this finding of Cooper indicated that the finding was a chance false positive or Type I error. Their failure also indicated that if desensitization did produce a worthwhile therapeutic response, *combining* the much improved

TABLE II

Symptom Improvement in Agoraphobic Patients and Patients with Circumscribed Phobias[a]

A. Agoraphobic patients	Treated with desensitization		Controls	
At end of treatment:	(N = 20)		(N = 20)	
Much improved	9	12	5	11
Improved	3		6	
No change	8		9	
One year following treatment:	(N = 17)		(N = 17)	
Much improved	9		5	
Improved	4		6	
No change	4		6	
B. Patients with circumscribed phobias				
At end of treatment:	(N = 11)		(N = 10)	
Much improved	6	11	2	3
Improved	5		1	
No change	0		7	
One year following treatment:	(N = 11)		(N = 10)	
Much improved	3	7	3	4
Improved	4		1	
No change	4		6	

[a]From Marks and Gelder (1965).

and improved groups did not provide a replicable measure of this response. Marks and Gelder did not comment on the failure of replication and followed Cooper's procedure of combining the responses of the much improved and improved group in patients with circumscribed phobias. In this way they obtained what they considered the major finding of their study. All 11 patients with circumscribed phobias improved with desensitization, whereas only 3 of 10 controls improved without the treatment. This difference was statistically significant, and although most of the difference had disappeared by 1-year follow-up, Marks and Gelder concluded on the basis of the findings of both studies that desensitization was useful in patients with circumscribed phobias but not in agoraphobic patients.

This conclusion provides an excellent example both of how a finding appearing in two studies and suggesting the presence of a valuable and persistent therapeutic effect is ignored because it fails to reach statistical significance due to the number of subjects used (a likely Type II error). This also shows how a finding that reaches or almost reaches statistical significance once (a possible Type I error) is awarded actual significance even when it indicates the presence of only a transient therapeutic effect.

In three further studies evaluating desensitization on phobic patients (Gelder & Marks, 1966; Gelder, Marks, Wolff, & Clarke, 1967; Marks, Gelder, & Edwards, 1968), the same trend continued to appear; that is, approximately 50% of patients showed *much improvement* with desensitization as against 25% with control therapies. The numbers of patients investigated were in the same range as in the previous studies, so the trend never reached significance. It was consistently ignored by the authors—almost certainly a false negative or Type II error. Gelder, with Bancroft, Gath, Johnston, Mathews, and Shaw (1973) carried out a further study that finally demonstrated at a significant level that agoraphobic patients responded better to desensitization than to nonspecific therapy. Patients with circumscribed phobias *did not.* In discussing his findings he seemed unaware that they contradicted his previous conclusions. The pessimistic evaluation given given desensitization in this series of studies, particularly in the treatment of agoraphobia, continues to be quoted (Luborsky, Barton, & Luborsky, 1975). If the findings of these studies, which were not stressed, are correct, it is the response to desensitization of patients with circumscribed phobias rather than with agoraphobia which is limited and transient. As will be discussed later in the present review, the finding is relevant to the treatment of homosexual subjects. Homosexuals are treated with desensitization for a postulated circumscribed phobia of members of the opposite sex.

Accepting unreplicated findings as valid because they are statistically significant, thus ignoring the possibility that they are Type I errors, and rejecting as due to chance findings that do not reach statistical significance, thus possibly committing Type II errors, are procedures that have occurred repeatedly in controlled studies evaluating behavioral therapy in homosexuality.

3. RATING SCALES

Another formalistic procedure which appears to have led to misinterpretation of the effects of behavioral therapy in homosexuality is the use of rating scales summing changes in several items of behavior in order to measure behavioral change, without first establishing that the items reflect the type of change the therapy produces. Again, presumably because of the replicatory studies they routinely carried out, therapists employing drugs were the first to draw attention to this problem in evaluating therapies. In double-blind drug evaluation studies, various indices were examined to determine which best discriminated the patients who were given an active drug from those given a placebo. The global clinical impression of physicians as to whether or not patients had improved proved superior to most rating scales that summed several items of behavioral change to measure patient improvement (Paredes, Baumgold, Hugh, & Ragland, 1966). Lipman, Cole, Park, and Rickels (1965) concluded that clinicians' global impression of change should be regularly utilized in studies evaluating therapies that influence behavior.

British workers, possibly due to their characteristic adherence to procedural rules, in contrast with the American bias toward empiricism, have proved much less willing to supplement itemized rating-scale assessments of change with global clinical judgment. As early as 1961, two British workers (Ashby & Collins, 1961) reported a controlled trial in which the itemized rating scale employed showed no significant difference between the response of patients to an active drug and a placebo, whereas "the more delicate perceptions of the clinician" did. They commented that the rating scale was an "objective but somewhat insensitive method of scoring." They preferred the estimate of improvement provided by the rating scale, presumably because of their belief that clinical judgment became "objective" when used to assess change on several items of behavior and the results were recorded on a rating scale. Preference for itemized rating-scale assessments rather than clinical impressions of change continues to characterize the research of British workers evaluating behavioral therapy in homosexuality.

Rating scales have the advantage of enabling the findings of different studies to be compared, since workers using the same scale itemize similar data. This advantage must be weighed against the danger that items of behavior scored by the scale may not be those that change with treatment. Until the rating scales employed in a therapeutic study are shown to be sensitive to the appropriate behavioral changes, these scales should be supplemented with clinical assessments of global change.

B. Theoretical Fixations

A formalistic attitude to methodology is often accompanied by rigid adherence to theoretical constructs, which has also hampered the reaching of a consensus concerning the value of behavioral treatments in homosexuality. Assumptions are unquestioned or advanced as established because they conform to current theoretical beliefs. These assumptions are therefore not subjected to empirical testing. Examples discussed later in this review include the delay in observing that "aversion" therapies rarely produce aversions; the failure to consider that behavioral therapies in homosexuality could produce worthwhile changes other than converting a homosexual orientation to a heterosexual one; and the conviction that aversive therapies acted by conditioning, leading to uncritical acceptance of all theoretical implications following from this conviction.

This reviewer does not suggest that theory be abandoned in favor of blind empiricism. Such empiricism can result in an inability to select the significant from the insignificant problems in research. The correct alternative is that important theoretical issues be recognized, but be adequately tested empirically before being accepted as established. A conclusion must not be accepted merely because it conforms to theoretical expectation or even if, in addition, it has emerged as statistically significant in a single study carried out with methodological perfection. Type I errors made in this way can be accepted as facts for a decade or more, initially retarding progress in that area of science. When they are ultimately discovered, a degree of cynicism and contempt results concerning the value of the application of the scientific method in that area. Cynicism concerning attempts to scientifically evaluate therapies that influence behavior is already widespread.

Theory and empiricism must be firmly united. Most importantly, the fact that a finding attains statistical significance in a single study must not be considered sufficient evidence to establish the validity of that finding. In the physical sciences a finding is accepted only after it has been adequately replicated. The time is overdue in the behavioral sciences for *adequate replication* to be similarly accepted as *the only criterion of validity.*

II. DEVELOPMENT OF AVERSIVE TECHNIQUES IN HOMOSEXUALITY

The first recognized behavioral therapy employed in homosexuality involved the administration of unpleasant physical stimuli (Max,

1935). The use of such aversive procedures in homosexuality has recently been criticized on the basis that their aim was to reduce patients' homosexual feelings and behavior rather than to attempt to increase their heterosexual feelings and behavior (Money, 1972; Wilson & Davison, 1974). In fact, almost all therapists using aversive techniques to treat homosexuality combined them with procedures intended to increase the patients' heterosexual behavior.

A. Freund's Study

The first influential study in which aversive therapy was employed to treat a significant number of homosexual patients was that carried out by Freund (1960). The treatment procedure was derived from a previously described aversive treatment of alcoholics, in which the production of nausea and vomiting by an emetic mixture was used as the unpleasant stimulus.

1. DETAILS OF TREATMENT

The first phase of Freund's therapy was daily administration to the patient (24 administrations in all) of an emetic mixture of emetine and apomorphine. While the emetic effects lasted, the patient was shown slides of dressed and undressed men. In the second phase of treatment, the patient was given 10 mg of testosterone propionate and 7 hours later was shown films of nude or seminude women.

Freund called the form of treatment he used a "conditioned reflex therapy," but he seems to have felt that it acted on a cognitive rather than a simple conditioning level. Pavlov (1927) recommended that for effective conditioning the conditioned stimulus should slightly precede the unconditioned stimulus. Presumably because Freund did not consider the conditioning element important in his treatment, he waited until the unconditioned stimulus was effective and emesis had occurred before he administered the conditioned stimulus, the slides of men.

2. RESPONSE TO TREATMENT

The only response to treatment Freund reported was the patients' heterosexual adaptation. Freund defined heterosexual adaptation as erotic behavior in which heterosexual intercourse was far more frequent than homosexual intercourse. It is not possible to know from his study if patients who failed to achieve this state reported other changes which they considered of value.

Ten patients (15%) made a short-term heterosexual adaptation (i.e., one lasting weeks or months) and 12 (18%) heterosexual adaptation lasting several years. Freund reported on the condition of these 12 patients at 3-years follow-up. Prior to treatment three were married; at follow-up all were. Three of the 12 patients had occasional desire for heterosexual intercourse with women other than their wives. None of the three had had homosexual relations following treatment, but only one claimed to have no homosexual desires. Freund considered that the homosexual desires of the other nine were greater than their heterosexual desires. Three had had regular homosexual relations for at least a period following treatment, three had had homosexual relations on three or less occasions, and three had had none. Freund (1960) concluded:

> The heterosexual adaptation of the whole group appears to consist mainly in the fact that the patients have learned to have intercourse without previous stimulation by the (for them) specific erotic object; this may be the reason why for some of them homosexual intercourse has become more infrequent. [p. 323]

Freund appeared to mean that there is a biological basis for homosexuality that determines that persons of the same rather than of the opposite sex are specific erotic objects. The treatment did not alter this biological basis of homosexuality in that women had not become the patients' specific erotic objects following treatment. Treatment merely enabled them to learn to have heterosexual intercourse without the stimulation produced by a specific erotic object. Men remained the specific sexual objects of the patients, but some patients had less frequent or no homosexual relations because they were discharging their sexual tension in heterosexual relations. In other words, Freund appeared to believe that the patients' *sexual behavior altered in a heterosexual direction, but their biologically determined sexual orientation did not.*

Freund attempted to compare the response of the patients he treated with that reported in studies by psychotherapists and concluded that, taking into account possible sources of error, there were no obvious differences either in quality or degree of therapeutic success. He regarded this as evidence for his belief that both therapies acted at a cognitive level by the common principle of encouragement of heterosexual and discouragement of homosexual behavior.

3. IMPLICATIONS OF FREUND'S STUDY

Freund's study raised questions of considerable interest, though not always explicitly. Some of these are:

a. Did the behavioral therapies act as conditioning techniques?

b. Did the behavioral therapies act at a cognitive level, altering the patient's evaluation of heterosexual and homosexual behavior, and persuading them to indulge in heterosexual fantasies and behavior and cease homosexual ones?

c. Did the results of the behavioral therapies differ from those of psychotherapy?

d. Is there a biologically determined sexual orientation of subjects which differs from their behavioral sexual orientation as indicated by their sexual practices?

e. If there is a biologically determined sexual orientation, is it altered by behavioral therapy?

The last two questions indicated Freund's adherence to a biological model. Such a model had no meaning to most of the theorists than advocating behavioral approaches to therapy. These theorists, though tacitly recognizing biological determinants of behavior, adopted the view then current in psychology that the significant variables determining behavior were environmental. These variables were conceived as operating by learning theory principles. A person's sexual orientation was therefore established by his previous experience and was demonstrated in his behavior. New learning experiences could alter his motivation to show certain types of sexual behavior and thus alter his sexual orientation. Behavioral theorists were so fixated on this view that they did not consider the possibility that biological factors could in part determine a person's sexual orientation and that these might not be susceptible to change by environmental variables. Hence they might not be capable of alteration by learning.

Unlike the issue raised by the biological model, that raised by Freund's first question—do behavioral therapies act by conditioning?—was, at the time Freund's work was published, an explicit article of faith for most behavioral therapists.

B. Aversive Therapy and Theoretical Fixations

The conviction that behavioral techniques acted according to laboratory-established laws of learning provided the basis for a stream of well-meant advice to therapists from learning theorists, many of whom had minimal experience with the use of behavioral therapies. In the highly influential book in which Freund's article was published, *Behaviour Therapy and the Neuroses,* the editor, Eysenck (1960) stated of aversive therapy:

> Learning theory does in part indicate that such punishment may be effective provided certain conditions are fulfilled. These conditions are quite strict, and relate to such technical matters as stimulus–response asynchronism; when they are disregarded—as unfortunately they usually have been in the past by practitioners ignorant of the principles of conditioning and learning theory—results may easily lead to a worsening, rather than to an improvement, of the condition requiring treatment . . . [p. 277]

Eysenck pointed out the difficulty of exactly timing the onset of the effect of emetic aversive agents and concluded that Freund would probably have obtained better results had he used electric shock. Eysenck advised therapists to assess patients' neuroticism since he felt Beech's study (1960) had shown that patients with high neuroticism could be made worse by aversive procedures.

In fact, what Beech showed was that three patients with high neuroticism scores responded poorly to an aversive procedure whereas one with moderate neuroticism responded marginally better. Beech's post hoc attribution of poor response to patients' high neuroticism is the type of procedure, as discussed in Section I, A, 1, likely to lead to Type I errors, and certainly seems to have done so in this case. The conclusion that aversive procedures may make patients with high neuroticism scores worse was widely accepted, and represents an example of how a weakly supported finding which is in conformity with theoretical preconceptions is not subject to reasonable scrutiny. Fortunately the acceptance was not universal. Thorpe, Schmidt, Brown, and Castell (1964) empirically tested the conclusion and rejected it.

Fortunately again, the dogma that electric shock would prove more efficacious than an emetic agent in aversive procedures was accepted without empirical testing. Following the publication of *Behaviour Therapy and the Neuroses,* an increasing number of studies utilized electric shock rather than emetic agents in aversive therapy of sexual disorders. Though evidence, to be discussed later, indicated that emetic agents and electric shock are equally effective as aversive stimuli, electric shock is considerably less unpleasant for the majority of patients. The pendulum is now swinging back regarding the aversive treatment of alcoholism. Because emetic agents establish taste aversions in animals, they are being increasingly employed as aversive stimuli with human subjects without empirical evidence that they are superior to electric shock.

C. Introduction of Electric Shock as the Aversive Agent

Following the use by Max (1935) of electric aversive therapy to treat a homosexual, the therapy was reintroduced by Rachman (1961) to treat a fetishist. Subsequently a group of workers at Banstead Hospital, England, having successfully treated a transvestite with an emetic aversive procedure (Lavin, Thorpe, Barker, Blakemore, & Conway, 1961), adopted electric aversion to treat another patient (Blakemore, Thorpe, Barker, Conway, & Lavin, 1963). These workers uncritically accepted Eysenck's conclusion concerning the greater efficacy of electric shock and rejected the emitic aversive procedure, not because it was ineffective, but because its efficacy could not be simply explained in terms of learning theory:

> Such practical difficulties are important also at the theoretical level, for they complicate any explanation of the exact nature of the learning process involved, and upon which the treatment is supposed to be rationally based. Despite the apparent success of Lavin *et al.* in the treatment of their patient, this critical evaluation of their procedure remains appropriate. [p. 29]

Workers at Banstead Hospital then reported the electrical aversive treatment of a homosexual patient (Thorpe, Schmidt, & Castell, 1963). Initially the patient was treated with a positive conditioning technique. He was instructed to masturbate and report when orgasm was being reached. He was then shown a picture of an attractive, scantily dressed female until he reported he had ejaculated. His masturbatory fantasy remained entirely homosexual.

Sessions of aversive therapy were then alternated with sessions of the conditioning procedure. During the aversive session pictures of nude males were shown 40 times (for 1-sec duration?) to the patient. On approximately a quarter of the occasions a painful electric shock was administered to the patient's feet .5 to 1 sec after the picture was shown. The patient subsequently reported great reluctance to use homosexual fantasy with masturbation in the positive conditioned trials. Following treatment he had "occasional homosexual patterns of behavior," presumably homosexual physical relations. He continued the new pattern of behavior of masturbating to female pictures and fantasies. In discussing the therapy, the author concluded that the patient showed an aversive response to young men and youths. They appeared not to have attributed this aversion to establishment of a conditioned response as such, but to the extinction of behavior that was negatively reinforced and to the strengthening of behavior that was positively reinforced.

This explanatory formulation suggested that this group of workers was in the process of abandoning adherence to a rigid learning theory formulation regarding the action of aversive therapy as they gained experience of its actual effects. Their adoption of this more flexible approach resulted in the development of a new and useful treatment technique, aversion-relief therapy.

D. Aversion-Relief Therapy

Thorpe *et al.* (1964) pointed out that one problem with behavior therapy arose from Eysenck's (1960) assertion that ". . . psychoanalysts show a preoccupation with psychological methods involving mainly *speech*, while behavior therapy concentrates on actual *behavior* as most likely to lead to the extinction of the unadaptive conditioned responses" (p. 11). Thorpe *et al.* considered that this assertion caused behavior therapists to go to great trouble and expense to reproduce the actual behavior to be extinguished, for example, obtaining female clothing to treat transvestites or suitable photographs of nude men and women to treat homosexuals. Thorpe *et al.* considered that as the use of these photographs resulted in symbolizing relevant behavior, rather than reproducing it, it would be much simpler to symbolize the behavior with words. They pointed out that the resultant technique might not be classified as behavior therapy, but emphasized that it would render possible the treatment of any type of maladaptation.

The previous experience of Thorpe *et al.* with aversive therapy was the basis for another innovation in technique that was subsequently utilized widely. They had noted that each time a patient being treated with aversive therapy recognized by a signal that a treatment session involving unpleasant stimuli was finished, he experienced great *relief.* They decided to attempt to utilize this relief in the treatment they developed, and therefore termed the treatment aversion-relief therapy.

With aversion-relief therapy, the patient was shown a series of words or phrases every 10 sec. All but the last word or phrase related to the behavior being treated, for example, "homosexual" or its synonyms. The last word related to behavior to be encouraged, such as "heterosexual." Each time the patient saw a word he was instructed to read it aloud. He then received a painful shock to his feet, except when the last word was shown. He soon learned that he received no shock with the last word and experienced marked relief. So that the last word signaled the beginning of a significant period in which the patient received no shocks, it was shown to him for 2 min. He then left the treatment room for a further 5 min. The series of words was shown to the patient five times in a treatment session. On average, 60 shocks were given in a session and sessions were carried out daily.

The response of three homosexuals was reported. One stated he felt aggression and disgust when he met homosexuals following treatment. There was no follow-up. The second reported that thinking about homosexuality was frightening and sickening during treatment. Three weeks after discharge he "had no problems about homosexual feelings." The third reported 4 weeks after discharge that he had no homosexual desires in situations where he normally would have experienced them. All three reported more heterosexual interest.

Workers at Banstead Hospital (Schmidt, Castell, & Brown, 1965) subsequently reported the behavioral treatment of 42 patients, 16 for homosexuality. Thirteen of the 16 were treated with aversion-relief therapy. Five refused to continue treatment. At completion of treatment, seven of the remaining eight showed marked improvement, defined as symptoms absent and normal activities resumed; and the other, moderate improvement, symptom present to a lesser degree and not interfering with normal activities. The authors state that the outcome of treatment was mainly refusal of treatment or success. They do not account for the high refusal rate.

E. Differential Conditioning with Electric Shock

More detailed information concerning homosexual patients' response to an aversion-relief procedure was provided by Solyom and Miller (1965). Of six patients treated, four who were having homosexual relations prior to treatment ceased them, *finding their homosexual desires easier to control.* The sexual feelings of the remaining two may have been unchanged. The authors concluded that their technique, designed to reduce homosexual interest and to diminish anxiety aroused by women, *did not necessarily awaken sexual interest in women.* They advised that it be used as a first step toward the establishment of heterosexual behavior.

F. Anticipatory Avoidance Aversion Therapy

1. THEORETICAL CONSIDERATIONS

The most elaborate electrical aversive therapy yet introduced was that of anticipatory avoidance, developed by Feldman and MacCulloch (1964) as an expression of their "firm conviction that if conditioning techniques are to be employed in psychiatry, they should represent the systematic application of the methods and findings of experimental psychology" (p. 170). A further conviction they held was that such findings could be transferred unmodified from the laboratory and applied to therapeutic procedures with human subjects.

Feldman and MacCulloch concluded from a review of the relevant literature that a conditioned avoidance technique should be used in the treatment of homosexuality as it would be most resistant to extinction, particularly if certain procedural rules were followed. Training trials should be well spaced. The conditioned stimulus should be presented with no distractions. Shock should be used rather than apomorphine. Reinforcement should be partial, with some but not all avoidance attempts being rewarded.

2. DETAILS OF TREATMENT

In Feldman and MacCulloch's technique the patient first rated a series of slides of men and women for attractiveness. About eight slides of members of each sex were then selected, ranging from mildly to highly attractive. The patient was seated in a quiet dark room and the slide of the least attractive male displayed. The patient was told that several seconds later he might receive a shock, that he could remove the slide of the male with a switch provided, and that when the slide disappeared the shock would cease. He should leave the slide showing as long as he found it attractive. If the patient left the male slide showing longer than 8 sec he received a shock to the calf. If the strength of the shock was not sufficiently great to cause him to remove the slide of the male immediately, it was increased until he did so.

After a number of presentations, the patient commenced to avoid the shock by rejecting the male slide within 8 sec. He was then placed on a schedule of reinforcement, which incorporated the variables considered by the authors to increase resistance to extinction. On one-third of the occasions on which the male slide was shown the patient could avoid the shock. These were called *reinforcement trials.* On one-third of the occasions his attempts to reject the male slide were prevented from being effective for 8 sec, so that he received the shock. These were called *nonreinforced trials.* One one-third of the occasions his attempts to reject the male slide were prevented from being effective for 4, 6, or $7\frac{1}{2}$ sec. If he continued to attempt to reject the slide he would succeed before the 8 sec had elapsed, so avoiding the shock. These were called *delayed trials.* The three types of trial appeared in random order and the intertrial interval was varied randomly. When the patient reported that his response to the male slide was one of indifference or dislike and he attempted to turn the slide off within 1 to 2 sec of its appearance, the slide was replaced by the next in the hierarchy of attractiveness.

Randomly on about half the occasions on which the patient rejected the slide of a male it was replaced with a slide of a female. This slide was removed by the therapist, but the patient was informed he could request its return. Randomly the request was granted for about half the occasions the patient made it.

3. RESPONSE TO TREATMENT

MacCulloch and Feldman (1967) reported the response of 41 male and 2 female homosexual patients 12 months following treatment. Patients received from 5 to 38 sessions of treatment, each lasting 20 to 25 min, during which a slide of a male was presented on about 24 occasions. Treatment continued until either a change of interest occurred or it became clear no change was likely. Seven patients terminated treatment after a few sessions. Of the remaining 36, at follow-up 13 were experiencing heterosexual intercourse and no homosexual fantasy or practice. A further 12 were using strong heterosexual fantasy or were involved in heterosexual relations short of intercourse. Twenty were not using homosexual fantasy and were not involved in homosexual relations. The authors concluded that 25 patients were significantly improved in that they showed Kinsey ratings of 0–2 (i.e., predominantly heterosexual). Prior to treatment no patients obtained Kinsey ratings in this range. Younger patients and those with experience of heterosexual activity were more likely to show a successful response.

4. POSTEXPERIMENTAL SEARCH FOR CORRELATIONS

MacCulloch, Feldman, and Pinshoff (1965) provided detailed data concerning the latency of the avoidance response to slides of males of four patients, the requests for slides of females of two patients, and the pulse rates during treatment of two patients. They related these data to aspects of personality, motivation, or response to treatment of the patients. This procedure is of the type referred to in Section I, as being likely to result in Type I errors. It is usually possible to find relationships in experimental data that were not predicted in advance but for which a plausible explanation is readily available. If the responses of a few selected experimental subjects are examined, the likelihood of finding such relationships is, of course, much greater. In view of the high probability that these relationships are due to chance, they should not be given significance until replicated. The appropriate procedure is to use them as a basis for prediction that similar relationships will emerge in a replicatory experiment, and for determining prior to the experiment how the relationships will be measured.

G. Electric Shock Contingent on Penile Responses

Bancroft (1969) reported the treatment of 10 male homosexuals. They were asked to produce homosexual fantasies to photographs of males and received painful electric shocks to the arm when they showed a distinguishable penile circumference increase, usually of about .6 mm. Following the initial shock, up to 4 further shocks were given at 15 sec intervals unless penile circumference decrease occurred. This procedure was repeated about 12 times in a session. On 3 occasions, the patient was encouraged to produce heterosexual fantasies to pictures of females, with the aim of reinforcing heterosexual responses by the "anxiety-relief" effect.

One year or more following therapy one patient had no homosexual desire and had commenced regular heterosexual intercourse which he had not experienced prior to treatment. Homosexual desire was still present in the other nine patients, but at reduced strength in two and possibly a third. Heterosexual feeling was increased in two of these three patients. Bancroft pointed out that two patients who became overtly homosexual for the first time following treatment were obviously more content than they had been prior to treatment. Three patients became sufficiently depressed to need antidepressant medication. Improvement was greater in older patients and was unrelated to previous heterosexual experience. These two prognostic relationships differed from those reported by MacCulloch and Feldman, a further indication that significance should not be attached to unpredicted findings noted on one occasion in experimental data.

H. Imaginary Aversive Therapy

Gold and Neufeld (1965) described an aversive technique they considered would be acceptable to therapists who had ethical and aesthetic objections to the induction of physically unpleasant sensations in patients.

A homosexual patient was trained to relax by the procedure used for systematic desensitization. While relaxed he was encouraged to visualize himself next to a most unattractive old man in a public lavatory. When he signaled that he visualized not soliciting this man, the image of the man was slowly changed to a more attractive form, but surrounded by prohibitions such as the image of a policeman standing nearby. The patient learned to reject the image of an attractive man in the absence of prohibitions. The patient then learned to visualize choosing an attractive young woman rather than an attractive young man. On follow-up the patient reported no compulsion to have homosexual relations and had formed a heterosexual relationship.

COVERT SENSITIZATION

Cautela (1966) described an elaboration of the method of imaginary aversive therapy which he termed covert desensitization. He later used it to treat three homosexuals (Cautela, 1967). Each patient was instructed to visualize being in a room with an attractive naked male. He approached the male and noticed he was covered with scabs and gave off a terrible stench. The odor made the patient feel sick and vomit all over his surroundings. He turned away and started to feel better. The patient was instructed to visualize at home scenes similar to those presented by the therapist. Two of the three homosexuals treated ceased homosexual behavior. The third who was not overtly homosexual experienced great reduction of homosexual fantasies.

III. CONTROLLED TRIALS OF AVERSIVE THERAPIES IN HOMOSEXUALITY

A. Comparison of Apomorphine and Aversion-Relief Therapies

The first comparison study of aversive procedures was reported by McConaghy (1969, 1970b). The study was commenced in 1964 and attempted to investigate the following problems then current: Do aversive therapies act by conditioning? Is apomorphine necessarily inferior to electric shock as an aversive stimulus? Is there a biological basis to homosexuality which is uninfluenced by aversive therapy?

1. MEASUREMENT OF CONDITIONABILITY AND SEXUAL ORIENTATION

A brief standardized investigatory procedure was developed to provide a measure both of subjects' ability to set up conditioned responses, their so-called "conditionability," and their biological sexual orientation. Subjects were shown a travelog type film in which were inserted in alternation at 1-min intervals 10-sec segments of moving pictures of a nude or seminude women and similar segments of a nude or seminude man. Segments of a picture of a red circle were inserted for 10 sec prior to the pictures of women and similar segments of a green triangle prior to those of men. While subjects viewed the film their penile volume changes were recorded by a modification of the method developed by Freund (1963). The procedure took less than 30 min and so could be conveniently repeated to monitor patients' progress.

In a study (McConaghy, 1967) validating the procedure, 11 heterosexual subjects each showed mean penile volume increases to the pictures of women and decreases to the pictures of men. The majority of 19 homosexual subjects showed the opposite responses. Penile volume responses appeared to the later presentations of the red circle and the green triangle similar to the responses to the nude figures. These were conditioned responses and were used to provide a measure of the degree to which the subject set up conditioned responses (McConaghy, 1970a). The statistical significance of the difference in penile changes to the pictures of women as compared to those of men was calculated using the Mann–Whitney U-test for each subject's responses. If all penile responses to pictures of women were greater than any to pictures of men, the U-score was 100, indicating maximal heterosexuality. If a patient's responses to pictures of men were greater than any to women, the U-score was 0, indicating maximal homosexuality. Scores of above 50 indicated predominantly heterosexual orientation and below 50 predominantly homosexual orientation. U-scores of 23 or less and 77 or more indicated a statistically significant difference between the penile responses to males and females (two-tailed). Utilizing this scoring method, all 11 heterosexual subjects were classified correctly, 10 obtaining U-scores of over 77. Fourteen of 19 homosexual subjects were classified as predominantly homosexual, one as bisexual, and four as predominantly heterosexual. Three of the four had stated they were predominantly heterosexual. Only one of these four obtained a U-score of over 77.

2. DETAILS OF THE STUDY

Forty men who requested aversive therapy to reduce homosexual impulses were randomly allocated to four groups, each of 10 subjects. Subjects in two groups received aversive treatment immediately following investigation of their conditionability and sexual orientation with the procedure just described. Those in the other two groups underwent the investigation twice at an interval of 3 weeks before receiving aversive treatment. The treatment was administered in one week. Two weeks following treatment all subjects underwent the investigation again. The subjects investigated for a second time without treatment intervening acted as controls for those treated immediately.

Two groups, one investigated once and one twice prior to treatment, were randomly allocated to receive apomorphine aversive treatment. The other two groups received aversive-relief therapy. The apomorphine procedure was based on that developed by Freund (1960). Patients were given 28 injections of apomorphine at 2-hr intervals during the day over 5 days. One minute prior to the expected onset of nausea the patient was instructed to illuminate the slide of a nude male and to attempt to respond to it with sexual arousal. Just prior to the nausea becoming maximal the patient was instructed to turn off the slide.

The aversion-relief procedure was based on that developed by Thorpe *et al.* (1964). Patients read aloud 14 phrases evocative of aspects of homosexuality, presented at 10-sec intervals. Immediately after they read each phrase they received a painful electric shock to two fingertips. A fifteenth phrase evocative of heterosexuality was then presented for 40 sec without shock. The series of phrases was presented five times in one session of treatment at intervals of $2\frac{1}{2}$ min. Three sessions were administered daily for 5 days.

3. SUBJECTIVE RESPONSE TO AVERSIVE THERAPIES

At 2 weeks following treatment, about half the patients considered their homosexual desire was reduced and a quarter that their heterosexual desire was increased. There was a trend for more patients to report decrease of homosexual desire following apomorphine and more to report increase of heterosexual desire following aversion-relief therapy. Neither trend was statistically significant, but, as discussed in Section I, A, with patient numbers of 20 per group, trends must be very strong to be statistically significant.

At 1 year following treatment, half the patients still considered their homosexual drive reduced but often not to the same extent as at 2 weeks following treatment. The number considering their heterosexual desire to be greater following treatment increased to a half. Mainly the same people reported both responses. The nonsignificant trend for more patients to report increased heterosexual desire following aversion-relief therapy as compared with apomorphine was still present. A quarter of the patients had had no homosexual relations since treatment and another quarter reported that the frequency of such relations was reduced. Slightly more patients reporting each of these responses had received apomorphine therapy. A quarter of the patients had increased the frequency of heterosexual intercourse. Only one experienced heterosexual intercourse for the first time following treatment. There was no relationship between previous heterosexual experience and reported reduction of homosexual feeling following treatment.

4. PENILE RESPONSE CHANGES

Using U-scores of the subjects' penile responses to the film assessment as a measure of their sexual orientation, 10 of the 40 patients showed a heterosexual orientation prior to treatment, but in only one of the 10 was the U-score over 77, that is, within the range obtained by 90% of heterosexual males (Barr & McConaghy, 1971; McConaghy, 1967). Following treatment, the U-scores of the majority of subjects shifted in the heterosexual direction to a small but statistically significant extent. Fifteen then obtained scores indicating a heterosexual orientation, but only in two were the scores above 77. No significant changes took place in the U-scores of the control group in the second assessment carried out prior to treatment. The change in U-scores of the treated subjects reflected the fact that, following treatment, their summed *penile responses to the pictures of men were significantly less* and those to the pictures of women significantly greater than they were prior to treatment. However, penile volume responses to pictures of women increased significantly only in those patients who, prior to treatment, showed penile volume decreases to pictures of women. In other words, those patients showed significantly less penile volume decrease to pictures of women following treatment. There was *no significant augmentation of penile volume increases to pictures of women in patients who showed such increases prior to treatment.* At 1-year follow-up the penile volume responses of patients showed no significant change from those at 2 weeks following treatment.

There was a significant relationship between change in U-score toward heterosexuality shown by patients following treatment and their reported increase of heterosexual and decrease of homosexual desire at 1-year follow-up. It has not proved possible to replicate this relationship in subsequent studies and it appears to have been a Type I error. This appears to be true also of the relationships found between conditionability and response to treatment.

5. CONDITIONABILITY AND RESPONSE TO TREATMENT

There are a variety of ways in which subjects' conditionability can be determined. As conditioned responses are based on unconditioned responses, they can presumably occur only in subjects who show unconditioned responses. In the case of the film assessment procedure, this means that true conditioned penile volume increases to the green triangle can be expected only in homosexual subjects who show mean penile volume increases to the pictures of nude males following the green triangles. Similarly, true conditioned penile volume decreases to the red circles can be expected only in homosexual subjects who show a decrease to the following pictures of women. Of the subjects who showed these types of unconditioned penile responses to pictures of men and women, over 20% showed penile volume responses to the preceding geometric figure which were opposite in direction to the following unconditioned response. Should this group of subjects be included in the group who condition poorly or be excluded from the analysis of the relationship between conditionability and response to treatment?

An additional problem is that conditioned penile volume responses correlated strongly with the unconditioned responses on which they were based (McConaghy, 1970a). Hence if amplitude of the conditioned response is used as a measure of conditionability, subjects who show strong unconditioned responses will be classified as showing good conditioning and those with weak unconditioned responses poor conditioning. Should a mathematical correction be made for this relationship? These decisions give a range of options as to how to measure conditionability. In the absence of information about which procedure is appropriate, the only possibility is to examine the relationship between all possible measures of conditionability and response to treatment. This, of course, means that the number of relationships examined will be sufficiently great, that some are likely to be statistically significant by chance, and therefore may result in Type I errors. Such appears to have occurred in McConaghy's study (1970a). He reported significant relationships between certain measures of conditionability and response to treatment, but stressed that they required replication. In the later studies he carried out these relationships did not reappear.

6. EFFECTS OF AVERSIVE PROCEDURES ON SEXUAL BEHAVIOR

The reduction in patients' homosexual feelings and behavior and in their penile volume increases to pictures of men following both aversive procedures suggested that the procedures reduced the strength of homosexual drive. Evidence that they produced increase in heterosexual feelings was less consistent. No augmentation of penile volume increases to pictures of women occurred in patients who showed such increases prior to treatment. Though at 1-year follow-up half the patients reported increased heterosexual interest, with one exception the only patients who engaged in heterosexual intercourse were those who had done so prior to treatment. At 2 weeks following treatment only a quarter of the patients reported increased heterosexual interest. If this change were produced by treatment it would be expected to be greater at 2 weeks than 1 year following treatment, as was the reported reduction in homosexual feelings. That it was greater at 1 year suggested it may have been secondary to the reduction in homosexual interest. Freund (1960) concluded of apomorphine therapy and Solyom and Miller (1965) of an aversive relief procedure that increased heterosexual feelings following their use was not primary, but secondary to decreased homosexual activity.

7. DOES AVERSIVE THERAPY PRODUCE AVERSION?

One reason that studies of aversive treatment in homosexuality failed to rapidly achieve a consensus concerning its therapeutic effects was that the early studies were carried out by workers who had clear expectations of what these effects would be. This prevented them investigating the effects the therapy actually produced. Freund (1960) expected the therapy he used to produce heterosexual adaptation. He did not report responses apart from this. Later workers under the influence of learning theorists expected aversive therapy to produce an aversion. Thorpe *et al.* (1963) concluded that the patient they treated showed an aversive response to young men and youths, though they did not report evidence of this response, but in fact stated that following treatment the patient had occasional homosexual patterns of behavior. Schmidt *et al.* (1965) reported that of eight homosexuals treated with aversion-relief therapy, seven showed marked improvement, defined as symptoms absent and normal activities resumed. Such a result suggested the change these patients showed was loss of homosexual feelings, not an actual aversion to homosexuality. Solyom and Miller (1965) reported only reduction of homosexual interest and diminished anxiety aroused by women in the homosexuals they treated with an aversion-relief procedure.

Feldman and MacCulloch (1971) considered that their technique set up a conditioned avoidance response that could cause the patient to avoid looking at attractive males. They did not report the presence of this response in treated patients, but rather a reduction or absence of homosexual interest.

McConaghy (1969) stressed the absence following aversive procedures of the conditioned responses that would be expected if the procedures acted by conditioning:

> The conditioned response to a stimulus reinforced with a painful electric shock to the hand is limb withdrawal and anxiety; to a stimulus reinforced with apomorphine is nausea. In the present investigation, patients aftet treatment did not report such responses to phrases associated with homosexuality or to photographs of attractive males. [p. 729]

Bancroft (1969) also pointed out that conditioned anxiety would be expected to result from associating electric shock with deviant stimuli or fantasies. Only one of the ten patients he treated showed any evidence of conditioned anxiety. Birk, Huddleston, Miller, and Cohler (1971), in a study to be discussed, reported reduction in homosexual feelings and interest but no aversion in five of eight patients following avoidance conditioning.

In over 200 patients the reviewer has treated with various aversive procedures, less than 5% have reported reactions that could be considered evidence of conditioned aversions. When such reactions were reported they were transient. Following apomorphine aversive therapy, a patient might report a brief feeling of nausea on one or two occasions when he noticed an attractive man. Following an aversive procedure using electric shock, a patient might report a feeling of receiving a shock when about to go into a public lavatory. The reviewer considered that these reactions were reported only by patients who showed other evidence of being emotionally unstable or who showed hysterical features. He attributed the reactions to suggestion, though of course such suggestion may have a basis in conditioning. In any case, such reactions were not related to the only persistent therapeutic effect of aversive procedures observed, namely, reduction in homosexual feelings and interest.

In view of the increasing acceptance (Hallam & Rachman, 1976; Lovibond, 1970) that therapies associating unpleasant stimuli with stimuli evoking the target behavior do not produce aversion but rather a reduction in desire to carry out the target behavior, it would seem preferable to abandon the term "aversion therapy" in favor of the alternative "aversive therapy." Part of the unfavorable publicity given aversive therapies results from *the belief that they produce aversions,* and hence that they reduce the patients' ability to carry out behavior they wish to carry out. The widely seen film of Anthony Burgess' novel, *A Clockwork Orange,* made this point unpleasantly explicit. In fact, aversive therapies only allow patients to limit behavior they do not wish to carry out. They in no way prevent the patient practicing behavior they *wish* to carry out.

B. Comparison of Apomorphine and Anticipatory Avoidance Therapies

The reviewer stressed in Section I, A, 1 the importance of not ignoring possibly meaningful trends that did not reach statistical significance in studies with relatively small numbers of subjects. In the study by McConaghy just discussed, there was a trend for more patients to report increased heterosexual desire following aversion-relief compared with apomorphine therapy and for more to report decreased homosexual desire and behavior following apomorphine therapy compared with aversion-relief. McConaghy, Proctor, and Barr (1972) attempted to determine if these findings could be replicated. MacCulloch and Feldman's report (1967) of a markedly superior response to anticipatory avoidance therapy suggested this would be a better procedure to investigate the efficacy of electric shock as an aversive stimulus and its termination as a relief procedure than the original aversion-relief paradigm. It was also decided to attempt to replicate the relationships found in the first study (McConaghy, 1970a) between the measures of the patients' conditionability derived from the film assessment and their response to aversive therapy.

1. DETAILS OF THE STUDY

Forty homosexual men were investigated with the film assessment procedure and were treated with apomorphine or anticipatory avoidance using the same experimental design as in the first study. Apomorphine therapy was carried out as in that study. The anticipatory avoidance procedure of Feldman and MacCulloch (1965), described in Section II, F, was followed except that 30 presentations of the male slide were given per session and patients received 14 sessions of treatment for 5 days.

2. SUBJECTIVE RESPONSE TO AVERSIVE THERAPIES

There was no consistent difference in efficacy of the two aversive procedures. There was a slight trend favoring anticipatory avoidance compared with apomorphine regarding the patients' report of increased heterosexual and decreased homosexual feelings, but a reverse trend occurred favoring apomorphine regarding reports of heterosexual and homosexual behavioral change.

At 6-months follow-up about half the patients reported decreased homosexual feelings and half, mostly the same patients, reported increased heterosexual feelings. A quarter ceased homosexual relations and in another quarter the frequency of such relations was reduced. The proportion of patients reporting these responses was similar to the proportion reporting similar responses at follow-up in the first study. No patients at follow-up reported complete absence of homosexual desire. This was a major difference in response to anticipatory avoidance from that reported by MacCulloch and Feldman (1967). These workers reported that at follow-up, 14 of 43 patients treated reported no homosexual feelings.

3. PENILE RESPONSE CHANGES

The U-scores of sexual orientation derived from the subjects' penile responses to the film assessments showed similar changes with treatment to those in the first study; namely, a small but statistically significant shift in the heterosexual direction for the majority of subjects. No significant change occurred in the U-scores derived from the responses in the first and second film assessment of those control subjects who had two assessments prior to receiving treatment. As in the first study, the shift in U-score reflected the fact that following treatment the summed penile responses of the patients to the pictures of men was significantly less and those to the pictures of women significantly greater than they were prior to treatment. Again, the change in penile responses to pictures of women in the assessment following treatment was not due to augmentation of the responses of subjects who showed penile volume increases to women in the assessment prior to treatment, but to diminution of the responses of subjects who showed penile volume decreases to women at that assessment.

4. DOES AVERSIVE THERAPY WORK BY CONDITIONING?

In the studies carried out by McConaghy (1969, 1970b) and McConaghy *et al.* (1972) for evaluating aversive therapies, no consistent relationship emerged between measures of patients' ability to establish conditioned responses in the assessment film and their response to aversive treatment. Such a finding provides evidence that the response to aversive treatment is not brought about by conditioning only if it has been established that people who condition well in one conditioning procedure condition well in another (i.e., there is a general factor of conditionability). Though from time to time evidence has been advanced that a general factor of conditionability exists (Barr & McConaghy, 1972), it has never been satisfactorily replicated.

More convincing evidence that aversive therapies do not work by conditioning was provided by the results of two studies by McConaghy (1970b) and McConaghy *et al.* (1972), indicating that three different procedures produced comparable therapeutic responses. The three procedures used different aversive stimuli, apomorphine, and electric shock, different stimuli to arouse homosexual feeling, phrases and slides of men, and differing numbers of trials, 28 with apomorphine therapy, 1050 with aversion-relief, and 420 with avoidance conditioning. The apomorphine and aversion-relief therapies were based on a classical conditioning paradigm rather than avoidance conditioning. Aversion-relief and avoidance conditioning included relief from shock to attempt to increase heterosexual arousal, whereas apomorphine therapy did not include any procedure to increase such arousal. Given this variation it seems impossible that the three techniques could be equally effective as conditioning procedures. That they were equally effective as therapies strongly suggests that they were not acting by conditioning. An additional study was carried out to obtain further evidence concerning this issue.

C. Comparison of Classical, Anticipatory Avoidance, and Backward Conditioning Procedures

1. DETAILS OF THE STUDY

The evidence that backward conditioning is a relatively ineffective conditioning procedure remains generally accepted (Hallam & Rachman, 1976). McConaghy and Barr (1973) reported a study in which 46 homosexual men were randomly allocated to receive one of the three following procedures:

a. Classical Conditioning. The patient was shown 3 slides of nude males each for 10 sec, at intervals of 4 min. During the final second of exposure to each slide and for 1 sec following its removal the patient received a painful electric shock to two fingers at a level he determined was definitely unpleasant but not unbearable.

b. Anticipatory Avoidance. This was carried out as in the second study by McConaghy *et al.* (1972) just described.

c. Backward Conditioning. This procedure was designed to act as a control for the anticipatory avoidance procedure. The patient received a shock of 1-sec duration. After $\frac{1}{2}$ sec the slide of a male was shown for 4 sec. Following a 2-sec interval either the slide of a female was shown for 16 sec or the screen was left blank for that period of time. The next shock was then administered. The sequence was repeated 30 times in a treatment session.

All patients received 14 sessions of treatment during 5 days.

2. RESPONSE TO TREATMENT

There were no consistent trends for one therapy to be more effective than another. The proportion of patients reporting decreased homosexual and increased heterosexual feeling was similar to those in the previous two studies reported by McConaghy (1970b) and McConaghy *et al.* (1972). The change in sexual orientation of the patients as determined by penile volume responses to the film assessment was also similar.

3. CRITICISMS

Hallam and Rachman (1976) criticized this study on the basis that the delay between the onset of the male slide and the shock was 9 sec with the classical conditioning procedure and 8 sec with the avoidance procedure. They stated that with classical conditioning the time interval between the CS and the UCS should be less than 1 sec. This widely promulgated statement is another example of the theoretical fixation on conclusions derived from limited laboratory evidence. The ideal CS–UCS interval varies widely depending on the stimulus modality (Mackintosh, 1974). It has been shown repeatedly that rapid conditioning of sexual arousal as measured by penile volume increase can be produced to neutral stimuli with CS–UCS intervals of 10 sec (Barr & McConaghy, 1971; McConaghy, 1970a, 1974b).

Hallam and Rachman also criticized the backward conditioning procedure on the basis that several minutes should be allowed to intervene between the pairing of the backward conditioning stimuli. In their fixation on procedural details, Hallam and Rachman seemed to have overlooked the primary intention of the study. Backward conditioning was used because it was believed to be a relatively ineffective conditioning procedure, to be compared with anticipatory avoidance, the procedure which has produced the best therapeutic response reported in the literature (MacCulloch & Feldman, 1967). If it is accepted that Hallam and Rachman are correct and the backward conditioning procedure was administered inefficiently, it would be an even less effective conditioning procedure. This would strengthen the argument that as the therapeutic response to backward conditioning was comparable to that of anticipatory avoidance, the therapeutic response to both procedures was not produced by conditioning.

D. Controlled Study of Avoidance Conditioning

1. DETAILS OF THE STUDY

Birk *et al.* (1971) randomly allocated 8 of 16 male homosexuals to avoidance conditioning, the other 8 receiving a control treatment. All patients received 20 to 25 sessions of treatment spaced over about 6 weeks, in the middle of a 2-year period of group psychotherapy. The avoidance conditioning procedure was developed from that of Feldman and MacCulloch (1965), the major modification allowing the patients for five 30-sec periods in a treatment session to keep the female picture displayed by repeatedly pressing a response key. This delayed the onset of the next male slide and the associated possibility of electric shock. The control procedure was the same as the avoidance conditioning except that the electric current that would be delivered to the patient in avoidance conditioning was passed through an amber signal light to the right of the projection screen. The patients were told this procedure would work by associative conditioning, and they pressed the response key to keep the female picture displayed, as did the patients who received the active treatment. Birk *et al.* advanced evidence that patients believed control treatment would be as effective as avoidance conditioning.

2. RESPONSE TO THE TWO PROCEDURES

What Birk *et al.* termed the "anecdotal" results were that during treatment five of eight patients receiving avoidance conditioning reported absence or marked diminution of homosexual urges, feelings, and behavior. In two of five the response persisted for at least 2 years. None of the eight patients receiving the control procedure reported this response. What the authors termed the "statistical" results were that during the first 2 months following treatment the

Kinsey ratings of patients receiving avoidance conditioning altered in the heterosexual direction by a total of 23 points, and those of the control group by 2 points. This difference was statistically significant. Both groups continued to receive psychotherapy for 1 year following conditioning treatments. At the end of that year the heterosexual Kinsey ratings of the patients treated by avoidance conditioning was reduced to 12 points and that of the controls increased to 5 points. The difference was no longer statistically significant. The frequency of homosexual cruising and petting remained significantly reduced in the patients treated with avoidance conditioning compared with the controls. There was no consistent trend for measures of heterosexual behavior to increase more in the group treated with avoidance.

3. INSENSITIVITY OF RATING SCALES

The patients' improvement 1 year after conditioning treatments was assessed on 16 rating scales both by themselves and by a psychiatrist not part of the treatment team. Those ratings did not significantly discriminate the group treated with avoidance from the controls. Birk *et al.* (1971) commented: "for change in homosexual feelings, and behavior the . . . ratings are in the predicted direction but not significant, and are much less impressive than one would have expected for examining the behavioral outcome data alone" (p. 322).

This study demonstrated the overvaluation of rating scale measures discussed in Section 1, A, 2. These measures were regarded as having some objective quality not shared by global clinical assessments of change. Such assessments were considered "anecdotal" rather than "statistical." The clinical assessment of behavioral outcome reported in the study by Birk *et al.* (1971) was that at 1 year following avoidance conditioning five of the eight patients showed significantly reduced homosexual cruising and petting. With the 8-point rating scale of homosexual behavior used by the authors, a change of 1 point was given for "somewhat less time cruising; less time feeling the urgency about homosexual desires" (p. 321). To obtain 3 points on the scale the patient needed to show "definite and unequivocal decrease in emphasis on males and a trend towards switching to females in masturbation fantasies . . ." (p. 321).

From the behavioral outcome data of the study, it can be determined that one or two of the five patients who improved with avoidance conditioning may have shown 3 or more points of change on the rating scale. The other three or four patients are likely to have obtained 1 or 2 points at most. The mean change on this rating scale for the response of all eight patients treated with avoidance conditioning would therefore be expected to be 1 to 2. In fact, the eight patients who received avoidance conditioning rated themselves on the scale as changing a mean of 2 points, while the psychiatrist rated them as changing slightly less. The change was not statistically significant in comparison with that in the control group. Birk *et al.* considered that though the clinically assessed change in behavioral outcome was statistically significant, its validity was in question because the rating scale measure of change was not statistically significant. In fact, the rating scale reflected the behavioral change perfectly. The problem was that the rating scale was insufficiently sensitive for the change to be statistically significant. Treatment outcomes will continue to fail to appear significant while rating scales used to measure outcomes are designed to be sensitive to the changes the therapist would like the treatment to produce rather than the changes the treatment *actually* produces.

E. Comparison of Anticipatory Avoidance, Classical Conditioning, and Psychotherapy

1. DETAILS OF THE STUDY

Feldman and MacCulloch (1971) randomly allocated 28 male and 2 female homosexuals to three groups, each to be treated with one of the following procedures:

a. Anticipatory Avoidance. Feldman and MacCulloch modified the procedure previously used, presenting pictures of men and women in movie form as well as by slides.

b. Classical Conditioning. A picture of a male was displayed for 2 sec and in the last $\frac{1}{2}$ sec of the 2-sec period the patient received an unpleasant electric shock to the calf. The picture of the male and the shock were removed simultaneously and a picture of a female shown for 10 sec.

In both procedures the picture of the male was shown 24 times in a treatment session and patients received 24 half-hour sessions.

c. Psychotherapy. Twelve hour sessions of exploration and discussion of the patients' sexual and associated personality difficulties were given.

2. RESPONSE TO TREATMENTS

Prior to and following treatment, the patients filled in a questionnaire termed the Sexual Orientation Method (SOM), developed by the authors to assess the subjects' degree of sexual interest in men and women. A 12-point improvement in the homosexual scale of the SOM was considered by the authors to indicate a successful response. With this measure, the two aversive procedures were equally effective and superior to psychotherapy, but not to a statistically significant extent. As regards the patients' improvement on the SOM heterosexual scale, there was little difference in the 3 treatments. Patients who failed to show a 12-point improvement on the SOM homosexual scale with psychotherapy were randomly assigned to one of the two aversive procedures. Patients who failed to show this degree of improvement with one form of aversive therapy were given the other.

Follow-up data on 27 patients who received at least one aversive treatment showed that some weeks to months after the last treatment, 16 were not engaged in homosexual practices or using homosexual fantasy. Four were having heterosexual intercourse. Sixteen showed Kinsey ratings of 0 to 2, whereas prior to treatment none obtained ratings in this range. Feldman and MacCulloch provided data on the relationship between aspects of the latency of patients' responses in the anticipatory avoidance procedure and their responses to treatment. For unstated reasons, the authors accepted a relationship to be statistically significant that had a probability of being due to chance of between 5 and 10%. It would be unwise to attach importance to these relationships until they have been precisely replicated.

3. CONCLUSIONS

a. SOM Rating Scale Measure. The trend found in this study for reduction in homosexual interest to occur in more patients following an aversive procedure than following psychotherapy alone was also found by Birk *et al.* (1971). In the study by Birk *et al.*, the rating scale measure of change in homosexual feelings and behavior failed to show the trend to be statistically significant, just as did the SOM score of change in homosexuality in the study by Feldman and MacCulloch. Feldman and MacCulloch stated that the SOM scale was not intended to supplant the clinical interview but to provide complementary data. It is unfortunate they did not provide clinical data, particularly global impressions of the change in strength of the patients' homosexual urges and behavior following the three treatments, as it was this type of data that demonstrated the differences between psychotherapy and aversive therapy to be significant in the study by Birk *et al.*

b. No Specific Increase in Heterosexual Feelings. Many psychotherapists would consider 12 hours of psychotherapy insufficient to produce significant specific therapeutic effects. If this is correct, the fact that there was no trend for patients in Feldman and MacCulloch's study to show more improvement on the SOM heterosexuality scales following aversive therapies, as compared with psychotherapy, is compatible with indications in many of the studies discussed that increase in heterosexual feelings and behavior following aversive therapies is a nonspecific effect.

c. Complete Absence of Homosexual Feelings. The major finding of this and of the previous study by MacCulloch and Feldman (1967) was that following aversive therapy about half the homosexual patients reported complete absence of homosexual feelings. Other workers who treated a series of patients with aversive therapies observed this degree of response in very few patients (Bancroft, 1969; Birk *et al.*, 1971; Freund, 1960; McConaghy, 1969; McConaghy & Barr, 1973; McConaghy *et al.*, 1972). The fact that in the study by Feldman and MacCulloch this degree of response followed both classical conditioning and anticipatory avoidance indicates that it cannot be attributed to special features of the latter therapy. Also, Birk *et al.* (1971); McConaghy *et al.* (1972); and McConaghy & Barr (1973) used anticipatory avoidance, though in modified form, as one of the therapies in their studies.

F. Shock Intensity in Aversive Treatments

Tanner (1973) randomly allocated 26 homosexual men to receive aversive therapy either with a 5-mA shock level, or with a level the patient chose as the maximum he could tolerate. All but one of the patients allocated to the latter procedure chose a level less than 5 mA. The only measure of outcome Tanner gave was the subjects' mean penile circumference increases to pictures of women and decreases to pictures of men following treatment as compared with pretreatment. One justification for reliance on this measure of outcome was a tentative conclusion by McConaghy (1970b) that subjects' penile volume responses at 2 weeks following treatment may be a better measure of long-term outcome than their reported changes in sexual feelings at that time. Subsequent evidence caused McConaghy (1975) to conclude that penile volume changes following treatment are unrelated to the therapeutic response of aversive procedures. In any case, as is discussed in Section IV, B, small changes in penile dimensions can be assessed quite differently by penile volume and circumference measures.

Tanner's study is to the reviewer's knowledge the only one which has attempted to answer this important question of whether level of shock is related to therapeutic response. Therefore the lack of data concerning the patients' actual therapeutic responses is particularly unfortunate.

G. Contingent Aversive Therapy and Covert Sensitization

Callahan and Leitenberg (1973), using a single subject design, treated three homosexuals with sessions of electric shock contingent on their showing penile circumference increases to pictures of males, and with covert sensitization. Two patients reported an increase and the third no change in homosexual urges during the contingent aversive procedure. As is clear from the studies already discussed, lack of change following aversive therapy for homosexuality is not unusual, but reported increases in homosexual urges is infrequent. Of 126 patients treated with aversive procedures in three studies, three reported increase and another three possible increase in homosexual feelings following treatment (McConaghy, 1969; McConaghy & Barr, 1973; McConaghy *et al.*, 1972). It would appear either that the three patients treated by Callahan and Leitenberg were not typical of the majority of male homosexuals who requested this treatment or that aversive therapy contingent on penile circumference increases is less effective than other forms (see Section V, A, 3, *e*).

Studies employing single subject design usually investigate only a small number of subjects. If the subjects are atypical, valid findings of the study will not reappear when attempts are made to replicate it with more typical subjects. The single subject design has recently been widely used in studies evaluating behavioral treatments in homosexuality. Replications of the findings have been rare. In these studies, penile circumference rather than volume measures usually have been used as a measure of outcome. In the reviewer's opinion, there are significant problems associated with the use of single subject design and with penile circumference measures that have resulted from failure to subject theoretical considerations concerning both procedures to empirical testing.

IV. THEORY AND PRACTICE IN RESEARCH DESIGN AND ASSESSMENT OF SEXUAL AROUSAL

A. Single Subject Design

Yates (1970) argued that the term *behavior therapy* should be restricted to therapy administered to patients in a single subject design. He (Yates, 1976) recently again recommended the design to behavior therapists, relating it to Bernard's model of research. Yates approvingly pointed out that for Bernard there was no such thing as error—every observation had its explanation. Yates appeared to suggest that it is possible at present to explain every observation concerning human behavior and that it is laudable to do so. The reviewer considers this view to be destructive to the scientific study of human behavior. Certainly, post hoc explanations can be provided for any item of human behavior in terms of learning theory just as they can be provided in psychoanalytic terms. It is precisely this tolerance of post hoc explanations that weakens single subject designs as they are used in studies evaluating therapies. One typical paradigm of this design as used in practise is as follows:

It is decided on the basis of Theory 1 to subject the patient to Procedure A. If the outcome is as predicted, Theory 1 is confirmed. If the outcome is not as predicted, Theory 2 is advanced to explain the patient's failure to respond and to justify his being given Procedure B. If the outcome is as predicted, Theories 1 and 2 are confirmed. If the outcome is not as predicted, Theory 3 is advanced. . . . Eventually by chance, the patient must show, at least temporarily, one predicted response and so all the theories are confirmed.

This criticism of course does not apply to the appropriate use of the single subject design. Such appropriate use requires the experimenter to have sufficient understanding of all variables involved so that prior to the study he predicts the precise outcome. He then manipulates the variables exactly as planned and obtains the predicted outcome. He replicates the procedure in a number of subjects. He thus proves conclusively that he has complete understanding of the variables involved. The reviewer believes that at present this degree of understanding is not possible concerning the variables in behavioral treatments. For this reason he considers the single subject design unsuitable for evaluation of behavior therapies.

Yates (1976) felt that to demonstrate valid behavior control the therapist using the single subject design needed to demonstrate a reversal effect when the therapeutic contingency was removed. This is possible only for a therapeutic response that disappears following cessation of treatment. Yates' approach seems dictated by rigid adherence to a nonbiological operant learning theory model of the mode of action of behavioral therapies. With this model, continued reinforcement is required for the effects of the therapies to persist. The possibility is ignored that stimuli could modify the activity of central nervous processes in a manner that would persist for long periods of time following cessation of the stimuli. Evidence for this possibility has been advanced within some learning theory models, for example, in relation to the phenomenon of incubation (Eysenck, 1968). If the possibility is accepted, failure of a therapeutic effect to disappear when the therapeutic contingency is removed is not evidence that the effect was not produced by the contingency.

Few therapists would be very interested in a response to treatment that disappears when the treatment is ceased, yet this is the only type of response in which a reversal effect can be demonstrated. This is perhaps the reason that the choice of the single subject design is associated with lack of emphasis on therapeutic outcome: "the validity of the (single subject) approach is established, not in terms of whether or not the client 'gets better,' but rather in terms of whether the behavior under study changes systematically in accordance with predictions . . ." (Yates, 1976).

The major consideration is not which theoretical argument seems most plausible concerning the value of single subject or group designs in the evaluation of therapy, but which design in practice leads to the correct evaluation of procedures, so that other workers obtain comparable results utilizing them. The reviewer had considered it was indisputable that group designs have produced much more information of value to therapists using behavioral techniques and was astonished that Yates (1976) stated the opposite view. The reader must reach his own conclusion concerning this question.

B. Penile Volume and Circumference Measures of Sexual Arousal

In assessing patients' sexual orientation and changes in sexual responsiveness with treatment, both penile volume and penile circumference responses to pictures of males and females have been employed. Validation has so far been reported only for penile volume changes as a measure of *individual* subjects' sexual orientation.

1. PENILE VOLUME MEASURES

Freund (1963) used the method he pioneered to investigate the responses of 65 relatively exclusive heterosexuals and 58 relatively exclusive homosexuals. All heterosexuals and 48 homosexuals were correctly classified. Some subjects were asked to fantasize in a way that would cause them to produce sexual arousal when pictures of the nonpreferred sex were shown and to diminish arousal when pictures of the preferred sex were shown. Five of 44 heterosexuals and 6 of 24 homosexuals were able to produce records which would have misclassified them.

2. PENILE CIRCUMFERENCE MEASURES

Bancroft, Jones, and Pullman (1966) described a strain-gauge transducer that measured change in penile circumference. They appeared to assume, as did others (Zuckerman, 1971), that the device measured penile erectile responses in the same manner as Freund's apparatus. Freund (1963) measured penile volume changes occurring during a period of less than 20 sec while the subjects viewed pictures of men and women. That such small short-term penile dimensional changes would be measured meaningfully by a circumference strain-gauge required empirical confirmation. However, the strain-gauge transducer should provide a valid indication of the presence of complete penile erection.

3. COMPARISON OF VOLUME AND CIRCUMFERENCE MEASURES

Freund, Langevin, and Barlow (1974a) compared a volumetric and penile circumference measure of penile change in 14 of 48 subjects and found the volumetric measure much more sensitive.

McConaghy (1974a) used the two measures to assess penile changes of subjects who watched 10-sec segments of moving pictures of men and women. He reported that some subjects showed circumference and volume changes that were reasonably similar; others showed circumference responses that had latencies several seconds longer than the equivalent volume responses; and still others showed responses that were mirror images, the volumetric responses being more consistent with the subjects' stated sexual orientation. To determine the significance of the responses that were mirror images, subjects who showed such responses to the 10-sec film segments were shown a series of erotic slides with the aim of causing them to have an erection. One response is shown in Fig 1. While the volume measure, as seen from Fig. 1, shows a slight increase within a few seconds of the onset of the first slide, the circumference measure shows a decrease until almost 2 min later. This suggests that sexual arousal is being accompanied by penile volume increase but initial circumference decrease. McConaghy (1974a) pointed out that this type of response could be explained if sexual arousal caused the penis to increase in length at a rate faster than its blood supply increased. This would result in the penis showing a volume increase but a concomitant decrease in circumference.

Bancroft (1974) reported that reduction in penile circumference frequently followed the presentation of an erotic stimulus and increase in circumference followed its cessation. He suggested explanations for these paradoxical changes, believing them to validly indicate the direction of the associated penile erectile changes. McConaghy's findings suggest the paradoxical responses in penile circumference noted by Bancroft are in the opposite direction to the actual erectile changes, which are measured correctly by penile volume measures.

If this paradoxical relationship between penile circumference and volume measures occurred in some subjects in Freund *et al.*'s study (1974a), Freund would not have reported it. He stated he rejected the responses of subjects in whom both measures did not indicate volume increase when the subjects reported they felt penile tumescence.

4. VALIDATION OF PENILE CIRCUMFERENCE MEASURES

Bancroft (1971) reported a study validating penile circumference changes as a measure of sexual interest. Thirty homosexuals were shown 5 pictures of men and 5 of women, each for 2 min, and were

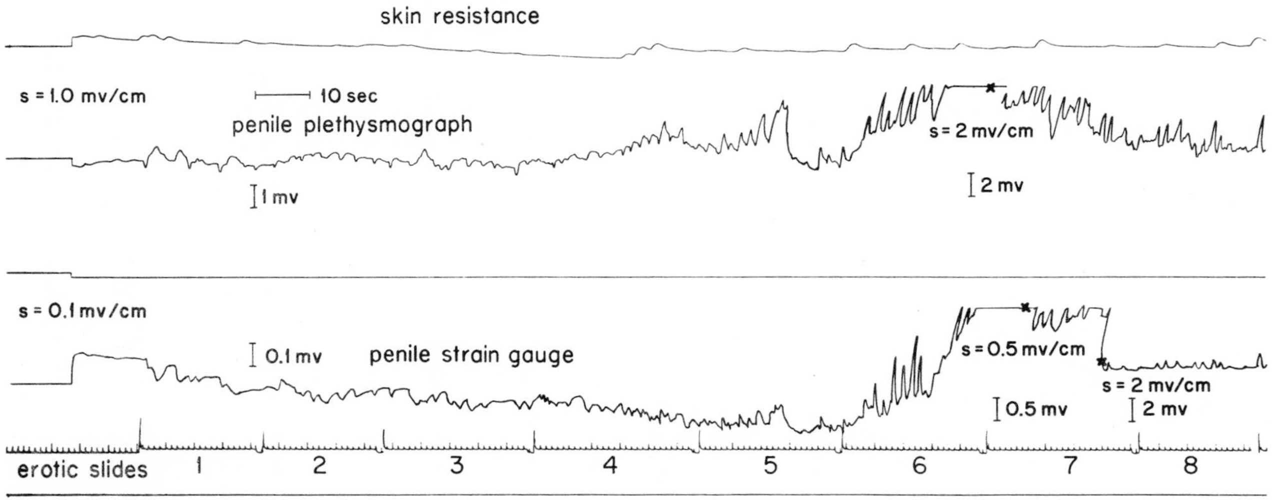

Fig. 1. Penile changes culminating in erection as determined by a plethysmograph measuring volume changes and a strain-gauge transducer measuring circumference changes.

asked to produce an erotic fantasy in association with each picture. Bancroft did not report the responses of individual subjects, but the mean penile response of the group was significantly greater to the pictures of men than to those of women. In only 14 of the 30 homosexuals was there a significant correlation between erectile response and the individual's subjective rating of their sexual interest in the series of slides. Subjects who failed to show a significant correlation between the two variables almost all showed a mean increase in penile diameter of less than .4 mm, indicating that diameter increases in this range have little validity as measures of subjects' sexual interest. Penile circumference measures would seem unsuitable to assess the response to treatment of subjects when a substantial proprotion do not show responses large enough to be validly assessed.

Mavissakalian, Blanchard, Abel, and Barlow (1975) reported mean penile circumference responses of six homosexual and six heterosexual males to 2-min black and white video moving pictures. Responses to pictures of single nude females displaying sexually provocative behavior did not distinguish the two groups of subjects at a statistically significant level. This finding suggests that penile circumference measures to such pictures are insufficiently sensitive to provide a valid measure of change in subjects' heterosexual and homosexual arousal with treatment. Penile circumference responses to such pictures have been used as the major objective index of change in studies evaluating techniques for increasing heterosexual arousal, as discussed in Section V.

5. DURATION OF MEASURED PENILE RESPONSES

Freund (1963) and McConaghy (1967) reported that volumetric measures of subjects' penile responses to less than 20-sec exposure to erotic stimuli meaningfully discriminated subjects' erotic preferences. Bancroft (1974), using a circumference measure, recommended that penile responses to 2-min exposure to the erotic stimuli be used. He reported mean *latencies* of penile circumference increases to slides and films to be in the range of 20 sec, with a standard deviation of 20 sec. Meaningful penile circumference responses would therefore not occur within the times used by Freund and McConaghy to obtain meaningful volume responses.

Laws and Rubin (1969), using a penile circumference measure, were able to record erections in four of seven subjects to erotic movie films of 10- −12-min duration. The four subjects, when instructed to attempt to prevent erection, were able to reduce the average degree of erection to a mean of 14% of the maximum, from a mean of 76% of the maximum without this instruction. They reported they did so by carrying out mental activity requiring concentration. They were able to produce partial erections with a mean of 13% of the maximum when instructed to do so in the absence of the erotic film. They did so by fantasizing erotic stimuli. The shortest latency of any increase in penile circumference under these conditions was slightly less than 1 min. It would seem likely that penile responses recorded within 20 sec as opposed to 2 or more minutes would be less subject to voluntary control by mental activity, as such activity would presumably take some seconds to be effectively established. Such an assertion requires experimental investigation.

6. CRITICISM OF VOLUMETRIC PENILE MEASURES

Despite the much stronger empirical support for penile volume changes than for circumference changes as valid measures of sexual interest, theoretically based objections have been directed only to the use of volume measures. The devices used to measure penile volume have been frequently criticized as cumbersome (Bancroft *et al.*, 1966; Barlow, in press). Certainly these devices are more bulky than strain-gauge transducers but should pose no problem in laboratory use. It might provoke comment if they were used to monitor penile responses in social situations. Volume measuring devices can be easily positioned by the patient himself, contrary to Barlow's (in press) belief. Abel and Blanchard (1976) pointed out the lack of functional value to the patient of penile increases less than 20% of full erection, the increases which have so far been the ones studied with volumetric devices. These authors considered the measurements of penile increases of 75% or more of full erection, usually made with circumference devices, would be likely to be clinically useful. This view has not yet been empirically supported.

Another criticism made is that workers using penile volume measures failed to calibrate them in terms of absolute volume change or as percentages of full erection and used rank-order rather than parametric statistics in data analysis (Abel & Blanchard, 1976; Bancroft, 1974; Zuckerman, 1971). Bancroft considered there was no satisfactory procedure for testing the significance of differences in U-scores derived from subjects' penile volume responses, used as a measure of sexual orientation by McConaghy. Bancroft does not state his theoretical reasons for this belief. In practice, differences in

U-scores analyzed by nonparametric procedures have demonstrated meaningful differences in subjects' levels of sexual arousal. Apart from the significant discrimination of heterosexual and homosexual subjects by U-scores, referred to in Section III, A, 1, Barr (1973) was able to demonstrate significant differences between the U-scores of homosexuals and transexuals. Another significant discrimination established by U-scores is that between homosexual subjects with varying degree of heterosexual behavior, discussed in Section V, B, 4.

It is possible that absolute measures of penile changes will prove more valuable than relative measures. If so, volumetric measures can be calibrated absolutely. From the data available at present, it would appear that relative measures are adequate to compare degrees of arousal produced in subjects by different erotic stimuli. Perhaps attempting to develop absolute measures of penile change will prove as meaningful as attempting to determine the exact length of an elastic telescope.

V. NONAVERSIVE TECHNIQUES IN HOMOSEXUALITY

A. Techniques to Reduce Anxiety

1. ASSERTIVE TRAINING

Stevenson and Wolpe (1960) reported the successful long-term response of two homosexual patients to encouragement of assertive behavior. Following treatment, one married and ceased homosexual behavior except for a period 2 years later when his wife was ill. The other after some months commenced heterosexual and ceased homosexual relations, and eventually married. In the first, reduction of anxiety and shame concerning homosexual behavior was noted to occur. The second became antagonistic to men, presumably only homosexual men.

2. SYSTEMATIC DESENSITIZATION

Kraft (1967) treated a 32-year-old man who had extensive homosexual relations since childhood. At 23 he married but had difficulty maintaining an erection in the heterosexual relationship. He was treated with systematic desensitization by Wolpe's (1958) method, except that relaxation was induced by methohexital sodium. For the first six treatment sessions the patient was desensitized to heterosexual intercourse. He became attached to the therapist. Following an episode of mutual exposure to a male patient which occurred during treatment and was strongly discouraged by the therapist, the patient had no further interest in homosexual activities. Nine months following treatment he was enjoying heterosexual intercourse. Other reports of reorientation of homosexual patients with systematic desensitization have been published (Huff, 1970; LoPiccolo, 1971).

3. COMPARISON OF SYSTEMATIC DESENSITIZATION AND CONTINGENT AVERSIVE ELECTRIC SHOCK

Bancroft (1971) compared systematic desensitization and aversive therapy in the treatment of homosexuality.

a. Subject Selection: Randomization or Matching. Bancroft (1974) criticized the studies of McConaghy (1969, 1970) and Birk *et al.* (1971) that evaluated aversive treatments in homosexuality because the patients in the studies were randomly allocated to different treatment procedures. Methodologists frequently advocate matching subjects in groups given different treatments in order to increase the probability that treatment effects will be statistically significant. In practice, matching of human subjects in treatment studies has not produced any more useful findings than random allocation because known measurable variables rarely affect a sufficient proportion of the treatment outcome to make matching on the variables of significance.

The findings of a single study may always be due to chance. Several replicatory studies must be carried out before the findings can be accepted. If in all the studies patients are randomly allocated to the two procedures to be evaluated, the differences between the patients receiving the two procedures in any one study will be determined by chance. Hence it is highly unlikely similar differences will occur between the patients receiving the two procedures in another study. It is often not realized even by methodologists (Frank, 1959) that *the characteristics of groups formed by randomization are not equivalent or equal.* They differ, but the ways in which they differ are *determined by chance.* These differences in the groups are allowed for in the statistical convention of significance by which the possibility that chance could have produced the outcome is taken into account.

It is methodologically unacceptable when groups of subjects are formed by randomization for differences between the groups to be sought and, if found, attributed significance in determining the outcome. Feldman and MacCulloch (1971), in the study discussed in Section III, randomly allocated subjects to three treatments, but reported the responses of the homosexuals with previous heterosexual experience separately from those without such experience. If the authors considered this variable of sufficient importance to affect the outcome, they should have matched the groups with this variable in mind. Alternatively, they should have regarded their study as a pilot and should have repeated it matching the groups on this variable. Once randomization is acceptable as the method of dealing with differences between subjects it must be adhered to when the outcome is statistically assessed.

In Bancroft's (1971, 1974) study, 18 homosexual patients were matched in pairs on variables of age, Eysenck Personality Inventory Score, and degree of previous heterosexual experience, to form two groups of nine subjects. Twelve additional patients were randomly allocated, six to each group, to make a total of 15 in each. Four of the 15 dropped out of the group allocated to receive systematic desensitization and three out of that allocated to receive the aversive procedure. The response to treatment of those who dropped out was not included in the comparison reported. Having decided it was of importance that the patients be matched, the methodologically appropriate procedure would be to discard the responses of the patients matched with those who dropped out. This was not done. Such a procedure would have made the patient numbers very small. This illustrates one of the difficultiees with matching small numbers of subjects. In addition to this attempt at matching, Bancroft demonstrated that the two groups of 15 subjects were comparable on several variables. Though such a comparison is methodologically pointless, if done at all, it should be based on a comparison of the groups of 11 and 12 subjects on whom the outcome was reported, not on the two groups of 15 who entered the study.

b. Details of Treatment. The contingent aversive procedure was based on that previously used by Bancroft (1969) and described in Section II, G. The patients received unpleasant levels of electric shock to the arm when they showed penile diameter increases of about .3 mm to pictures of men or to homosexual fantasies. The desensitization procedure was based on that introduced by Wolpe (1958). The aim was to reduce the patients' postulated fear of heterosexual approach behavior culminating in intercourse. Some patients must have found the treatment aim inappropriate as nine of the 15 allocated to desensitization had attempted heterosexual genital contact prior to treatment and five had achieved it without anxiety, revulsion, or impotence.

c. Response to Treatments. The outcome Bancroft reported was the change in itemized rating-scale measures of each subject's sexual behavior from that over the period 2 years to 2 months before treatment to that at 6 months following treatment. On the rating scales, each patient received a total score for homosexuality and a total score for heterosexuality, determined by adding points for various activities. On the heterosexual behavior scale, these activities included noticing women as sexually interesting, having dates, kissing, and having sexual relations with women; and on the homosexual scale the homosexual equivalent of these activities. Significant reduction in mean homosexual ratings followed treatment in both groups, but there was virtually no difference between the response of the group treated with the aversive procedure and that treated with desensitization. A nonsignificant increase in heterosexual score occurred in both groups.

Bancroft reported that patients showed mean penile diameter increases of .5 mm to pictures of women following desensitization, and of 1 mm following the aversive procedure. These changes were both statistically significant. Penile diameter decreases of .28 mm to pictures of men followed desensitization, and decreases of 1.45 mm followed the aversive procedure. Only the change following the aversive procedure was statistically significant.

Bancroft attached considerable significance to a finding that at the end of each aversive treatment session, patients showed significantly greater penile diameter increase to pictures of women than they had at the beginning of that session. Such a result did not occur at the end of desensitization sessions. Patients who showed this increase were significantly more likely to be classified as showing improvement on clinical assessment. Bancroft concluded that the facilitatory effect on heterosexual erections in the aversion group appeared to be related in some way to clinical outcome. However, the facilitatory effect may have been a transient response to the series of shocks, since it always disappeared by the next session of treatment. In any case, it was an unpredicted finding and requires replication before it is given attention.

d. Does Desensitization Have a Specific Therapeutic Effect in Homosexuality? Bancroft (1974) considered that desensitization specifically reduced fear of heterosexual behavior in the patients treated. However, as pointed out in Section I, A, 1, there is no consistent evidence that desensitization has a specific effect on patients with circumscribed phobias. Marks and Gelder (1965) reported an effect that largely disappeared within a year and which may have been a Type I error due to chance. Gelder *et al.* (1973) subsequently failed to demonstrate any specific effect of desensitization in patients with circumscribed phobias.

The evidence that desensitization has a specific effect on circumscribed phobias in nonpatients is also not as convincing as is widely accepted (Lick, 1975). Rachman (1973), in reviewing studies evaluating the effects of psychological treatment, selected as the model study of desensitization in the treatment of phobias that by Lang, Lazovik, and Reynolds (1965), in which students having a fear of snakes were treated. Rachman concluded that the study demonstrated a clear-cut specific effect of desensitization as compared with a pseudotherapy. It did not. On a test of students' ability to approach snakes, desensitization produced a mean improvement of .18 and the pseudotherapy .14, an insignificant difference. The authors of the study did not report this result, but combined it with the result of a previous study by Lang and Lazovik (1963) in which desensitization was compared with no treatment. They thus obtained the significant difference they reported of a mean improvement of .27 in the combined desensitization groups and −.23 in the combined no-treatment and pseudotherapy groups. Combining the results of two studies in this way is methodologically unacceptable.

If desensitization has no specific effect on the treatment of circumscribed phobias in patients, it would seem unlikely to have a specific effect on anxiety about heterosexual behavior in homosexuals. Certainly, the treatment appears to have no specific effect on anxiety about heterosexual behavior in heterosexuals. Desensitization produced no greater improvement than did routine therapy in impotent males (Kockott, Dittmar, & Nusselt, 1975).

It is possible that desensitization produces specific improvement in homosexuality by a mechanism other than that of reducing anxiety about heterosexuality. This needs demonstration by a controlled comparison of desensitization and a nonspecific treatment of homosexuality. Otherwise, Bancroft's conclusion that desensitization and an aversive procedure produced comparable results in homosexuality, if correct, throws strong doubt on the proposition that aversive therapy has a specific effect on homosexuality. The study by Birk *et al.* (1971) and rather less convincingly that of Feldman and MacCulloch (1971) indicate that aversive therapy does have a specific effect. Bancroft's conclusion therefore warrants careful scrutiny.

e. Criticisms of Bancroft's Study. (1) Technique. Electric shocks were given to the patients contingent on their showing penile diameter increases of .3 mm to homosexual stimuli. Further shocks were given if penile diameter reduction did not result. Bancroft (1974) pointed out that, in homosexuals, penile diameter increase of up to 1 mm can follow *cessation* of a homosexual stimulus and penile diameter decrease of more than 1 mm can follow the *onset* of such a stimulus. Data provided by McConaghy and discussed in Section IV, B, 3 indicate that these changes are mirror images of the true changes in penile erectile responses occurring at these times. If this is so, it would mean that with Bancroft's technique, the patient's penile diameter increases to homosexual stimuli that are being punished are at times accompanying penile detumescence. This may have made the treatment less effective. Bancroft (1971) in a separate study reported that penile diameter increases less than .4 mm had little validity as measures of subjects' sexual interest.

(2) Measures of outcome. Evidence already reviewed suggests that aversive therapies in homosexuality have no specific effect on heterosexual feelings or behavior, but reduce the intensity of homosexual drive in about half the patients treated, and lead to cessation of homosexual behavior in about a quarter of the patients. If in Bancroft's study the aversive but not the desensitization procedure produced this degree of change, would the measures of outcome used have detected this change? Bancroft assessed change in homosexual behavior by the alteration in total scores for homosexual behavior measured by an itemized rating scale for the period 2 years to 2 months prior to treatment and at 6 months following treatment. Assessing the patients' behavior on retrospective recollections seems likely to introduce error. It requires validation. Bancroft said that normally active homosexual males would obtain scores of about 25 on the scale he used. At 2 months prior to treatment the patients he treated obtained a mean score of about 13 on the scale. The sensitivity of the scale to change with treatment was therefore limited. Bancroft reported a mean reduction in homosexual rating of 9.4 with both desensitization and the aversive procedure. However, for an unexplained reason these figures were based on patient numbers of 14 and 15, respectively, rather than on the 11 and 12 who completed treatment. Bancroft also supplied a graph of the change in rating scale measures. The graph appears to show a slightly superior response with the aversive procedure. This degree of response could be meaningful. As discussed previously (Sections I, A, 3, III, D, 3, and

III, E, 3), rating scales have proved insensitive to changes produced by treatments, so that a minor difference on a rating scale can signify a meaningful difference in behavior.

f. Conclusion. The issue of whether aversive and anxiety-reducing techniques have equal effect in reducing homosexual feelings and behavior is of obvious theoretical and practical importance. In the reviewer's opinion, Bancroft's study leaves the issue unresolved. Further studies are clearly indicated. The aversive procedures investigated should be among those demonstrated to be as effective as any in general use, and measures of outcome should include one sensitive to the therapeutic change that has generally been found with aversive therapy, namely, reduction in intensity of awareness of homosexual feeling and in frequency of homosexual behavior.

B. Techniques Aimed at Increasing Heterosexual Arousal

In view of the lack of evidence that aversive procedures used in homosexuality directly increase heterosexual arousal, interest has developed in recent years in techniques that might have this effect.

1. ORGASMIC RECONDITIONING

Thorpe *et al.* (1963) introduced the technique which Marquis (1970) later termed orgasmic reconditioning. Details were given in Section II, A, 3. The patient immediately prior to reaching orgasm by masturbation was shown a picture of an attractive female. Thorpe *et al.* (1964) subsequently commenced the treatment of a homosexual patient by instructing him to masturbate as often as possible using heterosexual fantasies only. Initially he took a long time to reach orgasm, but later the time decreased and he reported satisfying fantasy. He was then treated with aversion-relief therapy. The patient experienced heterosexual interest for the first time in his life during and following treatment.

Bancroft (1974) reported that he used orgasmic reconditioning as an adjunct to aversive therapy. Many of his patients found it difficult to switch from deviant heterosexual fantasies once masturbation was under way. He advised them to commence with heterosexual fantasies and fight off the intrusion of deviant fantasies. Other workers (Lopiccolo, Steward, & Watkins, 1972; Marquis, 1970) have reported good results in increasing heterosexual arousal in male homosexuals by techniques which included advising them to use homosexual fantasies to attain erection and approach orgasm with masturbation, but to switch to heterosexual fantasies at the moment of orgasm. The patient treated by Lopiccolo *et al.* had difficulty fantasizing heterosexual stimuli and was told to use Polaroid pictures of his female sexual partner to aid these fantasies.

Conrad and Wincze (1976) evaluated orgasmic reconditioning in the treatment of four homosexuals, using a single subject design. Following a baseline phase, each patient had 20 sessions of treatment in which he masturbated until orgasm was imminent to slides depicting homosexual activity or to homosexual fantasy. He then switched to a slide of a nude woman or to heterosexual fantasy. After a second baseline period the first three patients had a second period of orgasmic reconditioning. The fourth patient, distressed by failure to improve and continued homosexual pedophiliac behavior, received aversive therapy. Baseline periods lasted 2 to 3 weeks, and during this time measures were taken of the patients' penile circumference increases to slides of males engaged in homosexual activity and to slides of nude women. All patients were requested to keep written records of the daily frequency and nature of sexual urges and fantasies. The first three patients were able to masturbate exclusively to pictures of nude women by the 30th to 35th session of treatment. They all reported increased heterosexual interest following treatment. This was not reflected in the second subject's written record of sexual feelings. Subjects 1 and 3 reported decreased homosexual interest, as did Subject 4 following aversive therapy. Subject 4's record of homosexual urges and masturbatory fantasies indicated that prior to aversive therapy, reduction had occurred which he presumably did not experience subjectively, as he felt unimproved and unable to control homosexual urges until after aversive therapy. Only in Subject 3 were penile circumference changes to homosexual and heterosexual stimuli consistent with reported change in sexual feelings.

The authors attached importance to failure of the patients' reported improvement, penile circumference measures, and their written records of sexual feelings to change in relation to the periods of withdrawal and reintroduction of active treatment. They imply that the patients may have reported changes they did not feel and that both the orgasmic reconditioning and aversive treatments were unsuccessful. As discussed in Section IV, A, the failure of a relationship to emerge between treatment effects and the cessation and reintroduction of treatment does not indicate that real treatment effects have not occurred. It does indicate that if such effects have occurred they persisted despite withdrawal of treatment, an eventuality that would delight most therapists. The major conclusion to be drawn from this study is that if the patients did subjectively experience increased heterosexual and decreased homosexual feelings, these changes were not reflected by penile circumference changes or by records made by the patients when requested to itemize sexual impulses in a notebook.

In the reviewer's opinion, the single subject design added nothing to this study. It is equivalent to an uncontrolled report of a positive response to orgasmic reconditioning in three patients and a negative response in a fourth, who subsequently responded to aversive therapy.

2. OPERANT CONDITIONING, FEEDBACK, AND EXPOSURE TO HETEROSEXUAL STIMULI

Quinn, Harbison, and McAllister (1970) reinforced a patient's penile circumference increases to slides of women by using drinks of water after having first induced thirst in the patient. Herman and Prewett (1974) reported improvement of erectile ability in a homosexual when he was given feedback concerning the extent of his penile circumference increases.

Barlow, Agras, Abel, Blanchard, and Young (1975) provided feedback to three patients of the amount of their penile circumference increases to slides of women. The first developed 80% of full erection to the slides of women. The second showed this response only after monetary reinforcement and social praise were added to feedback. The third did not develop this degree of erectile response. All three subjects reported increase in heterosexual and decrease in homosexual arousal. Barlow *et al.* used a single subject design and reported that erectile response following the use of feedback in the first subject did not weaken on withdrawal of feedback. They concluded that feedback was not responsible for the observed gains. This conclusion must be rejected on the grounds that feedback may have produced a persistent change not depending on continued treatment. The study, like that of Conrad and Wincze (1976), is equivalent to an uncontrolled clinical trial reporting positive findings.

Herman, Barlow, and Agras (1974b) reported that four homosexual subjects showed increased penile circumference responses after they had been repeatedly exposed to a 10-min movie of a nude, seductive woman assuming various sexual poses. The study provides a classical demonstration of how the single subject design can lead experimenters into the trap of unconsciously committing Type I errors by exploiting chance fluctuations in patients' responses; such experiments show a gambler's instinct always to quit when winning.

The exposure treatment was initially administered to each subject until he showed a large penile circumference increase to slides of women. Treatment was then ceased and the control procedure introduced. If chance fluctuation had contributed to the patient's large penile circumference increase at that session of treatment, his subsequent penile responses to slides of women would be likely to diminish. When during the control period the patient showed a small penile response to slides of women, the control procedure was stopped and the active treatment reintroduced until a large penile circumference increase again occurred. The procedure not open to criticism would be to administer the active treatment, the control procedure, and the second period of active treatment each in a fixed number of sessions. As the study was carried out, chance could have contributed to the initial response to treatment and produced the apparent reduction in response occurring with a variable delay after cessation of treatment. Chance could have contributed again to the return of response that occurred with a variable delay after treatment was reinstituted.

This study must also be regarded as an uncontrolled report of positive findings.

3. ASSOCIATION OF HETEROSEXUAL AND HOMOSEXUAL STIMULI

Heterosexual and homosexual stimuli in temporal association have been presented to homosexual subjects in a variety of paradigms with the aim of increasing heterosexual arousal.

a. Fading. Barlow and Agras (1973) reported the treatment of three patients with a fading procedure. Each patient was treated in a single subject design and a control procedure expected to be ineffective was introduced between the initial and a final stage of fading treatment.

(1) Details of treatment. In the fading procedure, the slide of a male to which the patient showed a large penile response was projected for him to view. The illumination of the slide was decreased and that of a slide of a female increased, contingent on the patient attaining 75% of a full erection as measured by penile circumference changes. The procedure lasted 2 min and was repeated 6 times in a treatment session. The degree of generalization of the

patient's response was tested the morning following treatment sessions. Penile circumference changes were measured while he viewed 3 slides of men and 3 of women, each for 2 min.

The first patient showed 75% of full erection to the female slide alone by the fifth session of treatment. In the test sessions, penile circumference changes to slides of women increased from 10 to 35%. As a control procedure, fading was then reversed, and illumination of the male slide increased, contingent on the patient attaining 75% of a full erection. By the fifth session he achieved 75% of full erection to the male slide alone. Paradoxically, penile circumference changes to slides of women in the test session continued to increase to 70% of full erection. Faced with a departure from the expected result, the authors decided to continue the reversed fading procedure "to confirm the trend." In the next 3 test trials following these added control treatment sessions, erections to slides of women fell to 15%, but then rose slightly. The authors reverted to the original fading procedure. The patient's erections to slides of women in test sessions commenced to fluctuate between about 30 to 55%. However, he reported a decrease in heterosexual urges and fantasies. Through the treatment procedure his erections to slides of men in the test sessions remained at about 50% of full erection. He was treated with an aversive procedure.

The second patient also showed penile circumference increases to pictures of women in the test sessions accompanying the fading procedure. A control procedure different from that used with the first subject was then introduced. The authors commented that penile circumference increase to pictures of women continued to rise, as in the first subject, before dropping to 34%. The third subject did not show this continued rise in penile response to women when the control procedure was introduced, but showed a rise on the fourth session of the control procedure. The authors did not comment on this discrepancy. Despite the second subject showing penile circumference increase to pictures of women, he did not report any heterosexual urges or fantasies throughout the treatment. In the months following treatment, he experienced increasing heterosexual urges and decreasing homosexual urges and reported that he had commenced heterosexual intercourse. The third patient also showed increased heterosexual and decreased homosexual urges following treatment, but was given aversive therapy to further reduce homosexual urges. The authors concluded that by the use of a single subject design they had demonstrated that fading was responsible for the increase in penile circumference responses to studies of women.

(2) Criticism. The study of Barlow and Agras (1973) in the reviewer's opinion is a further example of unconscious exploitation of the freedom provided by the single subject design, as discussed in Section IV, A. A large number of observations were made on each subject. Some by chance conformed to prediction. They were considered to have supported the hypothesis. Others did not. Some were unexplained: "It is not clear why this occurred. It is interesting to note, however . . ." (p. 364). Others were accounted for by plausible post hoc hypotheses: "Since (penile responses to slides of women) diminished when fading was reversed or stopped . . . why was heterosexual arousal sustained in two subjects after the experiment was over?—most probably because the subject encountered different contingencies after fading" (p. 364). "A divergence was also noted. . . . Presumably this was due to the 'therapeutic set' . . ." (p. 365).

In view of the modifications in procedure introduced when expected penile circumference changes failed to take place during the control procedures, the reviewer is unconvinced that this study demonstrated that the penile changes were under the control of the contingency that was varied.

(3) Do conditioned penile increases indicate sexual interest in the conditioned stimulus: Fetishism. An important finding of the study was that it is possible for a subject to show, possibly by conditioning, penile circumference increases up to 80% of full erection to pictures of women and be unaware of any heterosexual urges or fantasies. Penile responses produced by conditioning to a previously nonarousing stimulus have been equated to sexual arousal produced by a fetish (Rachman & Hodgson, 1968). The parallel is not a sound one. Sexual arousal to a fetishistic object is unlikely to have been initiated by sexual conditioning as most fetishists report their interest in the fetishistic object preceded puberty by some years and was initially not associated with sexual excitement.

b. Forward-Fading. McGrady (1973) reported the treatment of a homosexual by forward-fading. This was the reverse of the treatment procedure used by Barlow and Agras (1973). McGrady showed the patient a female image which was faded into a male image over 5 min. Meanwhile, the patient's penile circumference changes were monitored. The procedure was repeated 4 times in a session and the patient received 11 sessions of treatment, usually at weekly intervals. As the treatment progressed the patient showed maximum penile erection at an earlier stage in the fading procedure, until the ninth session when maximum erection occurred at $1\frac{1}{4}$ min, the time when the male image reached the patient's threshold of visibility.

One week following completion of treatment, the patient's penile circumference changes were recorded while he viewed 3 slides of nude females for 2 min each. He showed full erection to 2 of the 3 slides. However, when shown 10 slides of males and females he reported no increased arousal to those of females and slightly more to those of males compared to his response prior to treatment.

The patient engaged in no overt heterosexual activity and had two homosexual experiences during treatment. He reported several heterosexual fantasies, most accompanying masturbation. McGrady reported that when during treatment the patient found his penis could become erect to a female figure, he experienced an attitude change and ceased to regard himself as homosexual. No follow-up data were provided.

This study supports those of Barlow and Agras (1973) and Herman *et al.* (1974b) in demonstrating that homosexual subjects can show marked penile circumference increases to pictures of women following their repeatedly viewing such pictures, with or without the pictures being temporally associated with pictures of men. It also demonstrates that penile increases occurring in these conditions may not be associated with the development of sexual attraction to the female body shape.

c. Classical Conditioning. (1) Single subject evaluation. Herman, Barlow, and Agras (1974a) reported the treatment of three homosexuals by a classical conditioning procedure. The patients were shown pictures of women for 1 min followed by pictures of men or a film with homosexual content. Abel and Blanchard (1976) commented that an "outstanding feature of this report is that each subject was treated in a manner in which control conditions were included in order to isolate the critical variables" (p. 122). The reviewer was irresistibly reminded of Mae West's classic comment "What is this, propaganda?" Only the first of the three patients responded to the classical conditioning procedure without its being repeatedly modified on a post hoc basis. The third patient failed to respond even to repeated modifications. Hence, only the first patient's responses tested the unmodified procedure and only the strongly committed could conclude that his responses demonstrated that the control conditions isolated the critical variable.

After an initial baseline phase the control conditions were administered in the second and fourth phase of the treatment sequence. The active treatment was administered in the third and fifth phase. The heterosexual orientation measure (SOM) rose from 12 to 32 in the first control phase, from 32 to 40 in the first treatment phase, remained at 40 throughout the next control phase, and fell to 28 in the second treatment phase. In other words, the pattern in the second control and treatment phase was the reverse of that which would have demonstrated that the critical variable was isolated. The measure of heterosexual urges and fantasies rose from 0 to about 9.5 between the second and third session of initial treatment, but thereafter fluctuated between about 7 and 1.5, showing no change related to the second control and treatment phase. The third measure of heterosexual arousal used, the penile circumference changed to females, appeared to begin to increase in the first control phase. It could be considered to be affected by the second control and treatment phase only on the basis of a single high response in the second treatment phase, the other 8 responses fluctuating in the same range throughout the two periods.

The lack of relationship between changes in the outcome measures and the introduction and cessation of the contingency varied seems no less in this study than in those of Conrad and Wincze (1976) and Barlow *et al.* (1975), discussed earlier in this chapter. It indicates the degree of arbitrariness allowed by single subject designs that the authors of those studies decided the contingency varied was not responsible for the outcome, while the authors of this study decided that it was. A further problem with these single subject studies is that such a wealth of data are provided concerning the response of each subject that the reader, faced with the daunting task of examining the data in detail, is likely to accept the authors' conclusion, whether it is positive or negative.

In the reviewer's opinion, all the single subject studies discussed neither establish nor refute the possibility that the contingencies varied in them were responsible for the outcome. They can be considered no more than uncontrolled reports of positive responses.

(2) Comparison of positive and aversive classical conditioning. McConaghy (1975) reported a study in which 31 homosexual patients were randomly allocated to receive positive or aversive classical conditioning. The patients were further randomly allocated to receive each procedure in a forward or backward conditioning prardigm. With forward positive conditioning, the patients were shown slides of women for 10 sec followed also for 10 sec by sexually arousing slides of men or of couples in heterosexual physical relations. With backward positive conditioning, the slides of women followed the sexually arousing slides. With the forward aversive procedure, slides of men were shown to the patient for 10 sec, and 9 sec after the onset of each slide the patient received a 2-sec un-

pleasant electric shock. With backward aversive conditioning, the onset of the 2-sec shock preceded the onset of the male slide by 1 sec. The patients' penile volume responses were recorded throughout all procedures.

a. Response to Treatments. No penile response conditioning occurred to the slides of females in the positive-conditioning procedure though unconditioned penile volume increases to the sexually arousing slides persisted throughout treatment. There was no difference in the change in sexual feelings or behavior reported by patients who received positive conditioning in the forward as compared with the backward paradigm. It was concluded that the positive-conditioning treatment had no specific effect on the subjects' sexual feelings and acted as a placebo therapy.

At 3 weeks and at 1 year following treatment, more subjects who received the aversive treatment as compared with positive conditioning reported reduction in homosexual feelings and behavior. The difference was statistically significant for reduction of homosexual feelings at 3 weeks and reduction in homosexual behavior at 1 year. There was little difference in response following the forward compared with the backward aversive procedure. At 3 weeks following the aversive and positive-conditioning treatments a similar number of subjects reported increase in heterosexual feelings and behavior, but at 1 year there was a trend for more to report an increase following the aversive procedures.

It was concluded that the aversive procedures produced specific reduction of homosexual feelings and behavior in contrast to the placebo effect produced by positive conditioning. The increase in heterosexual feelings following the aversive procedure was considered a nonspecific consequence of the decrease in homosexual feelings.

b. Are Penile Volume Changes following Treatment Nonspecific? The changes in subjects' penile volume responses to 10-sec moving pictures of nude men and women following both the aversive and positive-conditioning procedures were similar to the changes following the aversive procedures in the three comparison studies previously reported by McConaghy and discussed in Section III, A, B, C. Statistically significant decrements occurred both in penile volume increases to pictures of men and in volume decreases to pictures of women.

If these penile volume changes were a specific effect of treatment related to the reduction of homosexual feelings and behavior, they should have been greater following the aversive as compared to the positive-conditioning procedure in the present study, since the treatment response was significantly greater following the aversive procedure. As the penile changes following the aversive and positive-conditioning procedures were comparable, it was concluded they were nonspecific and unrelated to the treatment effect.

Laws and Rubin (1969) showed that some subjects could markedly reduce the extent of their penile circumference increases in response to 10- to 12-min exposures of erotic movies. Freund (1971) considered that subjects could reduce their penile volume increase to erotic films of less than 20-sec duration. If this is so, the small but statistically significant reduction in subjects' penile volume increase to pictures of men which followed the positive- and aversive-conditioning treatments in McConaghy's study could have been induced unconsciously by expectation of improvement following treatment.

c. Penile Volume Decreases to Pictures of the Nonpreferred Sex. The change in penile volume decrease to pictures of women is more difficult to interpret in view of the limited study of negative penile responses to slides of members of the nonpreferred sex. They were originally reported by McConaghy (1970a) as occurring in both heterosexual and homosexual subjects, but were more common in the former. McConaghy suggested the responses might indicate the presence of an inhibitory sexual response to members of the nonpreferred sex. Penile volume decreases also occurred when subjects viewed slides of victims of road accidents (Colette, 1970) or received electric shocks (Barr & McConaghy, 1971). It was suggested that these responses were part of a fear response.

Freund *et al.* (1974a; Freund, Langevin, Cibiri, & Zajac, 1973) reported that penile volume decreases occurred to slides of members of the nonpreferred sex only when the slides were preceded by slides of members of the preferred sex. This has not been the reviewer's experience. Figure 2 shows negative penile responses in a heterosexual subject occurring repeatedly to slides of males.

Some heterosexual and homosexual subjects show the same degree of penile volume decreases to slides of members of the nonpreferred sex as to sexually neutral material such as landscapes. In such subjects, the penile decrease would seem part of a reticular arousal or orienting response to a stimulus. Other subjects show significantly greater volume decreases to slides of members of the nonpreferred sex than to landscapes, which suggests they experience some anxiety to slides of the nonpreferred sex at least in the context of a laboratory investigation. Still other subjects show penile volume increases to the nonpreferred sex which are significantly greater than their penile decreases to landscapes. This suggests they are sexually

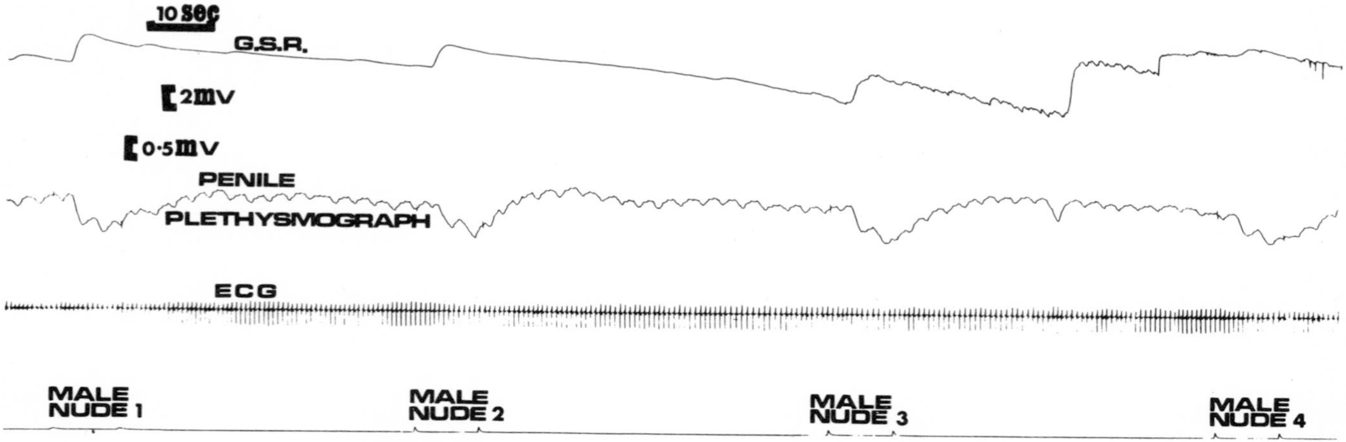

Fig. 2. Negative penile volume changes of a heterosexual subject to a series of pictures of male nudes.

aroused by the nonpreferred sex (i.e., that they have a bisexual component). Freund *et al.* (1973) did not examine the responses of individual subjects, but the mean responses of heterosexuals and homosexuals as groups. This procedure would have led them to sum negative with positive responses, and would have prevented them from observing the individual differences noted above.

Penile volume responses due to reticular arousal or anxiety would be expected to be reduced in subjects viewing the sexual assessment film for a second time. This could explain the reduction in penile volume decrease to pictures of women noted in homosexual patients following treatment in the study by McConaghy.

d. Conclusions. Reduction in homosexual feelings and behavior occurred to a significantly greater extent following aversive as compared with positive conditioning. It was concluded this was a specific response to aversive therapy. The response occurred to an equivalent extent after a forward or backward conditioning paradigm, and was not produced by conditioning. No significant difference was found in changes in penile measures of sexual orientation following aversive- as compared with positive-conditioning procedures. The penile measure remained a valid index of the subjects' sexual orientation following treatment, as it significantly differentiated the subjects from nonhomosexual subjects who had also received aversive therapy (McConaghy, 1975). It was concluded that the specific reduction in homosexual feelings and behavior following aversive treatment was not accompanied by change in the subjects' sexual orientation.

4. CAN HETEROSEXUAL STIMULI DECREASE HOMOSEXUAL ORIENTATION?

Most techniques for increasing subjects' heterosexual arousal have been based on a learning theory hypothesis, that is, causing subjects to be sexually aroused in the presence of heterosexual stimuli will result in their becoming more capable of heterosexual arousal and hence more heterosexual. If this is correct, homosexuals who have had extensive experience of heterosexual intercourse should be more heterosexual in orientation than those who lack such experience. A number of married homosexuals who have had frequent heterosexual intercourse, but with their wives only, report they experience no sexual interest in other women. The sexual orientation as measured by the film assessment procedure and the heterosexual experience of 181 subjects who requested behavioral treatment for homosexuality is reported in Table III.

TABLE III

U-Scores of Homosexual Subjects in Relation to Their Heterosexual Experience

Group	Sexual experience	Number of subjects	Mean U-score	Significance of difference between groups (Mann–Whitney U-test)
Single				
A	No heterosexual intercourse	79	28.0	A cf. B: $p = 0.05$
				A cf. C: $p = 0.18$,N.S.[a]
				A cf. D: $p = 0.03$
B	Heterosexual intercourse	58	35.0	B cf. C: $p = 0.008$
				B cf. D: $p = 0.38$,N.S.
Married				
C	Intercourse with wife only	24	19.1	C cf. D: $p = 0.02$
D	Intercourse with women additional to wife	20	41.7	
	Total	181		

[a]Not significant.

Married subjects with a history of intercourse with their wives only obtained U-scores indicative of a significantly more homosexual orientation than did single subjects with a history of heterosexual intercourse, and married men with a history of intercourse with women other than their wives. Almost all the married subjects had frequent and regular intercourse with their wives. The majority of single men who had experienced heterosexual intercourse and of married men who had experienced intercourse with women other than their wives had obtained this experience on less than 10 occasions. These findings are not compatible with the hypothesis that amount of experience of heterosexual arousal alters sexual orientation in the heterosexual direction. They are compatible with the hypothesis that sexual orientation is biologically determined and is not modified by adult sexual experience. On the basis of this hypothesis, homosexual subjects seeking heterosexual intercourse would be expected to have a more heterosexual biological orientation than those not seeking such intercourse. Some homosexual subjects with minimal heterosexual feelings would marry for companionship, social acceptance, or to father children. They would be less likely to have had intercourse with other women apart from their wives. Their sexual orientation would not differ from that of homosexual subjects who had not sought heterosexual intercourse.

If subjective awareness of sexual arousal to the female body shape is determined biologically and is not increased by heterosexual experience, behavioral techniques aimed at specifically increasing this form of heterosexual arousal will be ineffective. However, many homosexual males with a minimal heterosexual component are capable without any treatment of maintaining a sexual relationship with a woman. It is likely that homosexuals who wish to form such a relationship but do not do so are prevented by fear that they will prove impotent. The behavioral treatment which would seem most able to help them is that effective in the treatment of impotence in the heterosexual male. Comparison studies of such treatment have investigated small numbers of patients and their conclusions have been vitiated by Type II errors, but their findings suggest that a Masters and Johnson type of therapy is most effective (Ansari, 1976; Mathews, Bancroft, Whitehead, Hackmann, Julier, Bancroft, Gath, & Shaw, 1976).

VI. CONCLUSIONS

A. Efficacy of Behavioral Treatments in Homosexuality

At the beginning of this review of behavioral treatment in homosexuality it was stated that the major aim should be assessment of the efficacy of treatments. The extent to which this has been accomplished is summarized by the reviewer as follows:

1. FINDINGS ESTABLISHED BY MORE THAN ONE RESEARCH WORKER

a. Aversive therapy specifically reduces homosexual feelings and behavior, in comparison with psychotherapy (Birk *et al.*, 1971; Feldman & MacCulloch, 1971) and with positive conditioning (McConaghy, 1975).

b. Different forms of aversive therapy produce comparable responses (Feldman & MacCulloch, 1971; McConaghy, 1970b; McConaghy & Barr, 1973; McConaghy *et al.*, 1972).

c. Complete or almost complete penile erection can occur in homosexual subjects when viewing pictures of women without the subjects being aware of feelings of sexual arousal to the female body shape. (Barlow & Agras, 1973; McCrady, 1973).

2. FINDINGS ESTABLISHED BY ONE RESEARCH WORKER AND REQUIRING REPLICATION

a. Aversive therapies do not act by conditioning (McConaghy, 1975; McConaghy & Barr, 1973).

b. Subjects' sexual orientation is unaltered by aversive therapy (McConaghy, 1975).

c. Subjects with minimal heterosexual arousal to the female body shape can maintain a heterosexual relationship (McConaghy, in press).

3. UNESTABLISHED CONCLUSIONS OF BASIC THEORETICAL SIGNIFICANCE WHICH REQUIRE FURTHER INVESTIGATION

a. Sexual arousal to the body shape of the nonpreferred sex is biologically based and cannot be produced by behavioral techniques.

b. Systematic desensitization and orgasmic reconditioning produce reduction in homosexual feelings and behavior similar to that produced by aversive therapies (Bancroft, 1971; Conrad & Wincze, 1976).

B. Lack of Empirical Data

Though it appears established that aversive therapies reduce homosexual drive, it is premature to accept a mode of action for these therapies in which aversive stimuli play a specific role. If it can be demonstrated that aversive therapies produce significantly greater reduction in homosexual drive than do systematic desensitization and orgasmic reconditioning, such a mode of action would seem probable. A likely contender would be the hypothesis that aversive stimuli reduce secondary drive, leaving primary drive unaltered. The patients' sexual orientation would remain unchanged following aversive treatment, but stimuli which had attained secondary sexually arousing properties by learning would lose these properties, thus reducing the secondary or learned aspects of homosexual drive.

Alternatively, if it is established that there are no significant differences in responses to aversive therapies, systematic desensitization, and orgasmic reconditioning, a common mode of action of these therapies would seem probable. A likely contender would be the hypothesis that anxiety concerning homosexual behavior leads the patient compulsively to carry out the homosexual behavior he wants to limit but feels unable to do so. All these forms of treatment by reducing anxiety concerning homosexual behavior reduce the compulsive drive to carry out the behavior.

Further speculation concerning the mode of action of behavioral therapies in homosexuality remains an exercise in logical ingenuity, while the basis for such speculation in empirically established data is meager. This meagerness is particularly disappointing since behavioral treatments of homosexuals have been subject to investigation in numerous studies. The reviewer considers the failure of these studies to produce an accepted body of knowledge results from errors in their methodology. These errors have not been noted and corrected due to the excessive reliance placed on reaching conclusions by theoretical analysis at the expense of establishing empirical findings by replicatory studies. Man's ability to provide plausible theories to support any belief or explain any combination of data is unlimited. The aim of science is not merely to explain the nature of reality but to enable man to change and master it. The failure of thousands of years of philosophy to provide such achievements as compared with the success of a few hundred years of science should serve as an ever present reminder that theory is valueless when it is not constantly subjected to correction by empirical investigation.

While behavioral research fails to accept as its major criterion of validity the replication of experimental findings, the goal of achieving effective means to change human behavior "year by year recedes before us. It eluded us then, but that's no matter—tomorrow we will run faster, stretch out our arms further . . . and one fine morning—

So we beat on, boats against the current, borne back ceaselessly into the past."

ACKNOWLEDGMENTS

I would like to express my deep appreciation to Drs. J. Bancroft, D. H. Barlow, W. M. Freeman, and D. Kantorowitz for their kindness in supplying articles and thesis material, as yet unpublished, which proved of invaluable assistance in writing this review.

REFERENCES

Abel, G. G., & Blanchard, E. B. The measurement and generation of sexual arousal in male sexual deviates. In M. Hersen, R. M. Eisler, & P. M. Miller (Eds.), *Progress in behavior modification* (Vol. 2). New York: Academic Press, 1976. Pp. 99–136.

Ansari, I. M. A. Impotence: Prognosis (a controlled study). *British Journal of Psychiatry,* 1976, **128**, 194–198.

Ashby, W. R., & Collins, G. H. A clinical trial of imipramine (Tofranil) on depressed patients. *Journal of Mental Science,* 1961, **107**, 547–551.

Bancroft, J. Aversion therapy of homosexuality. *British Journal of Psychiatry,* 1969, **115**, 1417–1431.

Bancroft, J. Application of psychophysiological measures to the assessment and modification of sexual behaviour. *Behaviour Research and Therapy,* 1971, **9**, 119–130.

Bancroft, J. *Deviant sexual behaviour.* London & New York: Oxford University Press (Clarendon), 1974.

Bancroft, J., Jones, H. C., & Pullman, B. P. A simple transducer for measuring penile erections with comments on its use in the treatment of sexual disorders. *Behaviour Research and Therapy,* 1966, **4**, 239–241.

Barlow, D. H. Assessment of sexual behavior. In A. R. Ciminero, K. S. Calhoun, & H. E. Adams (Eds.), *Handbook of behavioral assessment.* New York: Wiley, 1977.

Barlow, D. H., & Agras, W. S. Fading to increase heterosexual responsiveness in homosexuals. *Journal of Applied Behavior Analysis,* 1973, **6**, 355–366.

Barlow, D. H., Agras, W. S., Abel, G. G., Blanchard, E. B., & Young, L. D. Biofeedback and reinforcement to increase heterosexual arousal in homosexuals. *Behaviour Research and Therapy,* 1975, **13**, 45–50.

Barr, R. F. Response to erotic stimuli of transsexual and homosexual males. *British Journal of Psychiatry,* 1973, **123**, 579–585.

Barr, R. F., & McConaghy, N. Penile volume responses to appetitive and aversive stimuli in relation to sexual orientation and conditioning performance. *British Journal of Psychiatry,* 1971, **119**, 377–383.

Barr, R. F., & McConaghy, N. A general factor of conditionability: A study of galvanic skin response and penile responses. *Behaviour Research and Therapy,* 1972, **10**, 215–227.

Beech, H. R. The symptomatic treatment of writer's cramp. In H. J. Eysenck (Ed.), *Behaviour therapy and neuroses.* Oxford: Pergamon, 1960. Pp. 349–372.

Birk, L., Huddleston, W., Miller, E., & Cohler, B. Avoidance conditioning for homosexuality. *Archives of General Psychiatry,* 1971, **25**, 314–323.

Blakemore, C. B., Thorpe, J. G., Barker, J. C., Conway, C. G., & Lavin, N. I. The application of faradic aversion conditioning in a case of transvestism. *Behaviour Research and Therapy,* 1963, **1**, 29–34.

Callahan, E. J., & Leitenberg, H. Aversion therapy for sexual deviation: Contingent shock and covert sensitization. *Journal of Abnormal Psychology,* 1973, **81**, 60–73.

Cautela, J. R. Treatment of compulsive behavior by covert sensitization. *Psychological Record,* 1966, **16**, 33–41.

Cautela, J. R. Covert sensitization. *Psychological Reports,* 1967, **20**, 459–468.

Clark, C. G., & Downie, C. C. A method for the rapid determination of the number of patients to include in a controlled clinical trial. *Lancet,* 1966, **11**, 1357–1358.

Colette, D. C. Negative penile volume responses. Unpublished master's thesis, School of Psychology, University of New South Wales, 1971.

Conrad, S. R., & Wincze, J. P. Orgasmic reconditioning: A controlled study of its effects upon the sexual arousal and behavior of adult male homosexuals. *Behavior Therapy,* 1976, **7,** 155–166.

Cooper, J. E. A study of behaviour therapy in thirty psychiatric patients *Lancet,* 1963, **1,** 411–415.

Cooper, J. E., Gelder, M. G., & Marks, I. M. Results in behaviour therapy in 77 psychiatric patients. *British Medical Journal,* 1965, **1,** 1222–1225.

Eysenck, H. J. Introduction. Summary and conclusions. In H. J. Eysenck (Ed.), *Behaviour therapy and the neuroses.* Oxford: Pergamon, 1960. Pp. 277; 461–467.

Eysenck, H. J. A theory of the incubation of anxiety/fear responses. *Behaviour Research and Therapy,* 1968, **6,** 309–321.

Feldman, M. P., & MacCulloch, M. J. A systematic approach to the treatment of homosexuality by conditioned aversion: preliminary report. *American Journal of Psychiatry,* 1964, **121,** 167–171.

Feldman, M. P., & MacCulloch, M. J. The application of anticipatory avoidance learning to the treatment of homosexuality: I. Theory, technique and preliminary results. *Behaviour Research and Therapy,* 1965, **2,** 165–183.

Feldman, M. P., & MacCulloch, M. J. *Homosexual behaviour: Therapy and assessment.* Oxford: Pergamon, 1971.

Frank, J. D. Problems of control in psychotherapy as examplified by the psychotherapy research project in the Phipps Psychiatric Clinic. *Research in Psychotherapy,* 1959, **11,** 10–26.

Freund, K. Some problems in the treatment of homosexuality. In H. J. Eysenck (Ed.), *Behavior therapy and the neuroses.* Oxford: Pergamon, 1960. Pp. 312–326.

Freund, K. A laboratory method of diagnosing predominance of homo- or hetero-erotic interest in the male. *Behaviour Research and Therapy,* 1963, **1,** 85–93.

Freund, K. A note on the use of the phallometric method of measuring mild sexual arousal in the male. *Behavior Therapy,* 1971, **2,** 223–228.

Freund, K., Langevin, R., & Barlow, D. Comparison of two penile measures of erotic arousal. *Behaviour Research and Therapy,* 1974, **12,** 355–359. (a)

Freund, K., Langevin, R., Cibiri, S., & Zajac, Y. Heterosexual aversion in homosexual males. *British Journal of Psychiatry,* 1973, **122,** 163–169.

Freund, K., Langevin, R., & Zajac, Y. Heterosexual arousal in homosexual males: A second experiment. *British Journal of Psychiatry,* 1974, **125,** 177–180. (b)

Gelder, M. G., Bancroft, J. H. J., Gath, D. H., Johnston, D. W., Mathews, A. M., & Shaw, P. M. Specific and non-specific factors in behavior therapy. *British Journal of Psychiatry,* 1973, **123,** 445–462.

Gelder, M. G., & Marks, I. M. Severe agoraphobia: A controlled prospective trial of behaviour therapy. *British Journal of Psychiatry,* 1966, **112,** 309–319.

Gelder, M. G., Marks, I. M., Wolff, H. H., & Clarke, M. Desensitization and psychotherapy in the treatment of phobic states: A controlled inquiry. *British Journal of Psychiatry,* 1967, **113,** 53–73.

Gold, S., & Neufeld, I. L. A learning approach to the treatment of homosexuality. *Behaviour Research and Therapy,* 1965, **2,** 201–204.

Hallam, R. S., & Rachman, S. Current status of aversion therapy. In M. Hersen, R. M. Eisler, & P. M. Miller (Eds.), *Progress in behavior modification* (Vol. 2). New York: Academic Press, 1976. Pp. 179–222.

Herman, S. H., Barlow, D. H., & Agras, W. S. An experimental analysis of classical conditioning as a method of increasing heterosexual arousal in homosexuals. *Behavior Therapy,* 1974, **5,** 33–47. (a)

Herman, S. H., Barlow, D. H., & Agaras, W. S. An experimental analysis of exposure to "elicit" heterosexual stimuli as an effective variable in changing arousal patterns in homosexuals. *Behaviour Research and Therapy*, 1974, **12**, 315–345. (b)

Herman, S. H., & Prewett, M. An experimental analysis of feedback to increase sexual arousal in a case of homo- and heterosexual impotence: A preliminary report. *Journal of Behavior Therapy and Experimental Psychiatry*, 1974, **5**, 271–274.

Huff, F. W. The desensitization of a homosexual. *Behaviour Research and Therapy*, 1970, **8**, 99–102.

Kockott, G., Dittmar, F., & Nusselt, L. Systematic desensitization of erectile impotence: A controlled study. *Archives of Sexual Behavior*, 1975, **4**, 493–500.

Kraft, T. A case of homosexuality treated by systematic desensitization. *American Journal of Psychotherapy*, 1967, **21**, 815–821.

Lang, P. J., & Lazovik, A. D. Experimental desensitization of a phobia. *Journal of Abnormal and Social Psychology*, 1963, **66**, 519–525.

Lang, P. J., Lazovik, A. D., & Reynolds, D. J. Desensitization, suggestibility and pseudotherapy. *Journal of Abnormal Psychology*, 1965, **70**, 395–402.

Lavin, N. I., Thorpe, J. G., Barker, J. C., Blakemore, C. B., & Conway, C. G. Behavior therapy in a case of transvestism. *Journal of Nervous and Mental Disease*, 1961, **133**, 346–352.

Laws, D. R., & Rubin, H. H. Instructional control of an autonomic sexual response. *Journal of Applied Behavior Analysis*, 1969, **2**, 93–99.

Lick, J. Expectancy, false galvanic skin response feedback, and systematic desensitization in the modification of phobic behavior. *Journal of Consulting and Clinical Psychology*, 1975, **43**, 557–567.

Lipman, R. S., Cole, J. O., Park, L. C., & Rickels, K. Sensitivity of symptom and non-symptom focused criteria of outpatient drug efficacy. *American Journal of Psychiatry*, 1965, **112**, 24–27.

LoPiccolo, J. Case study: Systematic desensitization of homosexuality. *Behavior Therapy*, 1971, **2**, 394–399.

LoPiccolo, J., Steward, R., & Watkins, B. Treatment of erectile failure and ejaculatory incompetence of homosexual etiology. *Journal of Behavior Therapy and Experimental Psychiatry*, 1972, **3**, 233–236.

Lovibond, S. H. Aversive control of behavior. *Behavior Therapy*, 1970, **1**, 80–91.

Luborsky, L., Barton, S., & Luborsky, L. Comparative studies of psychotherapies: Is it true that "everyone has won and all must have prizes"? *Archives of General Psychiatry*, 1975, **32**, 995–1008.

MacCulloch, M. J., & Feldman, M. P. Aversion therapy in the management of 43 homosexuals. *British Medical Journal*, 1967, **2**, 594–597.

MacCulloch, M. J., Feldman, M. P., & Pinshoff, J. M. The application of anticipatory avoidance learning to the treatment of homosexuality II. Avoidance response latencies and pulse rate changes. *Behaviour Research and Therapy*, 1965, **3**, 321–43.

Mackintosh, N. J. *The psychology of animal learning*. New York: Academic Press, 1974.

Marks, I. M., & Gelder, M. G. A controlled retrospective study of behaviour therapy in phobic patients. *British Journal of Psychiatry*, 1965, **111**, 561–573.

Marks, I. M., Gelder, M. G., & Edwards, G. Hypnosis and desensitization for phobias: A controlled prospective trial. *British Journal of Psychiatry*, 1968, **114**, 1263–1274.

Marquis, J. N. Orgasmic reconditioning: changing sexual object choice through controlling masturbation fantasies. *Journal of Behavior Therapy and Experimental Psychiatry*, 1970, **1**, 263–271.

Mathews, A., Bancroft, J., Whitehead, A., Hackmann, A., Julier, D., Bancroft, J., Gath, D.,

& Shaw, S. The behavioural treatment of sexual inadequacy: A controlled study. *Behaviour Research and Therapy,* 1976, **14,** 427–436.

Mavissakalian, M., Blanchard, E. B., Abel, G. G., & Barlow, D. H. Responses to complex erotic stimuli in homosexual and heterosexual males. *British Journal of Psychiatry,* 1975, **126,** 252–257.

Max, L. W. Breaking up a homosexual fixation by the conditioned reaction technique: A case study. *Psychological Bulletin,* 1935, **32,** 734.

McConaghy, N. Penile volume change to moving pictures of male and female nudes in heterosexual and homosexual males. *Behaviour Research and Therapy,* 1967, **5,** 43–48.

McConaghy, N. Subjective and penile plethysmograph responses following aversion-relief and apomorphine therapy for homosexual impulses. *British Journal of Psychiatry,* 1969, **145,** 723–730.

McConaghy, N. Penile response conditioning and its relationship to aversion therapy in homosexuals. *Behavior Therapy,* 1970, **1,** 213–221. (a)

McConaghy, N. Subjective and penile plethysmograph responses to aversion therapy for homosexuality: A follow-up study. *British Journal of Psychiatry,* 1970, **117,** 555–560. (b)

McConaghy, N. Measurements of change in penile dimensions. *Archives of Sexual Behavior,* 1974, **3,** 381–388. (a)

McConaghy, N. Penile volume responses to moving and still pictures of male and female nudes. *Archives of Sexual Behavior,* 1974, **3,** 565–570. (b)

McConaghy, N. Aversive and positive conditioning treatments of homosexuality. *Behaviour Research and Therapy,* 1975, **13,** 309–319.

McConaghy, N. Heterosexual experience, marital status and sexual orientation of homosexuals: Evidence of a biological basis for bisexuality. in press.

McConaghy, N., & Barr, R. F. Classical, avoidance and backward conditioning treatments of homosexuality. *British Journal of Psychiatry,* 1973, **122,** 151–162.

McConaghy, N., Proctor, D., & Barr, R. Subjective and penile plethysmography responses to aversion therapy for homosexuality: A partial replication. *Archives of Sexual Behaviour,* 1972, **2,** 65–78.

McCrady, R. E. A forward-fading technique for increasing heterosexual responsiveness in male homosexuals. *Journal of Behavior Therapy and Experimental Psychiatry,* 1973, **4,** 257–261.

Money, J. Strategy, ethics, behavior modification, and homosexuality. *Archives of Sexual Behavior,* 1972, **2,** 79–81.

Paredes, A., Baumgold, J., Hugh, L. A., & Ragland, R. Clinical judgment in the assessment of psychopharmacological effects. *Journal of Nervous and Mental Disease,* 1969, **142,** 153–160.

Pavlov, I. P. *Conditioned Reflexes.* C. V. Anrep (Tr. and Ed.) Oxford: University Press, 1927.

Quinn, J., Harbison, J., & McAllister, H. An attempt to shape human penile responses. *Behaviour Research and Therapy,* 1970, **8,** 213–216.

Rachman, S. Sexual disorders and behavior therapy. *American Journal of Psychiatry,* 1961, **118,** 235–240.

Rachman, S. J. The effects of psychological treatment. In H. J. Eysenck (Ed.), *Handbook of abnormal psychology.* London: Pitman, 1973. Pp. 805–861.

Rachman, S., & Hodgson, R. Experimentally induced "sexual fetishism": Replication and development. *Psychological Record,* 1968, **18,** 25–27.

Schmidt, E., Castell, D., & Brown, P. A retrospective study of 42 cases of behaviour therapy. *Behaviour Research and Therapy,* 1965, **3,** 9–19.

Solyom, L., & Miller, S. A differential conditioning procedure as the initial phase of behaviour therapy of homosexuality. *Behaviour Research and Therapy,* 1965, **3**, 147–160.

Stevenson, I., & Wolpe, J. Recovery from sexual deviations through overcoming non-sexual neurotic responses. *American Journal of Psychiatry,* 1960, **116**, 737–742.

Tanner, B. Shock intensity and fear of shock in the modification of homosexual behavior in males by avoidance learning. *Behaviour Research and Therapy,* 1973, **11**, 213–218.

Thorpe, J. G., Schmidt, E., Brown, P. T., & Castell, D. Aversion-relief therapy: A new method for general application. *Behaviour Research and Therapy,* 1964, **2**, 71–82.

Thorpe, J. G., Schmidt, E., & Castell, D. A comparison of positive and negative (aversive) conditioning in the treatment of homosexuality. *Behaviour Research and Therapy,* 1963, **1**, 357–362.

Wilson, T. G. T., & Davison, G. C. Behavior therapy and homosexuality: A critical perspective. *Behavior Therapy,* 1974, **5**, 16–28.

Wolpe, J. *Psychotherapy by reciprocal inhibition.* Stanford: Stanford University Press, 1958.

Yates, A. J. *Behavior therapy.* New York: Wiley, 1970.

Yates, A. J. Research methods in behavior modification: A comparative evaluation. In M. Hersen, R. M. Eisler, & P. M. Miller (Eds.), *Progress in behavior modification* (Vol. 2). New York: Academic Press, 1976. Pp. 279–306.

Zuckerman, M. Physiological measures of sexual arousal in the human. *Psychological Bulletin,* 1971, **75**, 297–329.

SUBJECT INDEX

E

F

G

H

I

L

M

T